KING
OF THE
COMICS

W9-BWB-506

Other *Pearls Before Swine* Collections

Breaking Stephan
Rat's Wars
Unsportsmanlike Conduct
Because Sometimes You Just Gotta Draw a Cover with Your Left Hand
Larry in Wonderland
When Pigs Fly
50,000,000 Pearls Fans Can't Be Wrong
The Saturday Evening Pearls
Macho Macho Animals
The Sopratos
Da Brudderhood of Zeeba Zeeba Eata
The Ratvolution Will Not Be Televised
Nighthogs
This Little Piggy Stayed Home
BLTs Taste So Darn Good

Treasuries

Pearls Falls Fast
Pearls Freaks the #%# Out*
Pearls Blows Up
Pearls Sells Out
The Crass Menagerie
Lions and Tigers and Crocs, Oh My!
Sgt. Piggy's Lonely Hearts Club Comic

Gift Books

Friends Should Know When They're Not Wanted
Da Crockydile Book o' Frendsheep

AMP! Comics for Kids

The Croc Ate My Homework
Beginning Pearls

KING OF THE COMICS

A
Pearls Before Swine
COLLECTION
BY STEPHAN PASTIS

Introduction

I had always wanted to meet *Garfield* creator Jim Davis, but I didn't know where to find him.

"He's somewhere toward Indianapolis," someone told me.

"No, he's an hour away from Indianapolis," someone else told me.

"No, he's near Muncie," someone else told me, which didn't help at all because I didn't know what a Muncie was.

So let me tell you how to find him, should the need ever arise:

Drive for hours and hours and do not stop until you have personally counted every stalk of corn growing in Indiana.

And then keep on driving until there are no more gas stations. And no more buildings.

And eventually, no more road signs.

It is as though the local officials are telling you, "Hell if I know."

And soon you will look around and see that you are the only car on the road. And then the road itself will end.

And you will find yourself in the middle of a cornfield. Where if the wind dies down, the only thing you will hear is the sound of your own heartbeat.

And the voice of Jim Davis.

"Welcome," he says from a structure that looks like a mirage; a massive building with a giant paw on the front of it, indicating that you are either at the studio of Jim Davis or the home of a very successful veterinarian.

And it is shocking to meet him.

Shocking in that he is Jim Davis. And shocking in that I never thought I would hear a human voice again.

But it really was Jim Davis. And I really was being welcomed into his studio. And there was even a sign prove it.

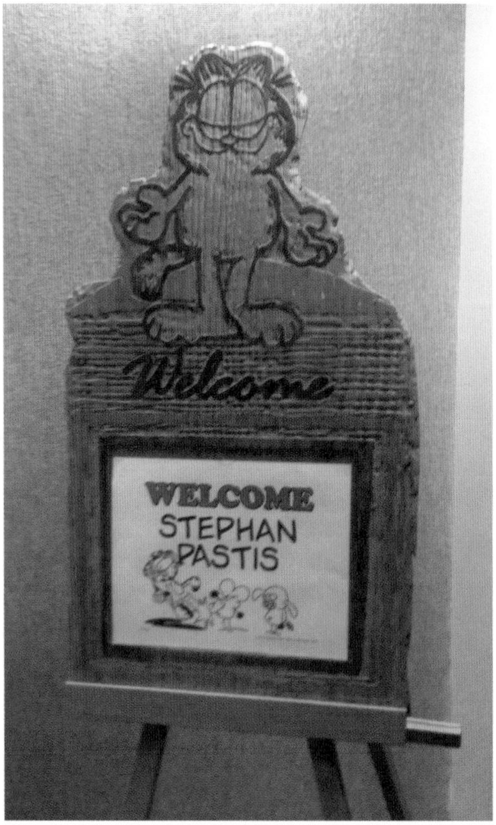
Welcome
WELCOME
STEPHAN
PASTIS

Then Jim introduced me to everyone on his staff. This too was shocking because I could not figure out where they came from.

Did they spring from sleeping pods in the basement? Live like little mice in the attic?

Surely, they did not commute. There was nowhere to commute *from*.

And they were all so *friendly*. They smiled. They joked. They laughed.

Jim even assembled them all in a giant room filled with thousands of *Garfield* products just so the staff could greet me and have me talk to them about *Pearls*.

And that's when it dawned on me.

What the warm greeting and the kind smiles and the remote location meant.

Jim Davis was going to kill me.

Here I was, the smart-ass cartoonist who thought it was okay to make fun of him and all his buddies like the creators of *Beetle Bailey* and *Family Circus* and *Cathy*.

"Get him somewhere remote," Mort Walker probably told him. "Like a cornfield, in the middle of nowhere."

"And welcome him with open arms," Bil Keane probably told him. "So he won't know what's coming."

"And then WHAM," Cathy Guisewite probably told him, "suffocate the little #&$# with a *Garfield* plush."

It all made so much sense.

So I started to do the calculations in my head:

— A good hitman in Indiana probably costs no more than $5,000;
— Jim Davis is a multi-millionaire;
— Jim Davis could have me killed thousands of times.

But then an even more sobering thought hit me.

Jim Davis doesn't have to hire anyone.

He is the most powerful man in Indiana.

He could kill me with his own hands and text a photo of it to the Governor, and the only ramification would be a reply text that said, "LOL."

So from that point on in the tour, I was careful.

I laughed at every one of his jokes. I praised all of his accomplishments.

And I never turned my back on him.

Except when taking this photo.

And even then, I was ready to spring like a cat. Not a fat, orange one. But a scared, nimble one.

Running through the cornfields.

Somewhere toward Indianapolis.

Stephan Pastis
March, 2015

Dedication

To Jim Davis,
for sparing me

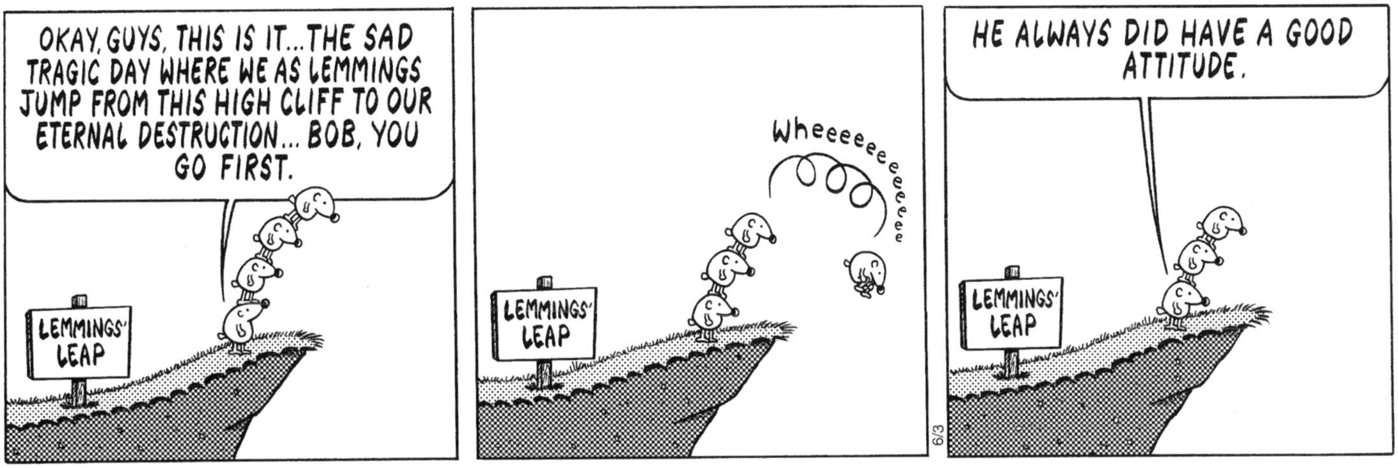
OKAY, GUYS, THIS IS IT...THE SAD TRAGIC DAY WHERE WE AS LEMMINGS JUMP FROM THIS HIGH CLIFF TO OUR ETERNAL DESTRUCTION... BOB, YOU GO FIRST.
LEMMINGS' LEAP
Wheeeeeeeeeeeeee
LEMMINGS' LEAP
6/3
HE ALWAYS DID HAVE A GOOD ATTITUDE.
LEMMINGS' LEAP

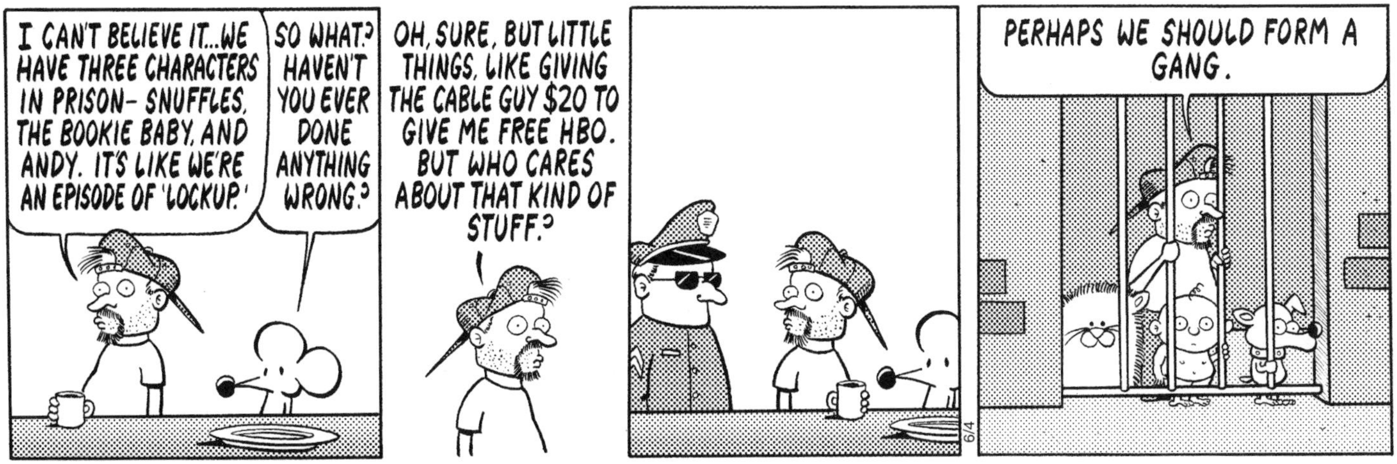
I CAN'T BELIEVE IT...WE HAVE THREE CHARACTERS IN PRISON– SNUFFLES, THE BOOKIE BABY, AND ANDY. IT'S LIKE WE'RE AN EPISODE OF 'LOCKUP.'
SO WHAT? HAVEN'T YOU EVER DONE ANYTHING WRONG?
OH, SURE, BUT LITTLE THINGS, LIKE GIVING THE CABLE GUY $20 TO GIVE ME FREE HBO. BUT WHO CARES ABOUT THAT KIND OF STUFF?
6/4
PERHAPS WE SHOULD FORM A GANG.

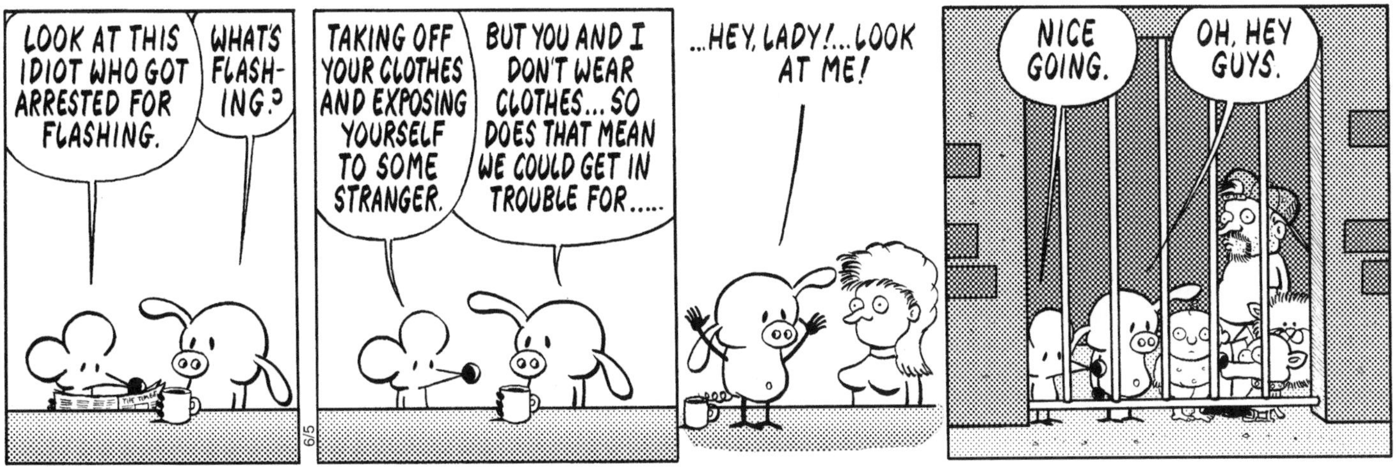
LOOK AT THIS IDIOT WHO GOT ARRESTED FOR FLASHING.
WHAT'S FLASHING?
6/5
TAKING OFF YOUR CLOTHES AND EXPOSING YOURSELF TO SOME STRANGER.
BUT YOU AND I DON'T WEAR CLOTHES... SO DOES THAT MEAN WE COULD GET IN TROUBLE FOR.....
...HEY, LADY!...LOOK AT ME!
NICE GOING.
OH, HEY GUYS.

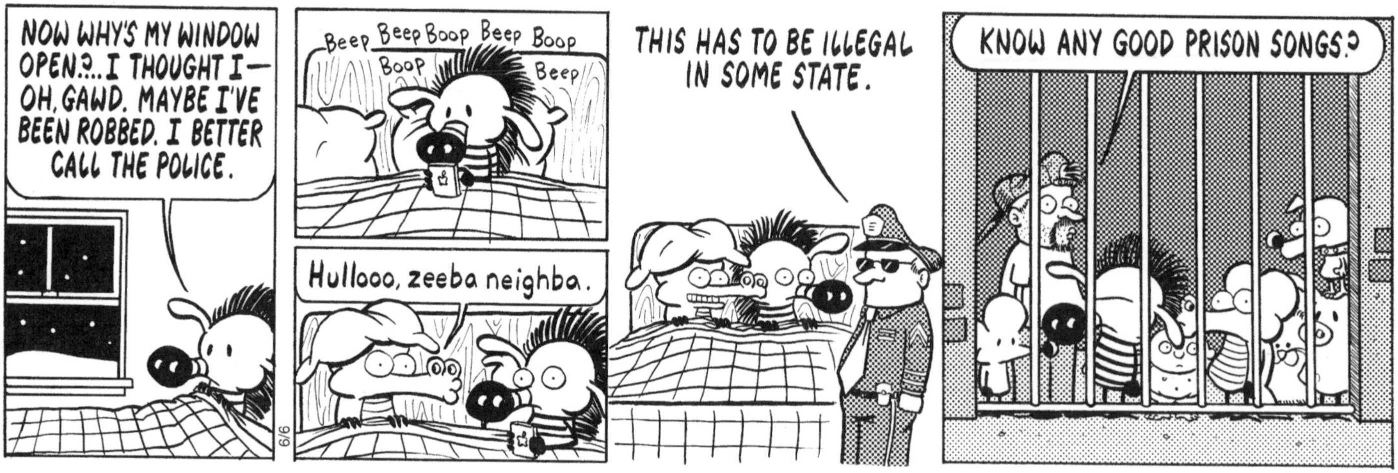
NOW WHY'S MY WINDOW OPEN?...I THOUGHT I— OH, GAWD. MAYBE I'VE BEEN ROBBED. I BETTER CALL THE POLICE.
6/6
Beep Beep Boop Beep Boop Boop Beep
Hullooo, zeeba neighba.
THIS HAS TO BE ILLEGAL IN SOME STATE.
KNOW ANY GOOD PRISON SONGS?

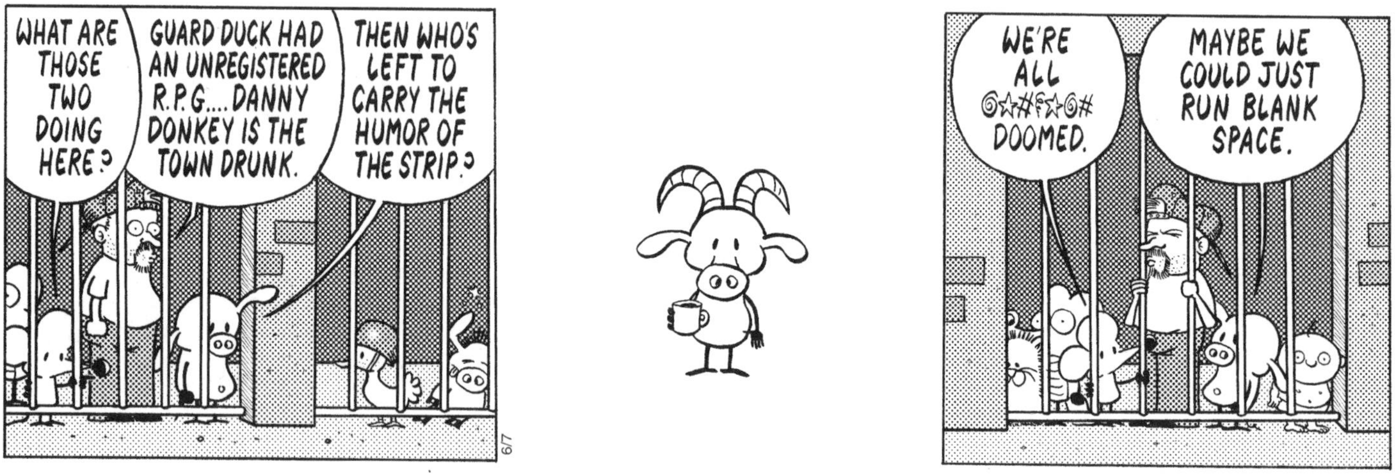
WHAT ARE THOSE TWO DOING HERE?
GUARD DUCK HAD AN UNREGISTERED R.P.G.... DANNY DONKEY IS THE TOWN DRUNK.
THEN WHO'S LEFT TO CARRY THE HUMOR OF THE STRIP?
6/7
WE'RE ALL @☆#f☆@# DOOMED.
MAYBE WE COULD JUST RUN BLANK SPACE.

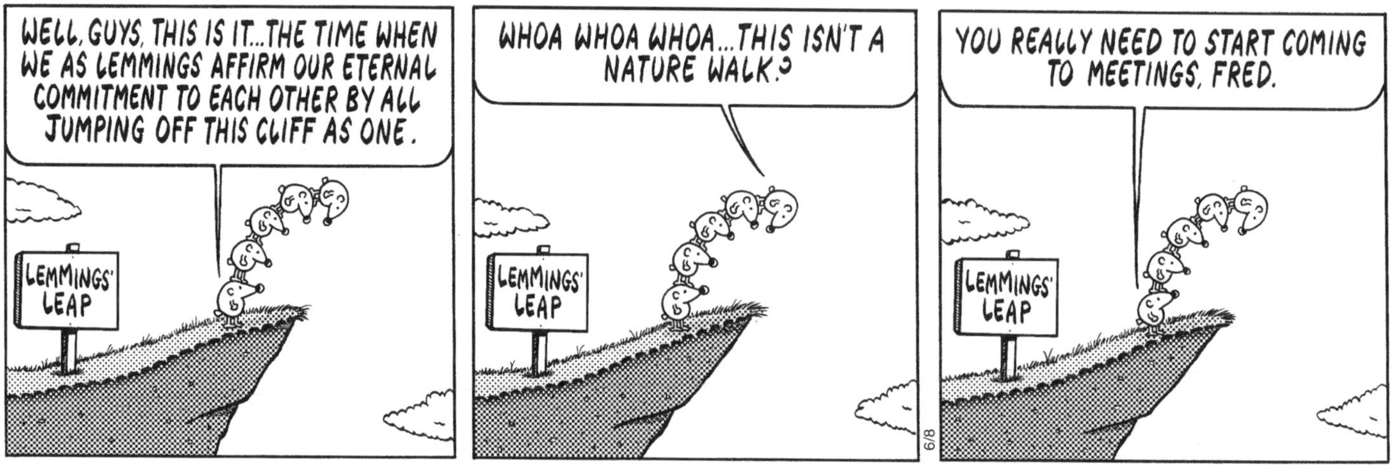
WELL, GUYS, THIS IS IT...THE TIME WHEN WE AS LEMMINGS AFFIRM OUR ETERNAL COMMITMENT TO EACH OTHER BY ALL JUMPING OFF THIS CLIFF AS ONE.
LEMMINGS' LEAP
WHOA WHOA WHOA...THIS ISN'T A NATURE WALK?
LEMMINGS' LEAP
6/8
YOU REALLY NEED TO START COMING TO MEETINGS, FRED.
LEMMINGS' LEAP

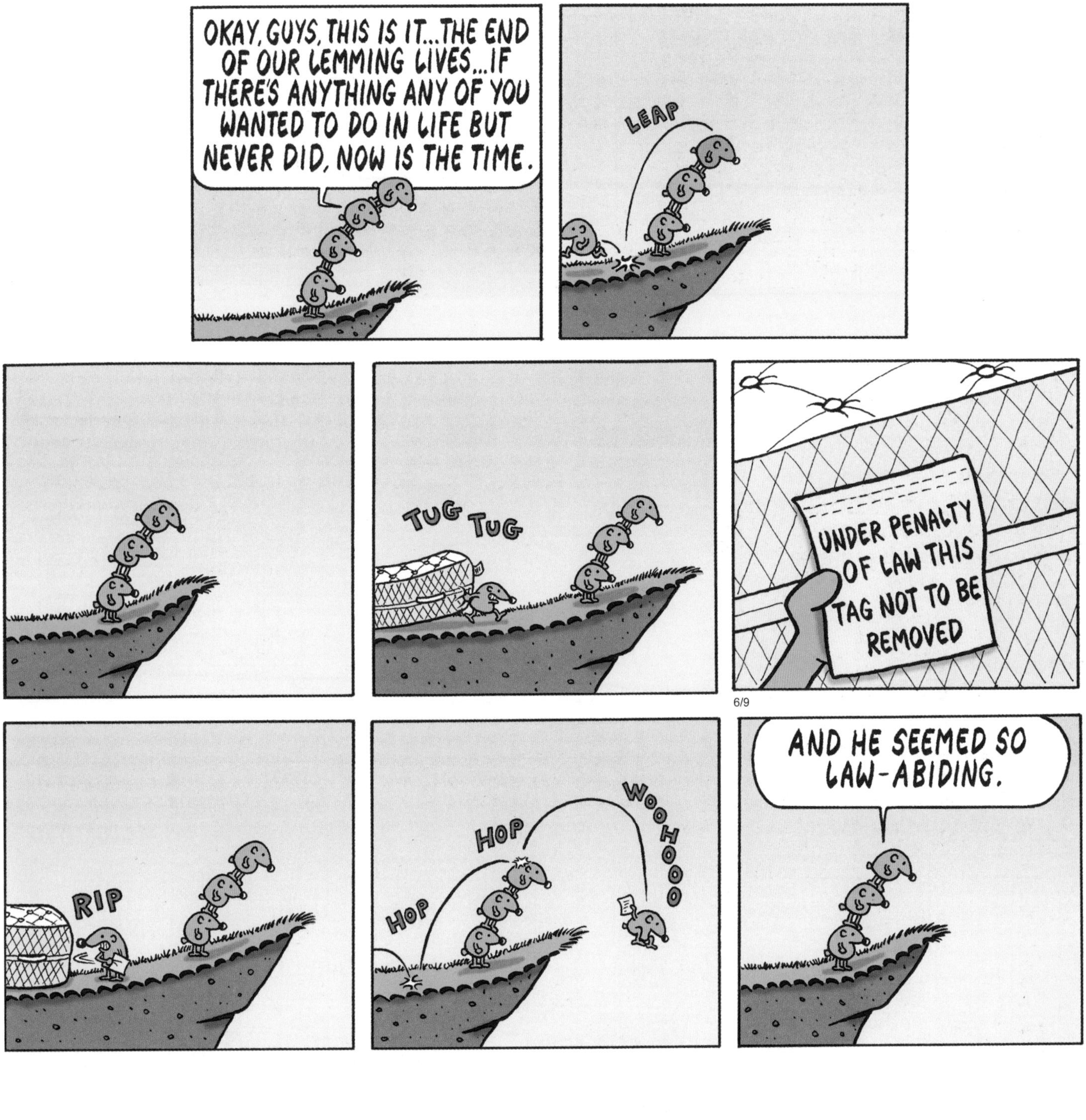
OKAY, GUYS, THIS IS IT...THE END OF OUR LEMMING LIVES...IF THERE'S ANYTHING ANY OF YOU WANTED TO DO IN LIFE BUT NEVER DID, NOW IS THE TIME.
LEAP
TUG TUG
UNDER PENALTY OF LAW THIS TAG NOT TO BE REMOVED
6/9
RIP
HOP
HOP
WOOHOOO
AND HE SEEMED SO LAW-ABIDING.

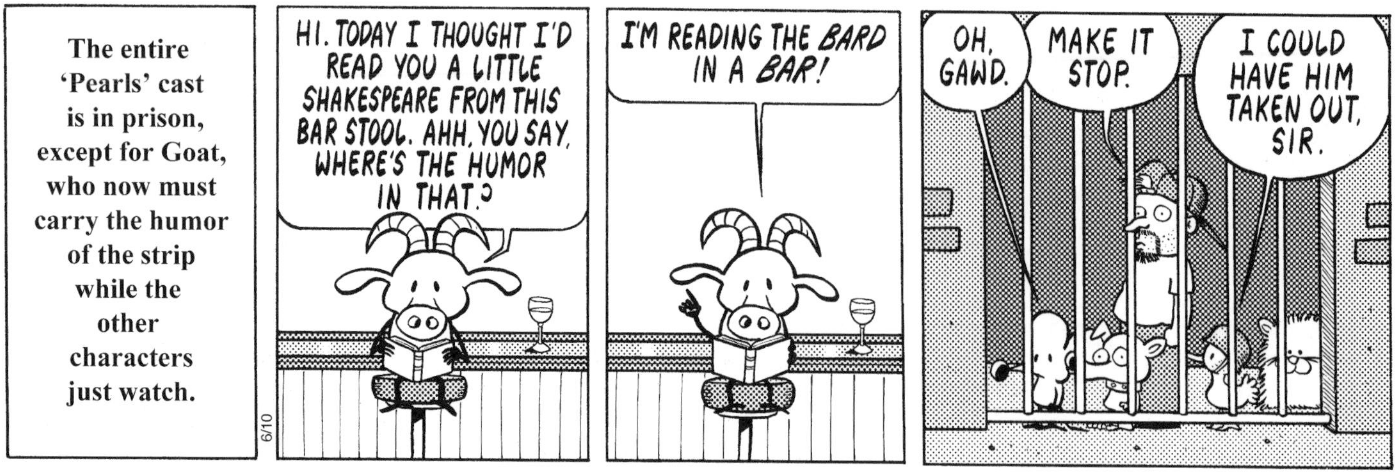
The entire 'Pearls' cast is in prison, except for Goat, who now must carry the humor of the strip while the other characters just watch.
HI. TODAY I THOUGHT I'D READ YOU A LITTLE SHAKESPEARE FROM THIS BAR STOOL. AHH, YOU SAY, WHERE'S THE HUMOR IN THAT?
I'M READING THE *BARD* IN A *BAR*!
OH, GAWD.
MAKE IT STOP.
I COULD HAVE HIM TAKEN OUT, SIR.
6/10

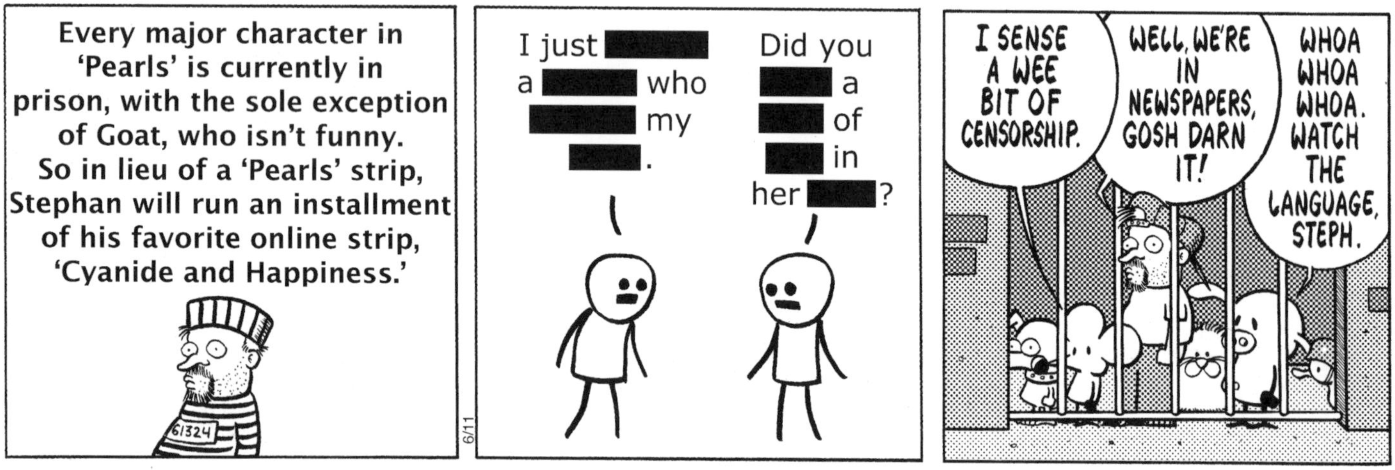
Every major character in 'Pearls' is currently in prison, with the sole exception of Goat, who isn't funny. So in lieu of a 'Pearls' strip, Stephan will run an installment of his favorite online strip, 'Cyanide and Happiness.'
61324
I just [redacted] a [redacted] who [redacted] my [redacted].
Did you [redacted] a [redacted] of [redacted] in her [redacted]?
I SENSE A WEE BIT OF CENSORSHIP.
WELL, WE'RE IN NEWSPAPERS, GOSH DARN IT!
WHOA WHOA WHOA. WATCH THE LANGUAGE, STEPH.
6/11

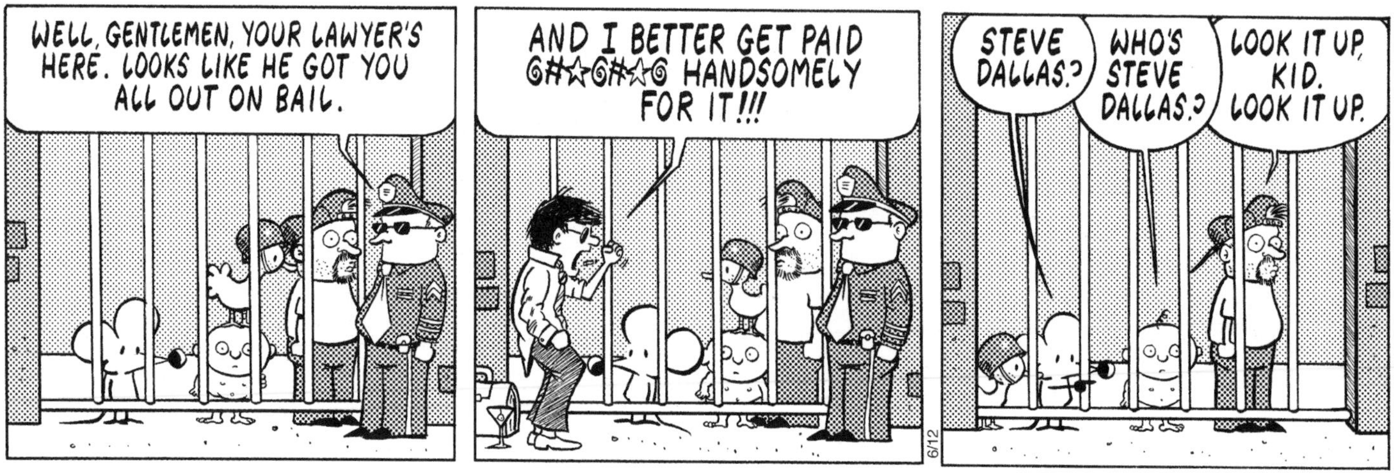
WELL, GENTLEMEN, YOUR LAWYER'S HERE. LOOKS LIKE HE GOT YOU ALL OUT ON BAIL.
AND I BETTER GET PAID @#☆@#☆@ HANDSOMELY FOR IT!!!
STEVE DALLAS?
WHO'S STEVE DALLAS?
LOOK IT UP, KID. LOOK IT UP.
6/12

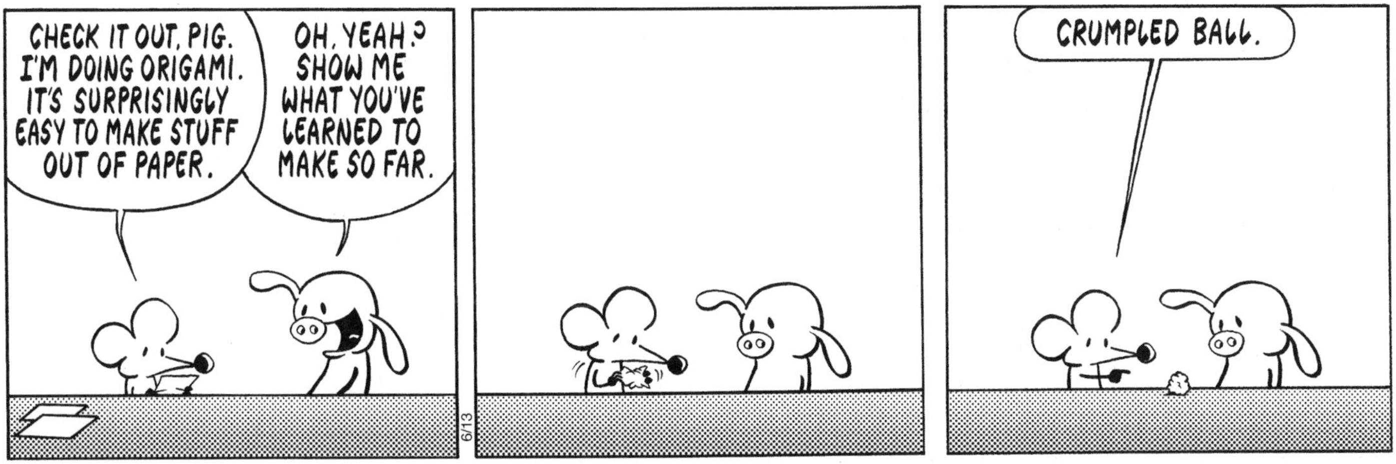
CHECK IT OUT, PIG. I'M DOING ORIGAMI. IT'S SURPRISINGLY EASY TO MAKE STUFF OUT OF PAPER.
OH, YEAH? SHOW ME WHAT YOU'VE LEARNED TO MAKE SO FAR.
6/13
CRUMPLED BALL.

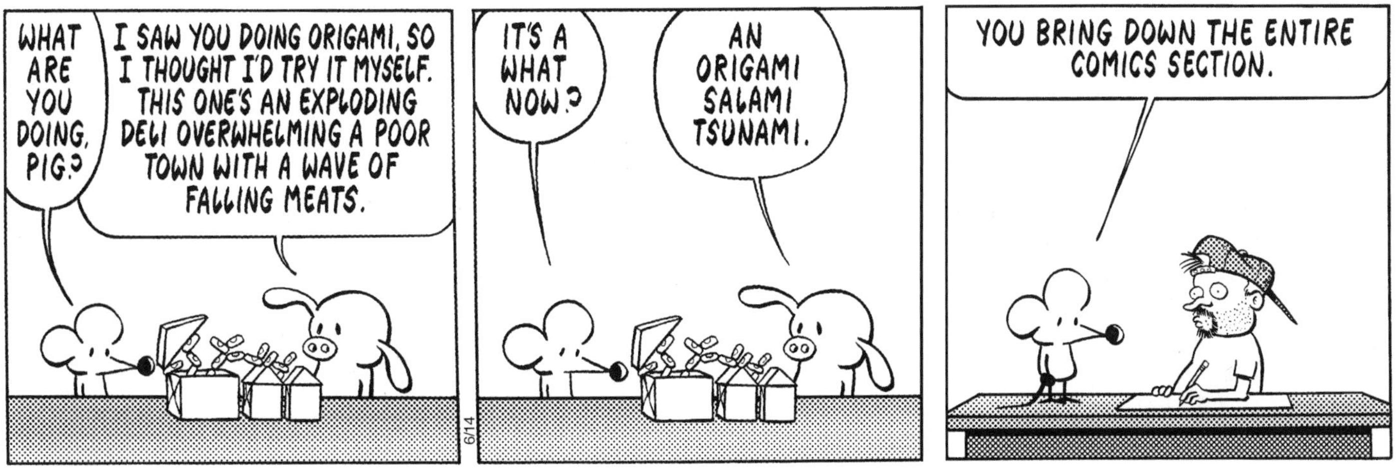
WHAT ARE YOU DOING, PIG?
I SAW YOU DOING ORIGAMI, SO I THOUGHT I'D TRY IT MYSELF. THIS ONE'S AN EXPLODING DELI OVERWHELMING A POOR TOWN WITH A WAVE OF FALLING MEATS.
IT'S A WHAT NOW?
AN ORIGAMI SALAMI TSUNAMI.
6/14
YOU BRING DOWN THE ENTIRE COMICS SECTION.

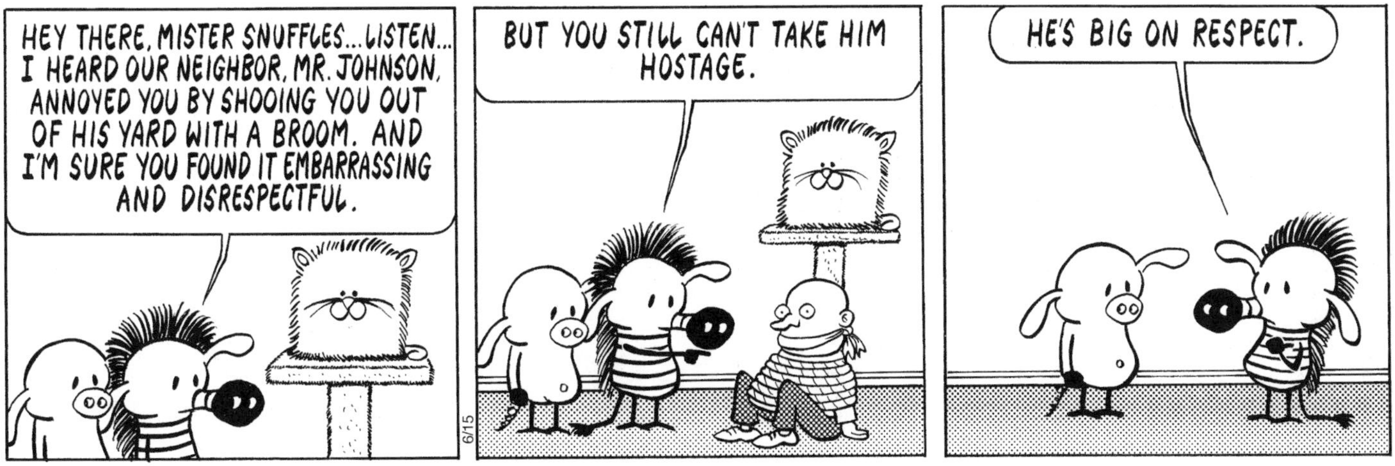
HEY THERE, MISTER SNUFFLES... LISTEN... I HEARD OUR NEIGHBOR, MR. JOHNSON, ANNOYED YOU BY SHOOING YOU OUT OF HIS YARD WITH A BROOM. AND I'M SURE YOU FOUND IT EMBARRASSING AND DISRESPECTFUL.
6/15
BUT YOU STILL CAN'T TAKE HIM HOSTAGE.
HE'S BIG ON RESPECT.

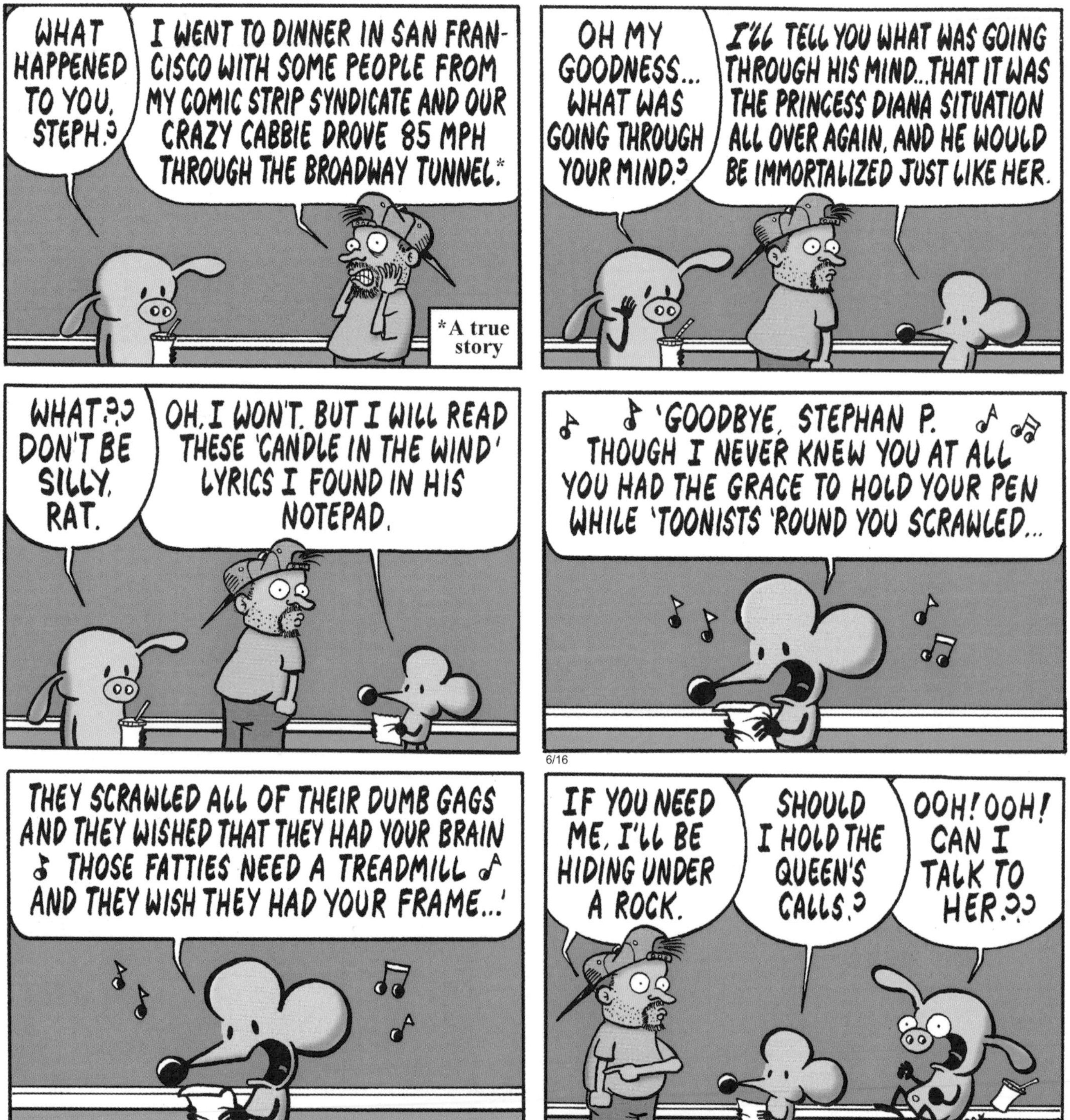
WHAT HAPPENED TO YOU, STEPH.?
I WENT TO DINNER IN SAN FRANCISCO WITH SOME PEOPLE FROM MY COMIC STRIP SYNDICATE AND OUR CRAZY CABBIE DROVE 85 MPH THROUGH THE BROADWAY TUNNEL.*
*A true story
OH MY GOODNESS... WHAT WAS GOING THROUGH YOUR MIND.?
I'LL TELL YOU WHAT WAS GOING THROUGH HIS MIND...THAT IT WAS THE PRINCESS DIANA SITUATION ALL OVER AGAIN, AND HE WOULD BE IMMORTALIZED JUST LIKE HER.
WHAT.?.? DON'T BE SILLY, RAT.
OH, I WON'T. BUT I WILL READ THESE 'CANDLE IN THE WIND' LYRICS I FOUND IN HIS NOTEPAD.
'GOODBYE, STEPHAN P. THOUGH I NEVER KNEW YOU AT ALL YOU HAD THE GRACE TO HOLD YOUR PEN WHILE 'TOONISTS 'ROUND YOU SCRAWLED...
6/16
THEY SCRAWLED ALL OF THEIR DUMB GAGS AND THEY WISHED THAT THEY HAD YOUR BRAIN THOSE FATTIES NEED A TREADMILL AND THEY WISH THEY HAD YOUR FRAME...'
IF YOU NEED ME, I'LL BE HIDING UNDER A ROCK.
SHOULD I HOLD THE QUEEN'S CALLS.?
OOH! OOH! CAN I TALK TO HER.?.?

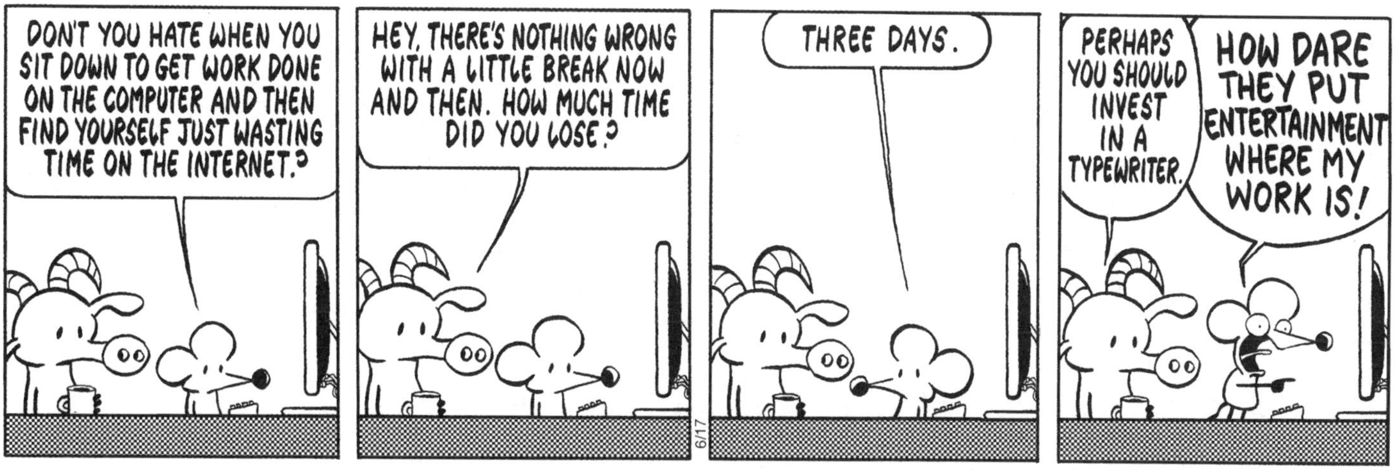
DON'T YOU HATE WHEN YOU SIT DOWN TO GET WORK DONE ON THE COMPUTER AND THEN FIND YOURSELF JUST WASTING TIME ON THE INTERNET?
HEY, THERE'S NOTHING WRONG WITH A LITTLE BREAK NOW AND THEN. HOW MUCH TIME DID YOU LOSE?
THREE DAYS.
6/17
PERHAPS YOU SHOULD INVEST IN A TYPEWRITER.
HOW DARE THEY PUT ENTERTAINMENT WHERE MY WORK IS!

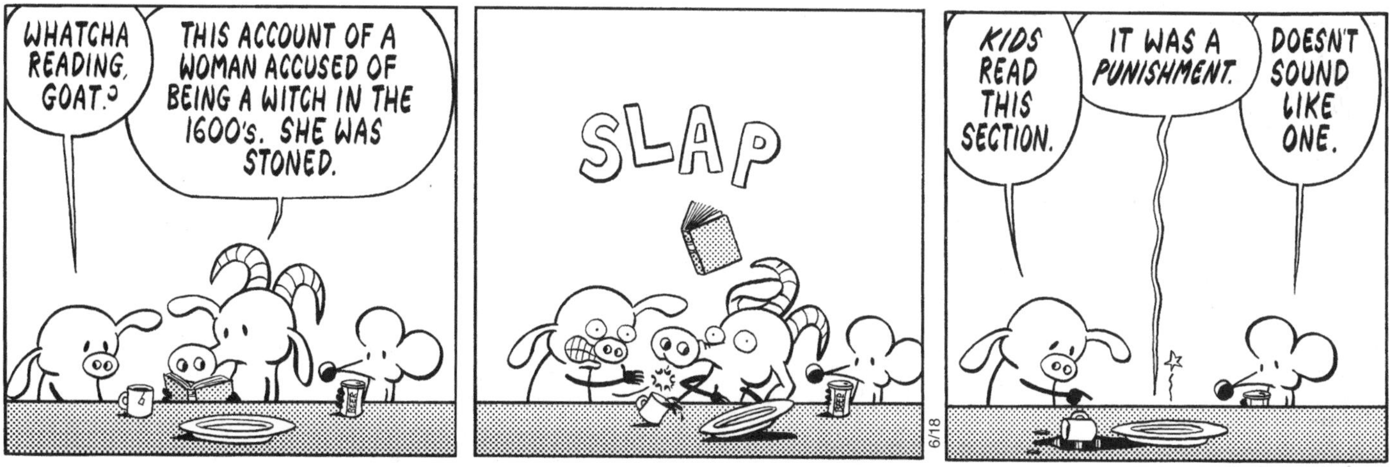
WHATCHA READING, GOAT?
THIS ACCOUNT OF A WOMAN ACCUSED OF BEING A WITCH IN THE 1600'S. SHE WAS STONED.
SLAP
6/18
KIDS READ THIS SECTION.
IT WAS A PUNISHMENT.
DOESN'T SOUND LIKE ONE.

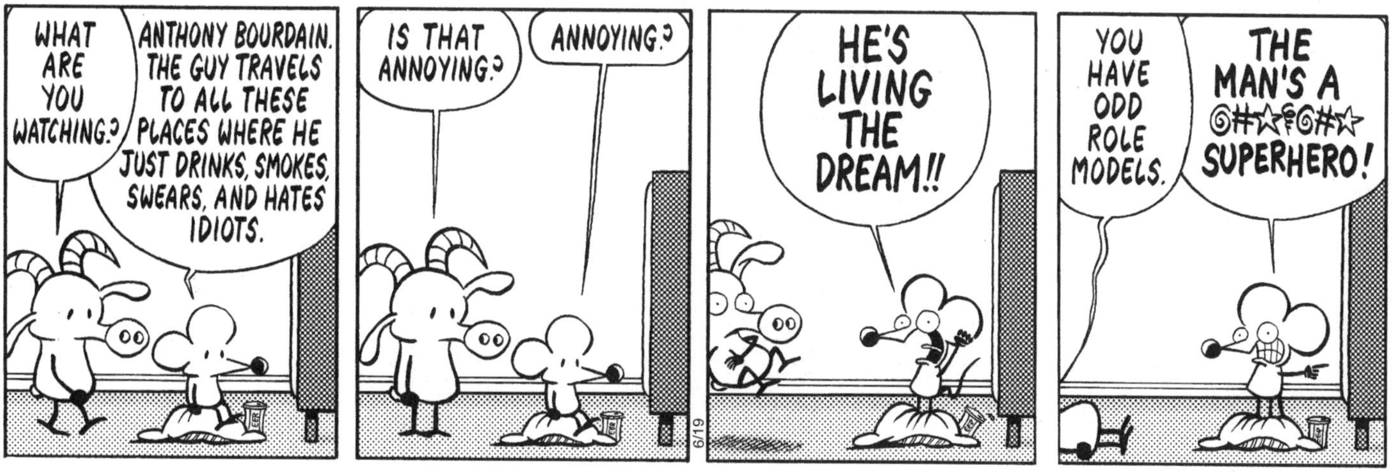
WHAT ARE YOU WATCHING?
ANTHONY BOURDAIN. THE GUY TRAVELS TO ALL THESE PLACES WHERE HE JUST DRINKS, SMOKES, SWEARS, AND HATES IDIOTS.
IS THAT ANNOYING?
ANNOYING?
6/19
HE'S LIVING THE DREAM!!
YOU HAVE ODD ROLE MODELS.
THE MAN'S A @#☆$@#☆ SUPERHERO!

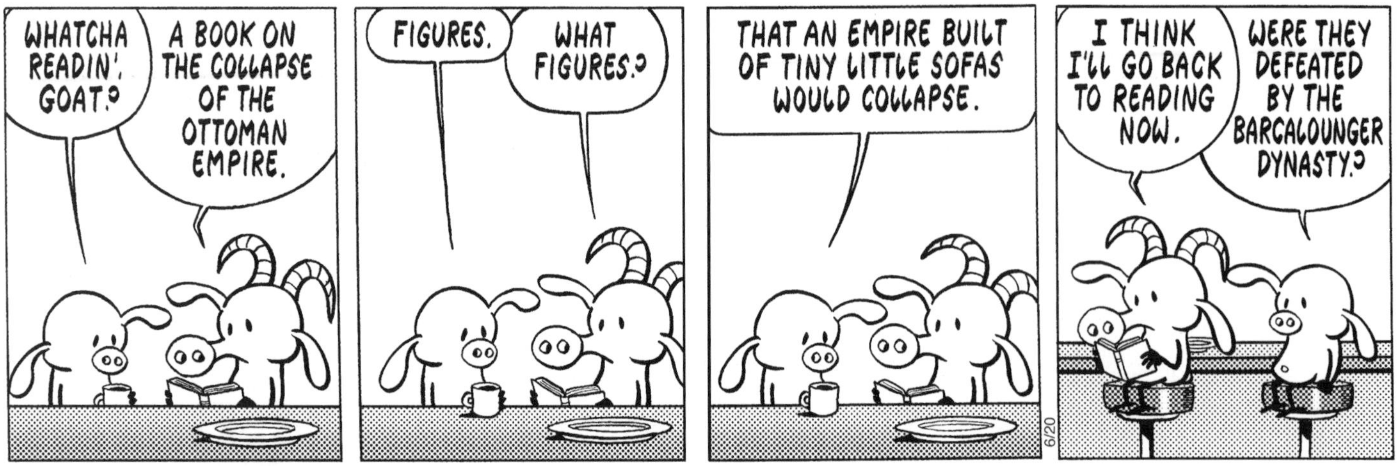
WHATCHA READIN', GOAT?
A BOOK ON THE COLLAPSE OF THE OTTOMAN EMPIRE.
FIGURES.
WHAT FIGURES?
THAT AN EMPIRE BUILT OF TINY LITTLE SOFAS WOULD COLLAPSE.
I THINK I'LL GO BACK TO READING NOW.
WERE THEY DEFEATED BY THE BARCALOUNGER DYNASTY?
6/20

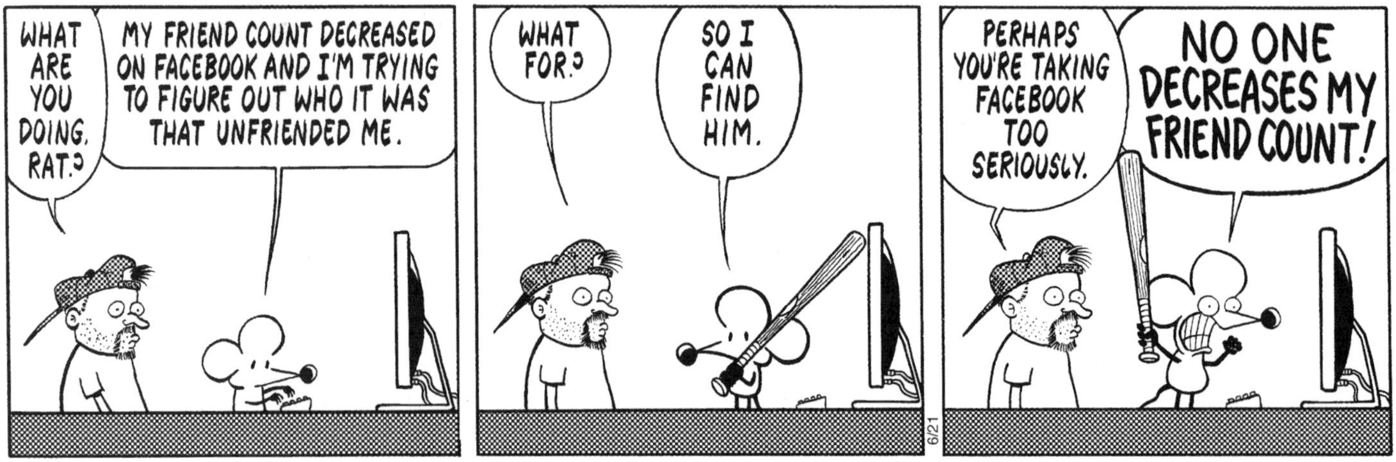
WHAT ARE YOU DOING, RAT?
MY FRIEND COUNT DECREASED ON FACEBOOK AND I'M TRYING TO FIGURE OUT WHO IT WAS THAT UNFRIENDED ME.
WHAT FOR?
SO I CAN FIND HIM.
6/21
PERHAPS YOU'RE TAKING FACEBOOK TOO SERIOUSLY.
NO ONE DECREASES MY FRIEND COUNT!

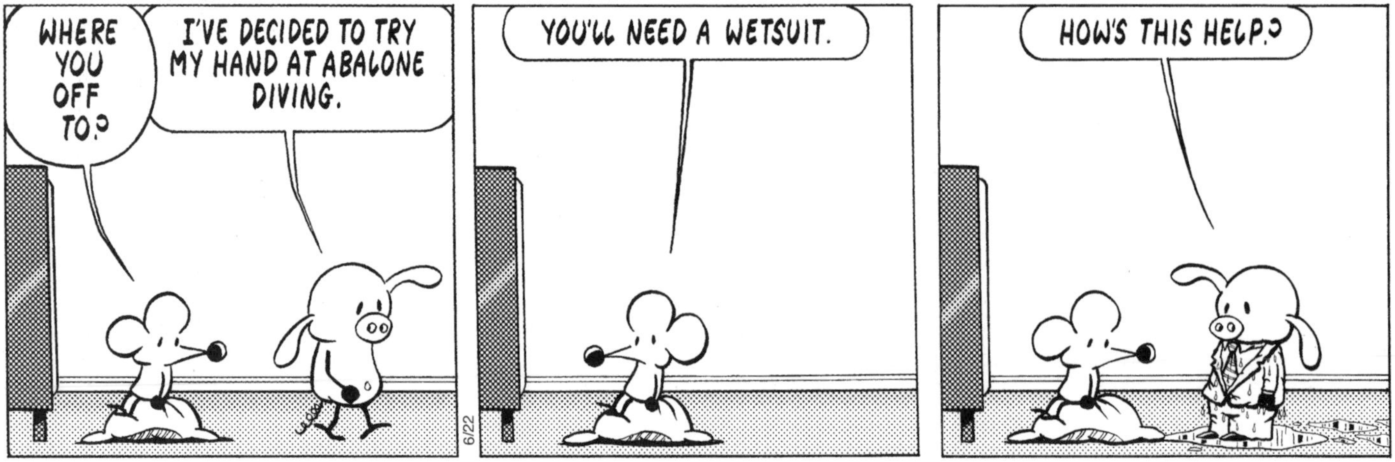
WHERE YOU OFF TO?
I'VE DECIDED TO TRY MY HAND AT ABALONE DIVING.
6/22
YOU'LL NEED A WETSUIT.
HOW'S THIS HELP?

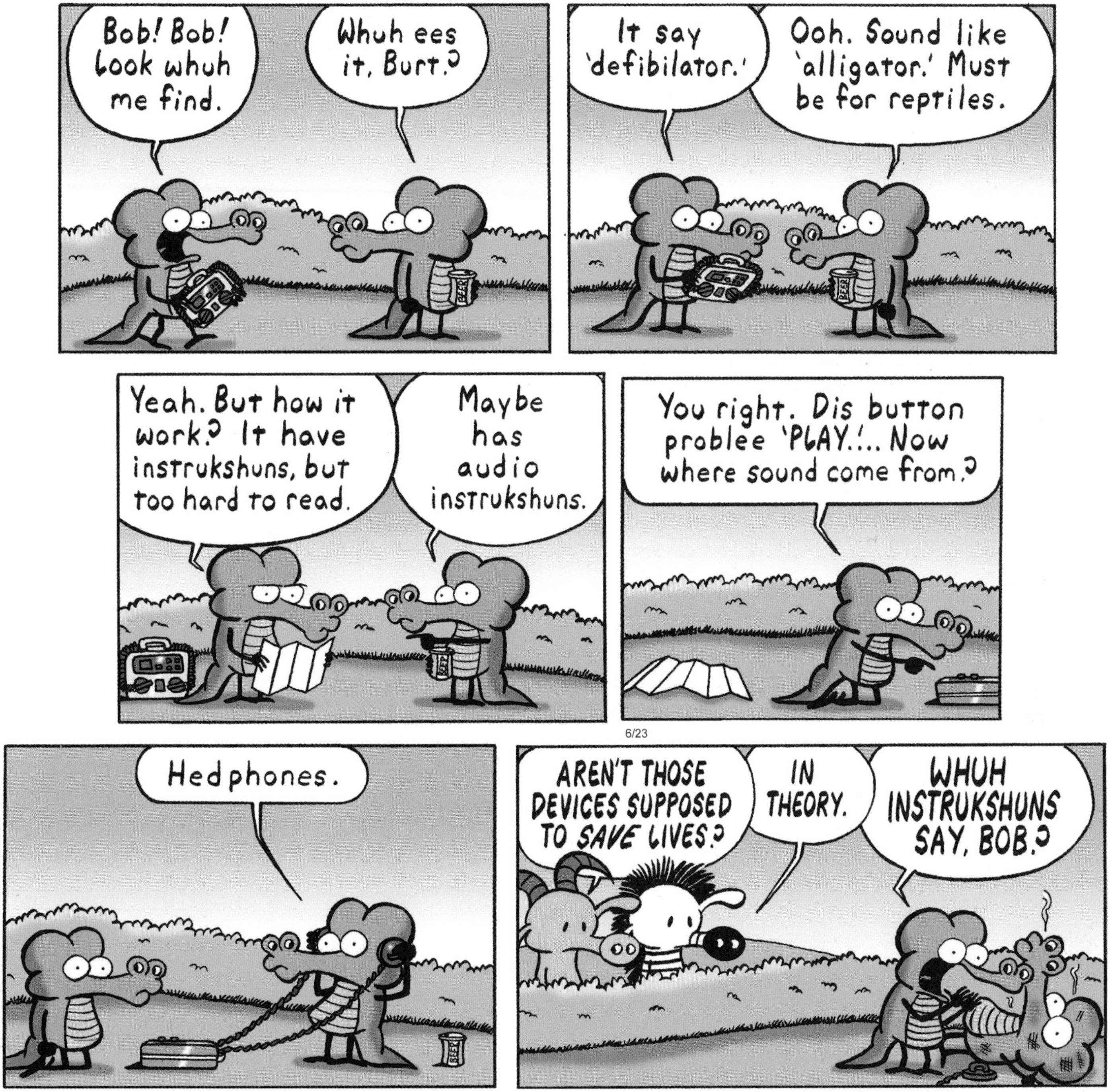
Bob! Bob! Look whuh me find.
Whuh ees it, Burt?
It say 'defibilator.'
Ooh. Sound like 'alligator.' Must be for reptiles.
Yeah. But how it work? It have instrukshuns, but too hard to read.
Maybe has audio instrukshuns.
You right. Dis button problee 'PLAY.'... Now where sound come from?
6/23
Hedphones.
AREN'T THOSE DEVICES SUPPOSED TO *SAVE* LIVES?
IN THEORY.
WHUH INSTRUKSHUNS SAY, BOB?

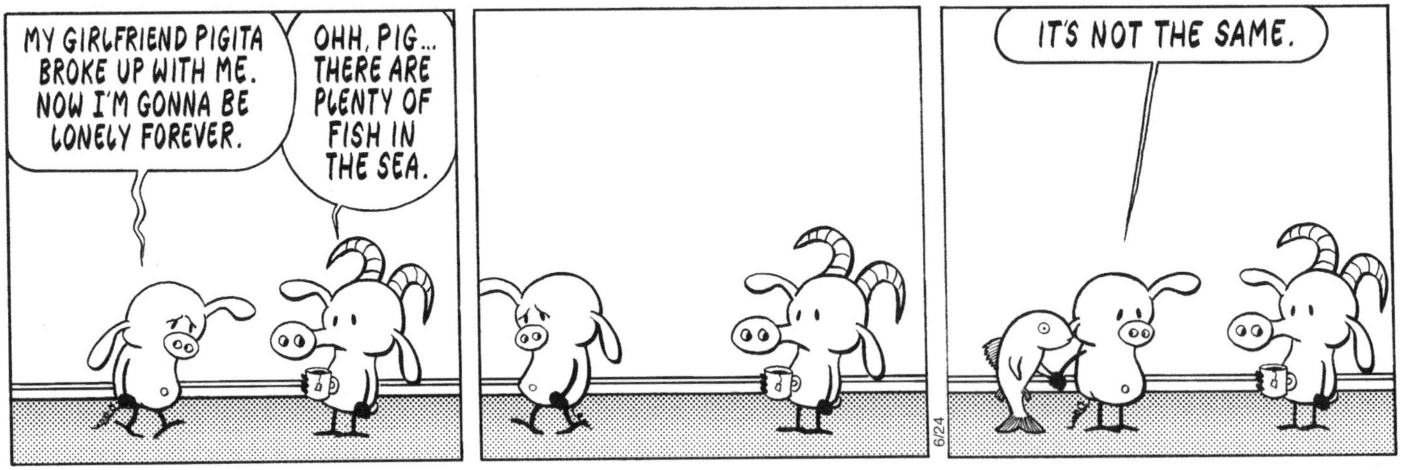
MY GIRLFRIEND PIGITA BROKE UP WITH ME. NOW I'M GONNA BE LONELY FOREVER.
OHH, PIG... THERE ARE PLENTY OF FISH IN THE SEA.
IT'S NOT THE SAME.
6/24

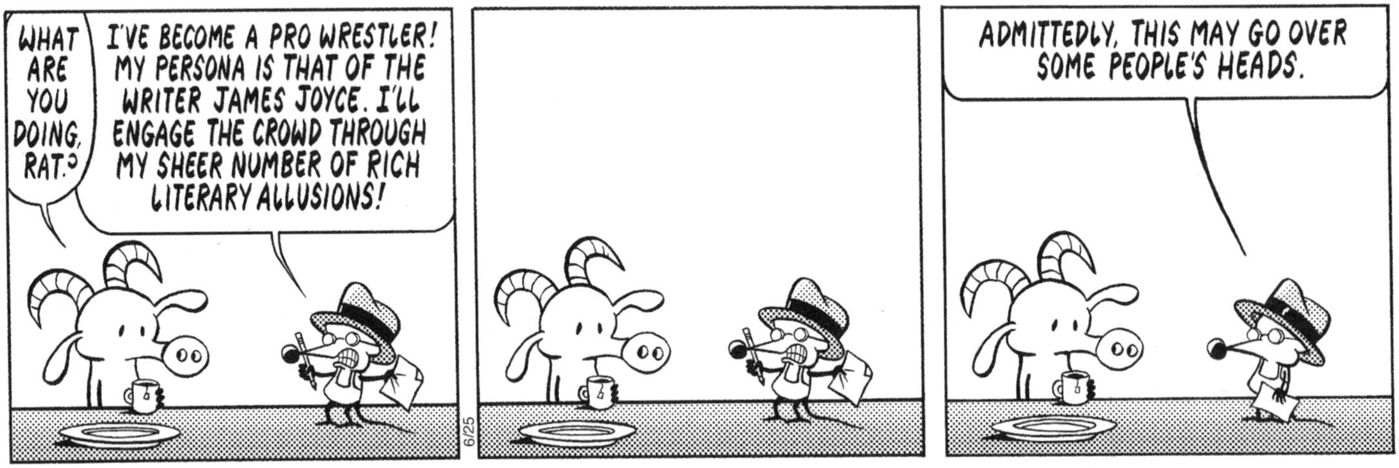
WHAT ARE YOU DOING, RAT?
I'VE BECOME A PRO WRESTLER! MY PERSONA IS THAT OF THE WRITER JAMES JOYCE. I'LL ENGAGE THE CROWD THROUGH MY SHEER NUMBER OF RICH LITERARY ALLUSIONS!
6/25
ADMITTEDLY, THIS MAY GO OVER SOME PEOPLE'S HEADS.

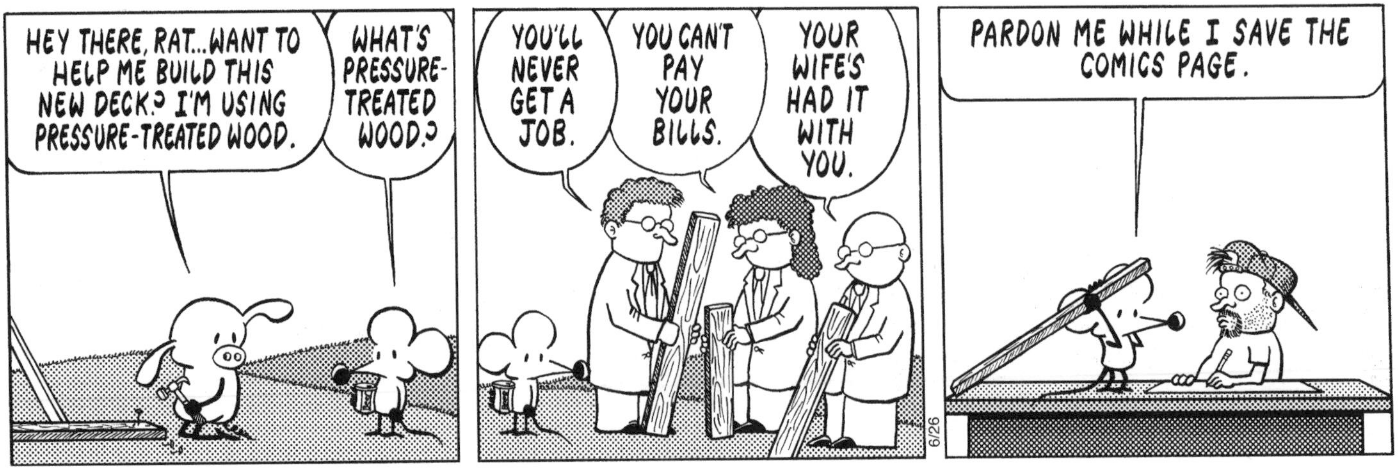
HEY THERE, RAT...WANT TO HELP ME BUILD THIS NEW DECK? I'M USING PRESSURE-TREATED WOOD.
WHAT'S PRESSURE-TREATED WOOD?
YOU'LL NEVER GET A JOB.
YOU CAN'T PAY YOUR BILLS.
YOUR WIFE'S HAD IT WITH YOU.
6/26
PARDON ME WHILE I SAVE THE COMICS PAGE.

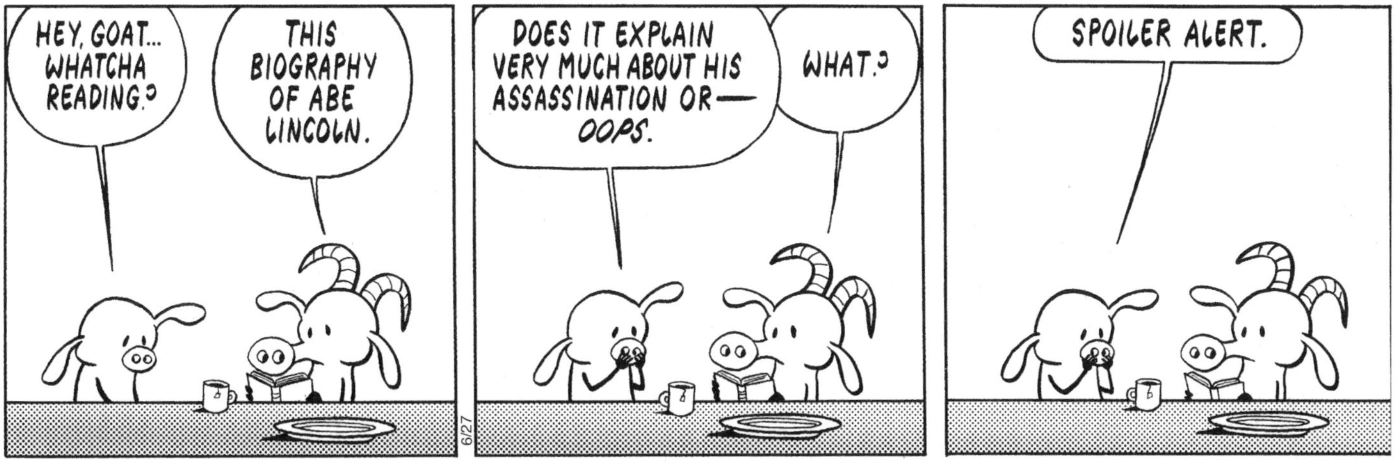
HEY, GOAT... WHATCHA READING?
THIS BIOGRAPHY OF ABE LINCOLN.
6/27
DOES IT EXPLAIN VERY MUCH ABOUT HIS ASSASSINATION OR— *OOPS.*
WHAT?
SPOILER ALERT.

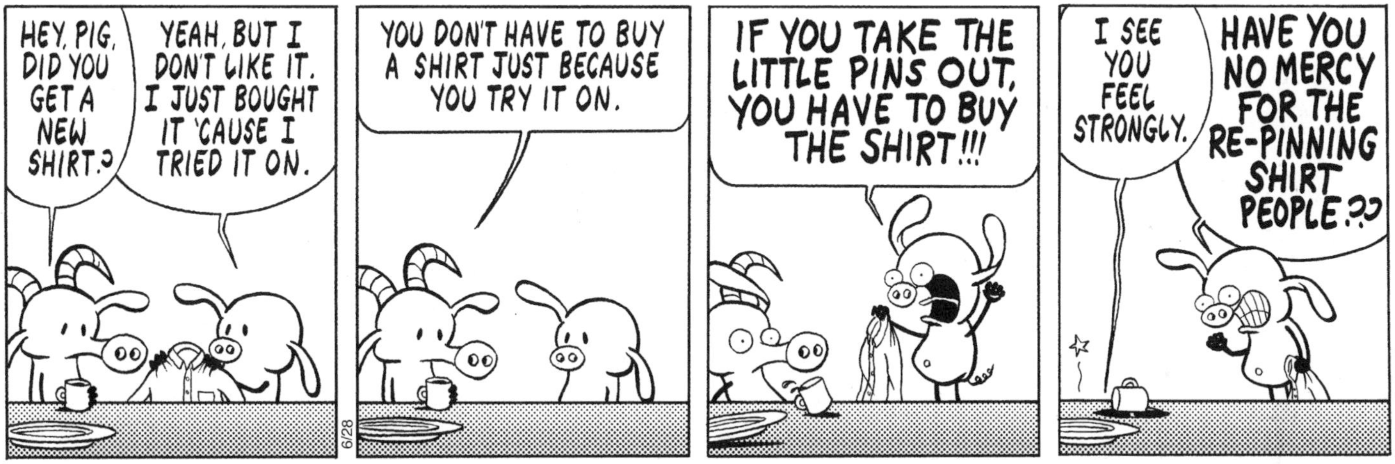
HEY, PIG, DID YOU GET A NEW SHIRT?
YEAH, BUT I DON'T LIKE IT. I JUST BOUGHT IT 'CAUSE I TRIED IT ON.
6/28
YOU DON'T HAVE TO BUY A SHIRT JUST BECAUSE YOU TRY IT ON.
IF YOU TAKE THE LITTLE PINS OUT, YOU HAVE TO BUY THE SHIRT!!!
I SEE YOU FEEL STRONGLY.
HAVE YOU NO MERCY FOR THE RE-PINNING SHIRT PEOPLE?!?

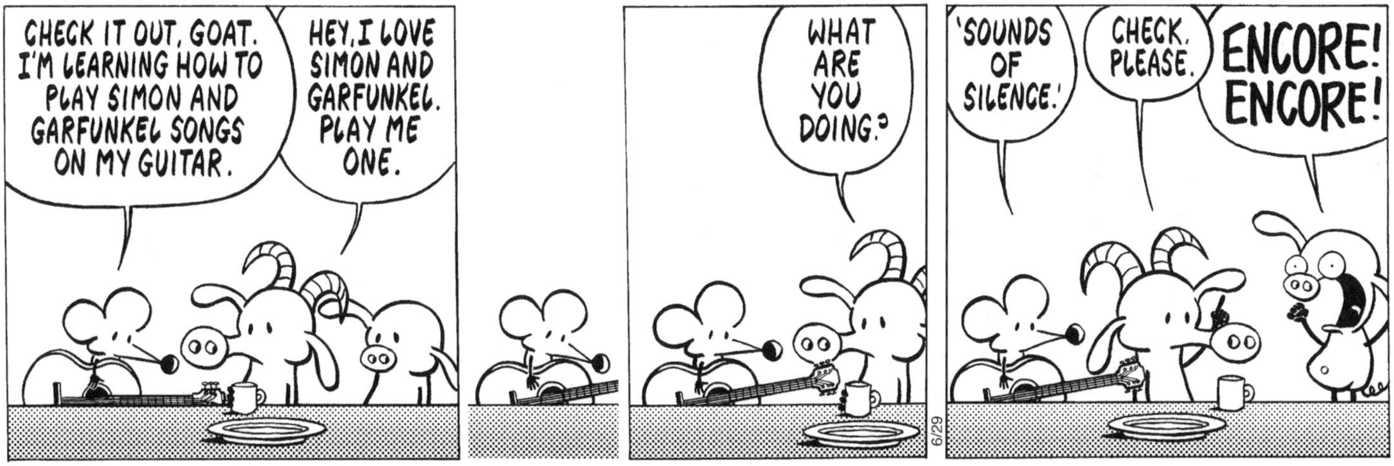
CHECK IT OUT, GOAT. I'M LEARNING HOW TO PLAY SIMON AND GARFUNKEL SONGS ON MY GUITAR.
HEY, I LOVE SIMON AND GARFUNKEL. PLAY ME ONE.
WHAT ARE YOU DOING?
6/29
'SOUNDS OF SILENCE.'
CHECK, PLEASE.
ENCORE! ENCORE!

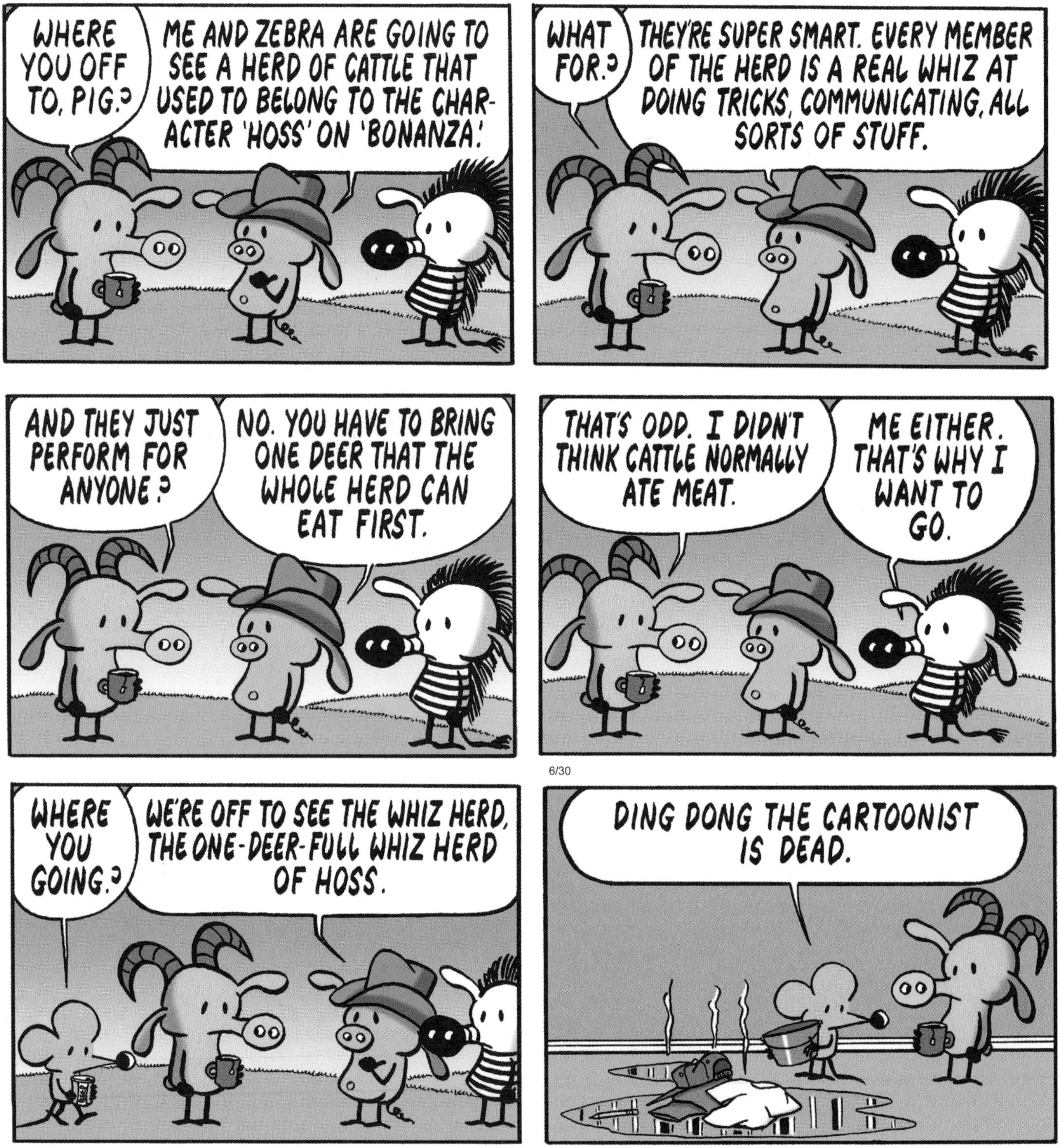
WHERE YOU OFF TO, PIG?
ME AND ZEBRA ARE GOING TO SEE A HERD OF CATTLE THAT USED TO BELONG TO THE CHARACTER 'HOSS' ON 'BONANZA.'
WHAT FOR?
THEY'RE SUPER SMART. EVERY MEMBER OF THE HERD IS A REAL WHIZ AT DOING TRICKS, COMMUNICATING, ALL SORTS OF STUFF.
AND THEY JUST PERFORM FOR ANYONE?
NO. YOU HAVE TO BRING ONE DEER THAT THE WHOLE HERD CAN EAT FIRST.
THAT'S ODD. I DIDN'T THINK CATTLE NORMALLY ATE MEAT.
ME EITHER. THAT'S WHY I WANT TO GO.
6/30
WHERE YOU GOING?
WE'RE OFF TO SEE THE WHIZ HERD, THE ONE-DEER-FULL WHIZ HERD OF HOSS.
DING DONG THE CARTOONIST IS DEAD.

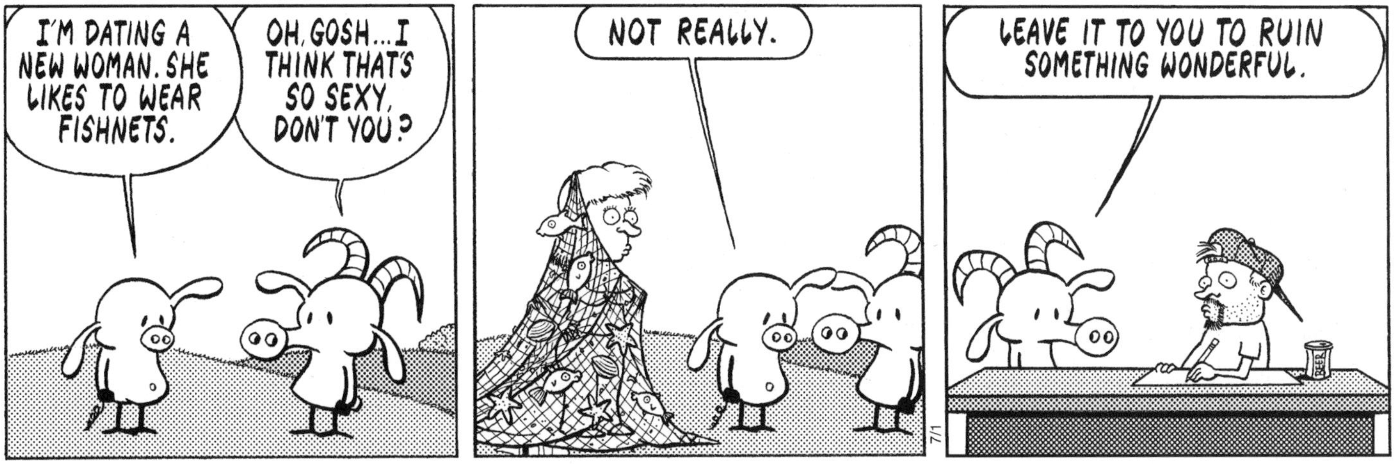
I'M DATING A NEW WOMAN. SHE LIKES TO WEAR FISHNETS.
OH, GOSH... I THINK THAT'S SO SEXY, DON'T YOU?
NOT REALLY.
LEAVE IT TO YOU TO RUIN SOMETHING WONDERFUL.
BEER
7/1

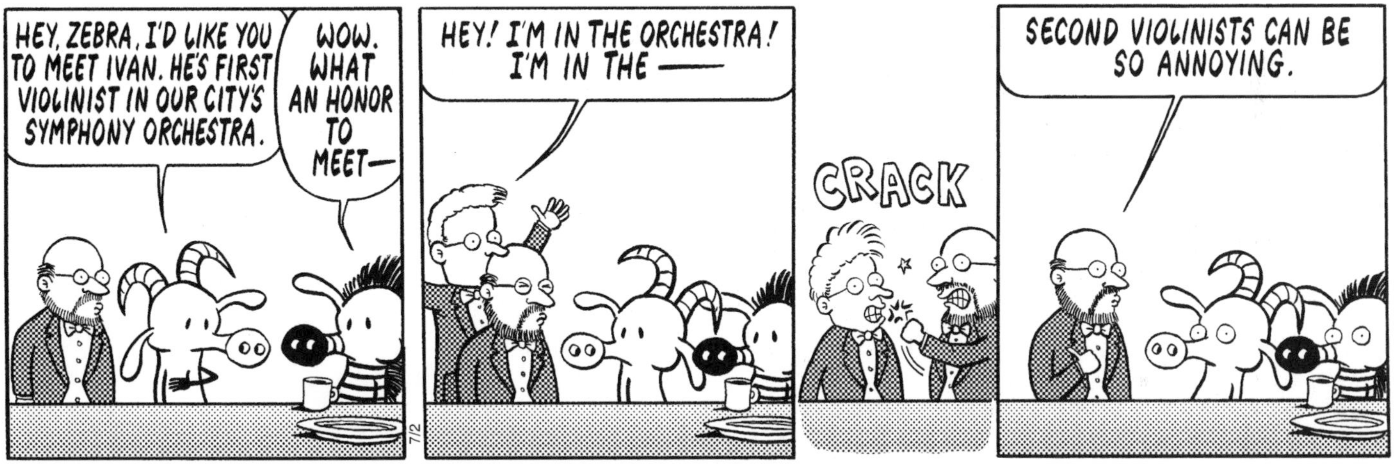
HEY, ZEBRA, I'D LIKE YOU TO MEET IVAN. HE'S FIRST VIOLINIST IN OUR CITY'S SYMPHONY ORCHESTRA.
WOW. WHAT AN HONOR TO MEET—
7/2
HEY! I'M IN THE ORCHESTRA! I'M IN THE ——
CRACK
SECOND VIOLINISTS CAN BE SO ANNOYING.

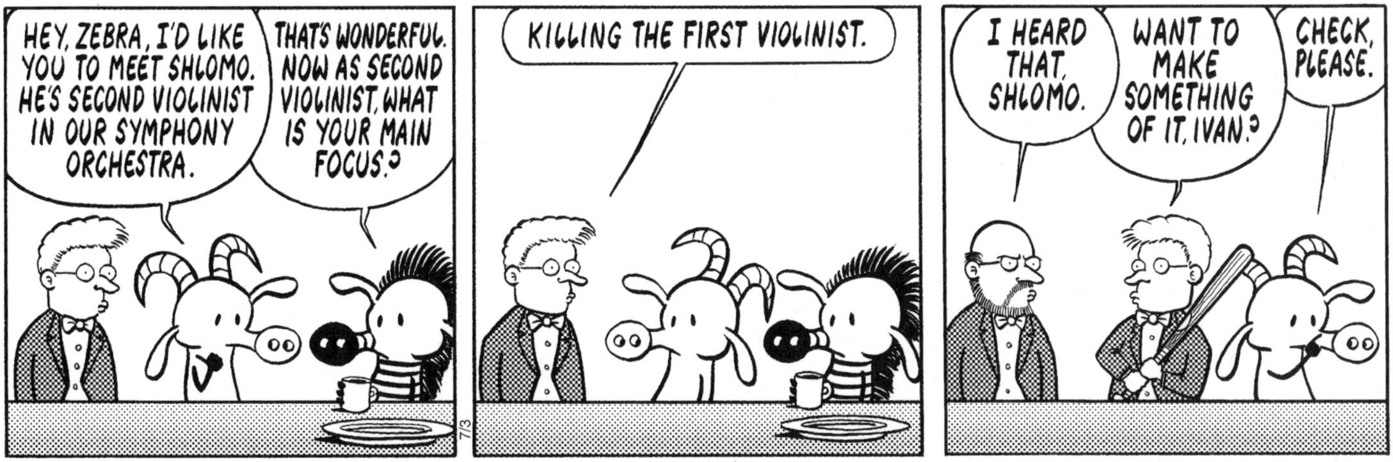
HEY, ZEBRA, I'D LIKE YOU TO MEET SHLOMO. HE'S SECOND VIOLINIST IN OUR SYMPHONY ORCHESTRA.
THAT'S WONDERFUL. NOW AS SECOND VIOLINIST, WHAT IS YOUR MAIN FOCUS?
7/3
KILLING THE FIRST VIOLINIST.
I HEARD THAT, SHLOMO.
WANT TO MAKE SOMETHING OF IT, IVAN?
CHECK, PLEASE.

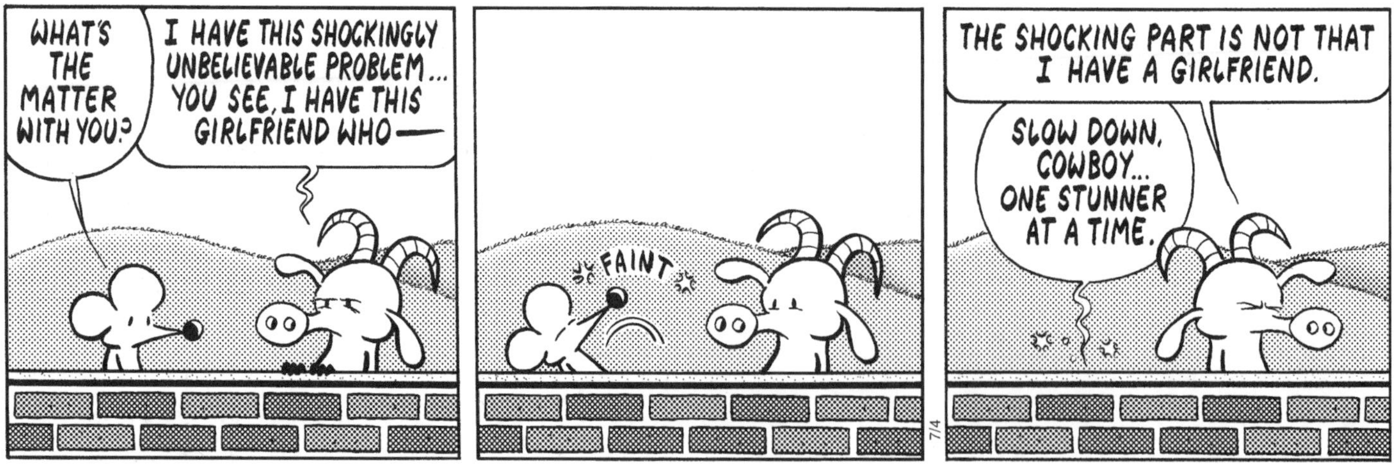
WHAT'S THE MATTER WITH YOU?
I HAVE THIS SHOCKINGLY UNBELIEVABLE PROBLEM... YOU SEE, I HAVE THIS GIRLFRIEND WHO—
FAINT
THE SHOCKING PART IS NOT THAT I HAVE A GIRLFRIEND.
SLOW DOWN, COWBOY... ONE STUNNER AT A TIME.
7/4

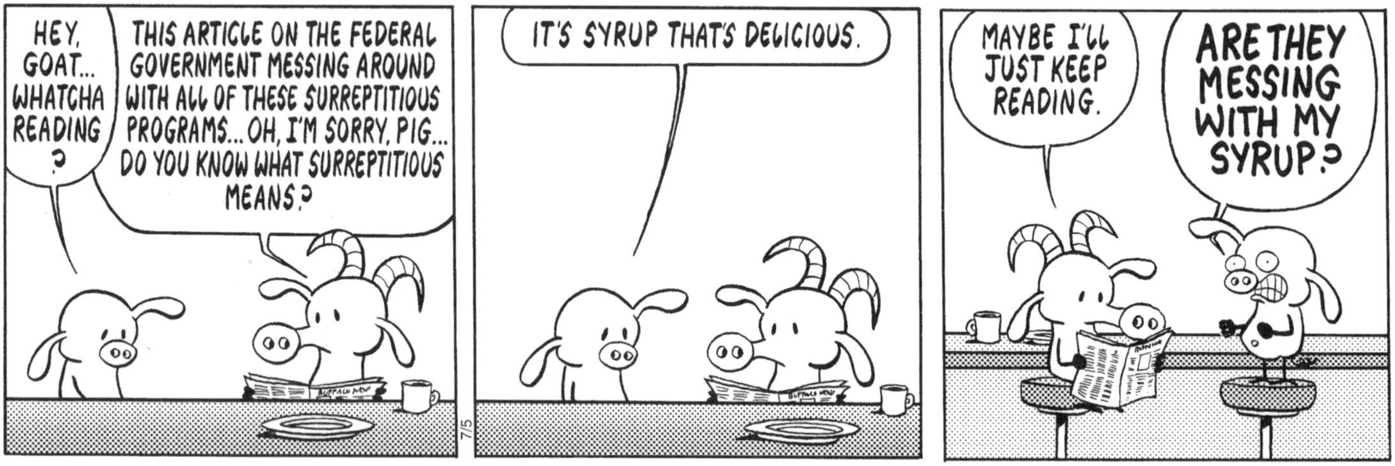
HEY, GOAT... WHATCHA READING?
THIS ARTICLE ON THE FEDERAL GOVERNMENT MESSING AROUND WITH ALL OF THESE SURREPTITIOUS PROGRAMS... OH, I'M SORRY, PIG... DO YOU KNOW WHAT SURREPTITIOUS MEANS?
IT'S SYRUP THAT'S DELICIOUS.
MAYBE I'LL JUST KEEP READING.
ARE THEY MESSING WITH MY SYRUP?
7/5

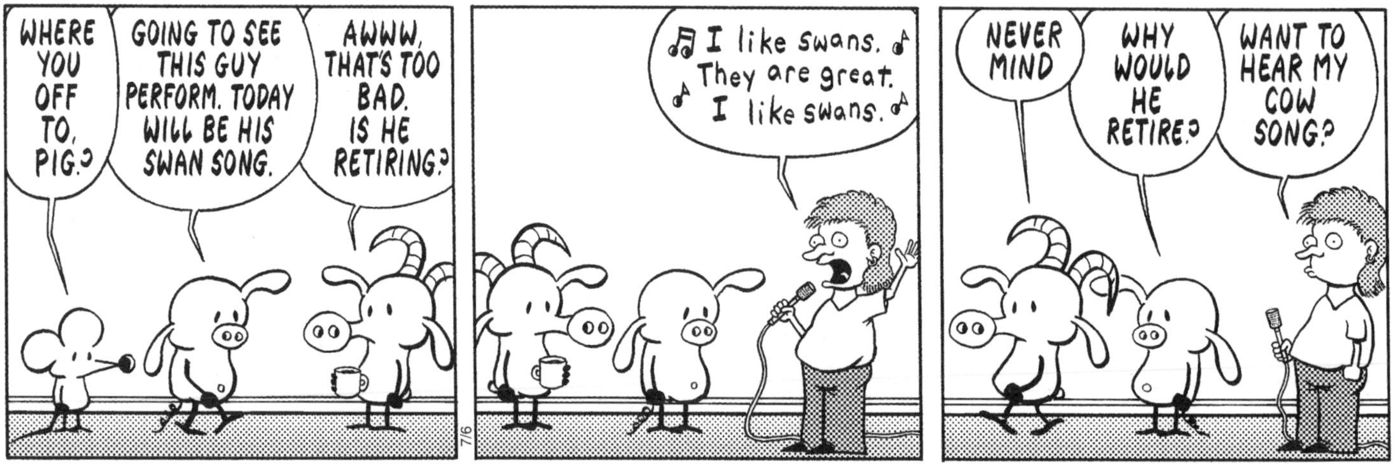
WHERE YOU OFF TO, PIG?
GOING TO SEE THIS GUY PERFORM. TODAY WILL BE HIS SWAN SONG.
AWWW, THAT'S TOO BAD. IS HE RETIRING?
I like swans. They are great. I like swans.
NEVER MIND
WHY WOULD HE RETIRE?
WANT TO HEAR MY COW SONG?
7/6

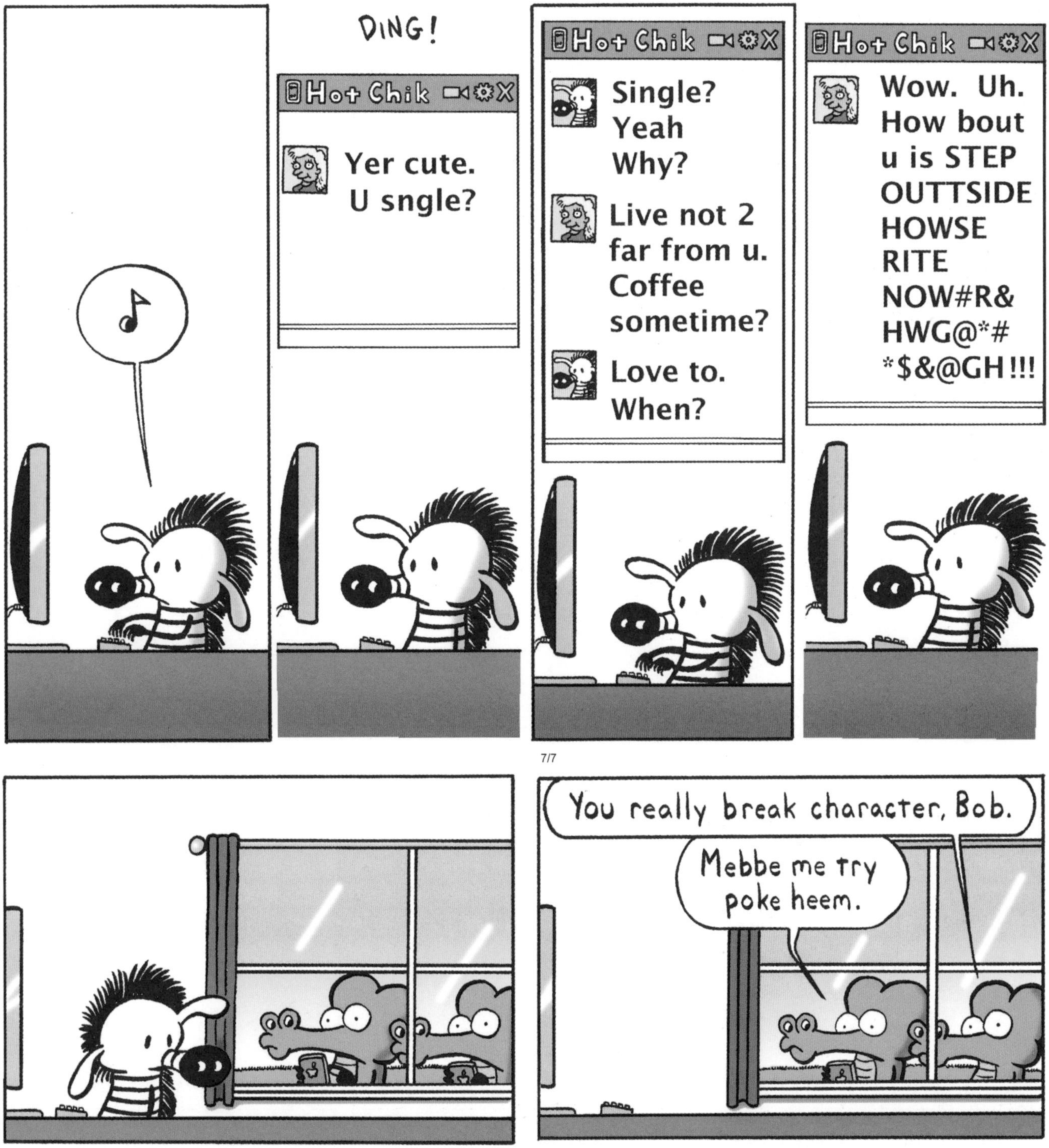
DING!
Hot Chik
Yer cute. U sngle?
Hot Chik
Single? Yeah Why?
Live not 2 far from u. Coffee sometime?
Love to. When?
Hot Chik
Wow. Uh. How bout u is STEP OUTTSIDE HOWSE RITE NOW#R& HWG@*# *$&@GH!!!
7/7
You really break character, Bob.
Mebbe me try poke heem.

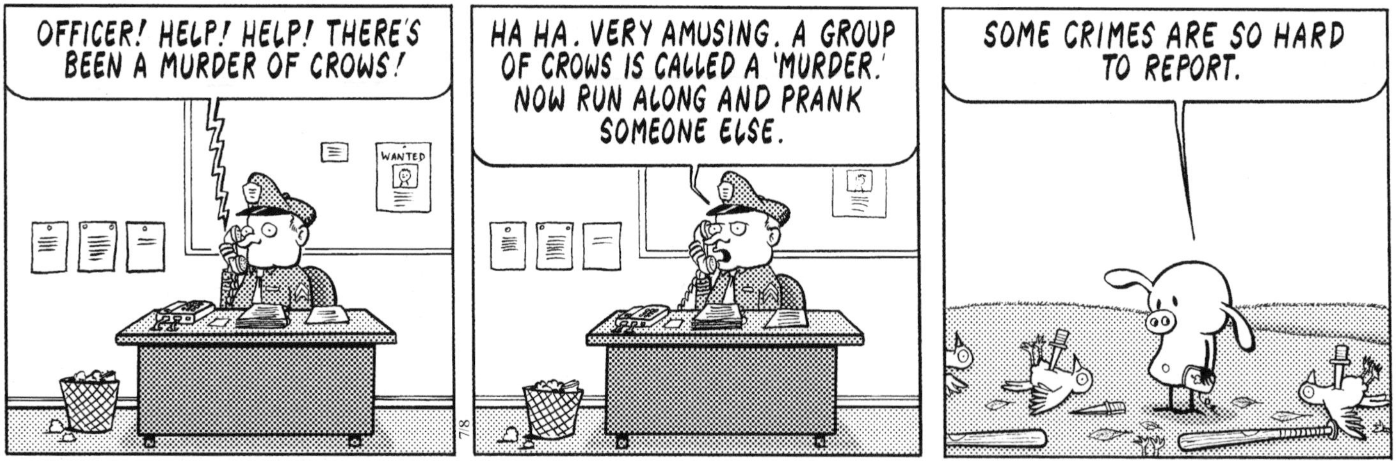
OFFICER! HELP! HELP! THERE'S BEEN A MURDER OF CROWS!
WANTED
7/8
HA HA. VERY AMUSING. A GROUP OF CROWS IS CALLED A 'MURDER.' NOW RUN ALONG AND PRANK SOMEONE ELSE.
SOME CRIMES ARE SO HARD TO REPORT.

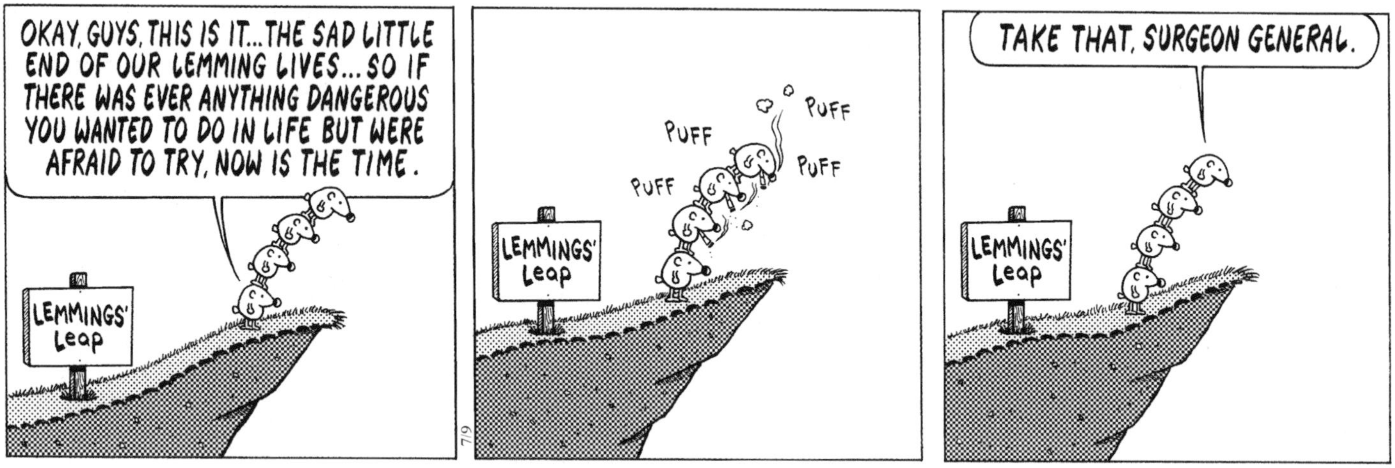
OKAY, GUYS, THIS IS IT...THE SAD LITTLE END OF OUR LEMMING LIVES... SO IF THERE WAS EVER ANYTHING DANGEROUS YOU WANTED TO DO IN LIFE BUT WERE AFRAID TO TRY, NOW IS THE TIME.
LEMMINGS' Leap
7/9
PUFF
PUFF
PUFF
PUFF
LEMMINGS' Leap
TAKE THAT, SURGEON GENERAL.
LEMMINGS' Leap

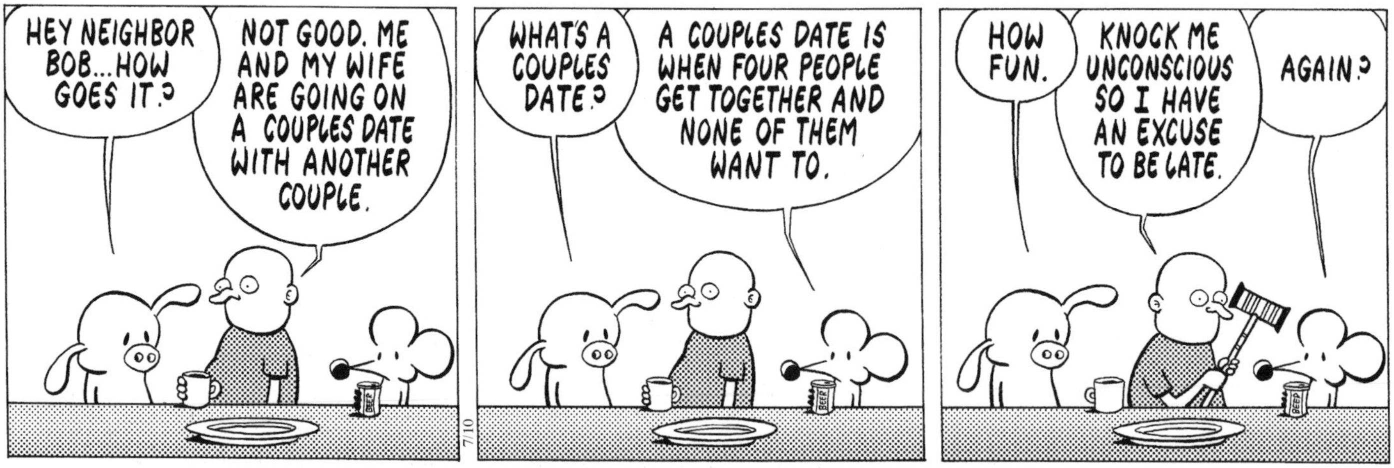
HEY NEIGHBOR BOB...HOW GOES IT?
NOT GOOD. ME AND MY WIFE ARE GOING ON A COUPLES DATE WITH ANOTHER COUPLE.
7/10
WHAT'S A COUPLES DATE?
A COUPLES DATE IS WHEN FOUR PEOPLE GET TOGETHER AND NONE OF THEM WANT TO.
HOW FUN.
KNOCK ME UNCONSCIOUS SO I HAVE AN EXCUSE TO BE LATE.
AGAIN?

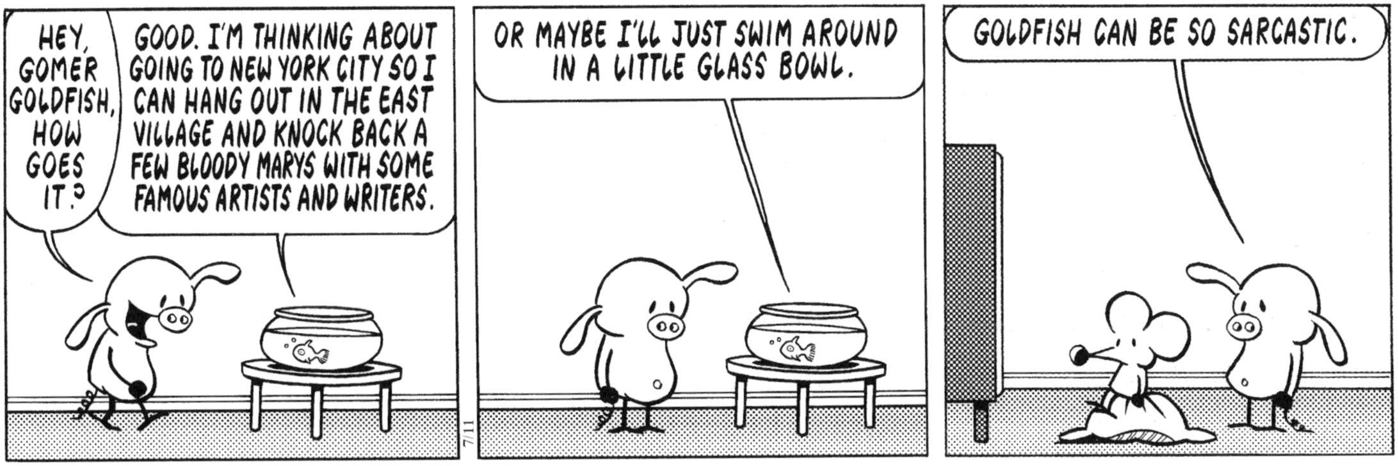

HEY, GOMER GOLDFISH, HOW GOES IT?
GOOD. I'M THINKING ABOUT GOING TO NEW YORK CITY SO I CAN HANG OUT IN THE EAST VILLAGE AND KNOCK BACK A FEW BLOODY MARYS WITH SOME FAMOUS ARTISTS AND WRITERS.
7/11
OR MAYBE I'LL JUST SWIM AROUND IN A LITTLE GLASS BOWL.
GOLDFISH CAN BE SO SARCASTIC.

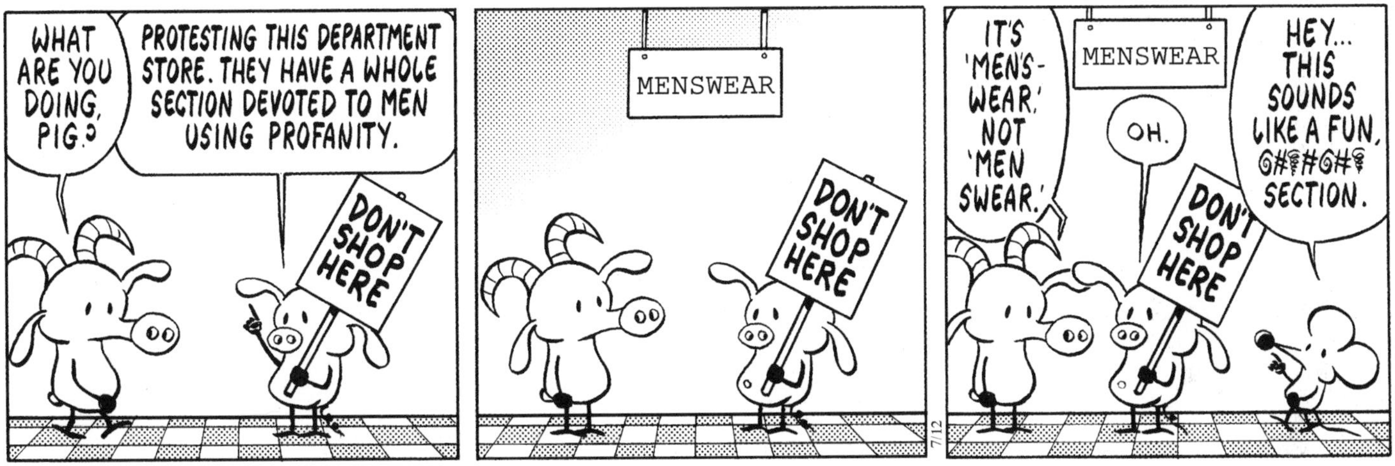

WHAT ARE YOU DOING, PIG?
PROTESTING THIS DEPARTMENT STORE. THEY HAVE A WHOLE SECTION DEVOTED TO MEN USING PROFANITY.
DON'T SHOP HERE
MENSWEAR
DON'T SHOP HERE
7/12
IT'S 'MENS-WEAR,' NOT 'MEN SWEAR.'
MENSWEAR
OH.
DON'T SHOP HERE
HEY... THIS SOUNDS LIKE A FUN,
SECTION.

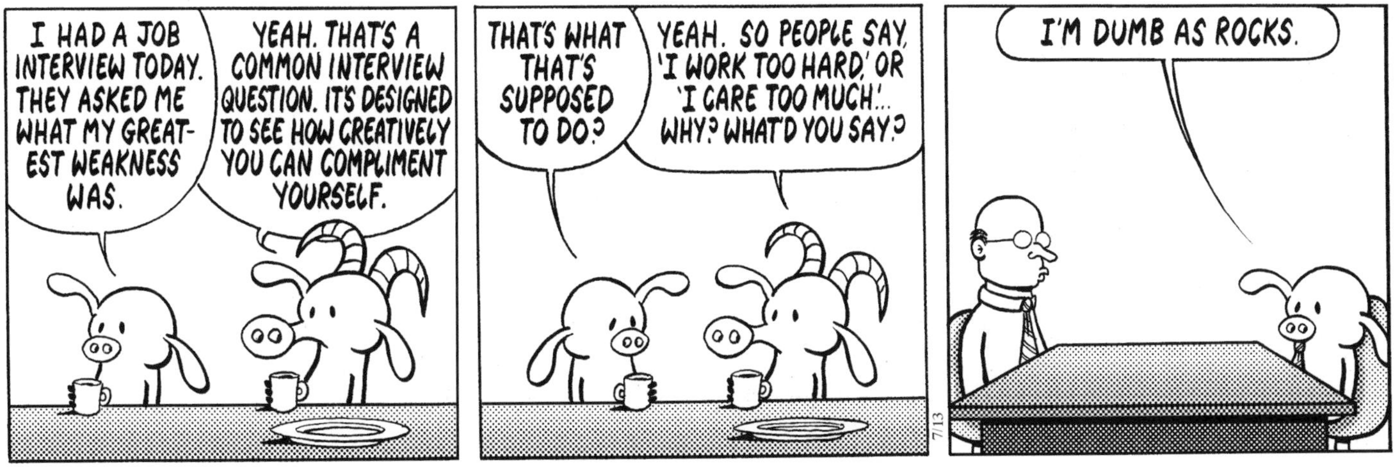

I HAD A JOB INTERVIEW TODAY. THEY ASKED ME WHAT MY GREAT-EST WEAKNESS WAS.
YEAH. THAT'S A COMMON INTERVIEW QUESTION. IT'S DESIGNED TO SEE HOW CREATIVELY YOU CAN COMPLIMENT YOURSELF.
THAT'S WHAT THAT'S SUPPOSED TO DO?
YEAH. SO PEOPLE SAY, 'I WORK TOO HARD,' OR 'I CARE TOO MUCH.'... WHY? WHAT'D YOU SAY?
7/13
I'M DUMB AS ROCKS.

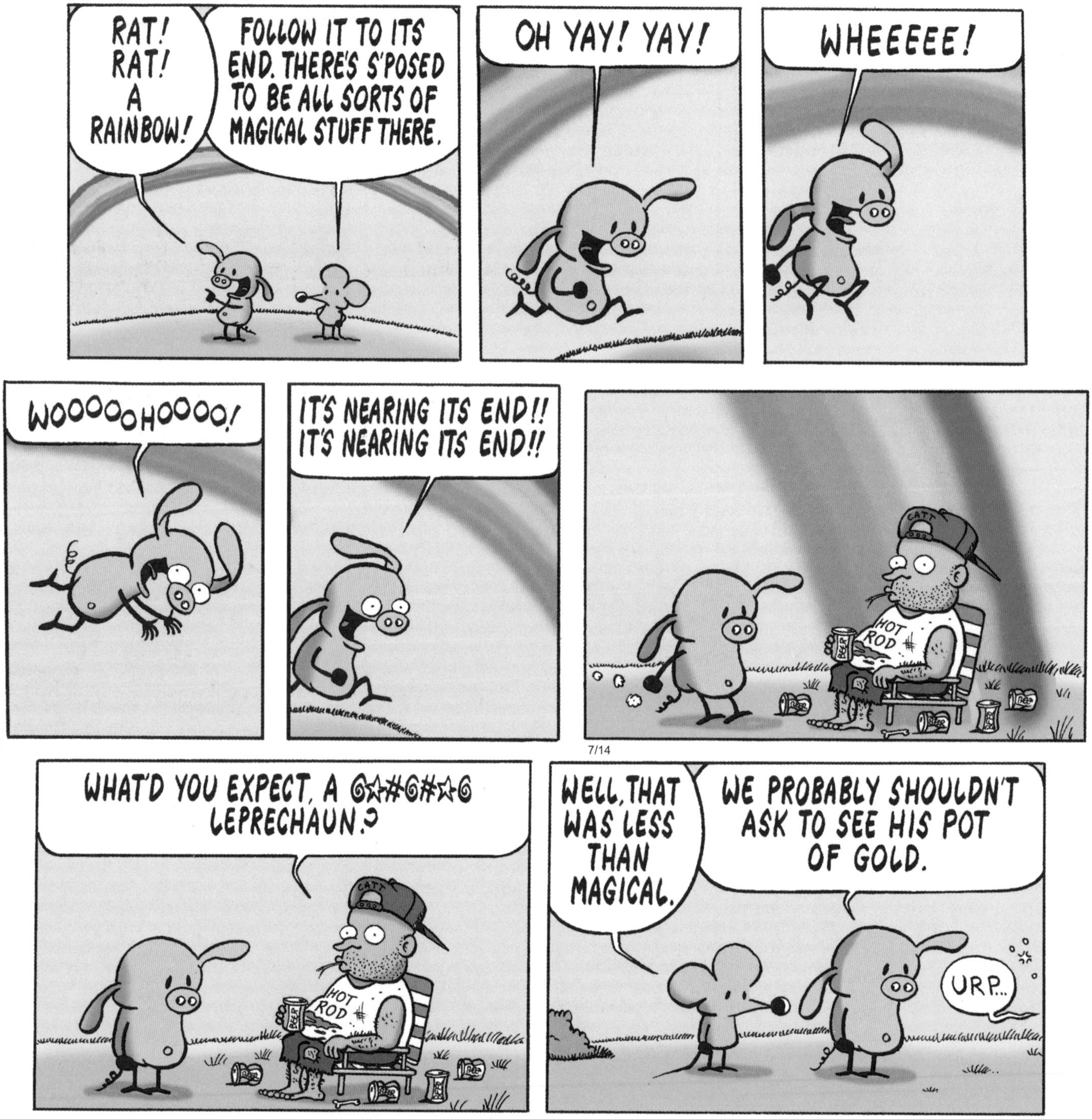
RAT! RAT! A RAINBOW!
FOLLOW IT TO ITS END. THERE'S S'POSED TO BE ALL SORTS OF MAGICAL STUFF THERE.
OH YAY! YAY!
WHEEEEE!
WOOOOOHOOOO!
IT'S NEARING ITS END!! IT'S NEARING ITS END!!
CATT
HOT ROD
BEER
7/14
WHAT'D YOU EXPECT, A G☆#G#☆G LEPRECHAUN?
WELL, THAT WAS LESS THAN MAGICAL.
WE PROBABLY SHOULDN'T ASK TO SEE HIS POT OF GOLD.
URP...

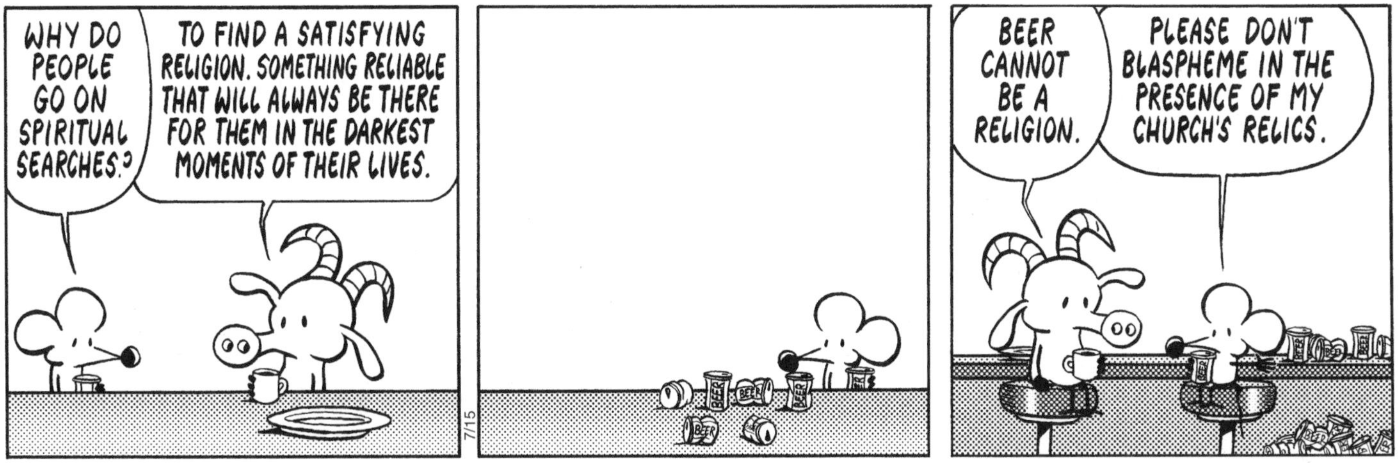
WHY DO PEOPLE GO ON SPIRITUAL SEARCHES?
TO FIND A SATISFYING RELIGION. SOMETHING RELIABLE THAT WILL ALWAYS BE THERE FOR THEM IN THE DARKEST MOMENTS OF THEIR LIVES.
7/15
BEER CANNOT BE A RELIGION.
PLEASE DON'T BLASPHEME IN THE PRESENCE OF MY CHURCH'S RELICS.

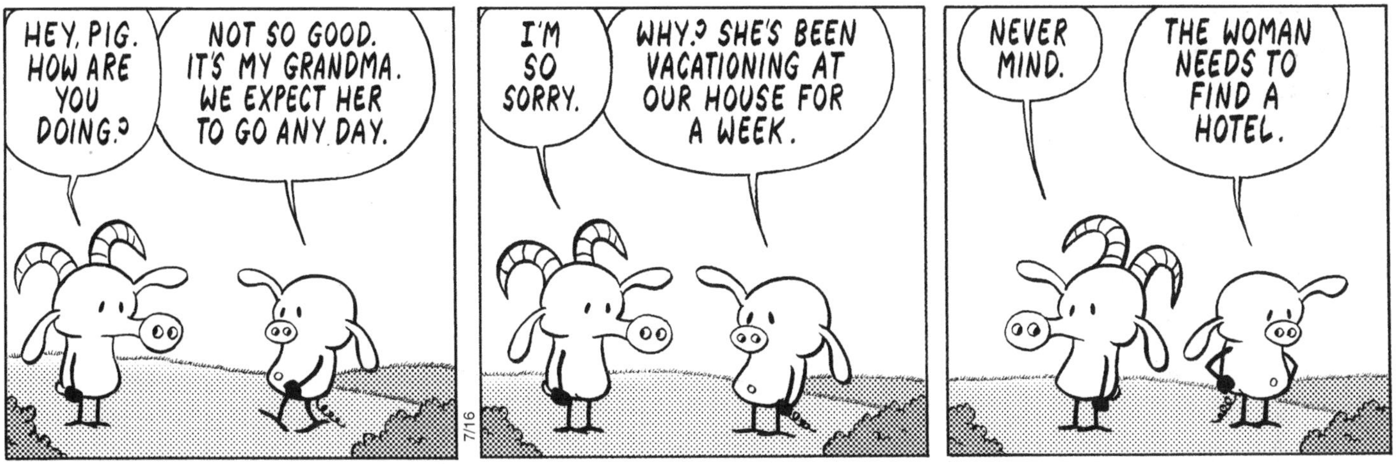
HEY, PIG. HOW ARE YOU DOING?
NOT SO GOOD. IT'S MY GRANDMA. WE EXPECT HER TO GO ANY DAY.
7/16
I'M SO SORRY.
WHY? SHE'S BEEN VACATIONING AT OUR HOUSE FOR A WEEK.
NEVER MIND.
THE WOMAN NEEDS TO FIND A HOTEL.

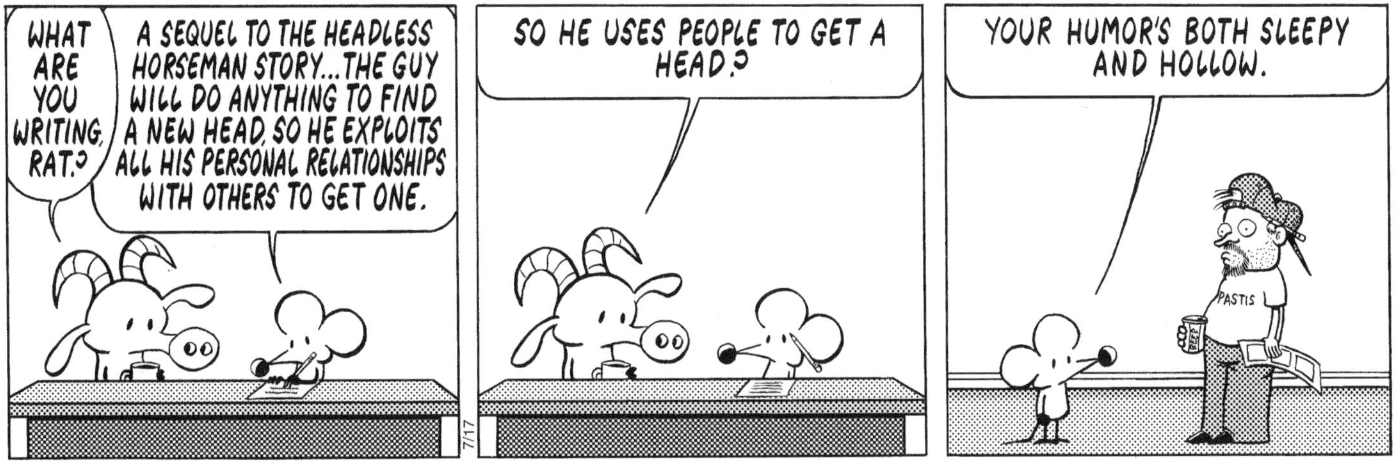
WHAT ARE YOU WRITING, RAT?
A SEQUEL TO THE HEADLESS HORSEMAN STORY... THE GUY WILL DO ANYTHING TO FIND A NEW HEAD, SO HE EXPLOITS ALL HIS PERSONAL RELATIONSHIPS WITH OTHERS TO GET ONE.
7/17
SO HE USES PEOPLE TO GET A HEAD?
YOUR HUMOR'S BOTH SLEEPY AND HOLLOW.
PASTIS

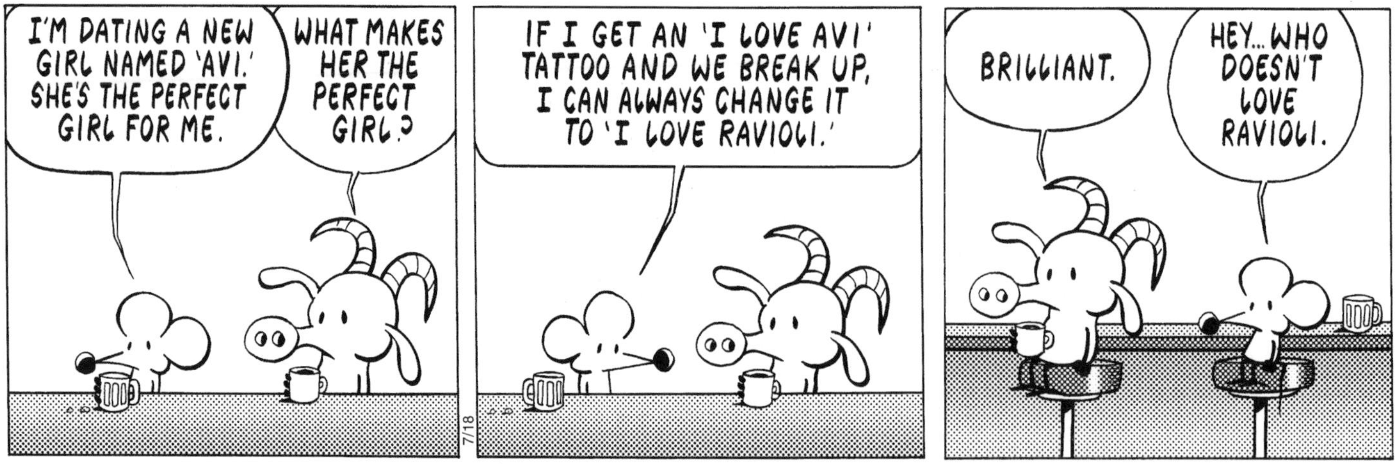
I'M DATING A NEW GIRL NAMED 'AVI.' SHE'S THE PERFECT GIRL FOR ME.
WHAT MAKES HER THE PERFECT GIRL?
IF I GET AN 'I LOVE AVI' TATTOO AND WE BREAK UP, I CAN ALWAYS CHANGE IT TO 'I LOVE RAVIOLI.'
7/18
BRILLIANT.
HEY... WHO DOESN'T LOVE RAVIOLI.

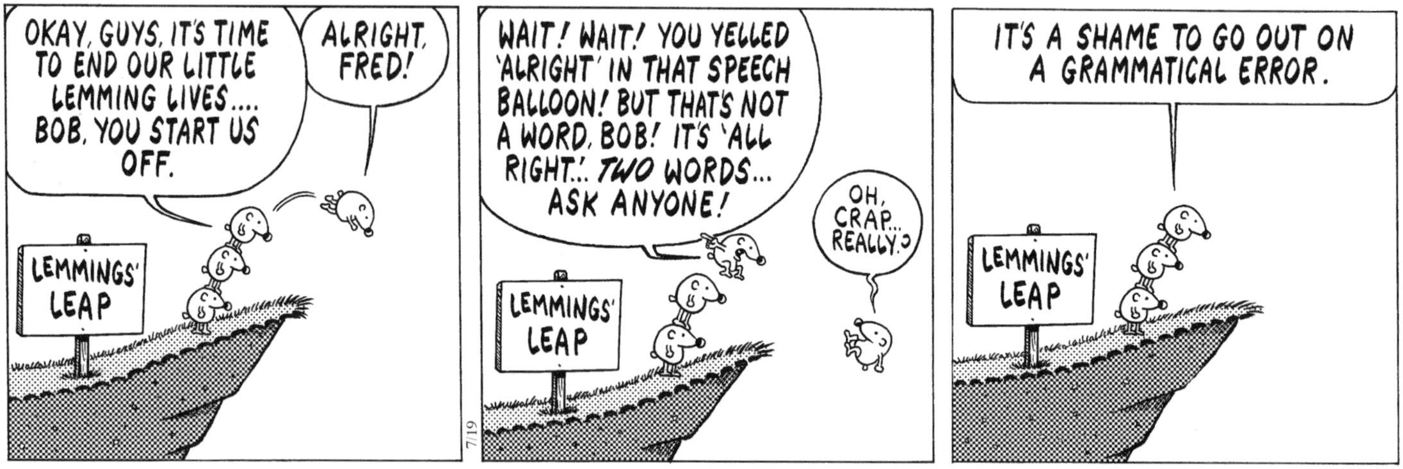
OKAY, GUYS, IT'S TIME TO END OUR LITTLE LEMMING LIVES.... BOB, YOU START US OFF.
ALRIGHT, FRED!
LEMMINGS' LEAP
7/19
WAIT! WAIT! YOU YELLED 'ALRIGHT' IN THAT SPEECH BALLOON! BUT THAT'S NOT A WORD, BOB! IT'S 'ALL RIGHT.' TWO WORDS... ASK ANYONE!
OH, CRAP... REALLY?
LEMMINGS' LEAP
IT'S A SHAME TO GO OUT ON A GRAMMATICAL ERROR.
LEMMINGS' LEAP

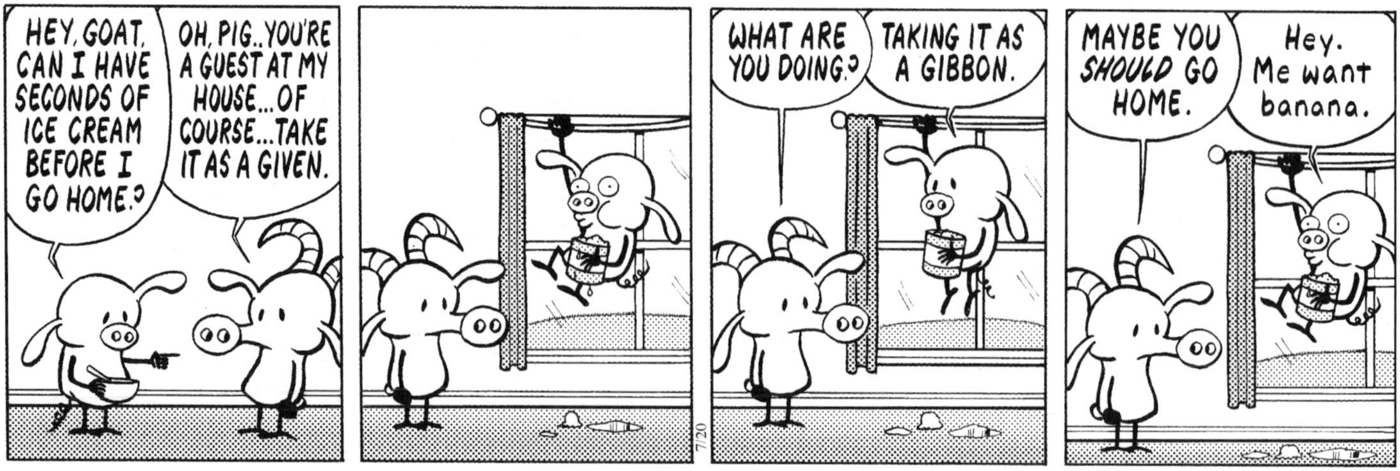
HEY, GOAT, CAN I HAVE SECONDS OF ICE CREAM BEFORE I GO HOME?
OH, PIG.. YOU'RE A GUEST AT MY HOUSE... OF COURSE... TAKE IT AS A GIVEN.
7/20
WHAT ARE YOU DOING?
TAKING IT AS A GIBBON.
MAYBE YOU SHOULD GO HOME.
Hey. Me want banana.

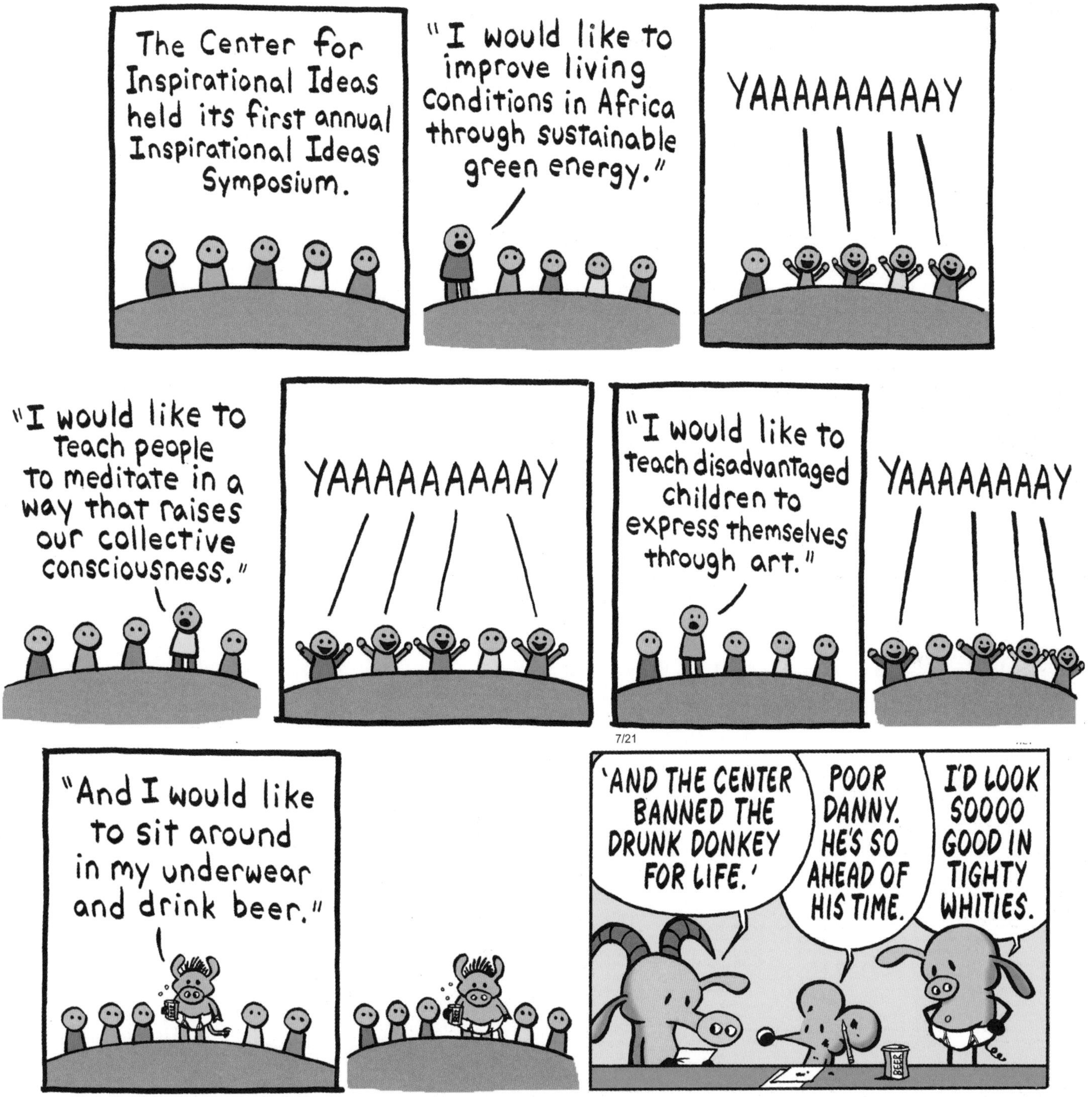
The Center for Inspirational Ideas held its first annual Inspirational Ideas Symposium.
"I would like to improve living conditions in Africa through sustainable green energy."
YAAAAAAAAY
"I would like to teach people to meditate in a way that raises our collective consciousness."
YAAAAAAAAAY
"I would like to teach disadvantaged children to express themselves through art."
YAAAAAAAAY
7/21
"And I would like to sit around in my underwear and drink beer."
'AND THE CENTER BANNED THE DRUNK DONKEY FOR LIFE.'
POOR DANNY. HE'S SO AHEAD OF HIS TIME.
I'D LOOK SOOOO GOOD IN TIGHTY WHITIES.
BEER

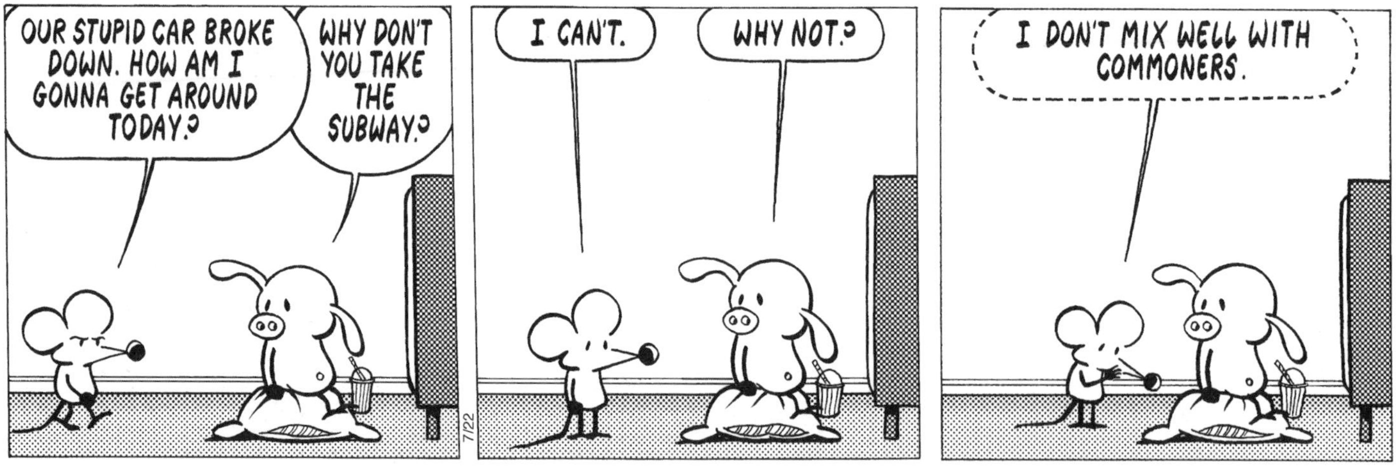
OUR STUPID CAR BROKE DOWN. HOW AM I GONNA GET AROUND TODAY?
WHY DON'T YOU TAKE THE SUBWAY?
I CAN'T.
WHY NOT?
I DON'T MIX WELL WITH COMMONERS.

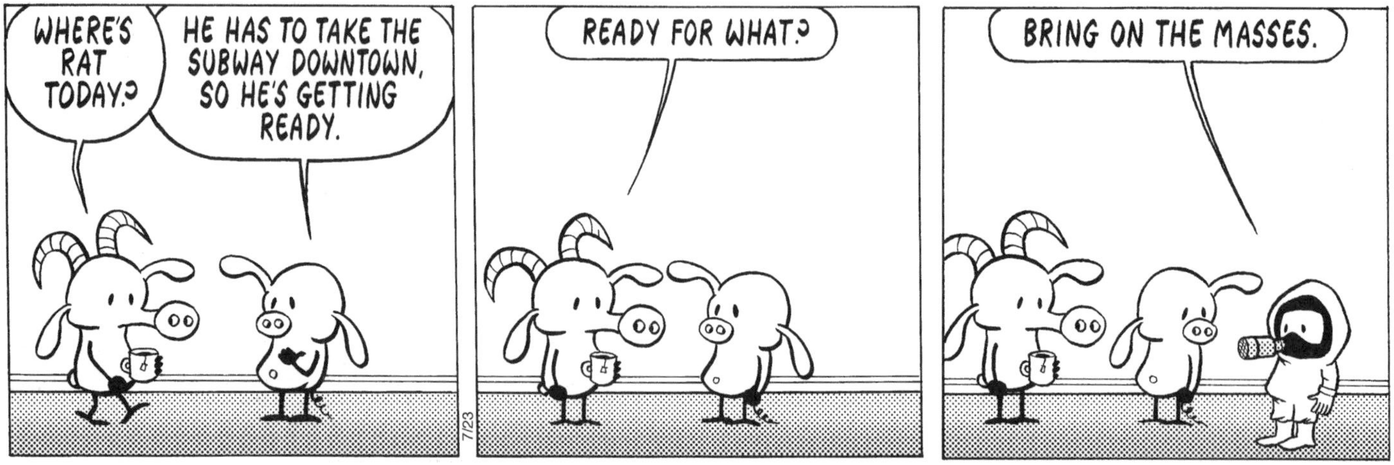
WHERE'S RAT TODAY?
HE HAS TO TAKE THE SUBWAY DOWNTOWN, SO HE'S GETTING READY.
READY FOR WHAT?
BRING ON THE MASSES.

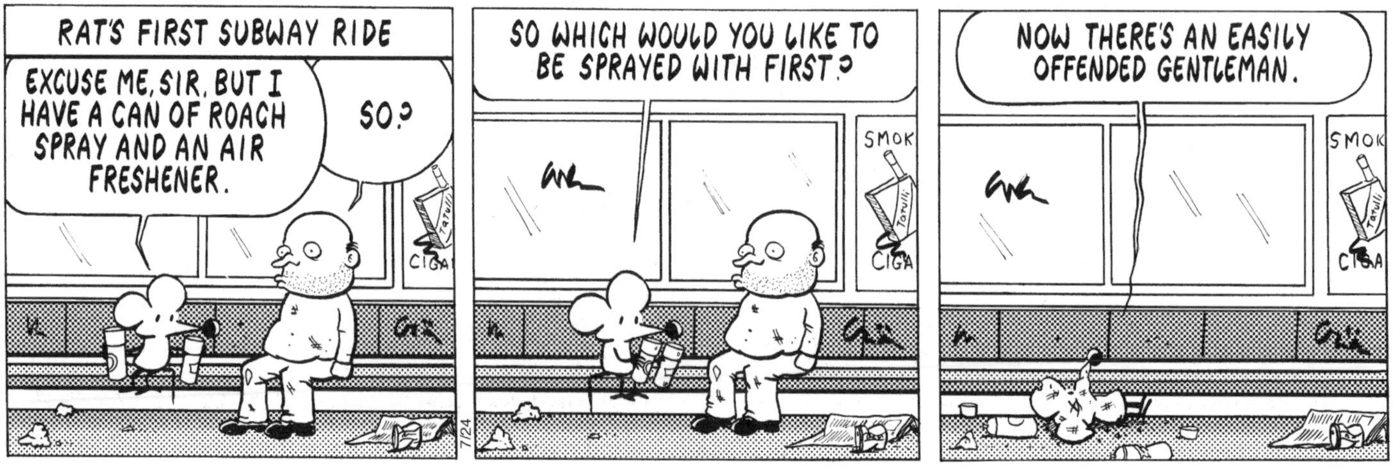
RAT'S FIRST SUBWAY RIDE
EXCUSE ME, SIR, BUT I HAVE A CAN OF ROACH SPRAY AND AN AIR FRESHENER.
SO?
SO WHICH WOULD YOU LIKE TO BE SPRAYED WITH FIRST?
NOW THERE'S AN EASILY OFFENDED GENTLEMAN.

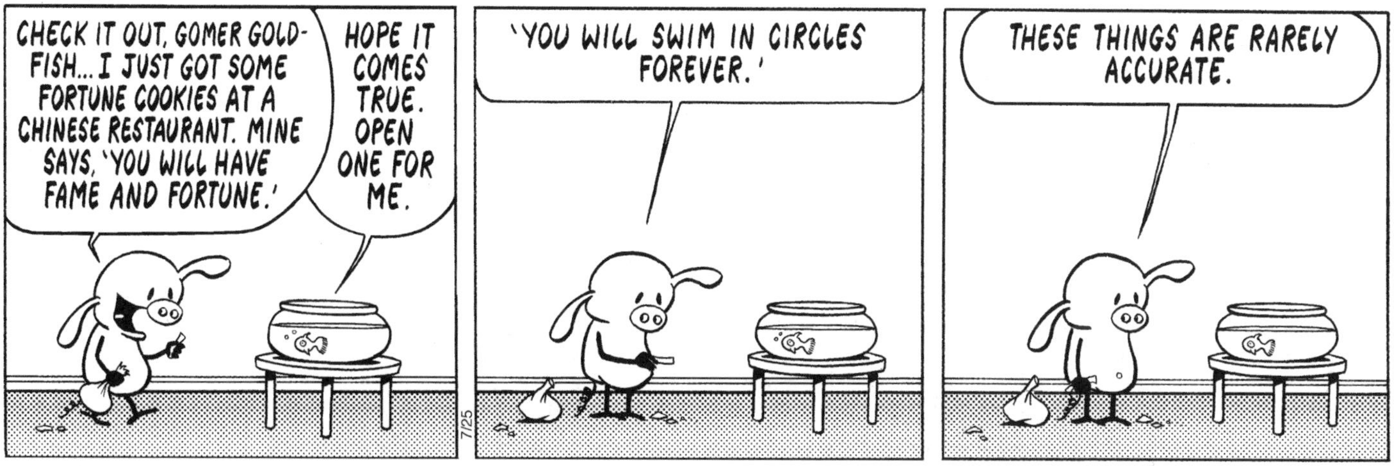
CHECK IT OUT, GOMER GOLDFISH... I JUST GOT SOME FORTUNE COOKIES AT A CHINESE RESTAURANT. MINE SAYS, 'YOU WILL HAVE FAME AND FORTUNE.'
HOPE IT COMES TRUE. OPEN ONE FOR ME.
7/25
'YOU WILL SWIM IN CIRCLES FOREVER.'
THESE THINGS ARE RARELY ACCURATE.

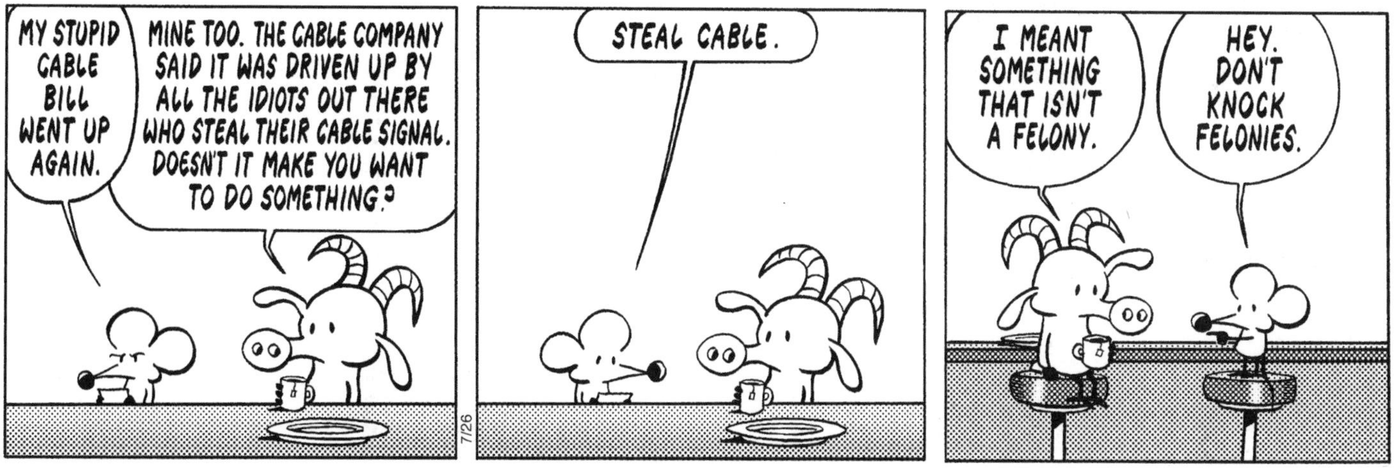
MY STUPID CABLE BILL WENT UP AGAIN.
MINE TOO. THE CABLE COMPANY SAID IT WAS DRIVEN UP BY ALL THE IDIOTS OUT THERE WHO STEAL THEIR CABLE SIGNAL. DOESN'T IT MAKE YOU WANT TO DO SOMETHING?
7/26
STEAL CABLE.
I MEANT SOMETHING THAT ISN'T A FELONY.
HEY. DON'T KNOCK FELONIES.

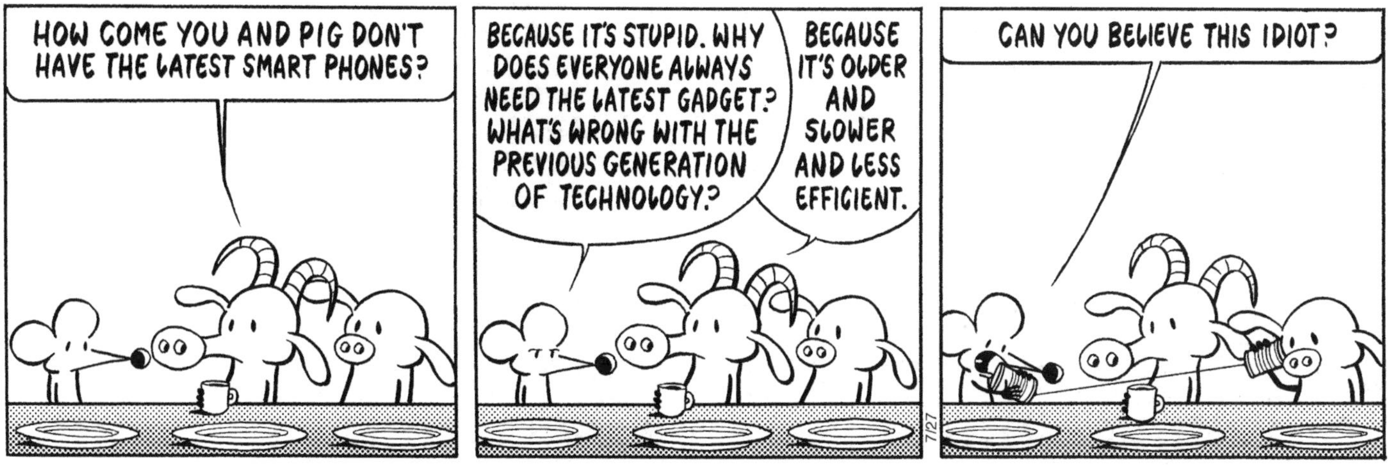
HOW COME YOU AND PIG DON'T HAVE THE LATEST SMART PHONES?
BECAUSE IT'S STUPID. WHY DOES EVERYONE ALWAYS NEED THE LATEST GADGET? WHAT'S WRONG WITH THE PREVIOUS GENERATION OF TECHNOLOGY?
BECAUSE IT'S OLDER AND SLOWER AND LESS EFFICIENT.
7/27
CAN YOU BELIEVE THIS IDIOT?

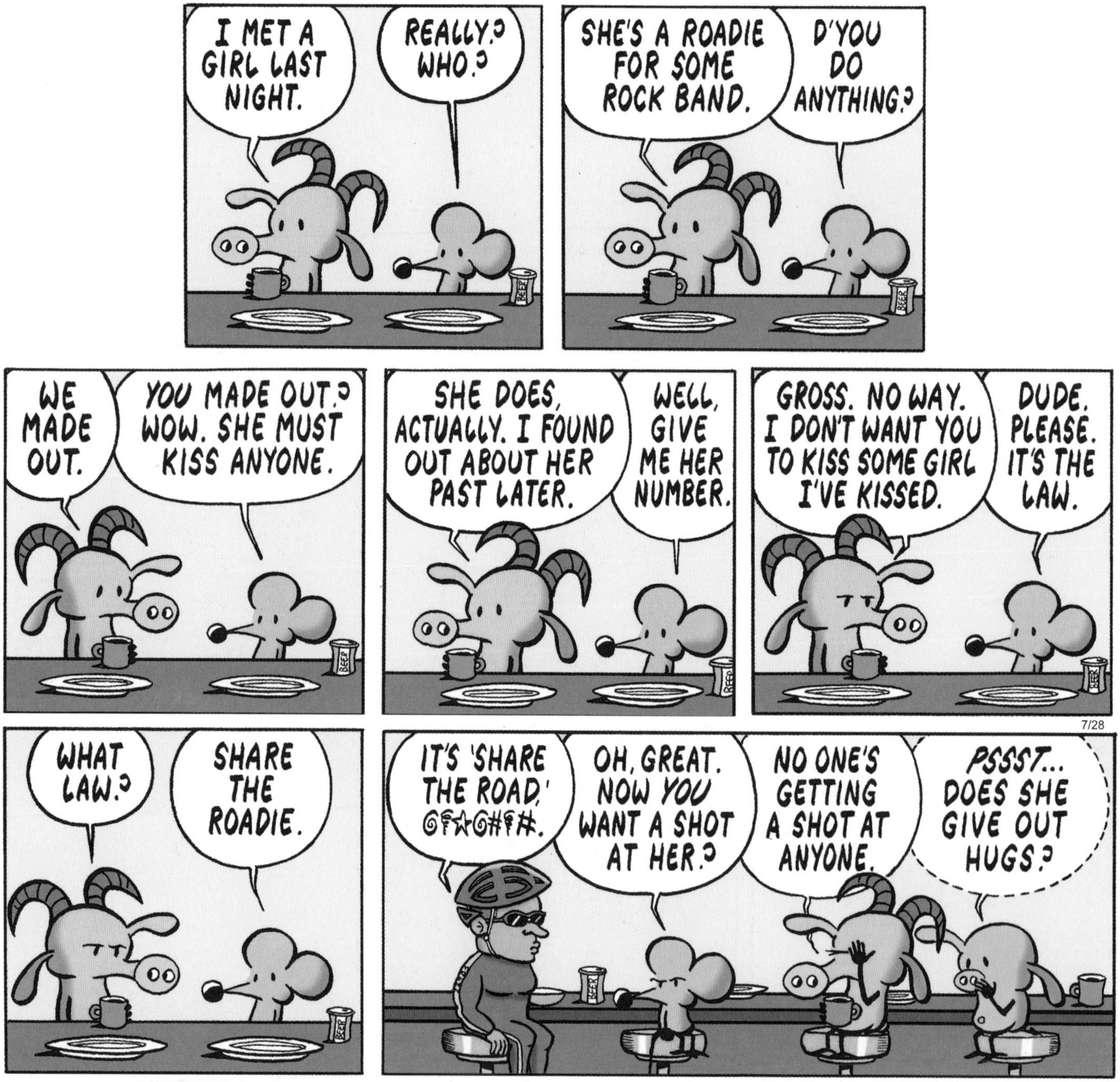
I MET A GIRL LAST NIGHT.
REALLY? WHO?
SHE'S A ROADIE FOR SOME ROCK BAND.
D'YOU DO ANYTHING?
WE MADE OUT.
YOU MADE OUT? WOW. SHE MUST KISS ANYONE.
SHE DOES, ACTUALLY. I FOUND OUT ABOUT HER PAST LATER.
WELL, GIVE ME HER NUMBER.
GROSS. NO WAY. I DON'T WANT YOU TO KISS SOME GIRL I'VE KISSED.
DUDE. PLEASE. IT'S THE LAW.
7/28
WHAT LAW?
SHARE THE ROADIE.
IT'S 'SHARE THE ROAD,' @$☆@#$#.
OH, GREAT. NOW *YOU* WANT A SHOT AT HER?
NO ONE'S GETTING A SHOT AT ANYONE.
PSSST... DOES SHE GIVE OUT HUGS?

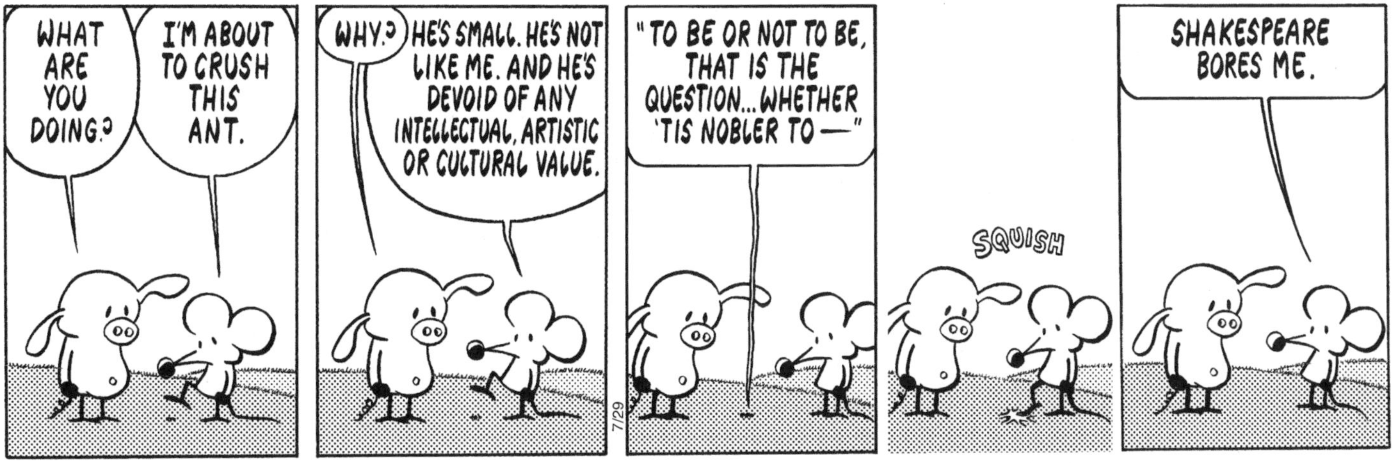
WHAT ARE YOU DOING?
I'M ABOUT TO CRUSH THIS ANT.
WHY?
HE'S SMALL. HE'S NOT LIKE ME. AND HE'S DEVOID OF ANY INTELLECTUAL, ARTISTIC OR CULTURAL VALUE.
7/29
"TO BE OR NOT TO BE, THAT IS THE QUESTION... WHETHER 'TIS NOBLER TO—"
SQUISH
SHAKESPEARE BORES ME.

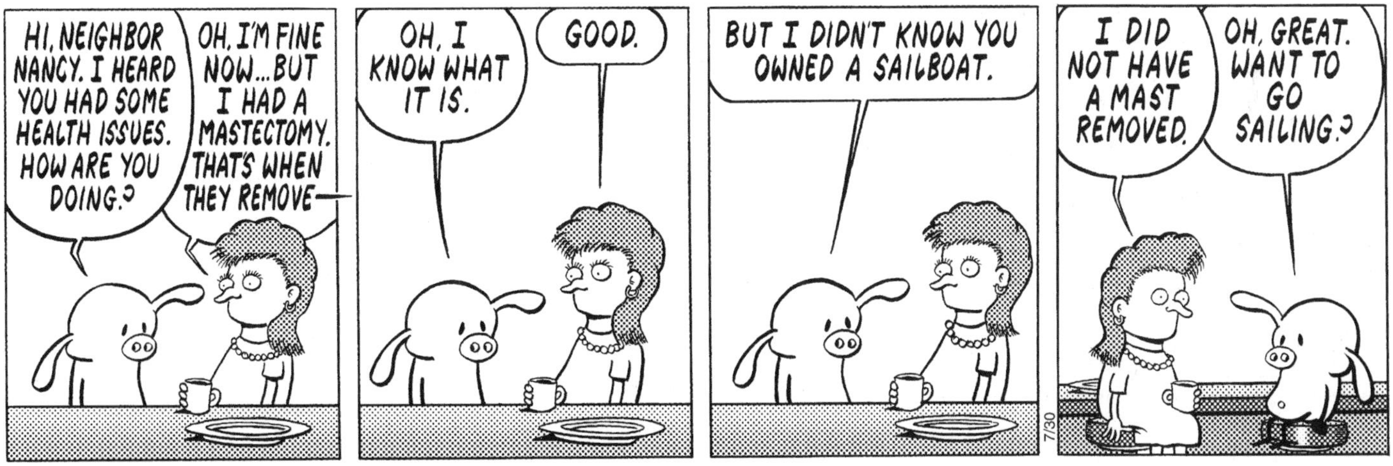
HI, NEIGHBOR NANCY. I HEARD YOU HAD SOME HEALTH ISSUES. HOW ARE YOU DOING?
OH, I'M FINE NOW... BUT I HAD A MASTECTOMY. THAT'S WHEN THEY REMOVE—
OH, I KNOW WHAT IT IS.
GOOD.
BUT I DIDN'T KNOW YOU OWNED A SAILBOAT.
7/30
I DID NOT HAVE A MAST REMOVED.
OH, GREAT. WANT TO GO SAILING?

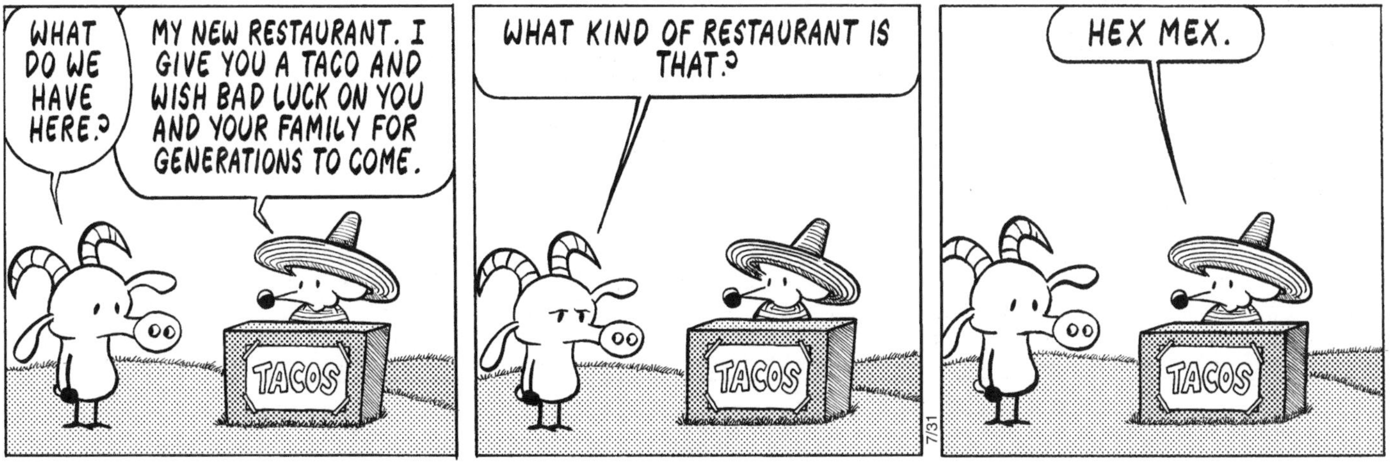
WHAT DO WE HAVE HERE?
MY NEW RESTAURANT. I GIVE YOU A TACO AND WISH BAD LUCK ON YOU AND YOUR FAMILY FOR GENERATIONS TO COME.
TACOS
WHAT KIND OF RESTAURANT IS THAT?
TACOS
7/31
HEX MEX.
TACOS

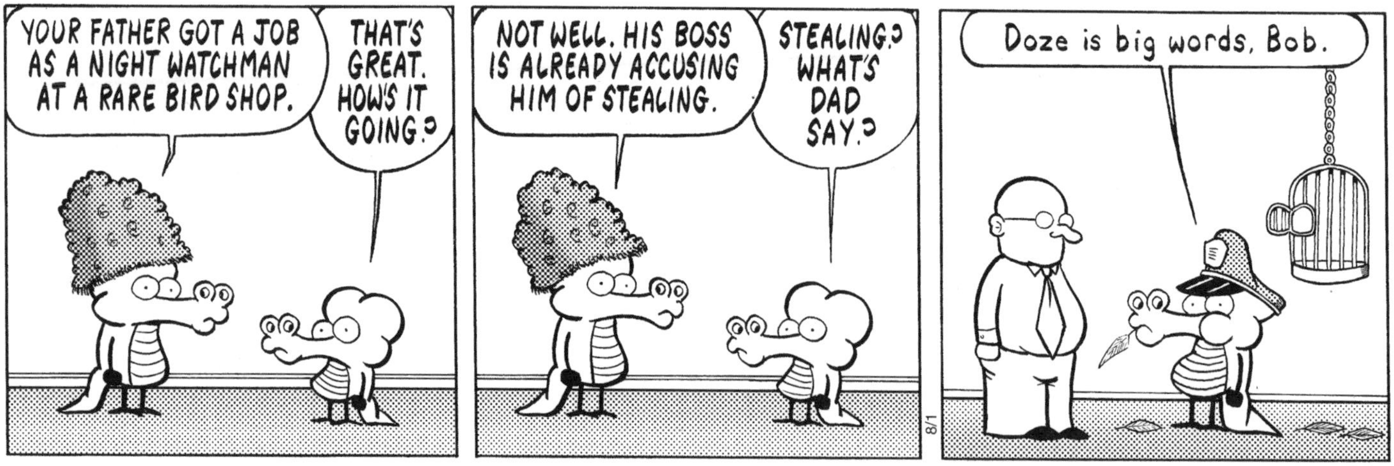
YOUR FATHER GOT A JOB AS A NIGHT WATCHMAN AT A RARE BIRD SHOP.
THAT'S GREAT. HOW'S IT GOING?
NOT WELL. HIS BOSS IS ALREADY ACCUSING HIM OF STEALING.
STEALING? WHAT'S DAD SAY?
Doze is big words, Bob.
8/1

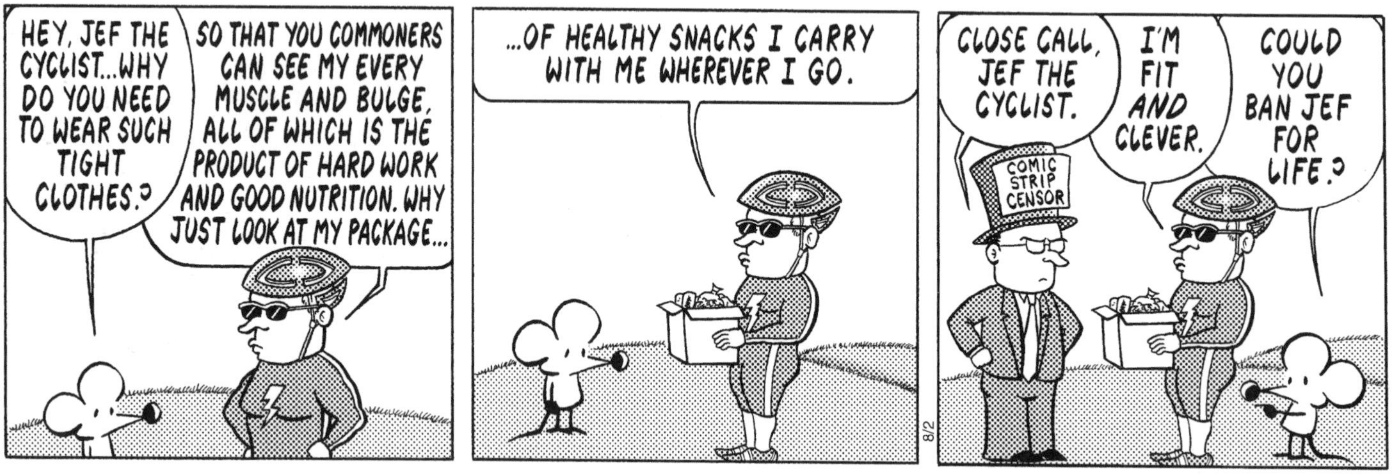
HEY, JEF THE CYCLIST...WHY DO YOU NEED TO WEAR SUCH TIGHT CLOTHES?
SO THAT YOU COMMONERS CAN SEE MY EVERY MUSCLE AND BULGE, ALL OF WHICH IS THE PRODUCT OF HARD WORK AND GOOD NUTRITION. WHY JUST LOOK AT MY PACKAGE...
...OF HEALTHY SNACKS I CARRY WITH ME WHEREVER I GO.
CLOSE CALL, JEF THE CYCLIST.
COMIC STRIP CENSOR
I'M FIT AND CLEVER.
COULD YOU BAN JEF FOR LIFE?
8/2

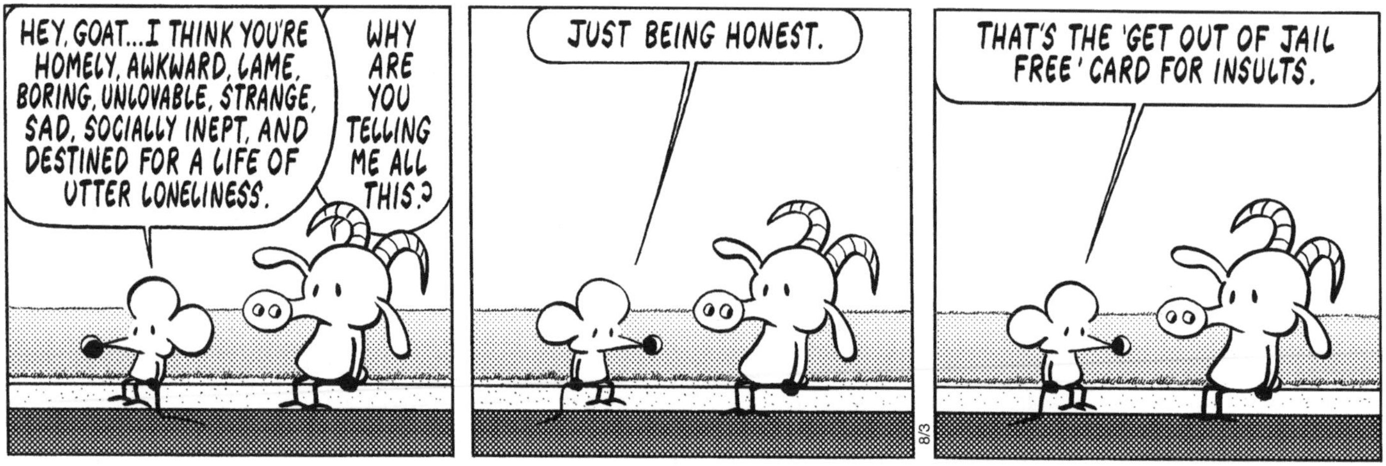
HEY, GOAT...I THINK YOU'RE HOMELY, AWKWARD, LAME, BORING, UNLOVABLE, STRANGE, SAD, SOCIALLY INEPT, AND DESTINED FOR A LIFE OF UTTER LONELINESS.
WHY ARE YOU TELLING ME ALL THIS?
JUST BEING HONEST.
THAT'S THE 'GET OUT OF JAIL FREE' CARD FOR INSULTS.
8/3

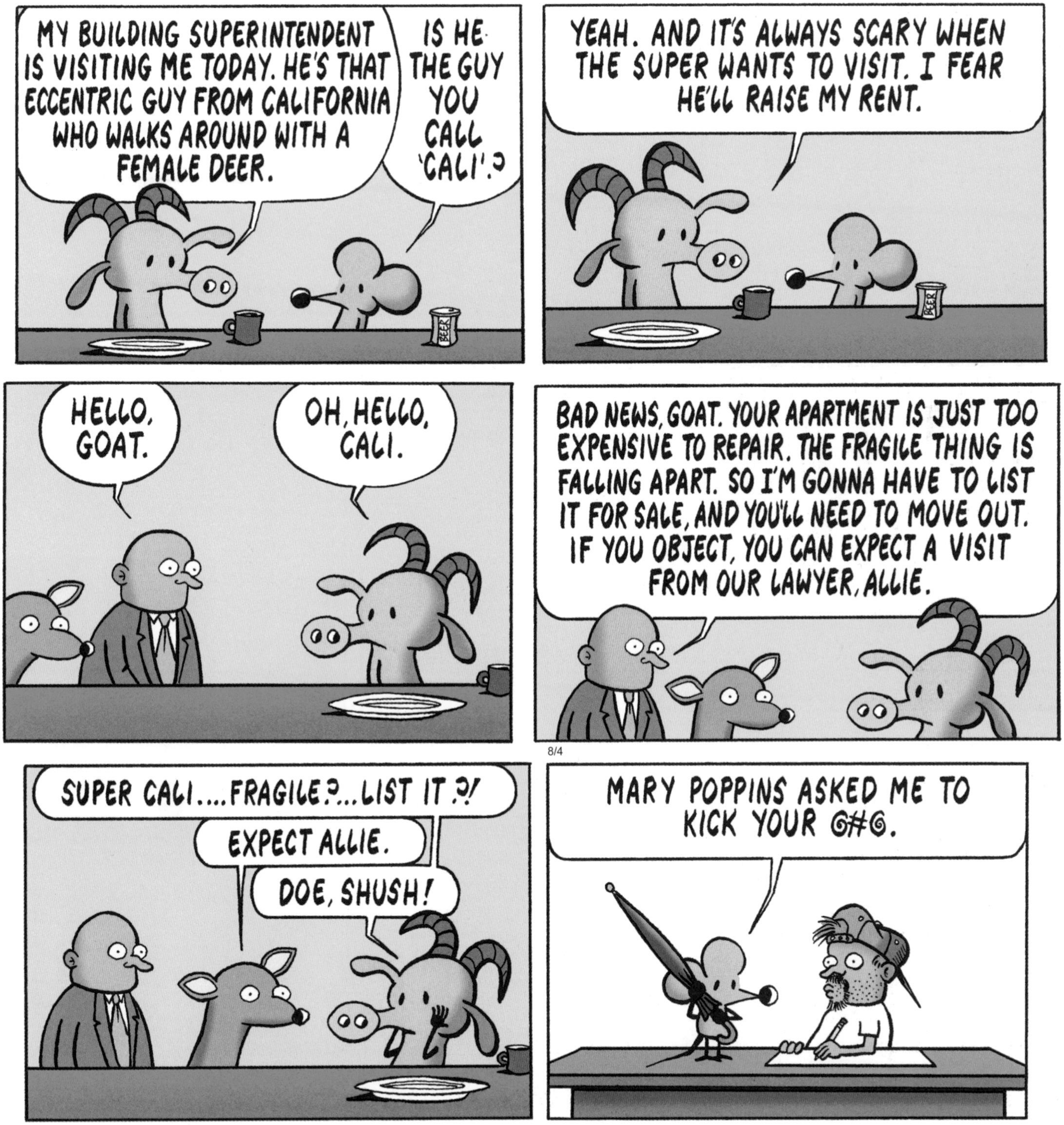
MY BUILDING SUPERINTENDENT IS VISITING ME TODAY. HE'S THAT ECCENTRIC GUY FROM CALIFORNIA WHO WALKS AROUND WITH A FEMALE DEER.
IS HE THE GUY YOU CALL 'CALI'?
YEAH. AND IT'S ALWAYS SCARY WHEN THE SUPER WANTS TO VISIT. I FEAR HE'LL RAISE MY RENT.
BEER
BEER
HELLO, GOAT.
OH, HELLO, CALI.
BAD NEWS, GOAT. YOUR APARTMENT IS JUST TOO EXPENSIVE TO REPAIR. THE FRAGILE THING IS FALLING APART. SO I'M GONNA HAVE TO LIST IT FOR SALE, AND YOU'LL NEED TO MOVE OUT. IF YOU OBJECT, YOU CAN EXPECT A VISIT FROM OUR LAWYER, ALLIE.
8/4
SUPER CALI....FRAGILE?...LIST IT?!
EXPECT ALLIE.
DOE, SHUSH!
MARY POPPINS ASKED ME TO KICK YOUR G#G.

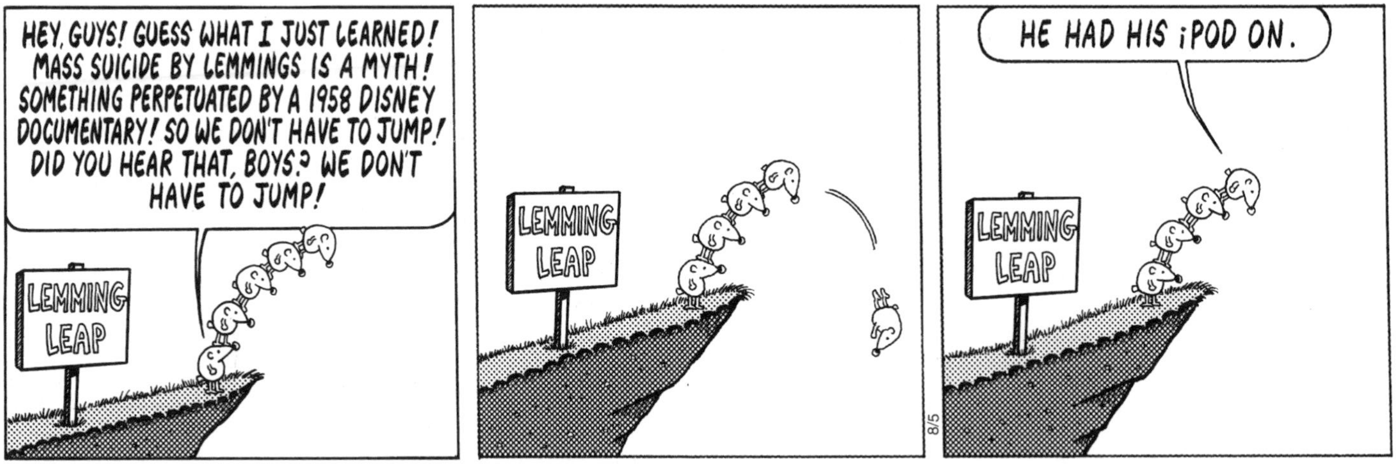
HEY, GUYS! GUESS WHAT I JUST LEARNED! MASS SUICIDE BY LEMMINGS IS A MYTH! SOMETHING PERPETUATED BY A 1958 DISNEY DOCUMENTARY! SO WE DON'T HAVE TO JUMP! DID YOU HEAR THAT, BOYS? WE DON'T HAVE TO JUMP!
LEMMING LEAP
LEMMING LEAP
LEMMING LEAP
HE HAD HIS iPOD ON.
8/5

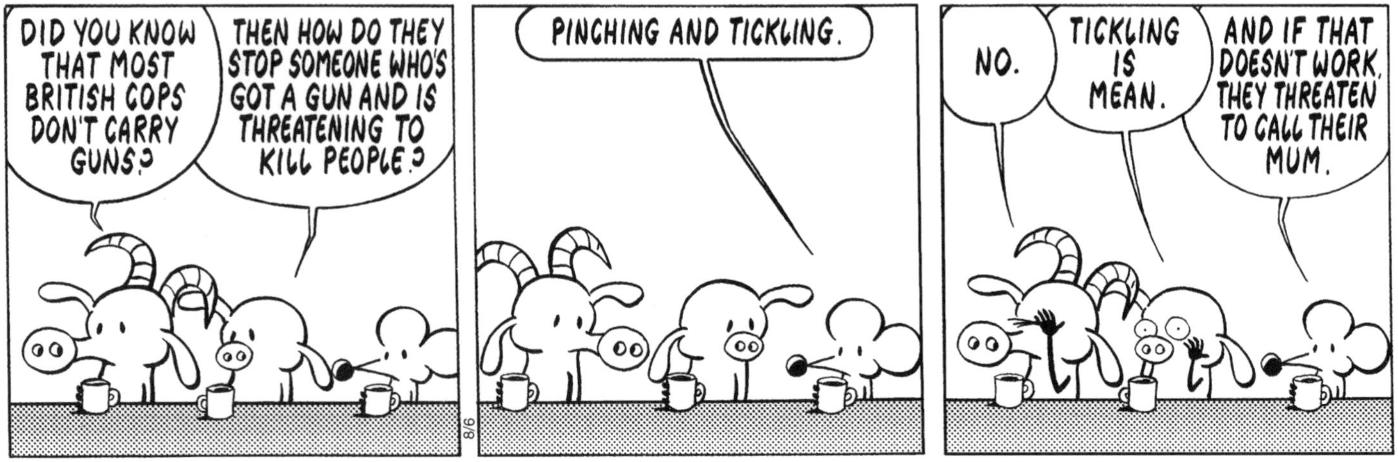
DID YOU KNOW THAT MOST BRITISH COPS DON'T CARRY GUNS?
THEN HOW DO THEY STOP SOMEONE WHO'S GOT A GUN AND IS THREATENING TO KILL PEOPLE?
8/6
PINCHING AND TICKLING.
NO.
TICKLING IS MEAN.
AND IF THAT DOESN'T WORK, THEY THREATEN TO CALL THEIR MUM.

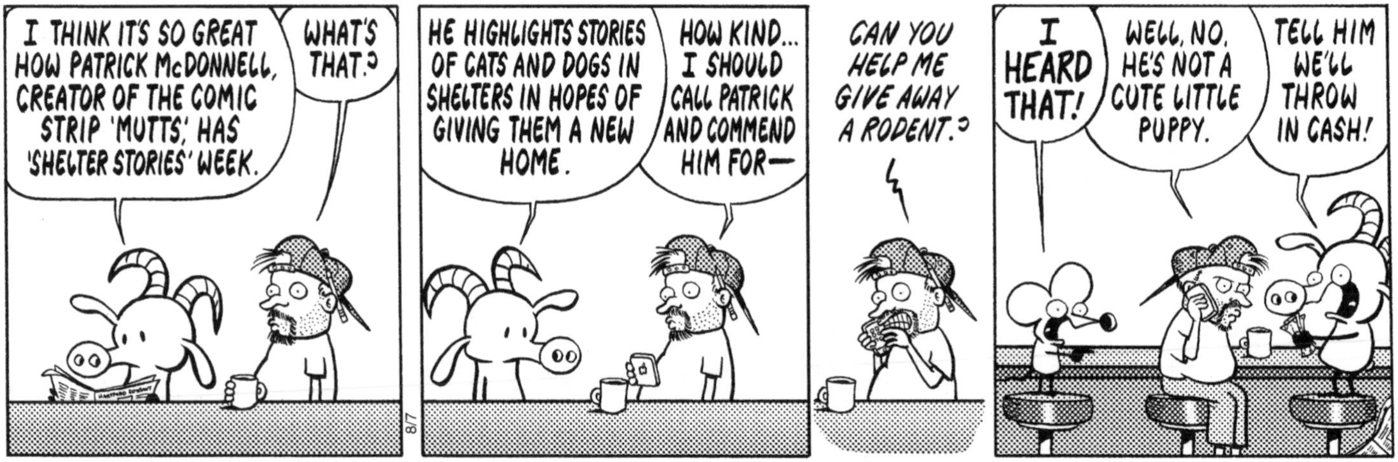
I THINK IT'S SO GREAT HOW PATRICK McDONNELL, CREATOR OF THE COMIC STRIP 'MUTTS,' HAS 'SHELTER STORIES' WEEK.
WHAT'S THAT?
8/7
HE HIGHLIGHTS STORIES OF CATS AND DOGS IN SHELTERS IN HOPES OF GIVING THEM A NEW HOME.
HOW KIND... I SHOULD CALL PATRICK AND COMMEND HIM FOR—
CAN YOU HELP ME GIVE AWAY A RODENT?
I HEARD THAT!
WELL, NO, HE'S NOT A CUTE LITTLE PUPPY.
TELL HIM WE'LL THROW IN CASH!

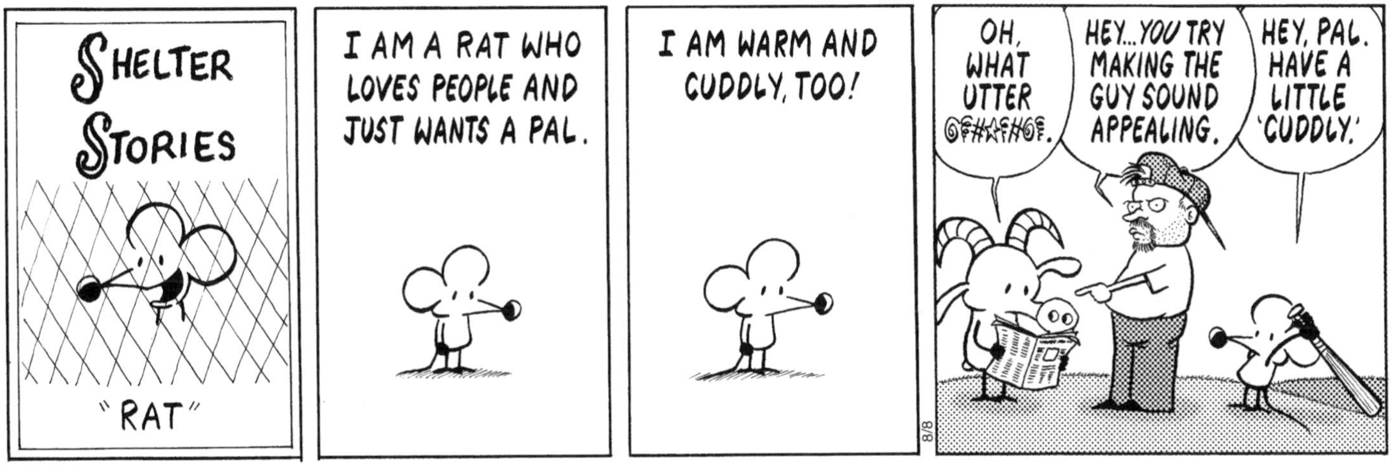
SHELTER STORIES
"RAT"
I AM A RAT WHO LOVES PEOPLE AND JUST WANTS A PAL.
I AM WARM AND CUDDLY, TOO!
OH, WHAT UTTER
HEY... YOU TRY MAKING THE GUY SOUND APPEALING.
HEY, PAL. HAVE A LITTLE 'CUDDLY.'
8/8

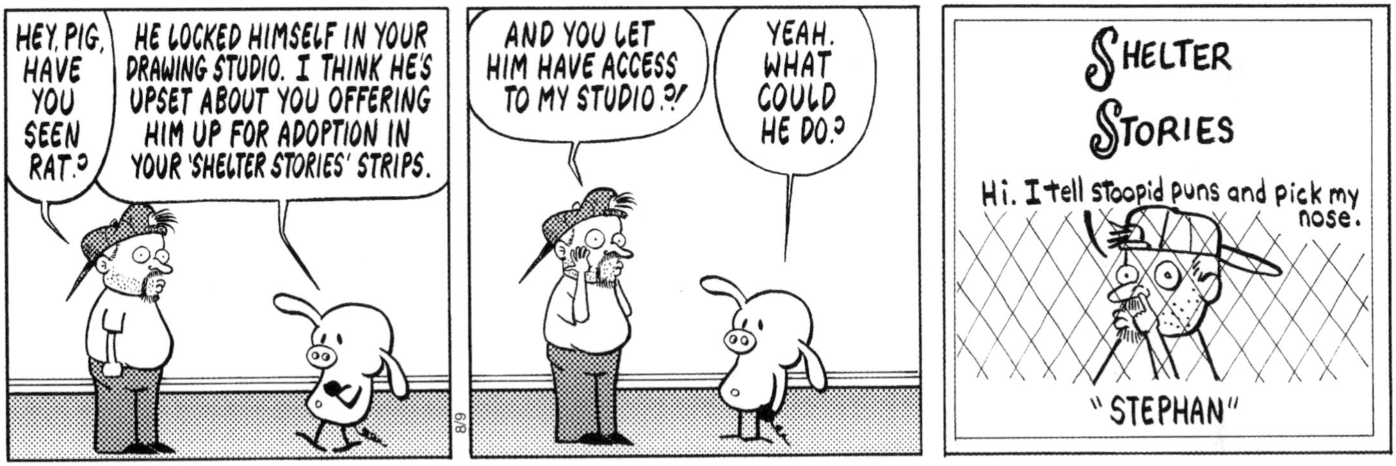
HEY, PIG, HAVE YOU SEEN RAT?
HE LOCKED HIMSELF IN YOUR DRAWING STUDIO. I THINK HE'S UPSET ABOUT YOU OFFERING HIM UP FOR ADOPTION IN YOUR 'SHELTER STORIES' STRIPS.
8/9
AND YOU LET HIM HAVE ACCESS TO MY STUDIO?!
YEAH. WHAT COULD HE DO?
SHELTER STORIES
Hi. I tell stoopid puns and pick my nose.
"STEPHAN"

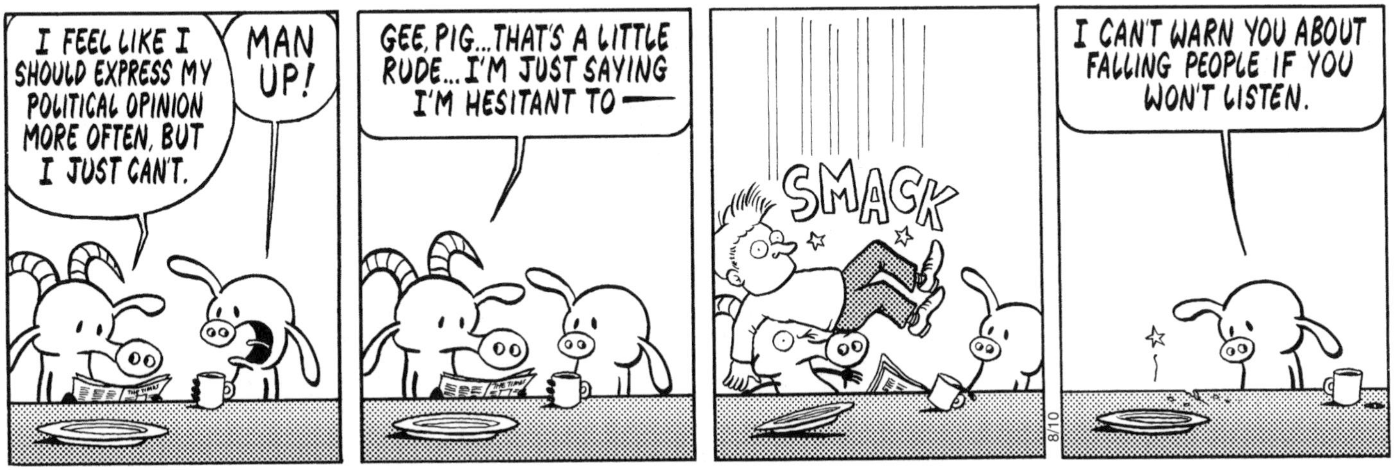
I FEEL LIKE I SHOULD EXPRESS MY POLITICAL OPINION MORE OFTEN, BUT I JUST CAN'T.
MAN UP!
GEE, PIG... THAT'S A LITTLE RUDE... I'M JUST SAYING I'M HESITANT TO —
SMACK
8/10
I CAN'T WARN YOU ABOUT FALLING PEOPLE IF YOU WON'T LISTEN.

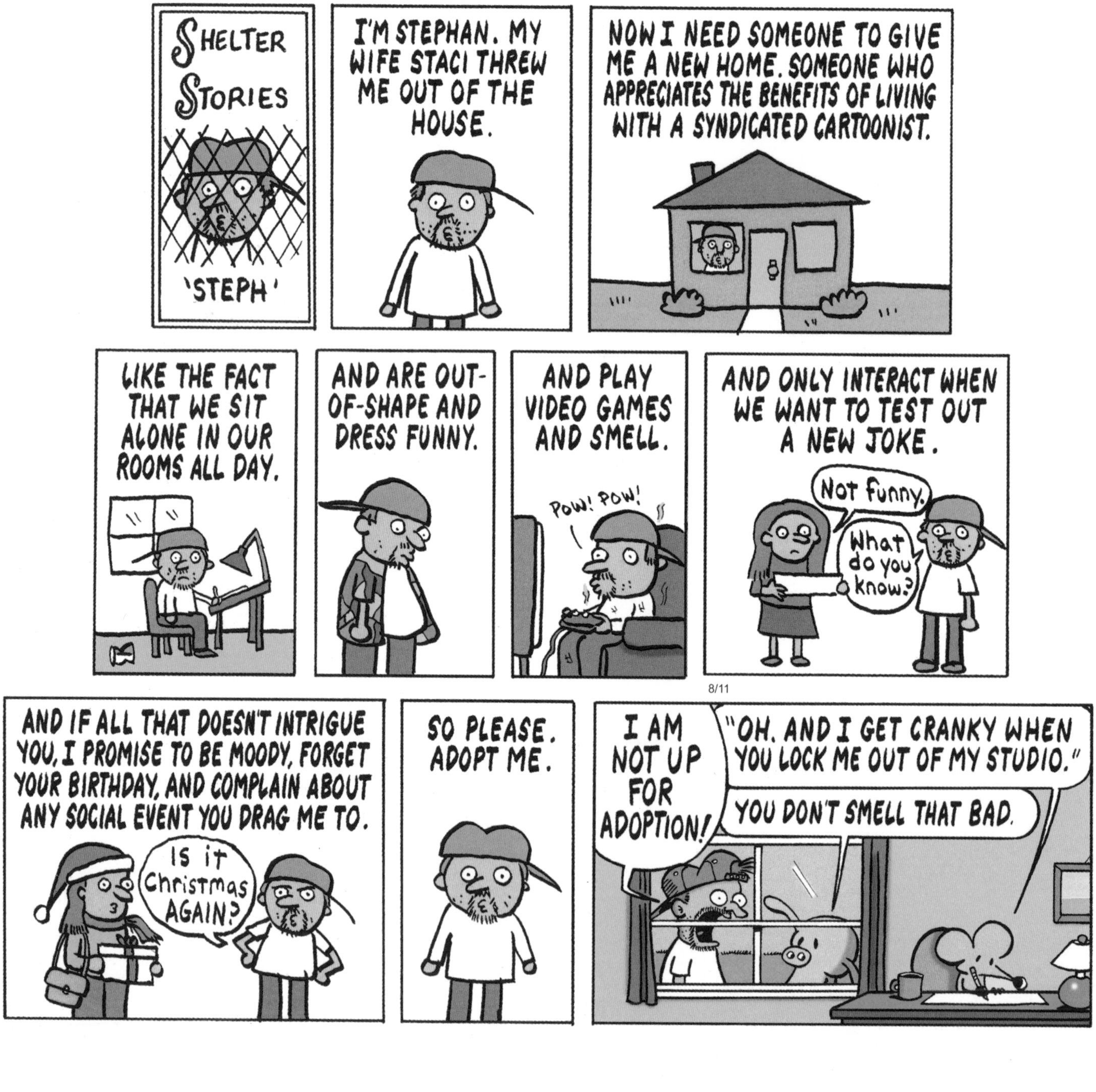
SHELTER STORIES
'STEPH'
I'M STEPHAN. MY WIFE STACI THREW ME OUT OF THE HOUSE.
NOW I NEED SOMEONE TO GIVE ME A NEW HOME. SOMEONE WHO APPRECIATES THE BENEFITS OF LIVING WITH A SYNDICATED CARTOONIST.
LIKE THE FACT THAT WE SIT ALONE IN OUR ROOMS ALL DAY.
AND ARE OUT-OF-SHAPE AND DRESS FUNNY.
AND PLAY VIDEO GAMES AND SMELL.
POW! POW!
AND ONLY INTERACT WHEN WE WANT TO TEST OUT A NEW JOKE.
Not funny.
What do you know?
8/11
AND IF ALL THAT DOESN'T INTRIGUE YOU, I PROMISE TO BE MOODY, FORGET YOUR BIRTHDAY, AND COMPLAIN ABOUT ANY SOCIAL EVENT YOU DRAG ME TO.
Is it Christmas AGAIN?
SO PLEASE. ADOPT ME.
I AM NOT UP FOR ADOPTION!
"OH. AND I GET CRANKY WHEN YOU LOCK ME OUT OF MY STUDIO."
YOU DON'T SMELL THAT BAD.

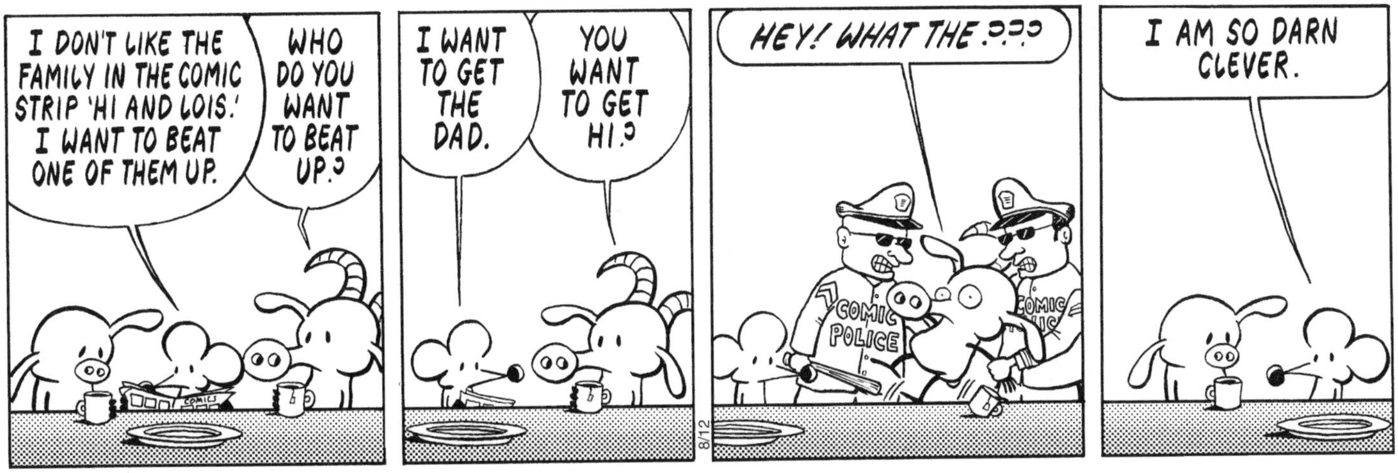
I DON'T LIKE THE FAMILY IN THE COMIC STRIP 'HI AND LOIS.' I WANT TO BEAT ONE OF THEM UP.
WHO DO YOU WANT TO BEAT UP?
COMICS
I WANT TO GET THE DAD.
YOU WANT TO GET HI?
HEY! WHAT THE ???
COMIC POLICE
I AM SO DARN CLEVER.
8/12

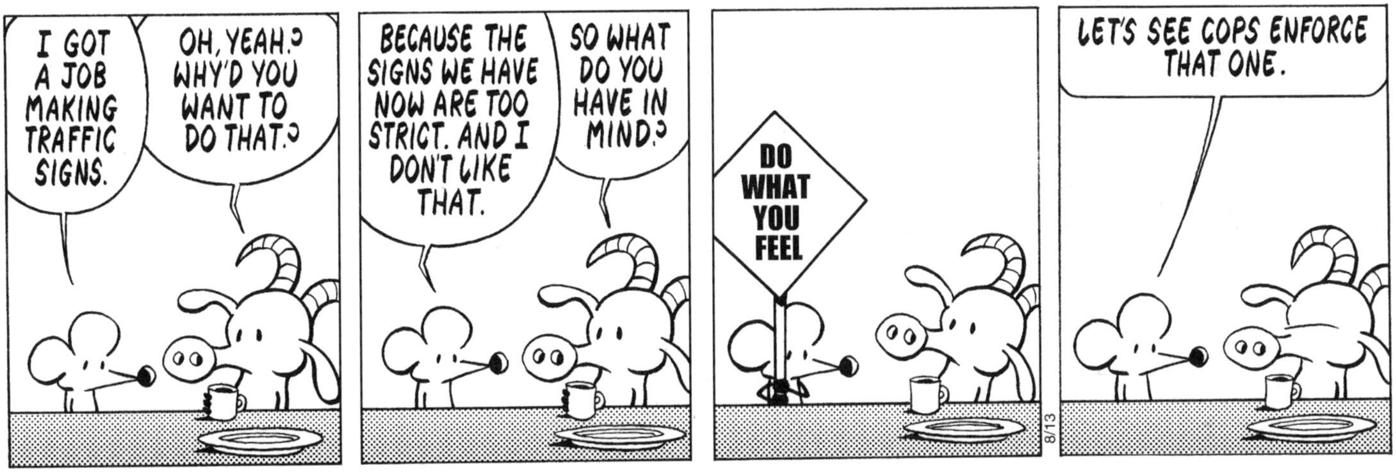
I GOT A JOB MAKING TRAFFIC SIGNS.
OH, YEAH? WHY'D YOU WANT TO DO THAT?
BECAUSE THE SIGNS WE HAVE NOW ARE TOO STRICT. AND I DON'T LIKE THAT.
SO WHAT DO YOU HAVE IN MIND?
DO WHAT YOU FEEL
LET'S SEE COPS ENFORCE THAT ONE.
8/13

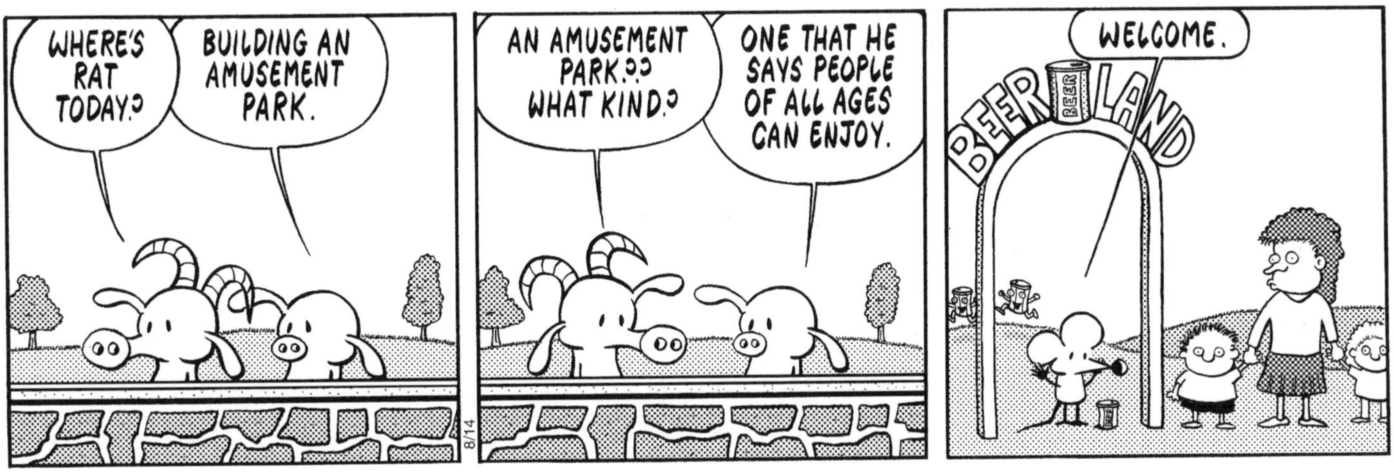
WHERE'S RAT TODAY?
BUILDING AN AMUSEMENT PARK.
AN AMUSEMENT PARK?? WHAT KIND?
ONE THAT HE SAYS PEOPLE OF ALL AGES CAN ENJOY.
WELCOME.
BEER LAND
BEER
8/14

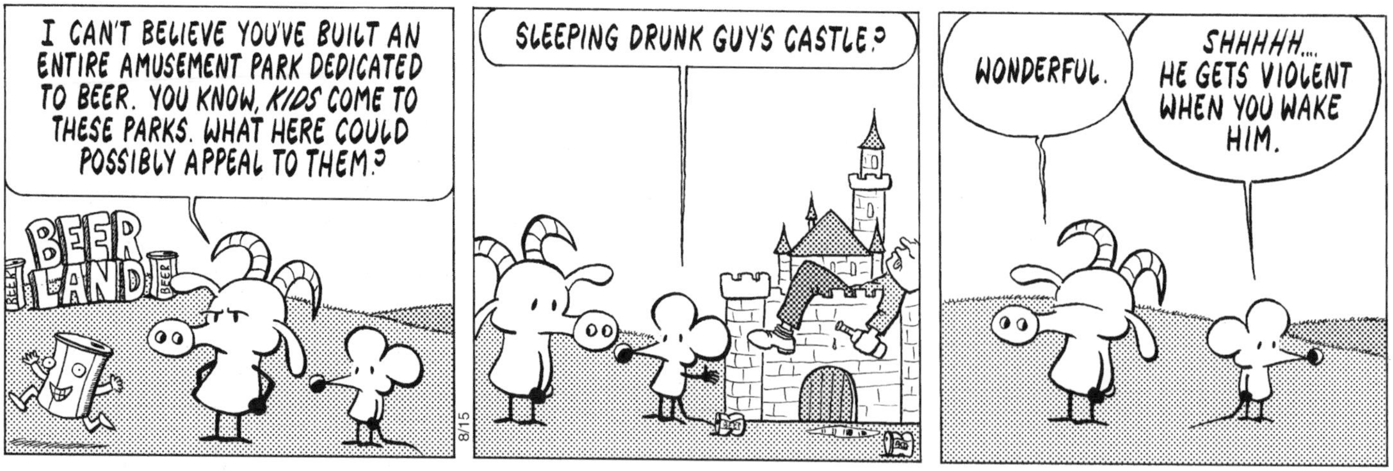
I CAN'T BELIEVE YOU'VE BUILT AN ENTIRE AMUSEMENT PARK DEDICATED TO BEER. YOU KNOW, KIDS COME TO THESE PARKS. WHAT HERE COULD POSSIBLY APPEAL TO THEM?
BEER LAND
BEER
8/15
SLEEPING DRUNK GUY'S CASTLE?
WONDERFUL.
SHHHHH.... HE GETS VIOLENT WHEN YOU WAKE HIM.

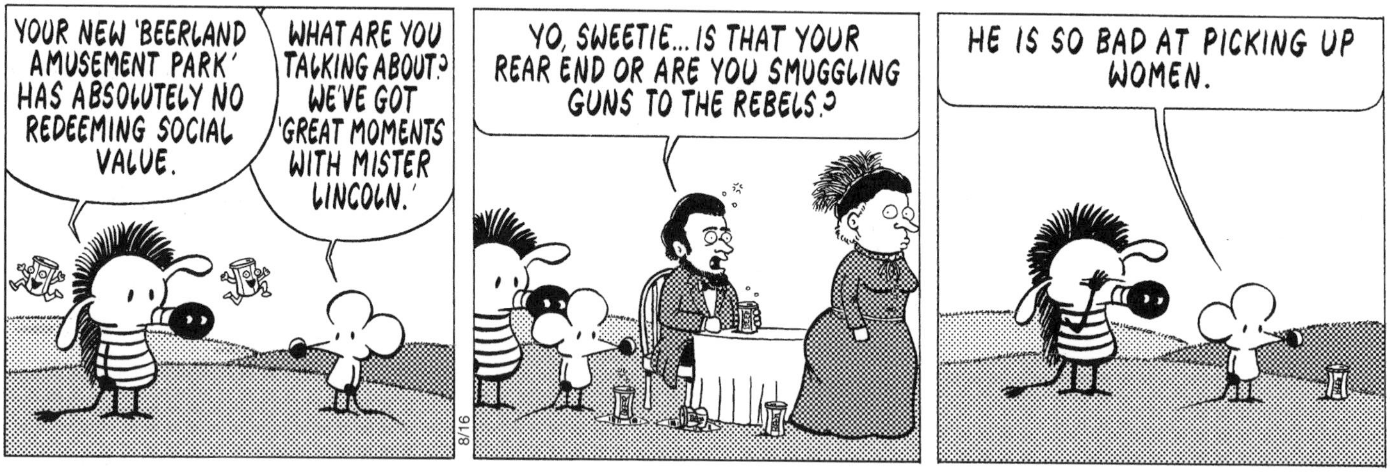
YOUR NEW 'BEERLAND AMUSEMENT PARK' HAS ABSOLUTELY NO REDEEMING SOCIAL VALUE.
WHAT ARE YOU TALKING ABOUT? WE'VE GOT 'GREAT MOMENTS WITH MISTER LINCOLN.'
8/16
YO, SWEETIE... IS THAT YOUR REAR END OR ARE YOU SMUGGLING GUNS TO THE REBELS?
HE IS SO BAD AT PICKING UP WOMEN.

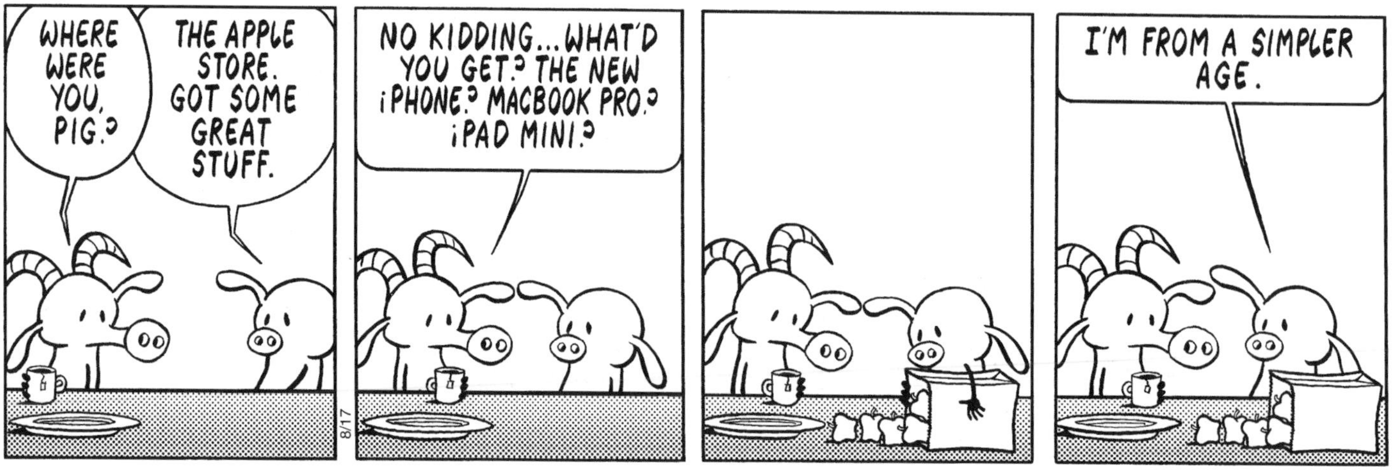
WHERE WERE YOU, PIG?
THE APPLE STORE. GOT SOME GREAT STUFF.
8/17
NO KIDDING... WHAT'D YOU GET? THE NEW iPHONE? MACBOOK PRO? iPAD MINI?
I'M FROM A SIMPLER AGE.

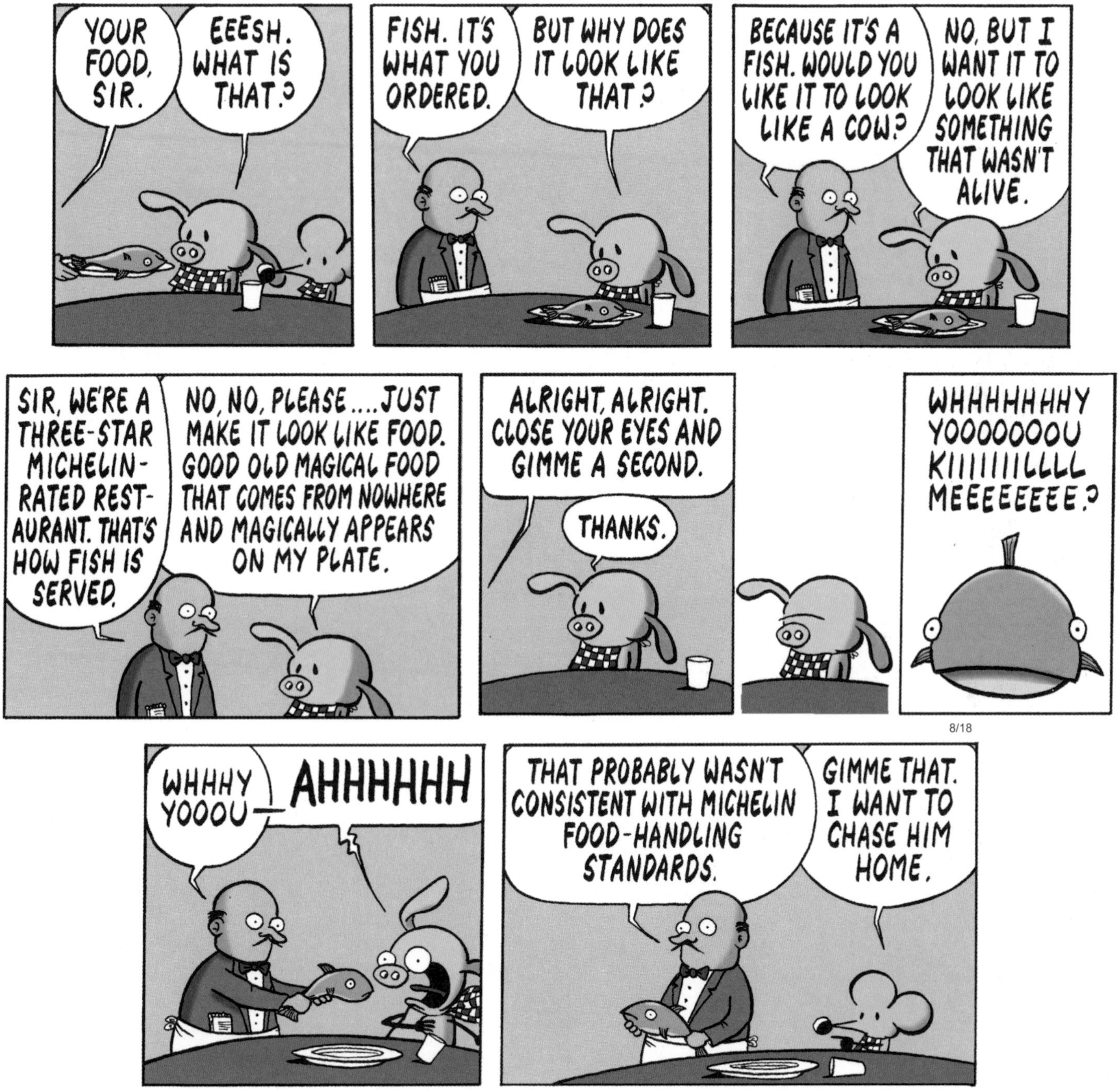
YOUR FOOD, SIR.
EEESH. WHAT IS THAT?
FISH. IT'S WHAT YOU ORDERED.
BUT WHY DOES IT LOOK LIKE THAT?
BECAUSE IT'S A FISH. WOULD YOU LIKE IT TO LOOK LIKE A COW?
NO, BUT I WANT IT TO LOOK LIKE SOMETHING THAT WASN'T ALIVE.
SIR, WE'RE A THREE-STAR MICHELIN-RATED RESTAURANT. THAT'S HOW FISH IS SERVED.
NO, NO, PLEASE.... JUST MAKE IT LOOK LIKE FOOD. GOOD OLD MAGICAL FOOD THAT COMES FROM NOWHERE AND MAGICALLY APPEARS ON MY PLATE.
ALRIGHT, ALRIGHT. CLOSE YOUR EYES AND GIMME A SECOND.
THANKS.
WHHHHHHHY YOOOOOOOU KIIIIIIILLLL MEEEEEEEE?
8/18
WHHHY YOOOU—
AHHHHHH
THAT PROBABLY WASN'T CONSISTENT WITH MICHELIN FOOD-HANDLING STANDARDS.
GIMME THAT. I WANT TO CHASE HIM HOME.

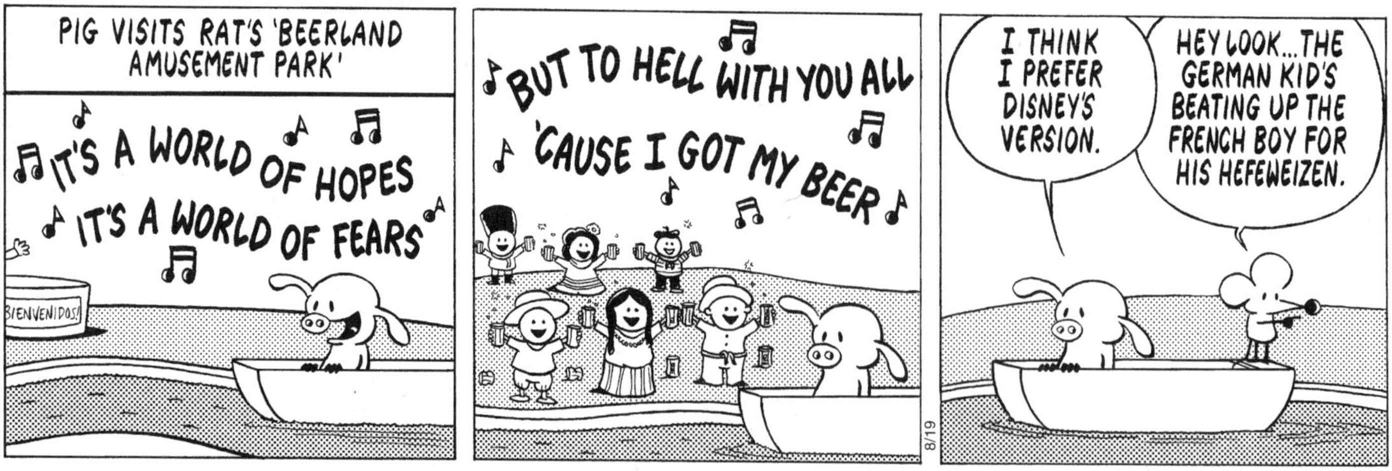
PIG VISITS RAT'S 'BEERLAND AMUSEMENT PARK'
IT'S A WORLD OF HOPES
IT'S A WORLD OF FEARS
BIENVENIDOS!
BUT TO HELL WITH YOU ALL
'CAUSE I GOT MY BEER
I THINK I PREFER DISNEY'S VERSION.
HEY LOOK...THE GERMAN KID'S BEATING UP THE FRENCH BOY FOR HIS HEFEWEIZEN.
8/19

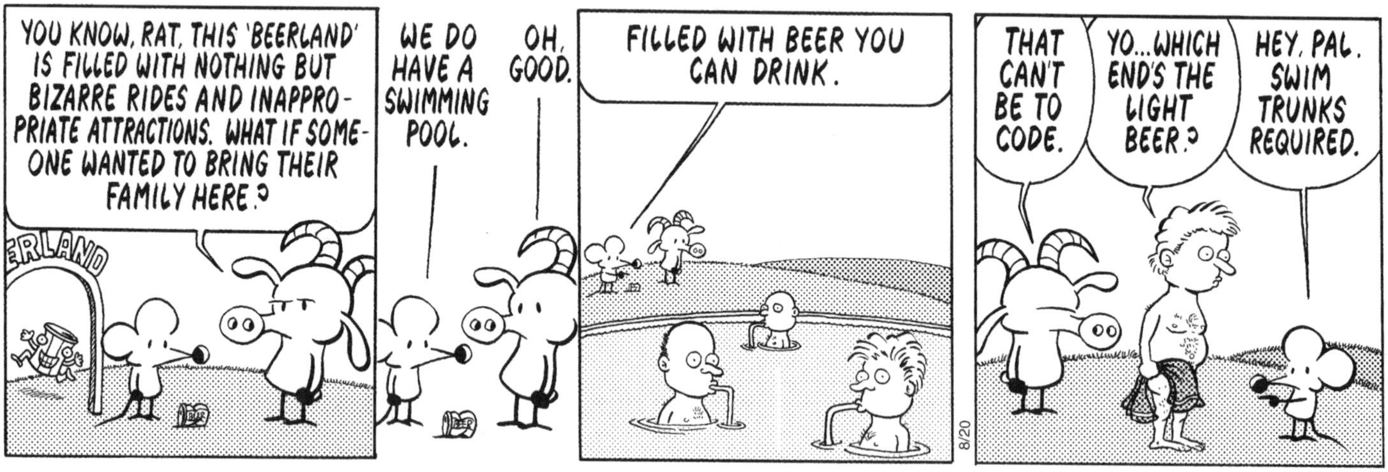
YOU KNOW, RAT, THIS 'BEERLAND' IS FILLED WITH NOTHING BUT BIZARRE RIDES AND INAPPROPRIATE ATTRACTIONS. WHAT IF SOMEONE WANTED TO BRING THEIR FAMILY HERE?
ERLAND
WE DO HAVE A SWIMMING POOL.
OH, GOOD.
FILLED WITH BEER YOU CAN DRINK.
THAT CAN'T BE TO CODE.
YO...WHICH END'S THE LIGHT BEER?
HEY, PAL. SWIM TRUNKS REQUIRED.
8/20

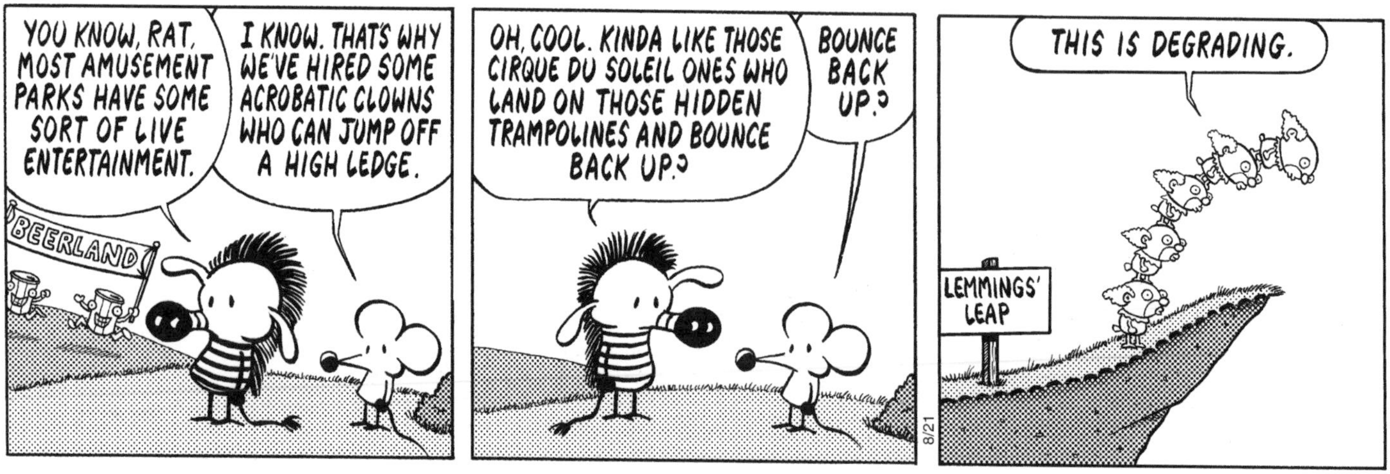
YOU KNOW, RAT, MOST AMUSEMENT PARKS HAVE SOME SORT OF LIVE ENTERTAINMENT.
I KNOW. THAT'S WHY WE'VE HIRED SOME ACROBATIC CLOWNS WHO CAN JUMP OFF A HIGH LEDGE.
BEERLAND
OH, COOL. KINDA LIKE THOSE CIRQUE DU SOLEIL ONES WHO LAND ON THOSE HIDDEN TRAMPOLINES AND BOUNCE BACK UP?
BOUNCE BACK UP?
8/21
THIS IS DEGRADING.
LEMMINGS' LEAP

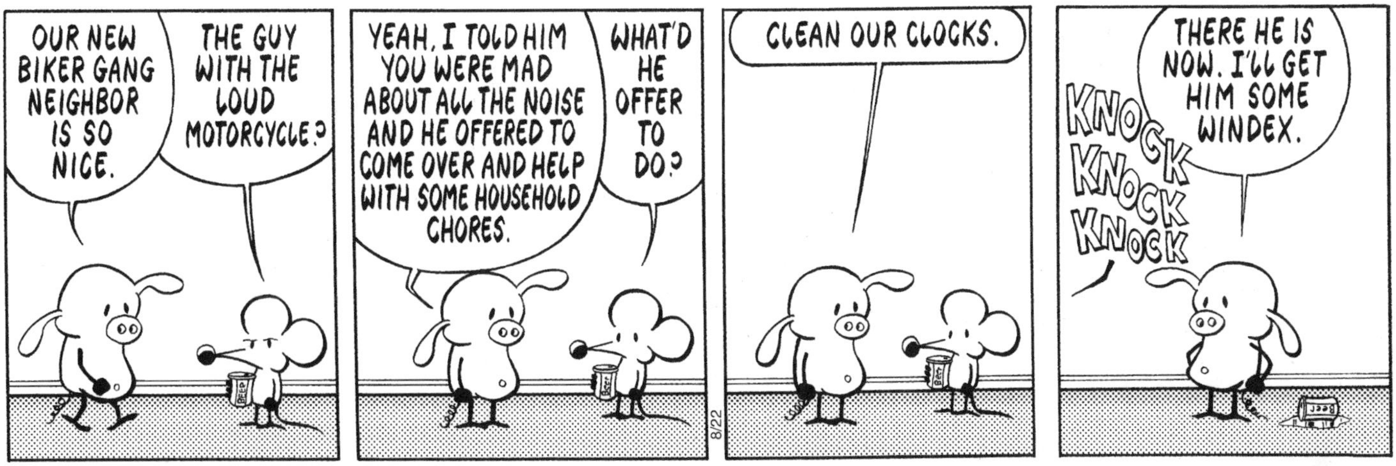
OUR NEW BIKER GANG NEIGHBOR IS SO NICE.
THE GUY WITH THE LOUD MOTORCYCLE?
YEAH, I TOLD HIM YOU WERE MAD ABOUT ALL THE NOISE AND HE OFFERED TO COME OVER AND HELP WITH SOME HOUSEHOLD CHORES.
WHAT'D HE OFFER TO DO?
CLEAN OUR CLOCKS.
KNOCK KNOCK KNOCK
THERE HE IS NOW. I'LL GET HIM SOME WINDEX.
8/22

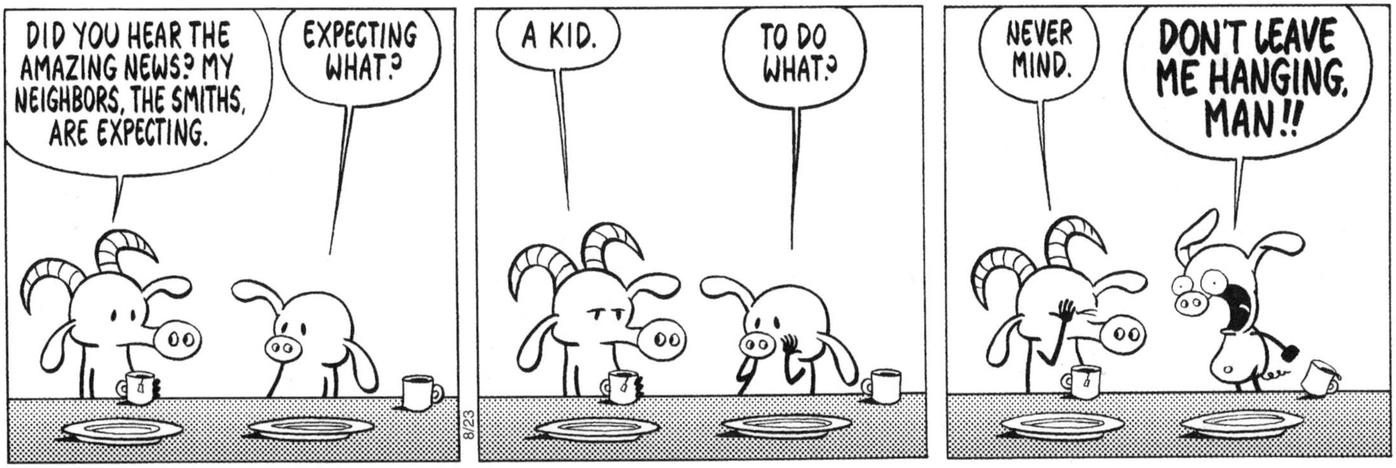
DID YOU HEAR THE AMAZING NEWS? MY NEIGHBORS, THE SMITHS, ARE EXPECTING.
EXPECTING WHAT?
A KID.
TO DO WHAT?
NEVER MIND.
DON'T LEAVE ME HANGING, MAN!!
8/23

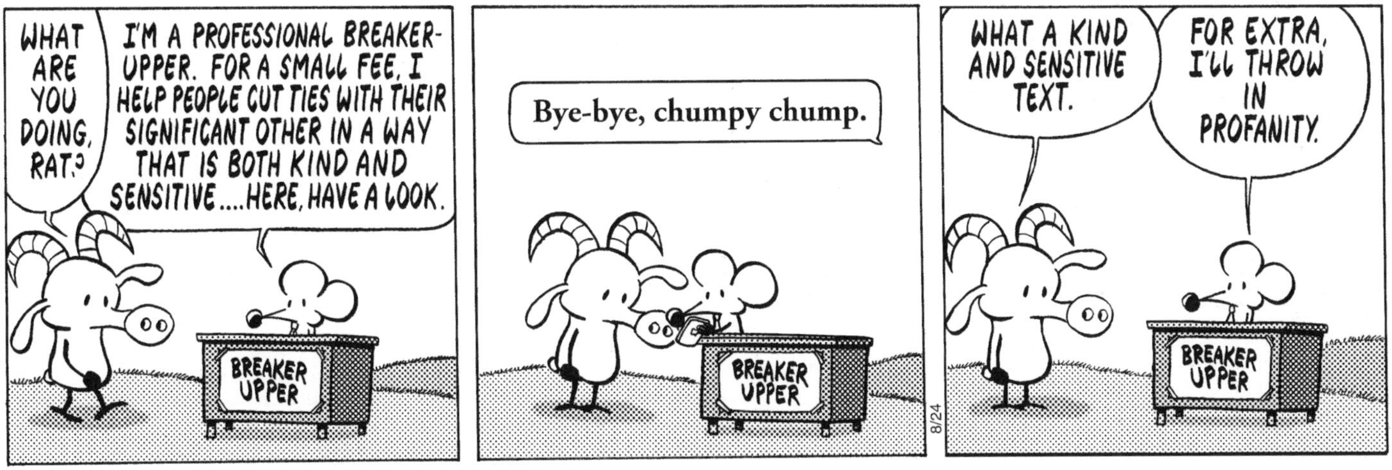
WHAT ARE YOU DOING, RAT?
I'M A PROFESSIONAL BREAKER-UPPER. FOR A SMALL FEE, I HELP PEOPLE CUT TIES WITH THEIR SIGNIFICANT OTHER IN A WAY THAT IS BOTH KIND AND SENSITIVE....HERE, HAVE A LOOK.
BREAKER UPPER
Bye-bye, chumpy chump.
WHAT A KIND AND SENSITIVE TEXT.
FOR EXTRA, I'LL THROW IN PROFANITY.
8/24

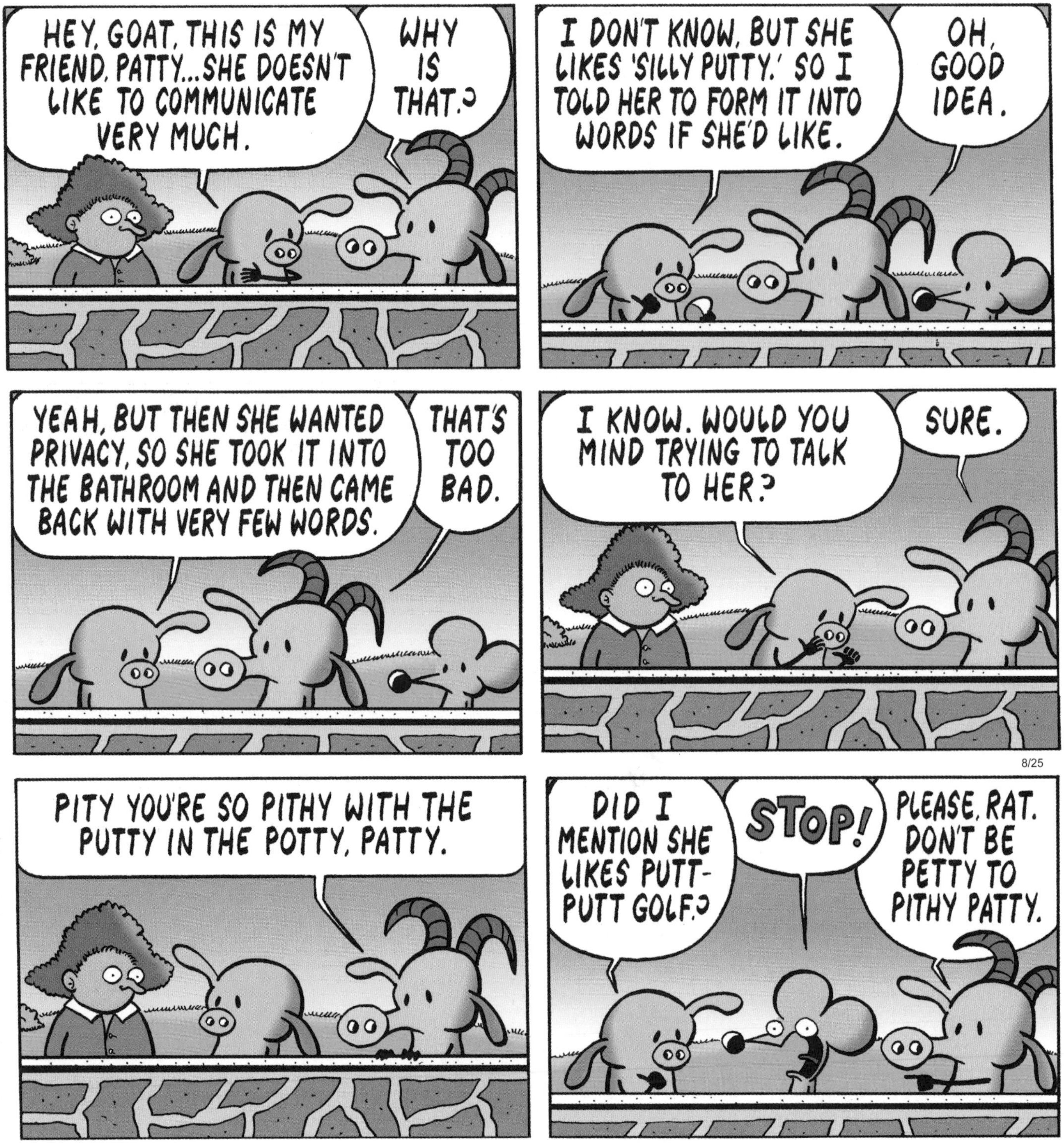
HEY, GOAT, THIS IS MY FRIEND, PATTY...SHE DOESN'T LIKE TO COMMUNICATE VERY MUCH.
WHY IS THAT?
I DON'T KNOW, BUT SHE LIKES 'SILLY PUTTY.' SO I TOLD HER TO FORM IT INTO WORDS IF SHE'D LIKE.
OH, GOOD IDEA.
YEAH, BUT THEN SHE WANTED PRIVACY, SO SHE TOOK IT INTO THE BATHROOM AND THEN CAME BACK WITH VERY FEW WORDS.
THAT'S TOO BAD.
I KNOW. WOULD YOU MIND TRYING TO TALK TO HER?
SURE.
8/25
PITY YOU'RE SO PITHY WITH THE PUTTY IN THE POTTY, PATTY.
DID I MENTION SHE LIKES PUTT-PUTT GOLF?
STOP!
PLEASE, RAT. DON'T BE PETTY TO PITHY PATTY.

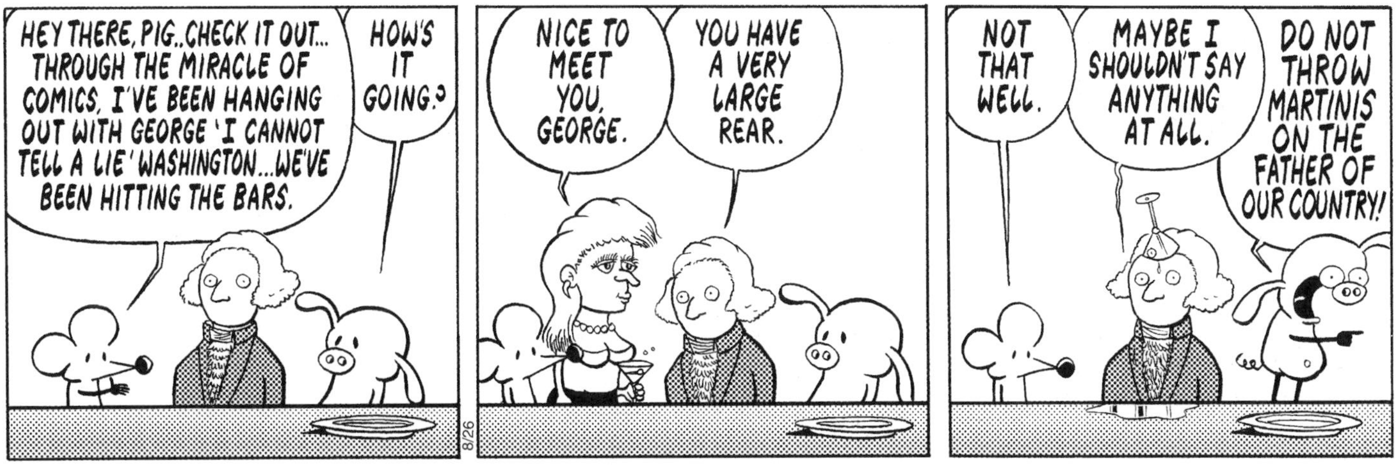
HEY THERE, PIG..CHECK IT OUT... THROUGH THE MIRACLE OF COMICS, I'VE BEEN HANGING OUT WITH GEORGE 'I CANNOT TELL A LIE' WASHINGTON...WE'VE BEEN HITTING THE BARS.
HOW'S IT GOING?
8/26
NICE TO MEET YOU, GEORGE.
YOU HAVE A VERY LARGE REAR.
NOT THAT WELL.
MAYBE I SHOULDN'T SAY ANYTHING AT ALL.
DO NOT THROW MARTINIS ON THE FATHER OF OUR COUNTRY!

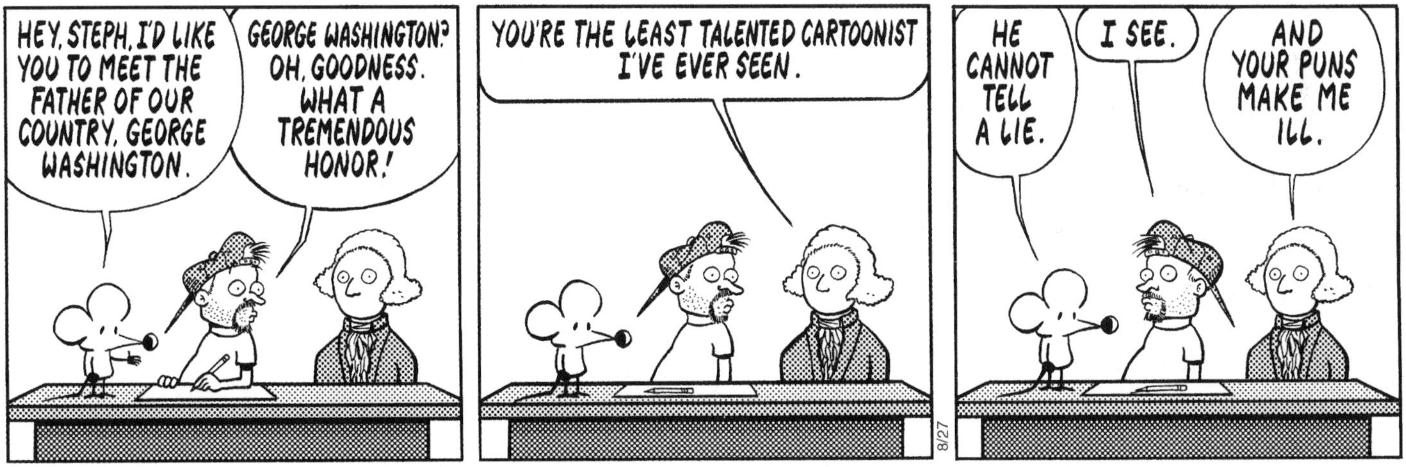
HEY, STEPH, I'D LIKE YOU TO MEET THE FATHER OF OUR COUNTRY, GEORGE WASHINGTON.
GEORGE WASHINGTON? OH, GOODNESS. WHAT A TREMENDOUS HONOR!
YOU'RE THE LEAST TALENTED CARTOONIST I'VE EVER SEEN.
8/27
HE CANNOT TELL A LIE.
I SEE.
AND YOUR PUNS MAKE ME ILL.

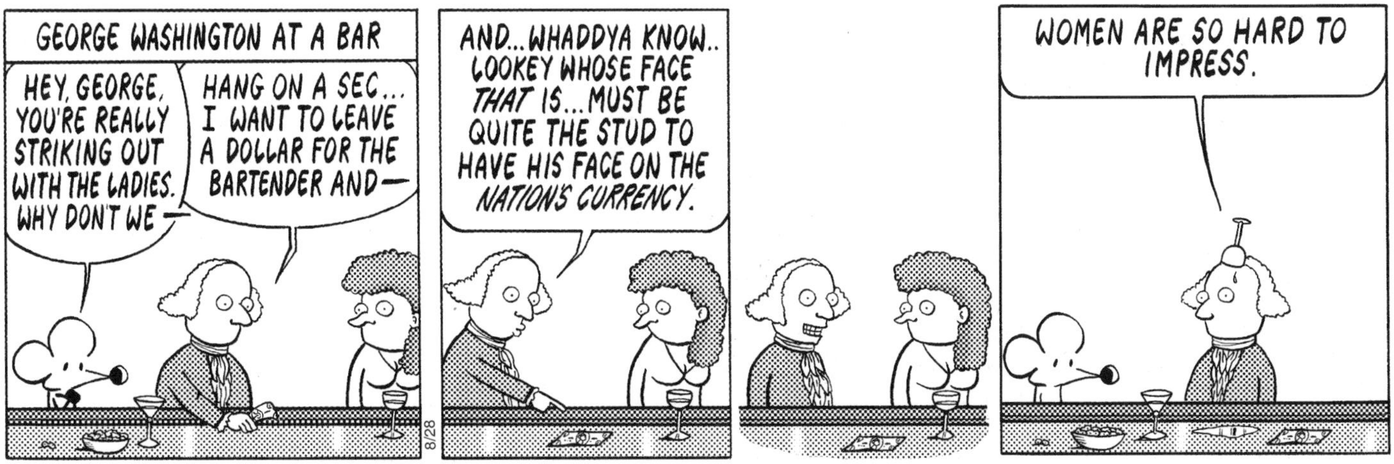
GEORGE WASHINGTON AT A BAR
HEY, GEORGE, YOU'RE REALLY STRIKING OUT WITH THE LADIES. WHY DON'T WE—
HANG ON A SEC... I WANT TO LEAVE A DOLLAR FOR THE BARTENDER AND—
8/28
AND...WHADDYA KNOW.. LOOKEY WHOSE FACE THAT IS...MUST BE QUITE THE STUD TO HAVE HIS FACE ON THE NATION'S CURRENCY.
WOMEN ARE SO HARD TO IMPRESS.

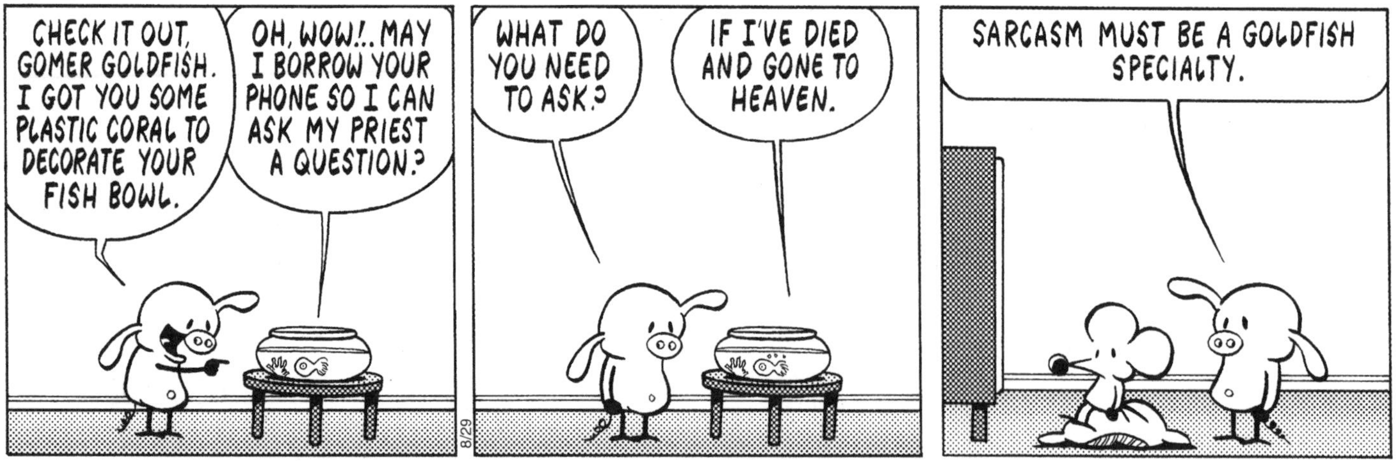
CHECK IT OUT, GOMER GOLDFISH. I GOT YOU SOME PLASTIC CORAL TO DECORATE YOUR FISH BOWL.
OH, WOW!.. MAY I BORROW YOUR PHONE SO I CAN ASK MY PRIEST A QUESTION?
8/29
WHAT DO YOU NEED TO ASK?
IF I'VE DIED AND GONE TO HEAVEN.
SARCASM MUST BE A GOLDFISH SPECIALTY.

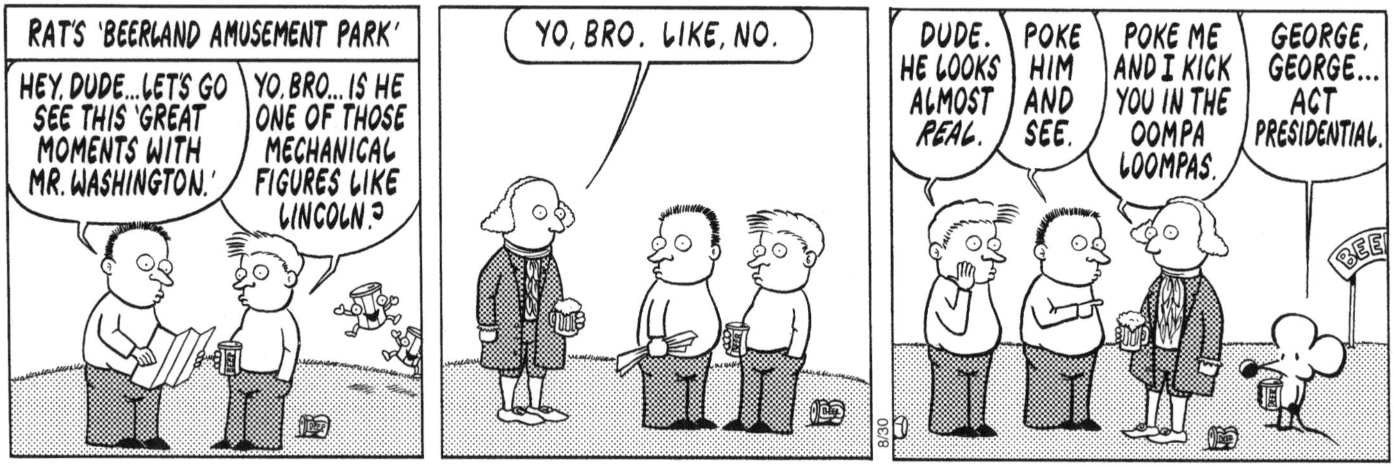
RAT'S 'BEERLAND AMUSEMENT PARK'
HEY, DUDE... LET'S GO SEE THIS 'GREAT MOMENTS WITH MR. WASHINGTON.'
YO, BRO... IS HE ONE OF THOSE MECHANICAL FIGURES LIKE LINCOLN?
YO, BRO. LIKE, NO.
8/30
DUDE. HE LOOKS ALMOST *REAL*.
POKE HIM AND SEE.
POKE ME AND I KICK YOU IN THE OOMPA LOOMPAS.
GEORGE, GEORGE... ACT PRESIDENTIAL.

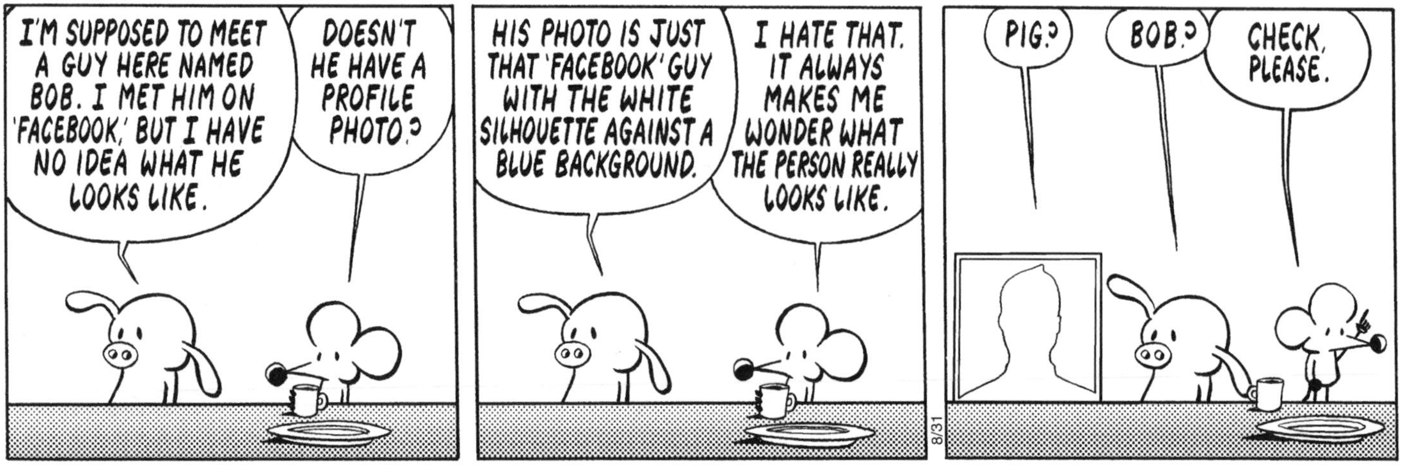
I'M SUPPOSED TO MEET A GUY HERE NAMED BOB. I MET HIM ON 'FACEBOOK,' BUT I HAVE NO IDEA WHAT HE LOOKS LIKE.
DOESN'T HE HAVE A PROFILE PHOTO?
HIS PHOTO IS JUST THAT 'FACEBOOK' GUY WITH THE WHITE SILHOUETTE AGAINST A BLUE BACKGROUND.
I HATE THAT. IT ALWAYS MAKES ME WONDER WHAT THE PERSON REALLY LOOKS LIKE.
8/31
PIG?
BOB?
CHECK, PLEASE.

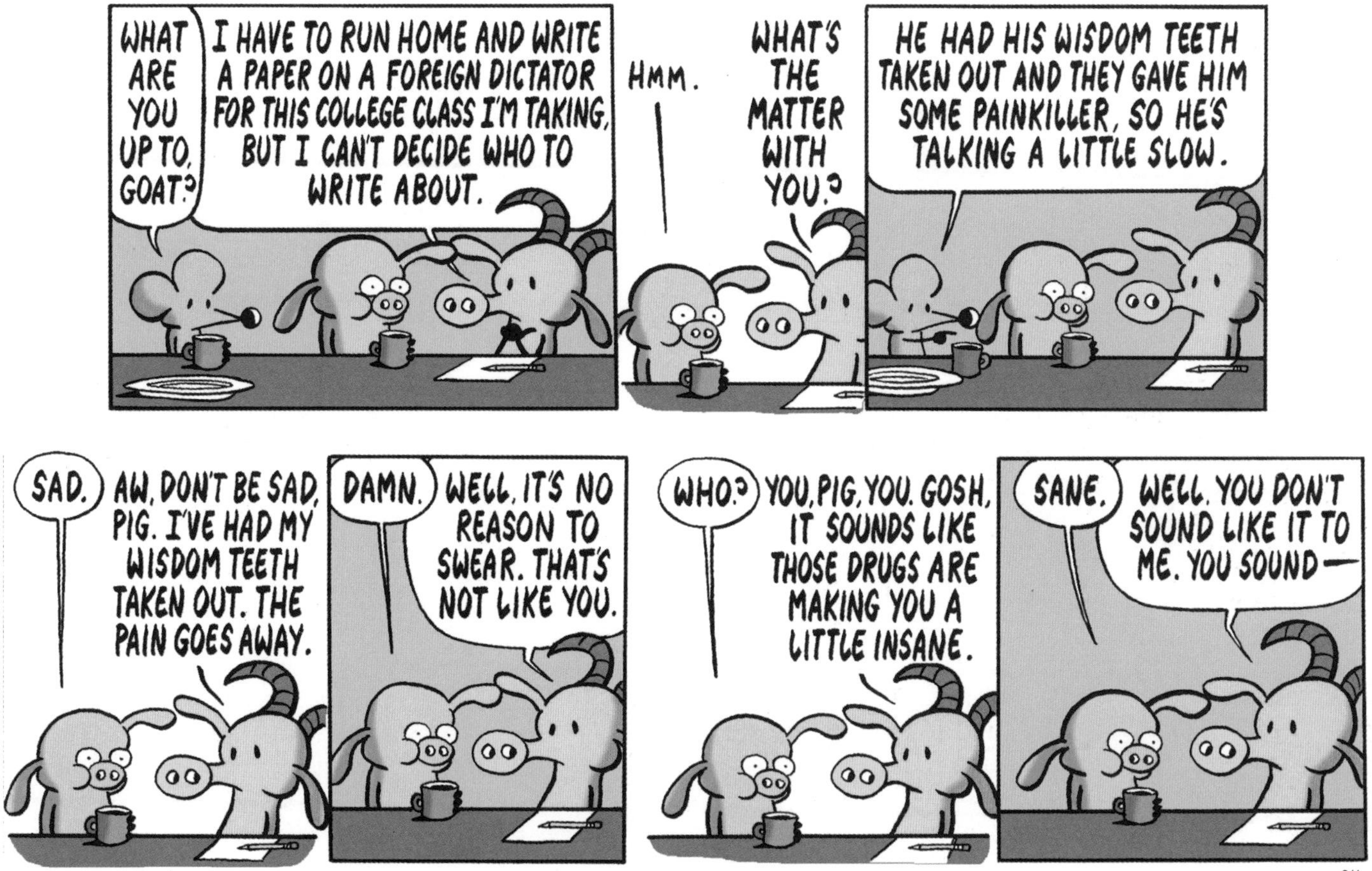
WHAT ARE YOU UP TO, GOAT?
I HAVE TO RUN HOME AND WRITE A PAPER ON A FOREIGN DICTATOR FOR THIS COLLEGE CLASS I'M TAKING, BUT I CAN'T DECIDE WHO TO WRITE ABOUT.
HMM.
WHAT'S THE MATTER WITH YOU?
HE HAD HIS WISDOM TEETH TAKEN OUT AND THEY GAVE HIM SOME PAINKILLER, SO HE'S TALKING A LITTLE SLOW.
SAD.
AW, DON'T BE SAD, PIG. I'VE HAD MY WISDOM TEETH TAKEN OUT. THE PAIN GOES AWAY.
DAMN.
WELL, IT'S NO REASON TO SWEAR. THAT'S NOT LIKE YOU.
WHO?
YOU, PIG, YOU. GOSH, IT SOUNDS LIKE THOSE DRUGS ARE MAKING YOU A LITTLE INSANE.
SANE.
WELL, YOU DON'T SOUND LIKE IT TO ME. YOU SOUND—
9/1

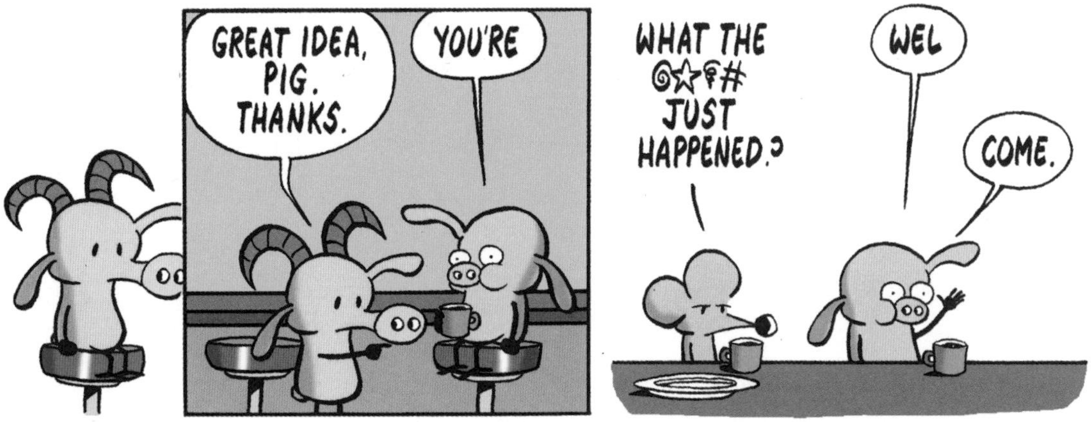
GREAT IDEA, PIG. THANKS.
YOU'RE
WHAT THE @☆?# JUST HAPPENED?
WEL
COME.

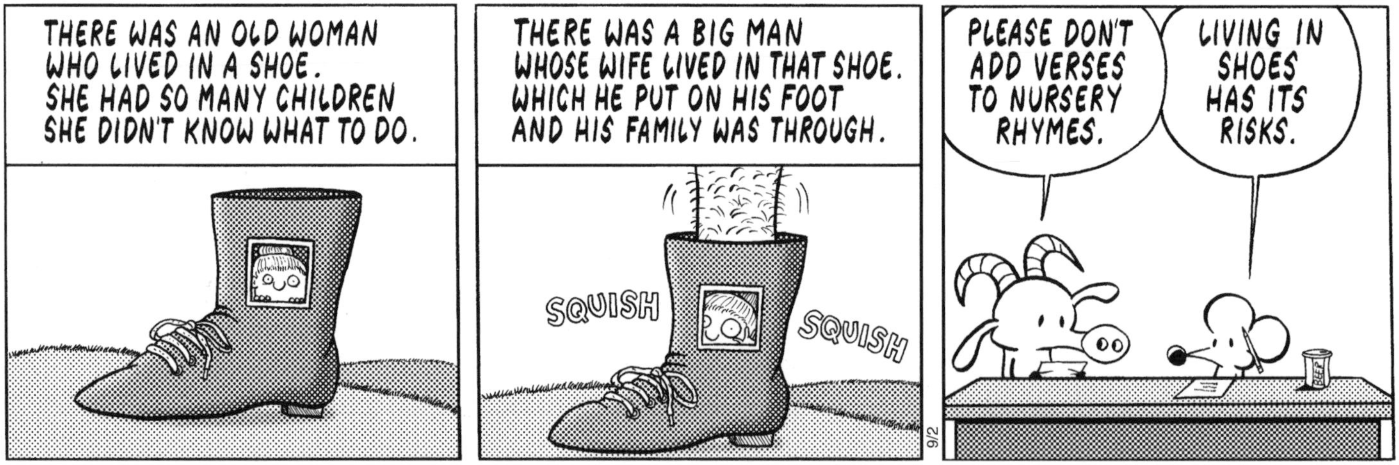
THERE WAS AN OLD WOMAN WHO LIVED IN A SHOE. SHE HAD SO MANY CHILDREN SHE DIDN'T KNOW WHAT TO DO.
THERE WAS A BIG MAN WHOSE WIFE LIVED IN THAT SHOE. WHICH HE PUT ON HIS FOOT AND HIS FAMILY WAS THROUGH.
SQUISH
SQUISH
PLEASE DON'T ADD VERSES TO NURSERY RHYMES.
LIVING IN SHOES HAS ITS RISKS.

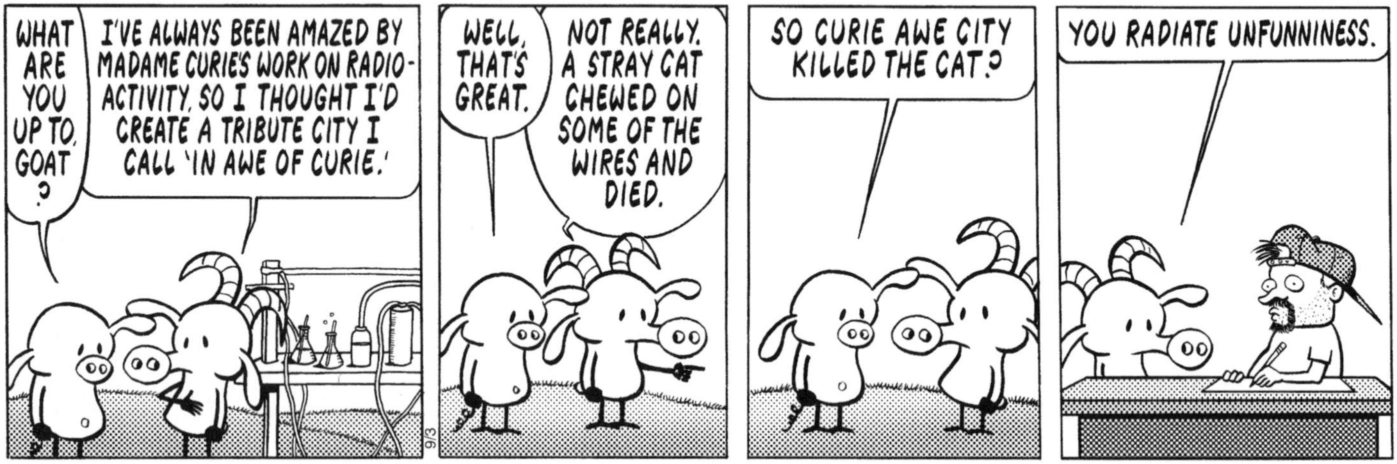
WHAT ARE YOU UP TO, GOAT?
I'VE ALWAYS BEEN AMAZED BY MADAME CURIE'S WORK ON RADIO-ACTIVITY, SO I THOUGHT I'D CREATE A TRIBUTE CITY I CALL 'IN AWE OF CURIE.'
WELL, THAT'S GREAT.
NOT REALLY. A STRAY CAT CHEWED ON SOME OF THE WIRES AND DIED.
SO CURIE AWE CITY KILLED THE CAT?
YOU RADIATE UNFUNNINESS.

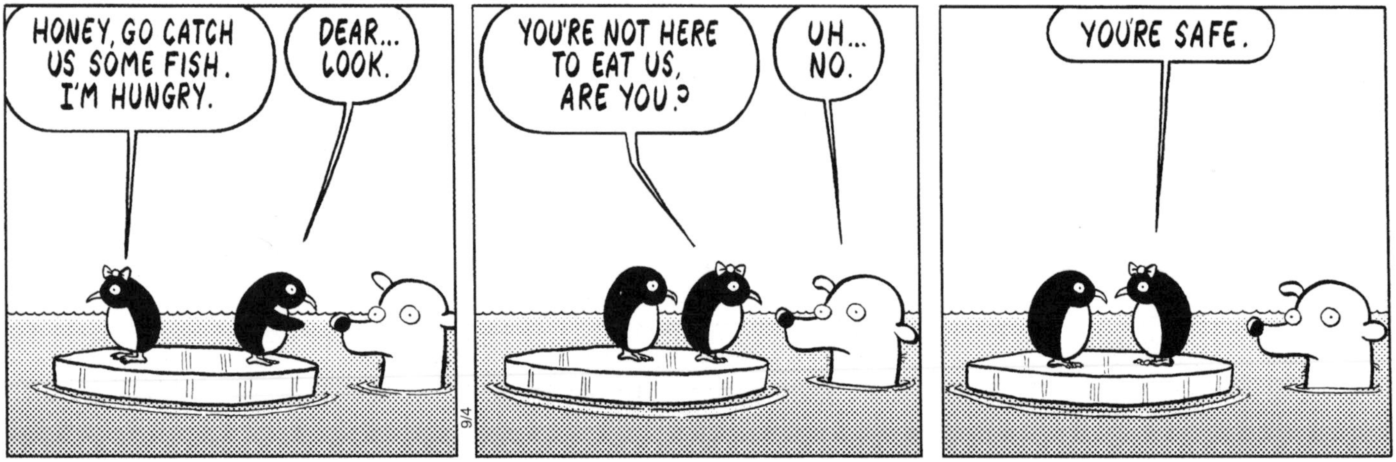
HONEY, GO CATCH US SOME FISH. I'M HUNGRY.
DEAR... LOOK.
YOU'RE NOT HERE TO EAT US, ARE YOU?
UH... NO.
YOU'RE SAFE.

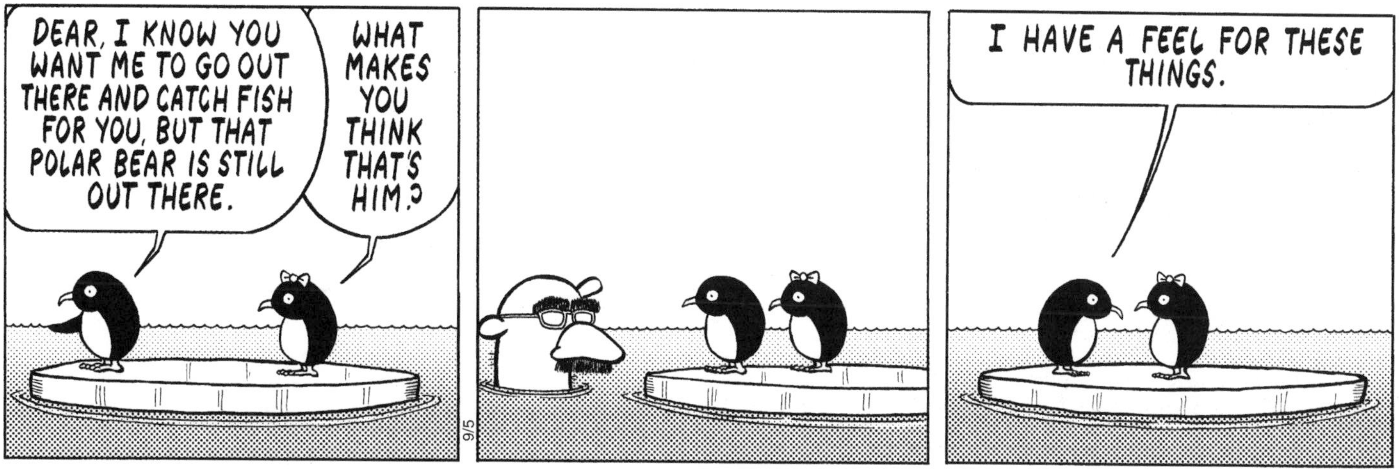
DEAR, I KNOW YOU WANT ME TO GO OUT THERE AND CATCH FISH FOR YOU, BUT THAT POLAR BEAR IS STILL OUT THERE.
WHAT MAKES YOU THINK THAT'S HIM?
9/5
I HAVE A FEEL FOR THESE THINGS.

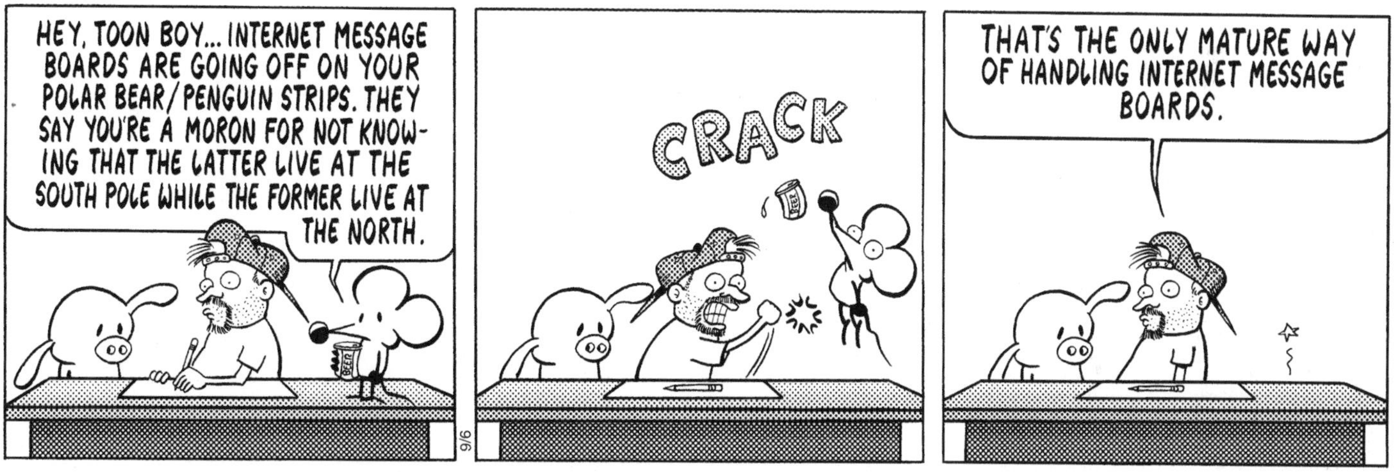
HEY, TOON BOY... INTERNET MESSAGE BOARDS ARE GOING OFF ON YOUR POLAR BEAR/PENGUIN STRIPS. THEY SAY YOU'RE A MORON FOR NOT KNOWING THAT THE LATTER LIVE AT THE SOUTH POLE WHILE THE FORMER LIVE AT THE NORTH.
BEER
9/6
CRACK
BEER
THAT'S THE ONLY MATURE WAY OF HANDLING INTERNET MESSAGE BOARDS.

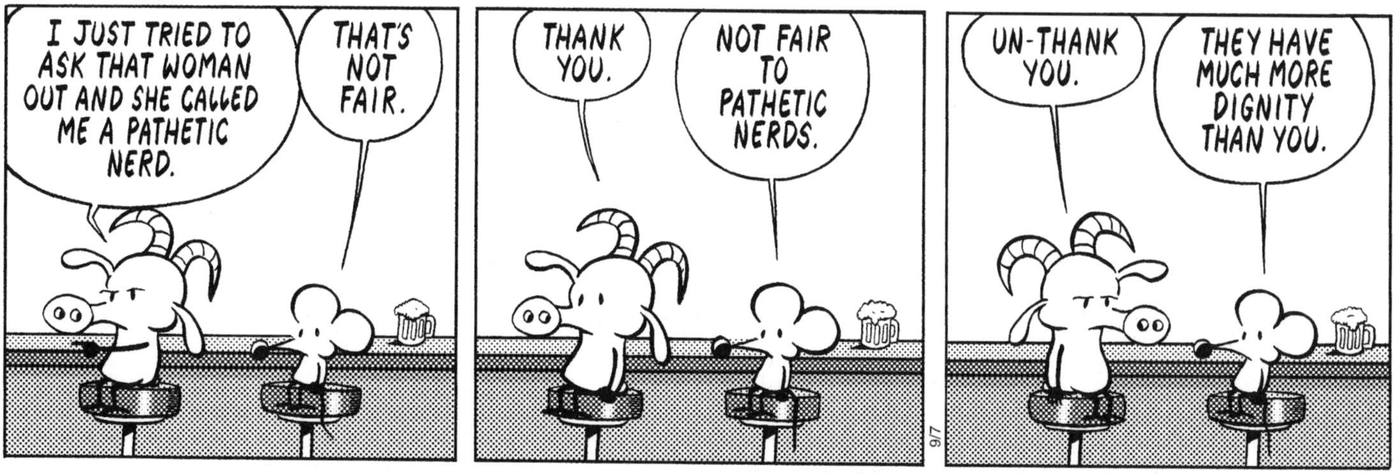
I JUST TRIED TO ASK THAT WOMAN OUT AND SHE CALLED ME A PATHETIC NERD.
THAT'S NOT FAIR.
THANK YOU.
NOT FAIR TO PATHETIC NERDS.
9/7
UN-THANK YOU.
THEY HAVE MUCH MORE DIGNITY THAN YOU.

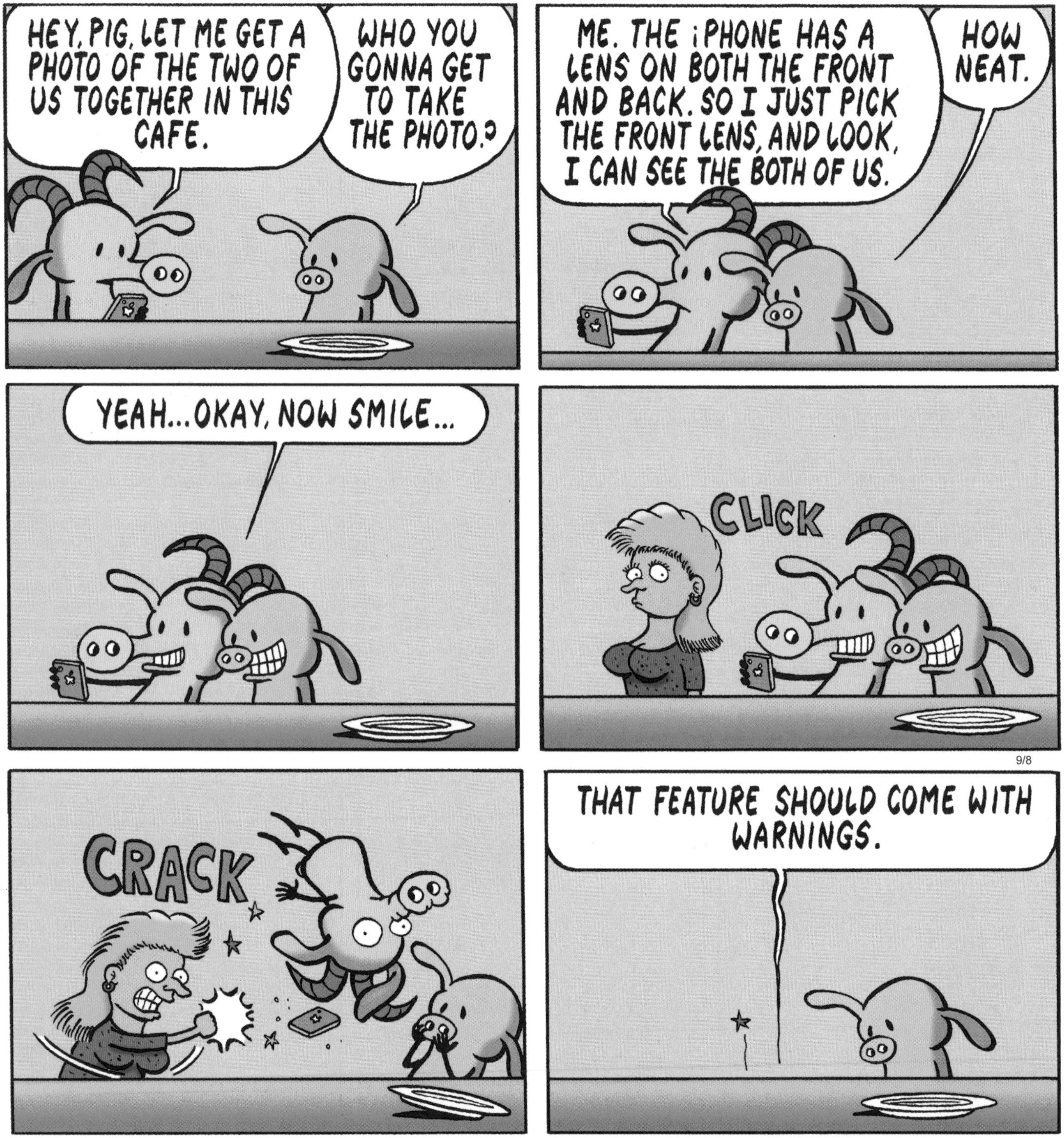
HEY, PIG, LET ME GET A PHOTO OF THE TWO OF US TOGETHER IN THIS CAFE.
WHO YOU GONNA GET TO TAKE THE PHOTO?
ME. THE iPHONE HAS A LENS ON BOTH THE FRONT AND BACK. SO I JUST PICK THE FRONT LENS, AND LOOK, I CAN SEE THE BOTH OF US.
HOW NEAT.
YEAH...OKAY, NOW SMILE...
CLICK
9/8
CRACK
THAT FEATURE SHOULD COME WITH WARNINGS.

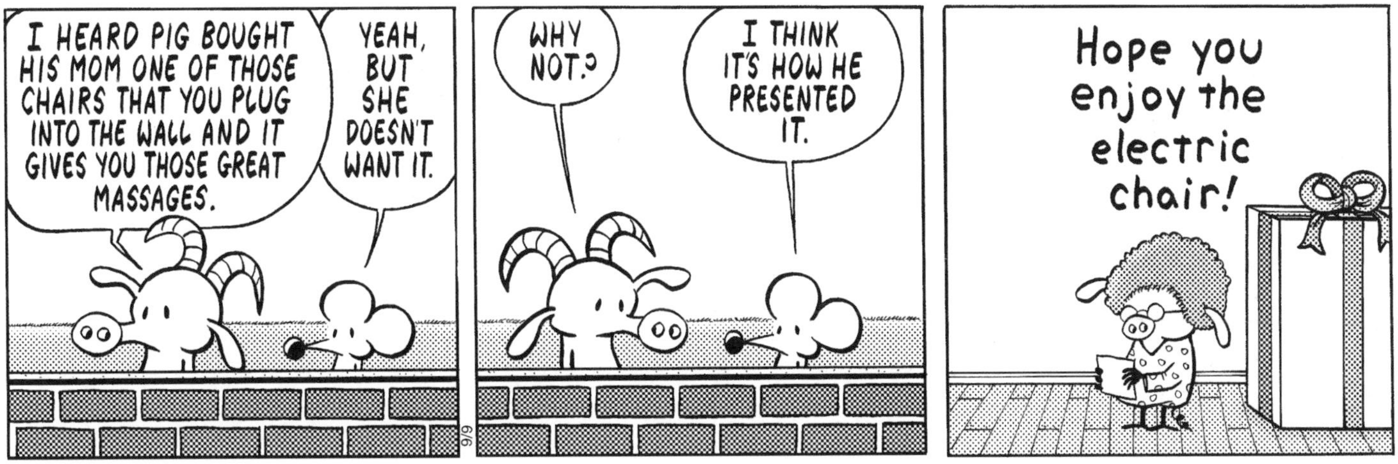
I HEARD PIG BOUGHT HIS MOM ONE OF THOSE CHAIRS THAT YOU PLUG INTO THE WALL AND IT GIVES YOU THOSE GREAT MASSAGES.
YEAH, BUT SHE DOESN'T WANT IT.
9/9
WHY NOT?
I THINK IT'S HOW HE PRESENTED IT.
Hope you enjoy the electric chair!

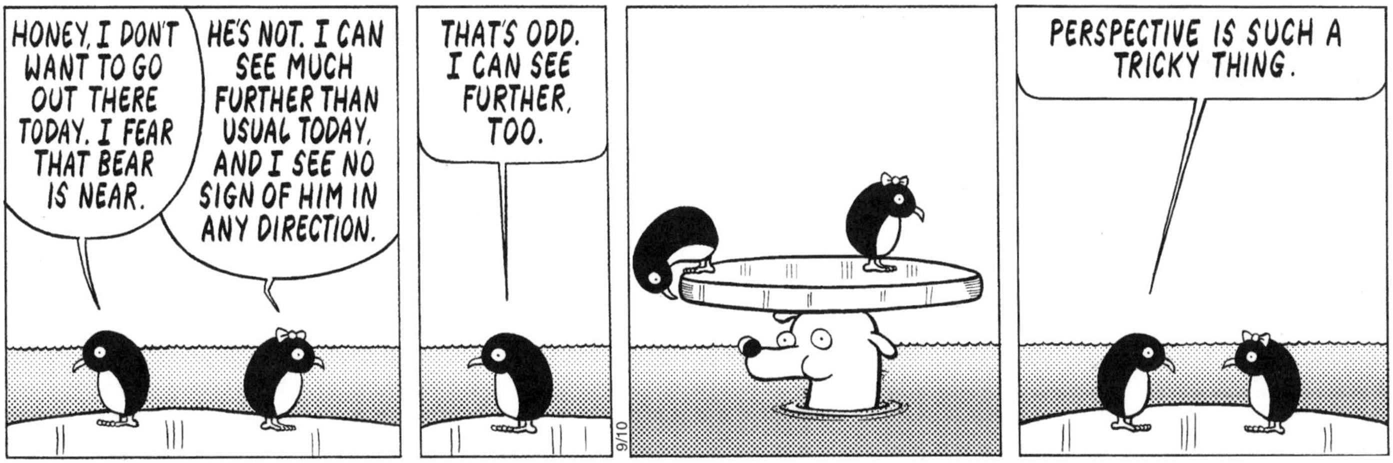
HONEY, I DON'T WANT TO GO OUT THERE TODAY. I FEAR THAT BEAR IS NEAR.
HE'S NOT. I CAN SEE MUCH FURTHER THAN USUAL TODAY, AND I SEE NO SIGN OF HIM IN ANY DIRECTION.
THAT'S ODD. I CAN SEE FURTHER, TOO.
9/10
PERSPECTIVE IS SUCH A TRICKY THING.

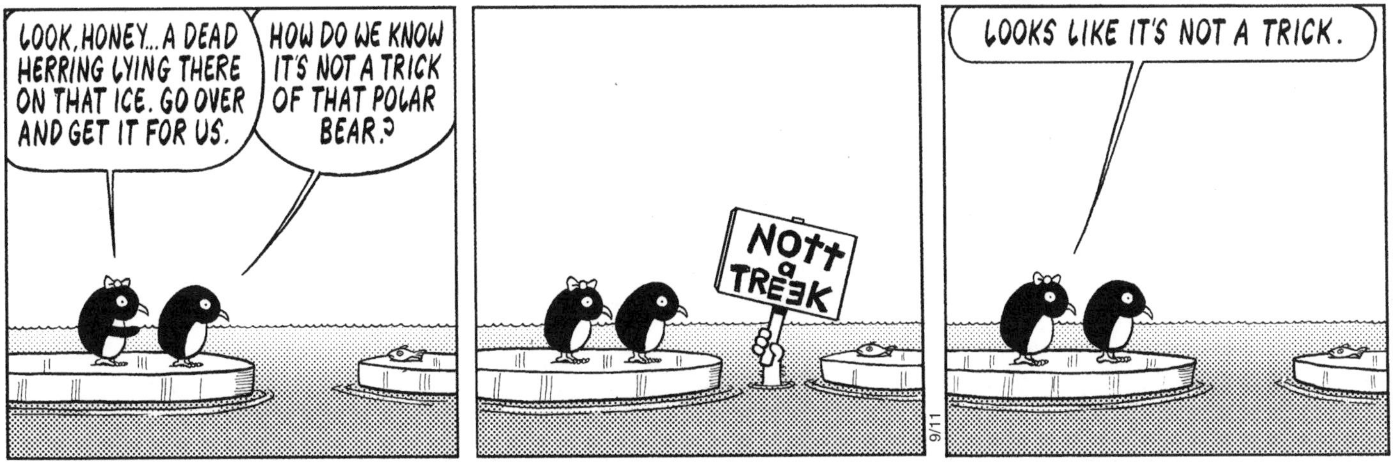
LOOK, HONEY... A DEAD HERRING LYING THERE ON THAT ICE. GO OVER AND GET IT FOR US.
HOW DO WE KNOW IT'S NOT A TRICK OF THAT POLAR BEAR?
NOtt a TREEK
9/11
LOOKS LIKE IT'S NOT A TRICK.

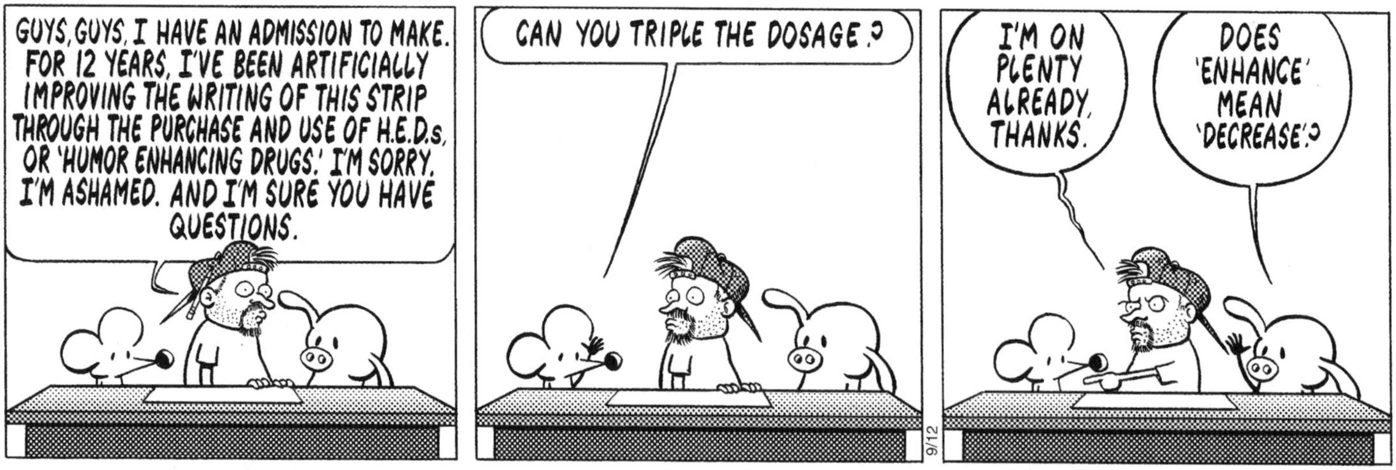
GUYS, GUYS. I HAVE AN ADMISSION TO MAKE. FOR 12 YEARS, I'VE BEEN ARTIFICIALLY IMPROVING THE WRITING OF THIS STRIP THROUGH THE PURCHASE AND USE OF H.E.D.s, OR 'HUMOR ENHANCING DRUGS.' I'M SORRY. I'M ASHAMED. AND I'M SURE YOU HAVE QUESTIONS.
CAN YOU TRIPLE THE DOSAGE?
I'M ON PLENTY ALREADY, THANKS.
DOES 'ENHANCE' MEAN 'DECREASE'?
9/12

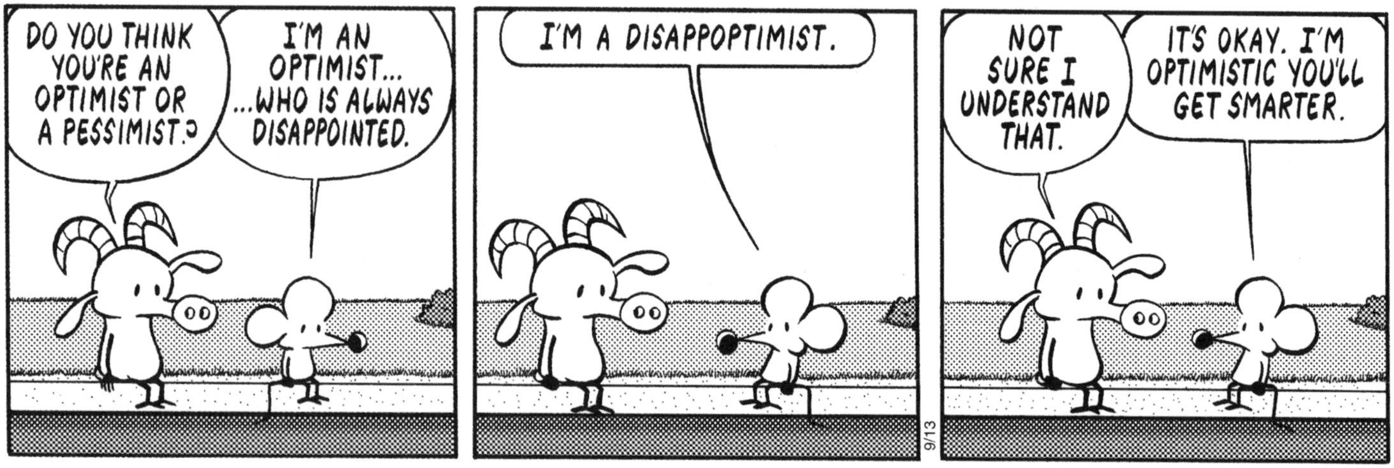
DO YOU THINK YOU'RE AN OPTIMIST OR A PESSIMIST?
I'M AN OPTIMIST... ...WHO IS ALWAYS DISAPPOINTED.
I'M A DISAPPOPTIMIST.
NOT SURE I UNDERSTAND THAT.
IT'S OKAY. I'M OPTIMISTIC YOU'LL GET SMARTER.
9/13

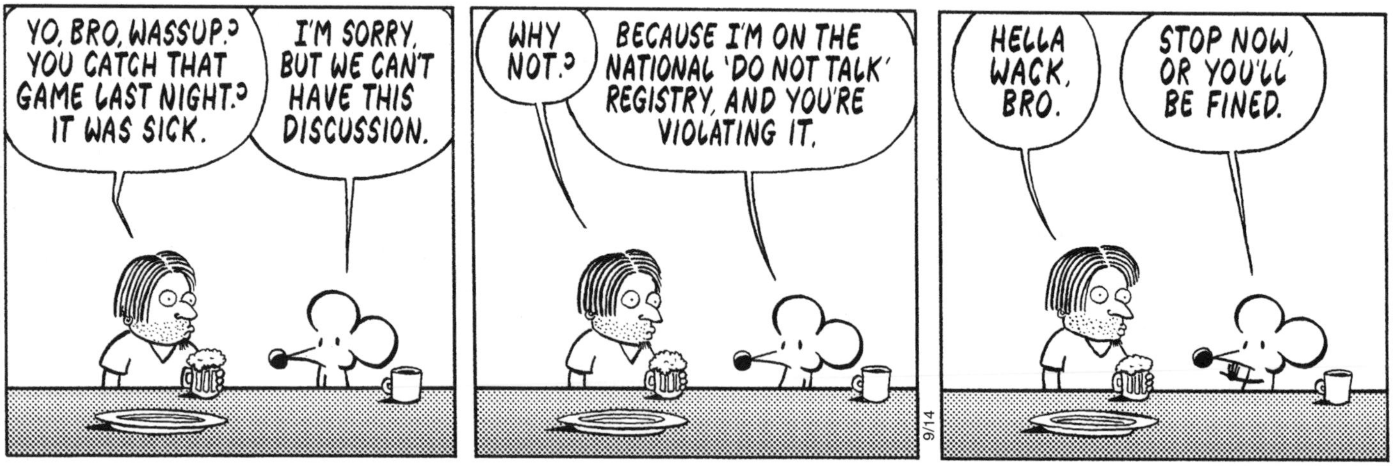
YO, BRO, WASSUP? YOU CATCH THAT GAME LAST NIGHT? IT WAS SICK.
I'M SORRY, BUT WE CAN'T HAVE THIS DISCUSSION.
WHY NOT?
BECAUSE I'M ON THE NATIONAL 'DO NOT TALK' REGISTRY, AND YOU'RE VIOLATING IT.
HELLA WACK, BRO.
STOP NOW, OR YOU'LL BE FINED.
9/14

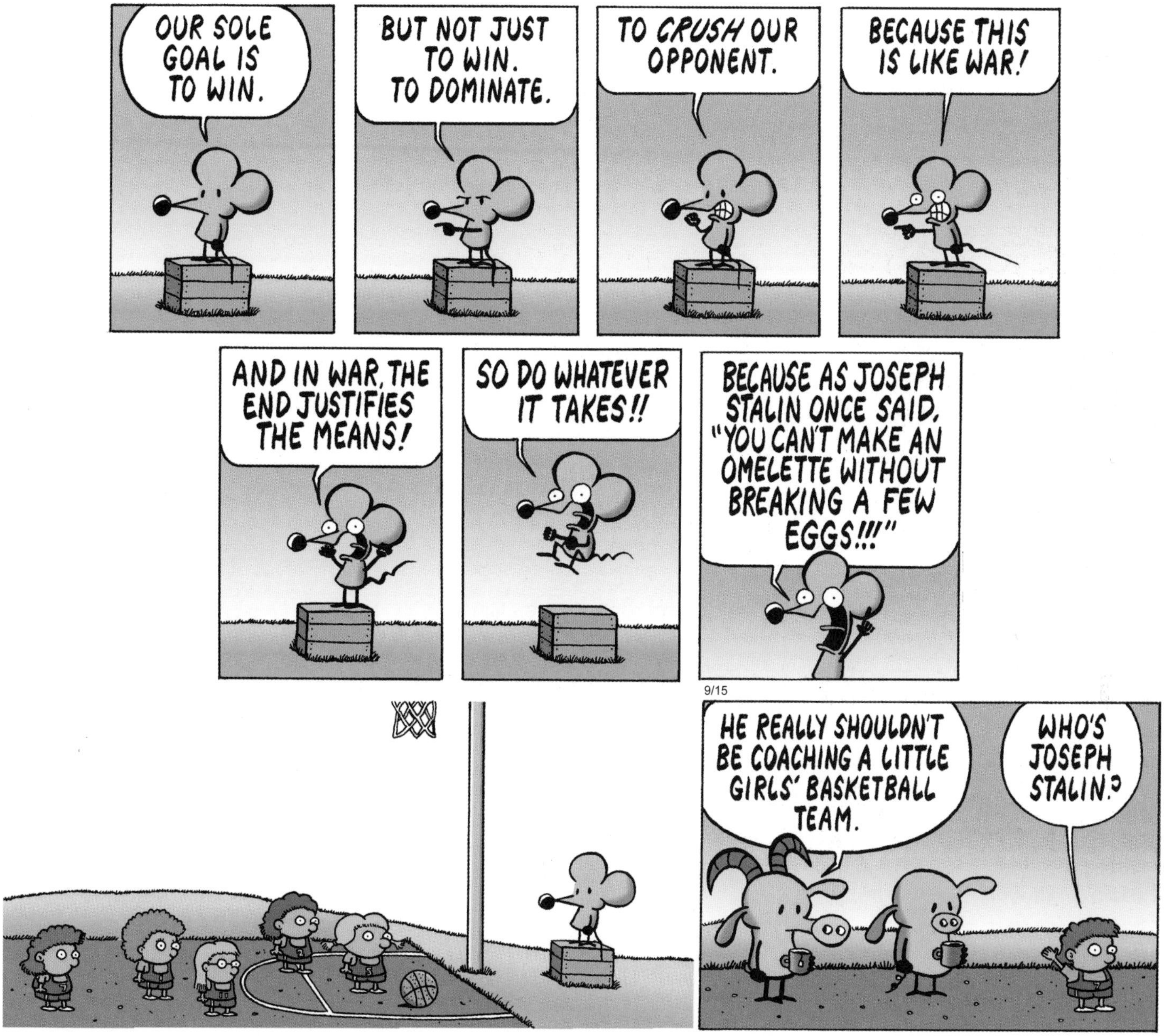
OUR SOLE GOAL IS TO WIN.
BUT NOT JUST TO WIN. TO DOMINATE.
TO CRUSH OUR OPPONENT.
BECAUSE THIS IS LIKE WAR!
AND IN WAR, THE END JUSTIFIES THE MEANS!
SO DO WHATEVER IT TAKES!!
BECAUSE AS JOSEPH STALIN ONCE SAID, "YOU CAN'T MAKE AN OMELETTE WITHOUT BREAKING A FEW EGGS!!!"
9/15
HE REALLY SHOULDN'T BE COACHING A LITTLE GIRLS' BASKETBALL TEAM.
WHO'S JOSEPH STALIN?

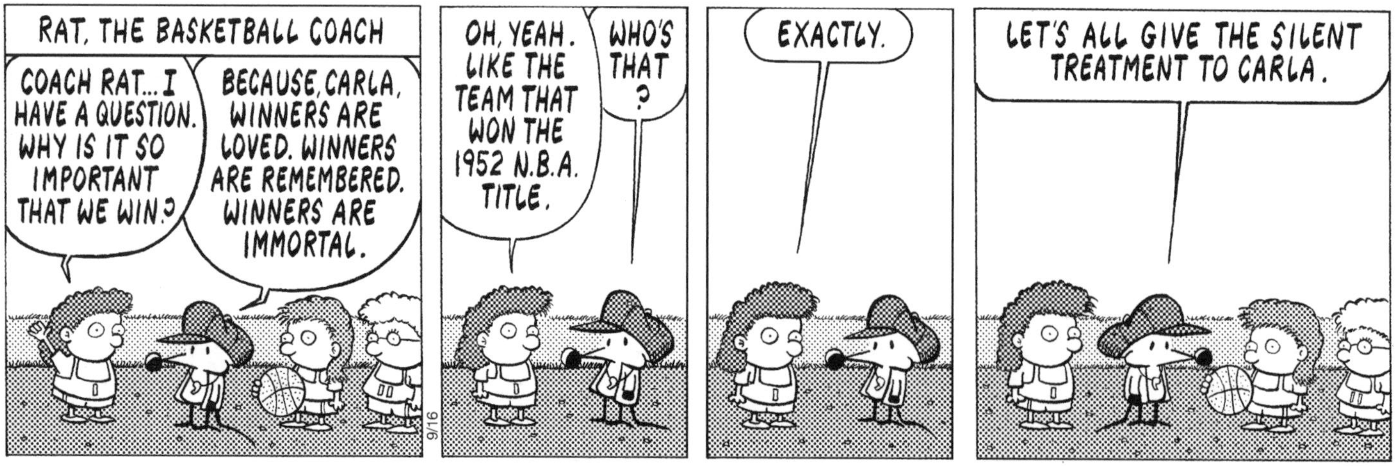
RAT, THE BASKETBALL COACH
COACH RAT... I HAVE A QUESTION. WHY IS IT SO IMPORTANT THAT WE WIN?
BECAUSE, CARLA, WINNERS ARE LOVED. WINNERS ARE REMEMBERED. WINNERS ARE IMMORTAL.
9/16
OH, YEAH. LIKE THE TEAM THAT WON THE 1952 N.B.A. TITLE.
WHO'S THAT?
EXACTLY.
LET'S ALL GIVE THE SILENT TREATMENT TO CARLA.

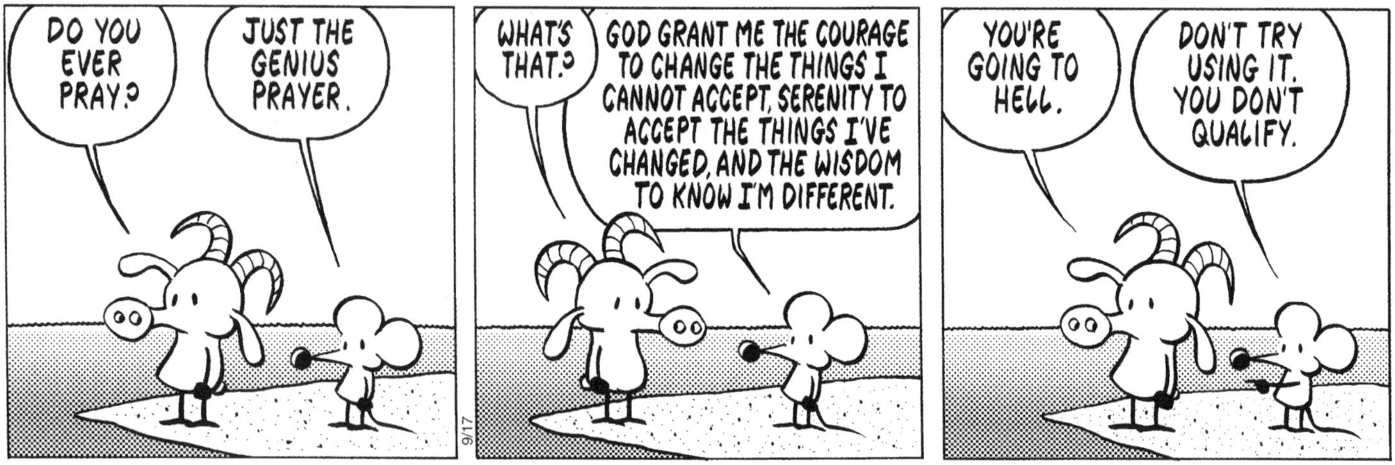
DO YOU EVER PRAY?
JUST THE GENIUS PRAYER.
9/17
WHAT'S THAT?
GOD GRANT ME THE COURAGE TO CHANGE THE THINGS I CANNOT ACCEPT, SERENITY TO ACCEPT THE THINGS I'VE CHANGED, AND THE WISDOM TO KNOW I'M DIFFERENT.
YOU'RE GOING TO HELL.
DON'T TRY USING IT. YOU DON'T QUALIFY.

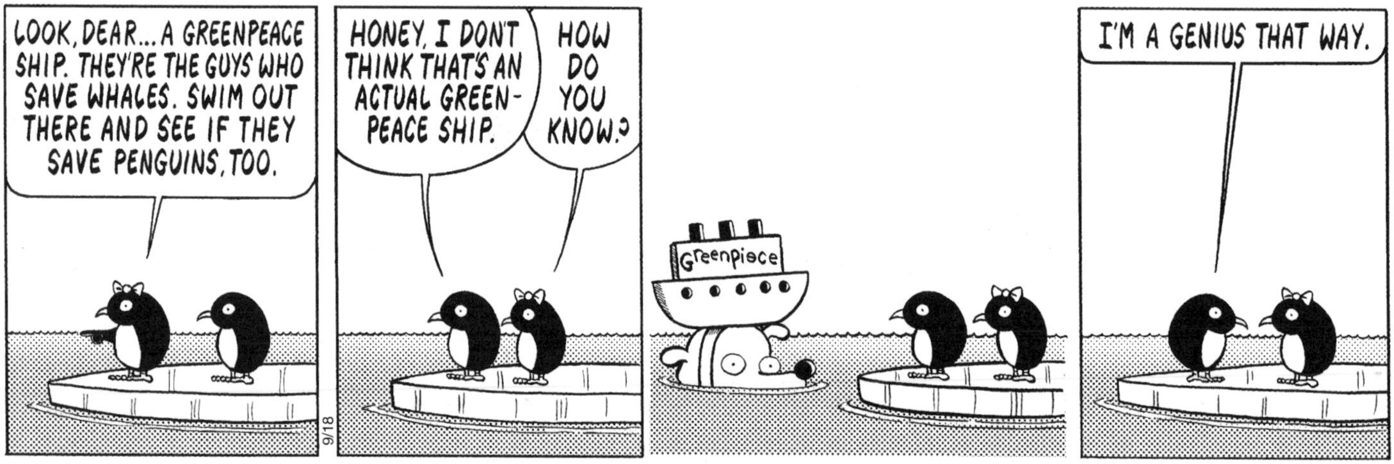
LOOK, DEAR... A GREENPEACE SHIP. THEY'RE THE GUYS WHO SAVE WHALES. SWIM OUT THERE AND SEE IF THEY SAVE PENGUINS, TOO.
9/18
HONEY, I DON'T THINK THAT'S AN ACTUAL GREEN-PEACE SHIP.
HOW DO YOU KNOW?
Greenpiece
I'M A GENIUS THAT WAY.

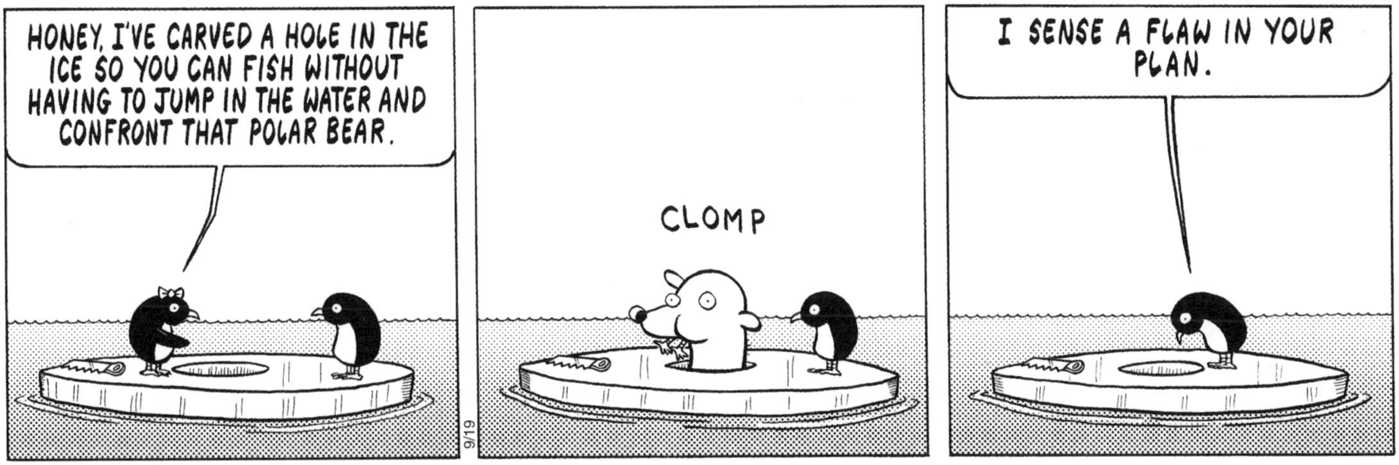
HONEY, I'VE CARVED A HOLE IN THE ICE SO YOU CAN FISH WITHOUT HAVING TO JUMP IN THE WATER AND CONFRONT THAT POLAR BEAR.
9/19
CLOMP
I SENSE A FLAW IN YOUR PLAN.

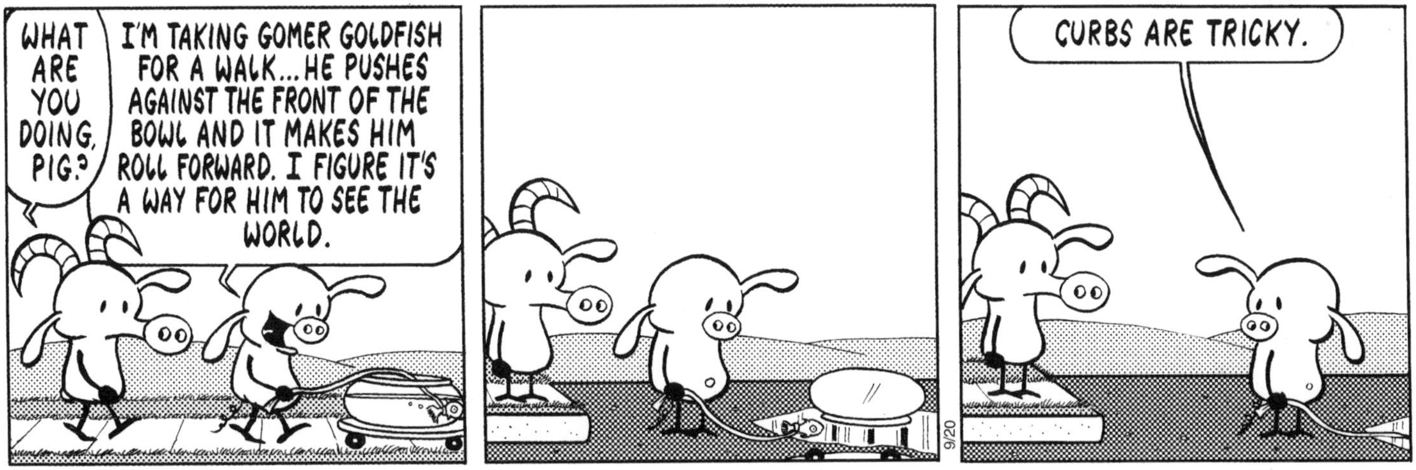
WHAT ARE YOU DOING, PIG?
I'M TAKING GOMER GOLDFISH FOR A WALK... HE PUSHES AGAINST THE FRONT OF THE BOWL AND IT MAKES HIM ROLL FORWARD. I FIGURE IT'S A WAY FOR HIM TO SEE THE WORLD.
9/20
CURBS ARE TRICKY.

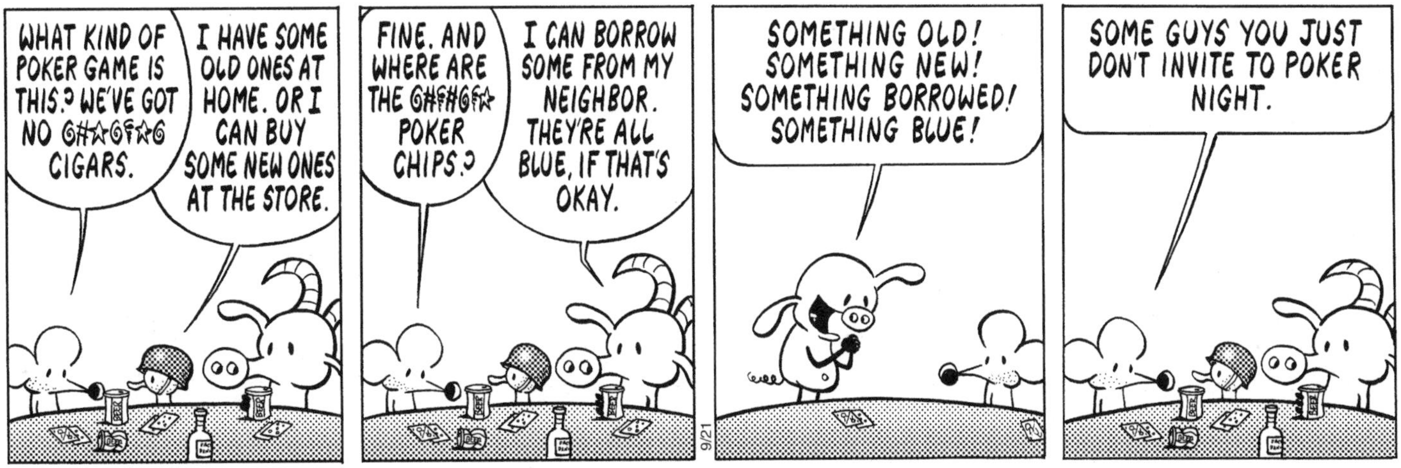
WHAT KIND OF POKER GAME IS THIS? WE'VE GOT NO @#☆@$☆@ CIGARS.
I HAVE SOME OLD ONES AT HOME. OR I CAN BUY SOME NEW ONES AT THE STORE.
FINE. AND WHERE ARE THE @#$#@$☆ POKER CHIPS?
I CAN BORROW SOME FROM MY NEIGHBOR. THEY'RE ALL BLUE, IF THAT'S OKAY.
9/21
SOMETHING OLD! SOMETHING NEW! SOMETHING BORROWED! SOMETHING BLUE!
SOME GUYS YOU JUST DON'T INVITE TO POKER NIGHT.

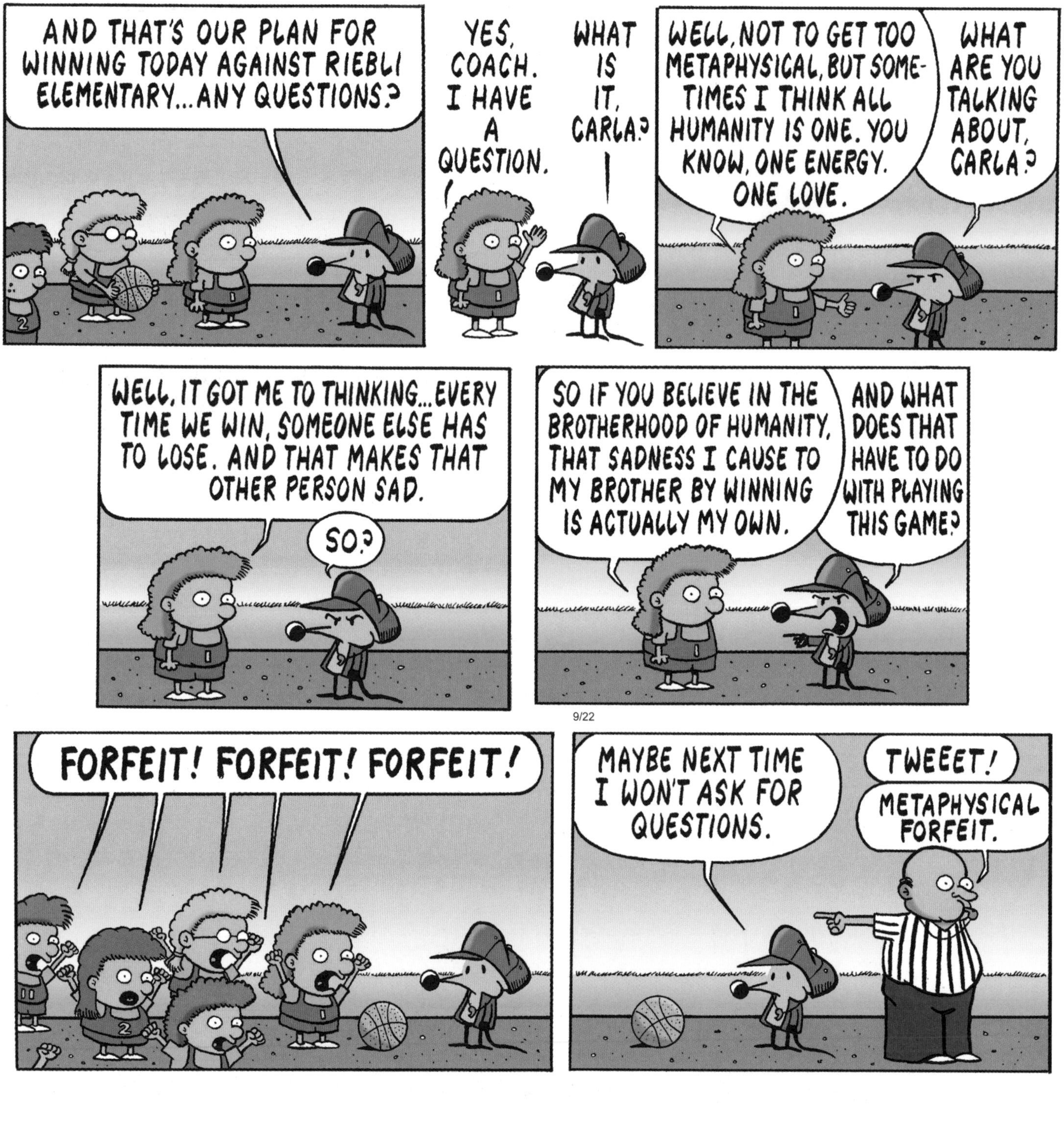
AND THAT'S OUR PLAN FOR WINNING TODAY AGAINST RIEBLI ELEMENTARY... ANY QUESTIONS?
YES, COACH. I HAVE A QUESTION.
WHAT IS IT, CARLA?
WELL, NOT TO GET TOO METAPHYSICAL, BUT SOMETIMES I THINK ALL HUMANITY IS ONE. YOU KNOW, ONE ENERGY. ONE LOVE.
WHAT ARE YOU TALKING ABOUT, CARLA?
WELL, IT GOT ME TO THINKING... EVERY TIME WE WIN, SOMEONE ELSE HAS TO LOSE. AND THAT MAKES THAT OTHER PERSON SAD.
SO?
SO IF YOU BELIEVE IN THE BROTHERHOOD OF HUMANITY, THAT SADNESS I CAUSE TO MY BROTHER BY WINNING IS ACTUALLY MY OWN.
AND WHAT DOES THAT HAVE TO DO WITH PLAYING THIS GAME?
9/22
FORFEIT! FORFEIT! FORFEIT!
MAYBE NEXT TIME I WON'T ASK FOR QUESTIONS.
TWEEET!
METAPHYSICAL FORFEIT.

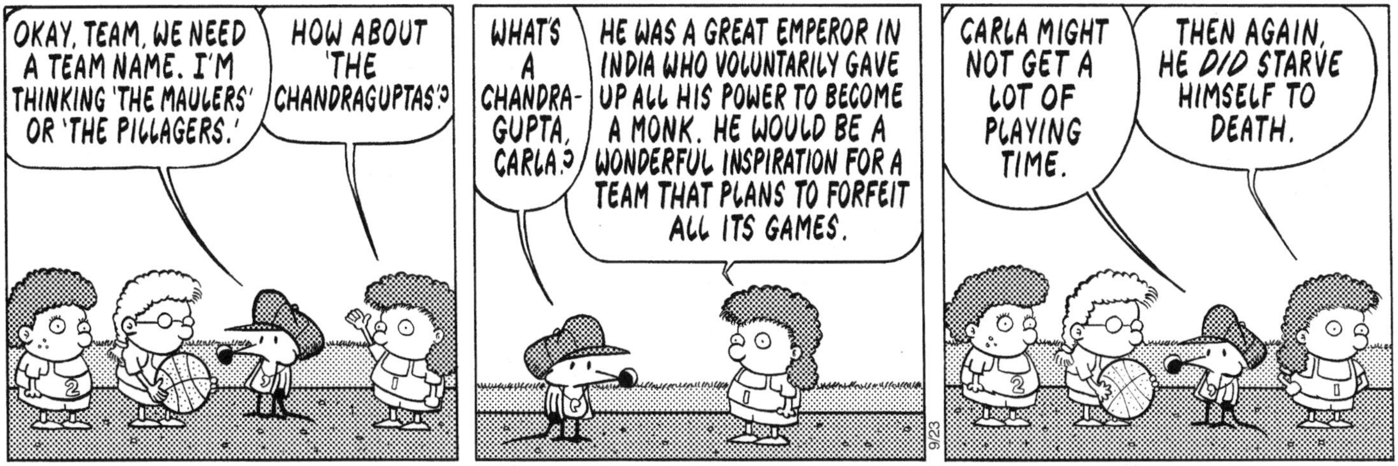
OKAY, TEAM, WE NEED A TEAM NAME. I'M THINKING 'THE MAULERS' OR 'THE PILLAGERS.'
HOW ABOUT 'THE CHANDRAGUPTAS'?
WHAT'S A CHANDRA-GUPTA, CARLA?
HE WAS A GREAT EMPEROR IN INDIA WHO VOLUNTARILY GAVE UP ALL HIS POWER TO BECOME A MONK. HE WOULD BE A WONDERFUL INSPIRATION FOR A TEAM THAT PLANS TO FORFEIT ALL ITS GAMES.
9/23
CARLA MIGHT NOT GET A LOT OF PLAYING TIME.
THEN AGAIN, HE *DID* STARVE HIMSELF TO DEATH.

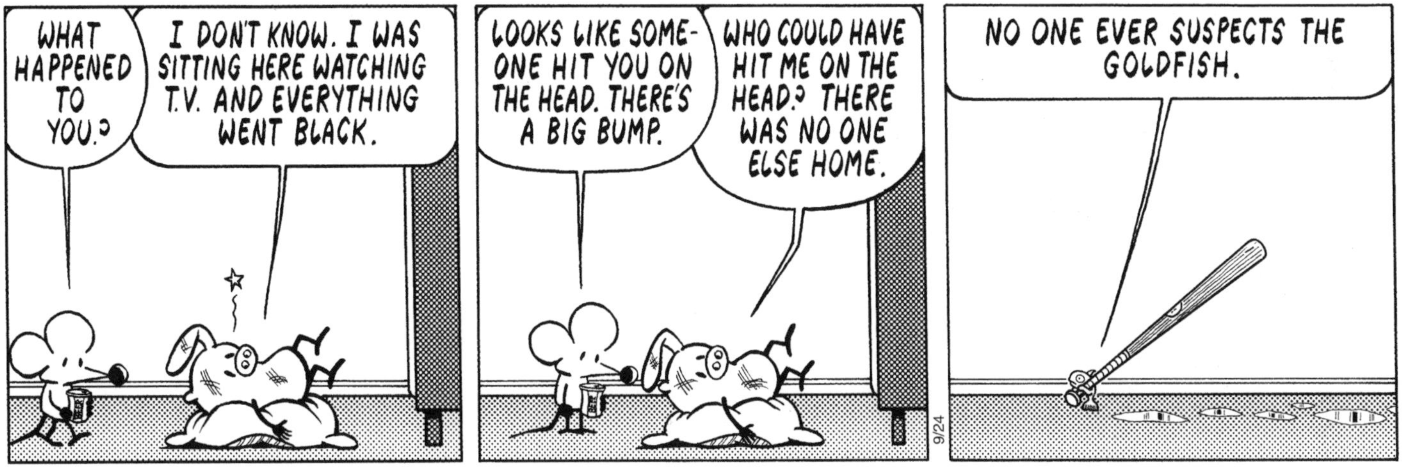
WHAT HAPPENED TO YOU?
I DON'T KNOW. I WAS SITTING HERE WATCHING T.V. AND EVERYTHING WENT BLACK.
LOOKS LIKE SOME-ONE HIT YOU ON THE HEAD. THERE'S A BIG BUMP.
WHO COULD HAVE HIT ME ON THE HEAD? THERE WAS NO ONE ELSE HOME.
9/24
NO ONE EVER SUSPECTS THE GOLDFISH.

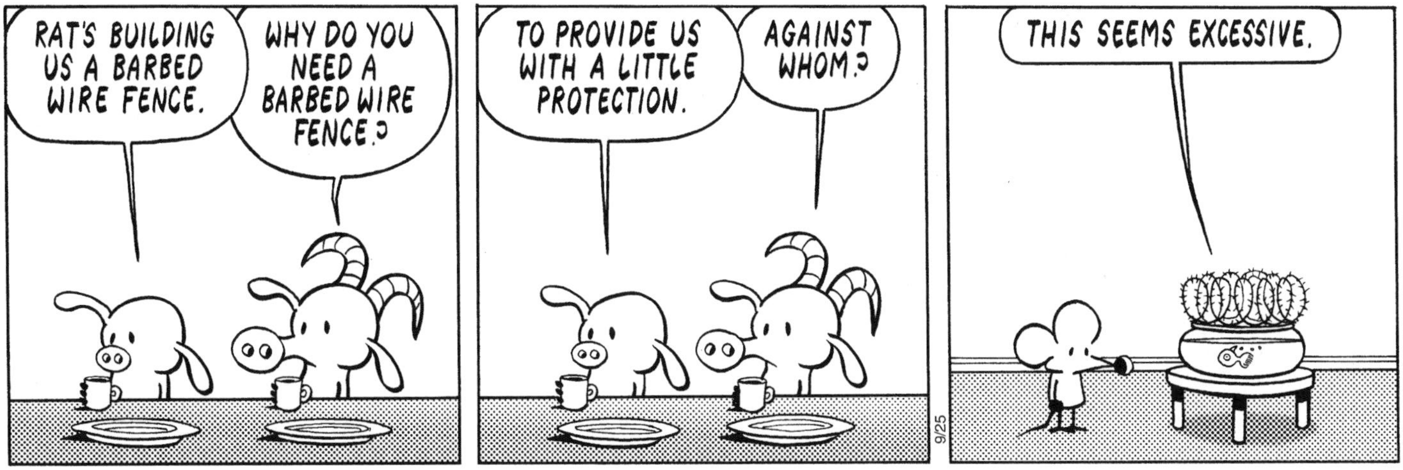
RAT'S BUILDING US A BARBED WIRE FENCE.
WHY DO YOU NEED A BARBED WIRE FENCE?
TO PROVIDE US WITH A LITTLE PROTECTION.
AGAINST WHOM?
9/25
THIS SEEMS EXCESSIVE.

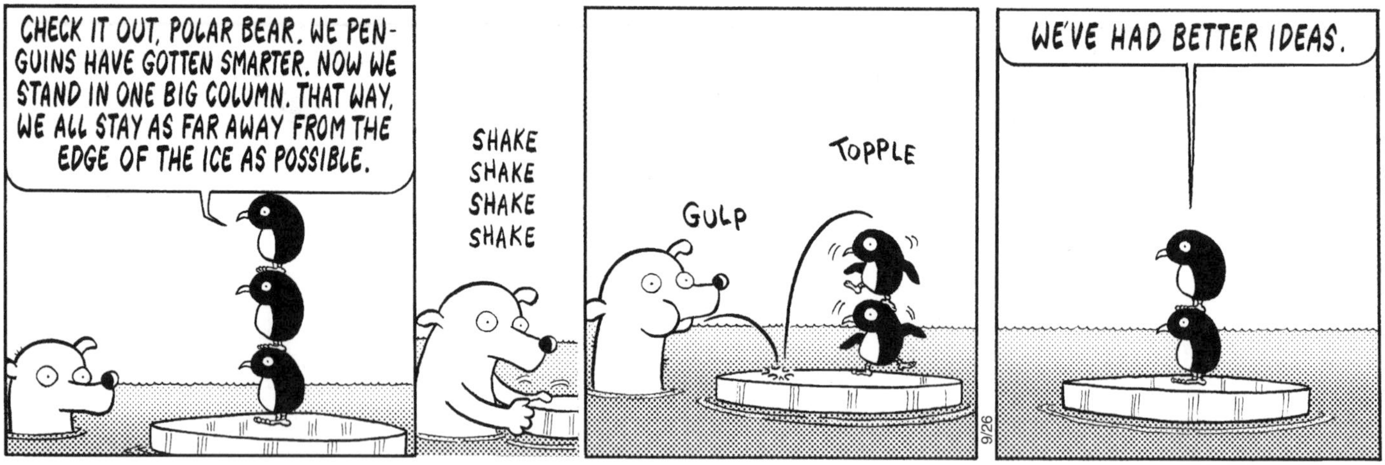
CHECK IT OUT, POLAR BEAR. WE PENGUINS HAVE GOTTEN SMARTER. NOW WE STAND IN ONE BIG COLUMN. THAT WAY, WE ALL STAY AS FAR AWAY FROM THE EDGE OF THE ICE AS POSSIBLE.
SHAKE SHAKE SHAKE SHAKE
GULP
TOPPLE
WE'VE HAD BETTER IDEAS.
9/26

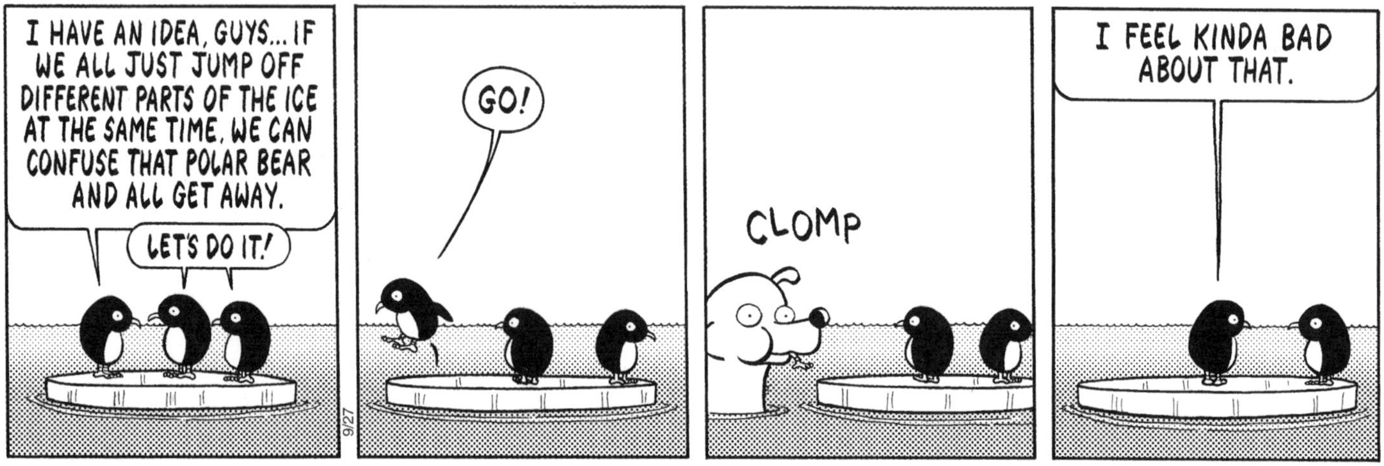
I HAVE AN IDEA, GUYS... IF WE ALL JUST JUMP OFF DIFFERENT PARTS OF THE ICE AT THE SAME TIME, WE CAN CONFUSE THAT POLAR BEAR AND ALL GET AWAY.
LET'S DO IT!
9/27
GO!
CLOMP
I FEEL KINDA BAD ABOUT THAT.

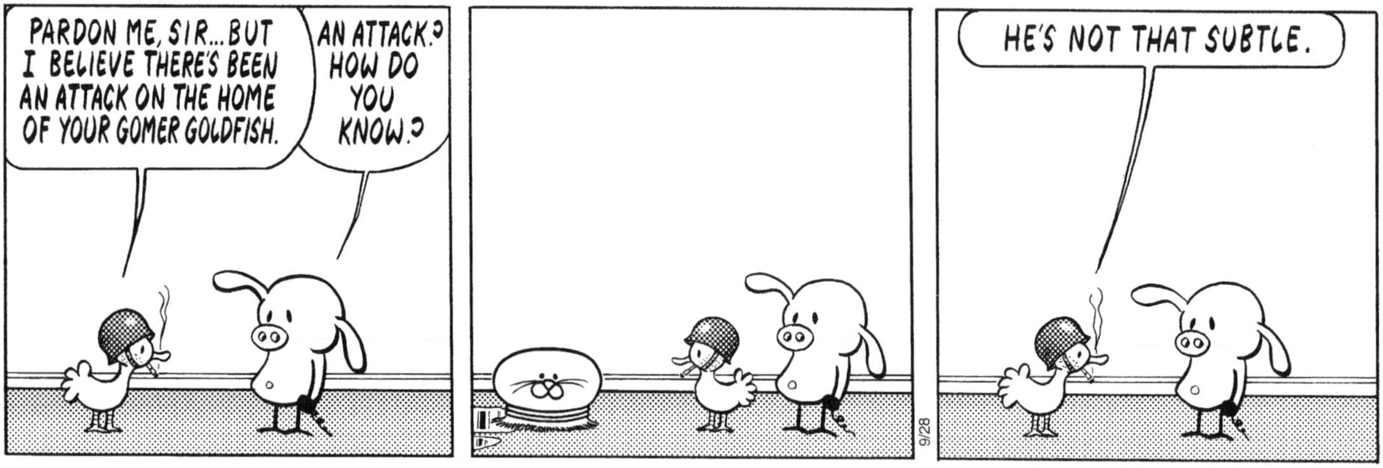
PARDON ME, SIR... BUT I BELIEVE THERE'S BEEN AN ATTACK ON THE HOME OF YOUR GOMER GOLDFISH.
AN ATTACK? HOW DO YOU KNOW?
9/28
HE'S NOT THAT SUBTLE.

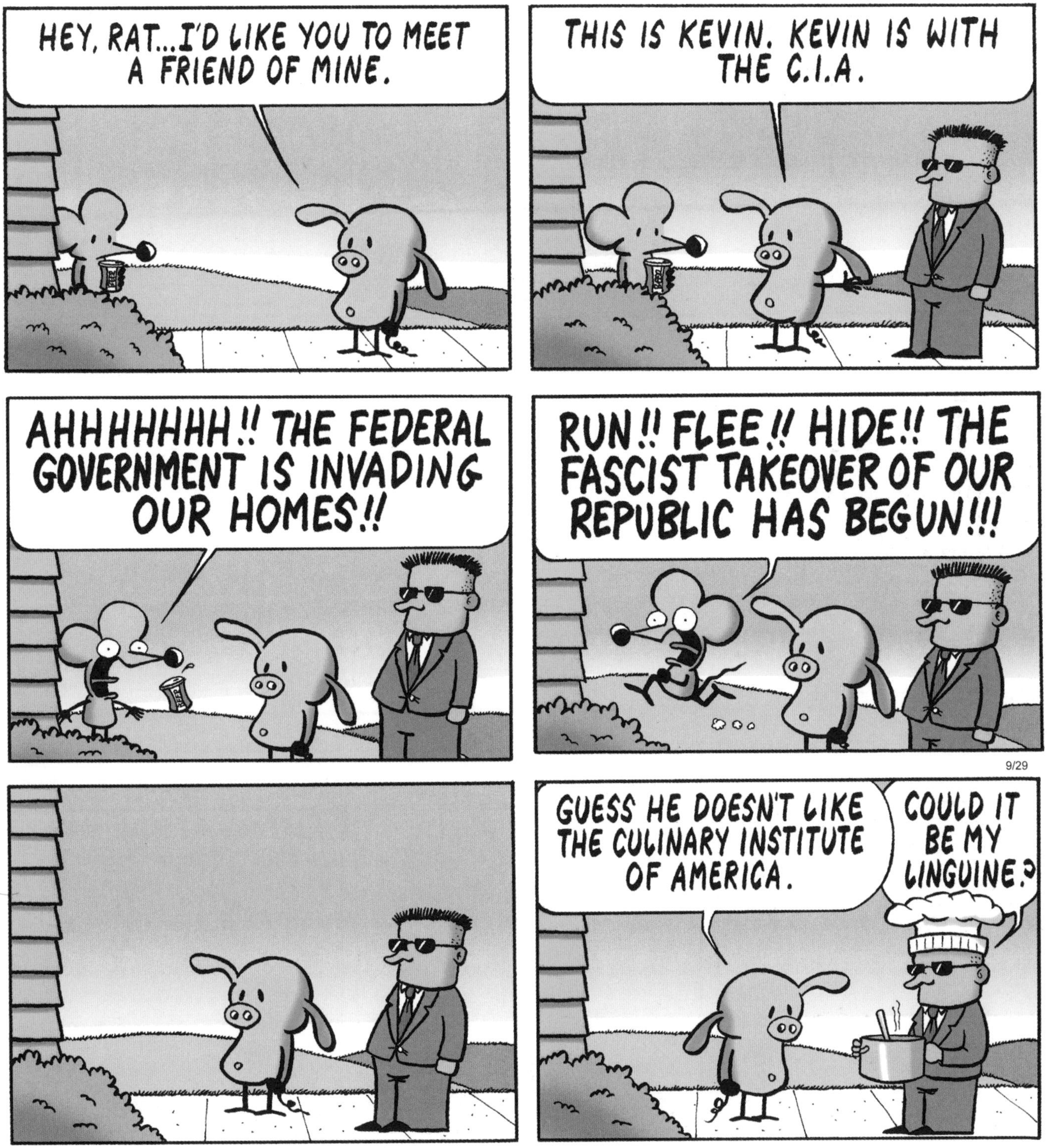

HEY, RAT...I'D LIKE YOU TO MEET A FRIEND OF MINE.
THIS IS KEVIN. KEVIN IS WITH THE C.I.A.
AHHHHHHH!! THE FEDERAL GOVERNMENT IS INVADING OUR HOMES!!
RUN!! FLEE!! HIDE!! THE FASCIST TAKEOVER OF OUR REPUBLIC HAS BEGUN!!!
9/29
GUESS HE DOESN'T LIKE THE CULINARY INSTITUTE OF AMERICA.
COULD IT BE MY LINGUINE?

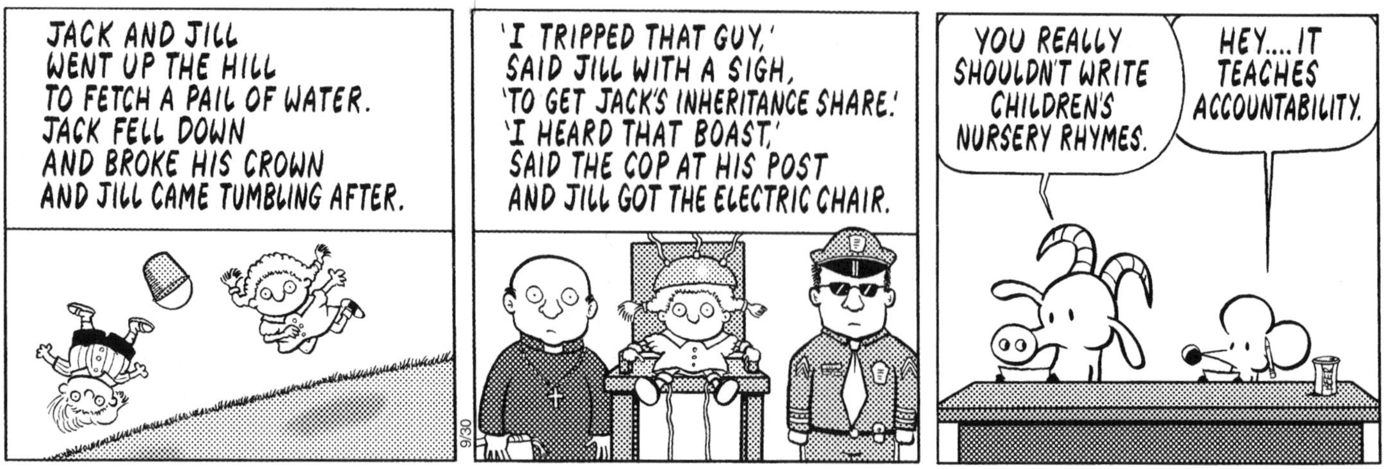
JACK AND JILL
WENT UP THE HILL
TO FETCH A PAIL OF WATER.
JACK FELL DOWN
AND BROKE HIS CROWN
AND JILL CAME TUMBLING AFTER.
'I TRIPPED THAT GUY,'
SAID JILL WITH A SIGH,
'TO GET JACK'S INHERITANCE SHARE.'
'I HEARD THAT BOAST,'
SAID THE COP AT HIS POST
AND JILL GOT THE ELECTRIC CHAIR.
9/30
YOU REALLY SHOULDN'T WRITE CHILDREN'S NURSERY RHYMES.
HEY.... IT TEACHES ACCOUNTABILITY.

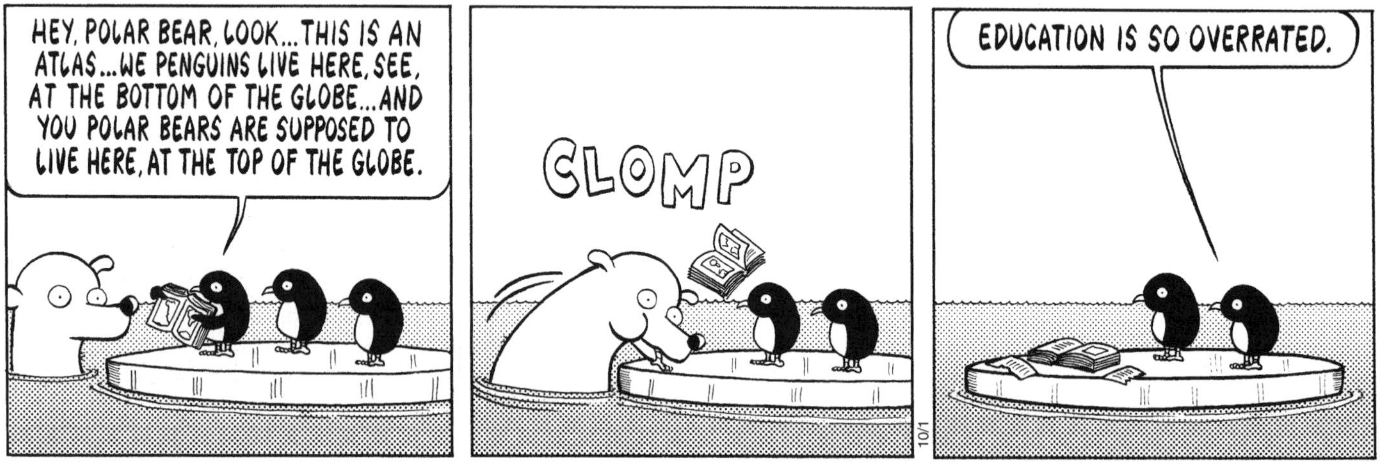
HEY, POLAR BEAR, LOOK... THIS IS AN ATLAS... WE PENGUINS LIVE HERE, SEE, AT THE BOTTOM OF THE GLOBE... AND YOU POLAR BEARS ARE SUPPOSED TO LIVE HERE, AT THE TOP OF THE GLOBE.
CLOMP
10/1
EDUCATION IS SO OVERRATED.

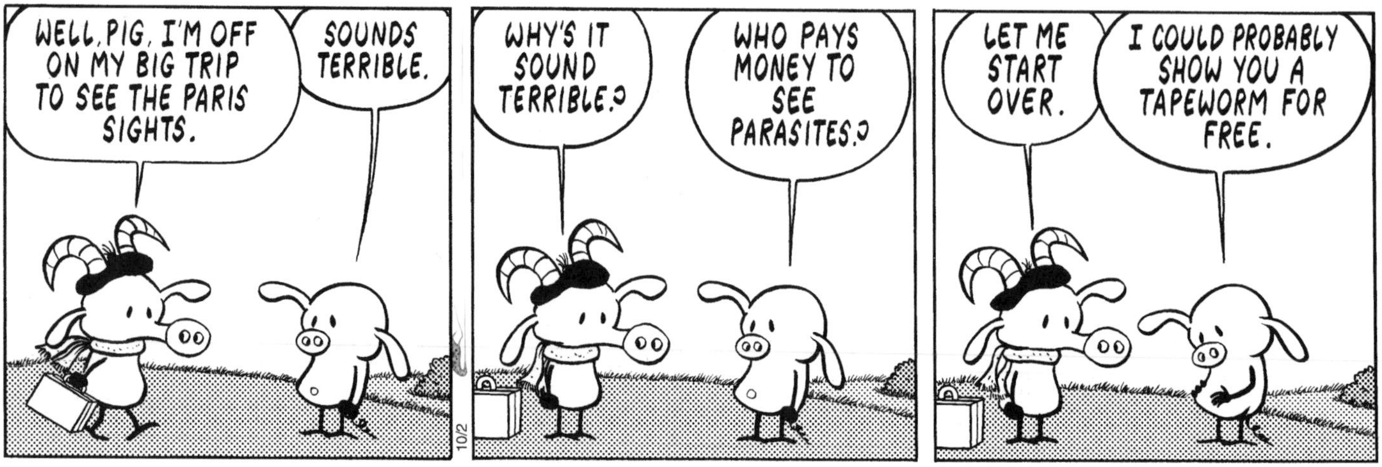
WELL, PIG, I'M OFF ON MY BIG TRIP TO SEE THE PARIS SIGHTS.
SOUNDS TERRIBLE.
10/2
WHY'S IT SOUND TERRIBLE?
WHO PAYS MONEY TO SEE PARASITES?
LET ME START OVER.
I COULD PROBABLY SHOW YOU A TAPEWORM FOR FREE.

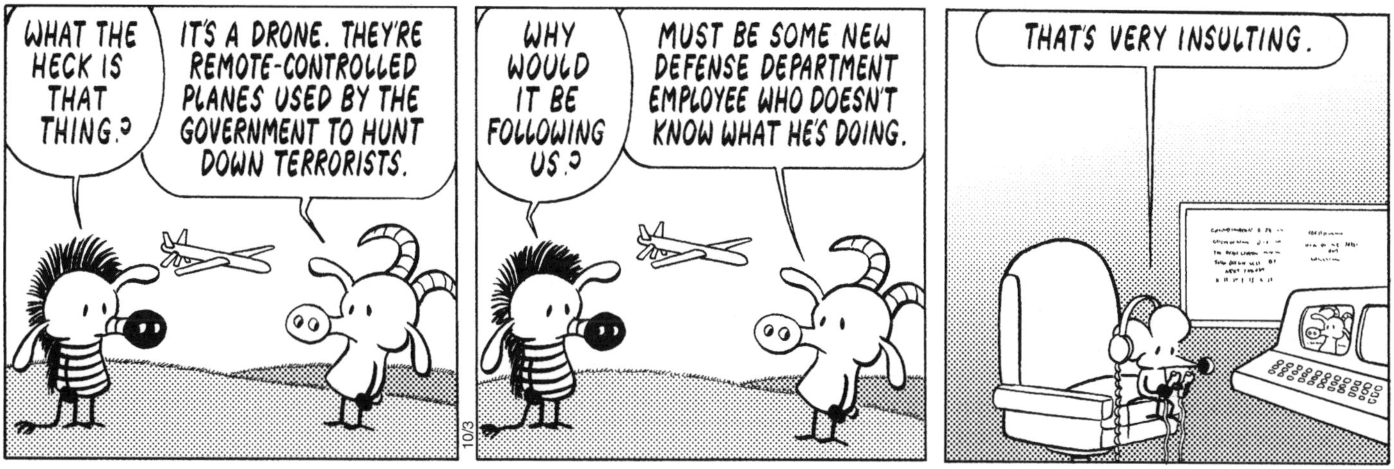
WHAT THE HECK IS THAT THING?
IT'S A DRONE. THEY'RE REMOTE-CONTROLLED PLANES USED BY THE GOVERNMENT TO HUNT DOWN TERRORISTS.
WHY WOULD IT BE FOLLOWING US?
MUST BE SOME NEW DEFENSE DEPARTMENT EMPLOYEE WHO DOESN'T KNOW WHAT HE'S DOING.
THAT'S VERY INSULTING.
10/3

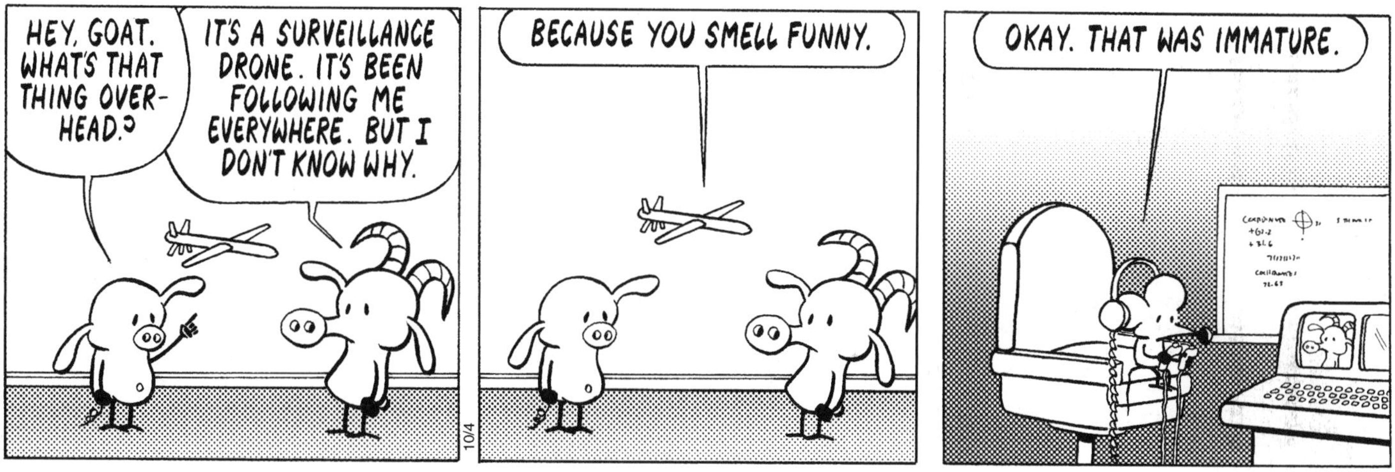
HEY, GOAT. WHAT'S THAT THING OVER-HEAD?
IT'S A SURVEILLANCE DRONE. IT'S BEEN FOLLOWING ME EVERYWHERE. BUT I DON'T KNOW WHY.
BECAUSE YOU SMELL FUNNY.
OKAY. THAT WAS IMMATURE.
10/4

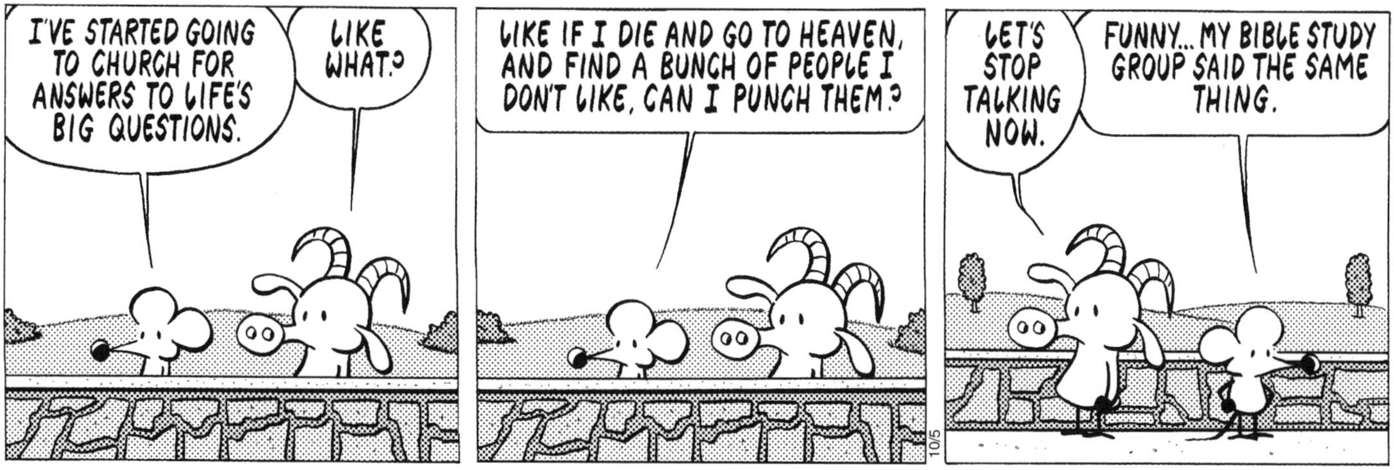
I'VE STARTED GOING TO CHURCH FOR ANSWERS TO LIFE'S BIG QUESTIONS.
LIKE WHAT?
LIKE IF I DIE AND GO TO HEAVEN, AND FIND A BUNCH OF PEOPLE I DON'T LIKE, CAN I PUNCH THEM?
LET'S STOP TALKING NOW.
FUNNY... MY BIBLE STUDY GROUP SAID THE SAME THING.
10/5

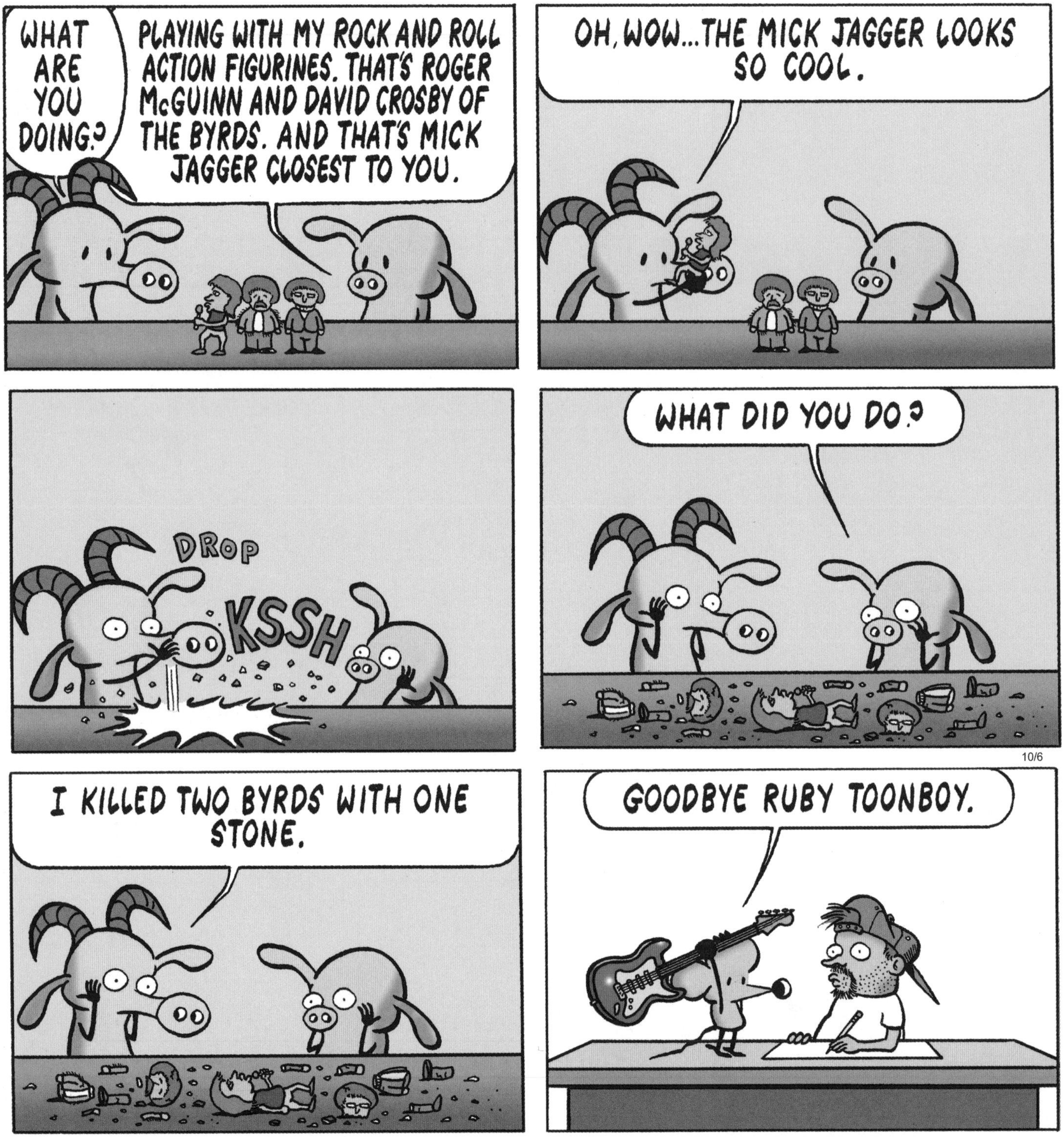
WHAT ARE YOU DOING?
PLAYING WITH MY ROCK AND ROLL ACTION FIGURINES. THAT'S ROGER McGUINN AND DAVID CROSBY OF THE BYRDS. AND THAT'S MICK JAGGER CLOSEST TO YOU.
OH, WOW...THE MICK JAGGER LOOKS SO COOL.
DROP
KSSH
WHAT DID YOU DO?
10/6
I KILLED TWO BYRDS WITH ONE STONE.
GOODBYE RUBY TOONBOY.

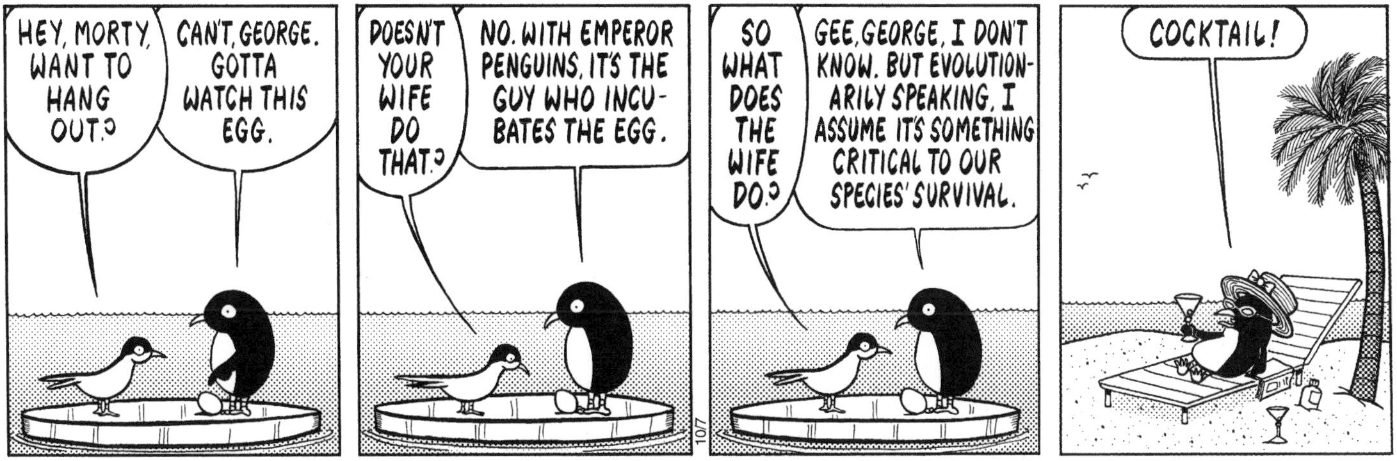
HEY, MORTY, WANT TO HANG OUT?
CAN'T, GEORGE. GOTTA WATCH THIS EGG.
DOESN'T YOUR WIFE DO THAT?
NO. WITH EMPEROR PENGUINS, IT'S THE GUY WHO INCUBATES THE EGG.
SO WHAT DOES THE WIFE DO?
GEE, GEORGE, I DON'T KNOW. BUT EVOLUTIONARILY SPEAKING, I ASSUME IT'S SOMETHING CRITICAL TO OUR SPECIES' SURVIVAL.
10/7
COCKTAIL!

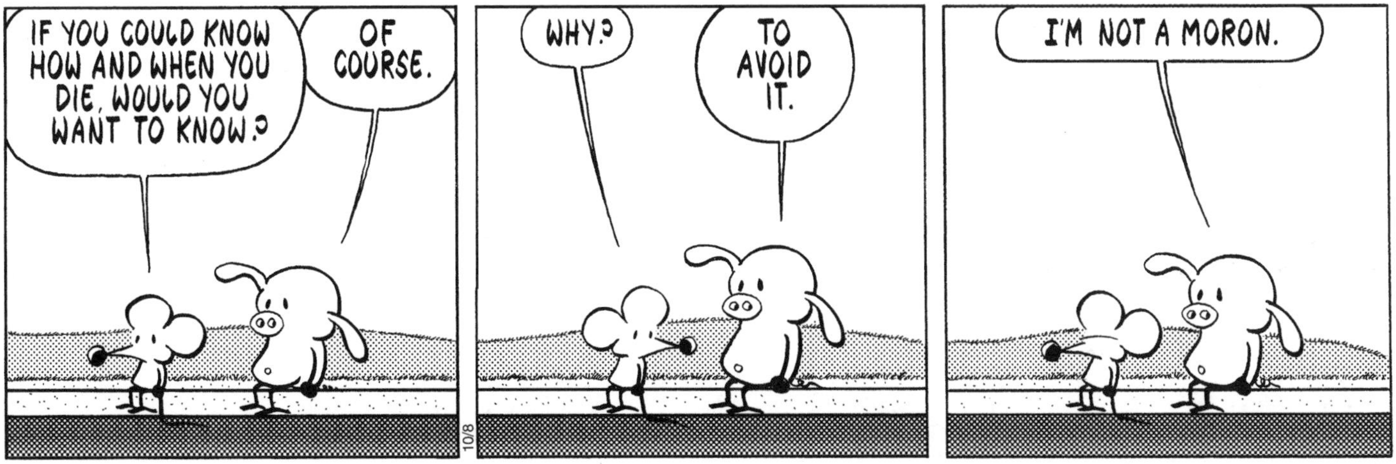
IF YOU COULD KNOW HOW AND WHEN YOU DIE, WOULD YOU WANT TO KNOW?
OF COURSE.
10/8
WHY?
TO AVOID IT.
I'M NOT A MORON.

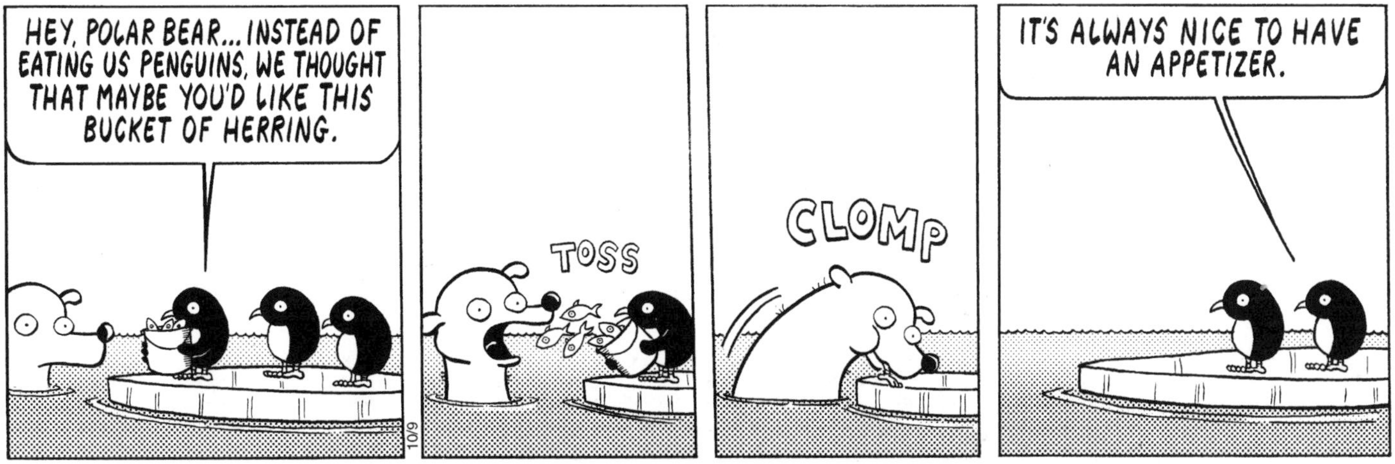
HEY, POLAR BEAR... INSTEAD OF EATING US PENGUINS, WE THOUGHT THAT MAYBE YOU'D LIKE THIS BUCKET OF HERRING.
10/9
TOSS
CLOMP
IT'S ALWAYS NICE TO HAVE AN APPETIZER.

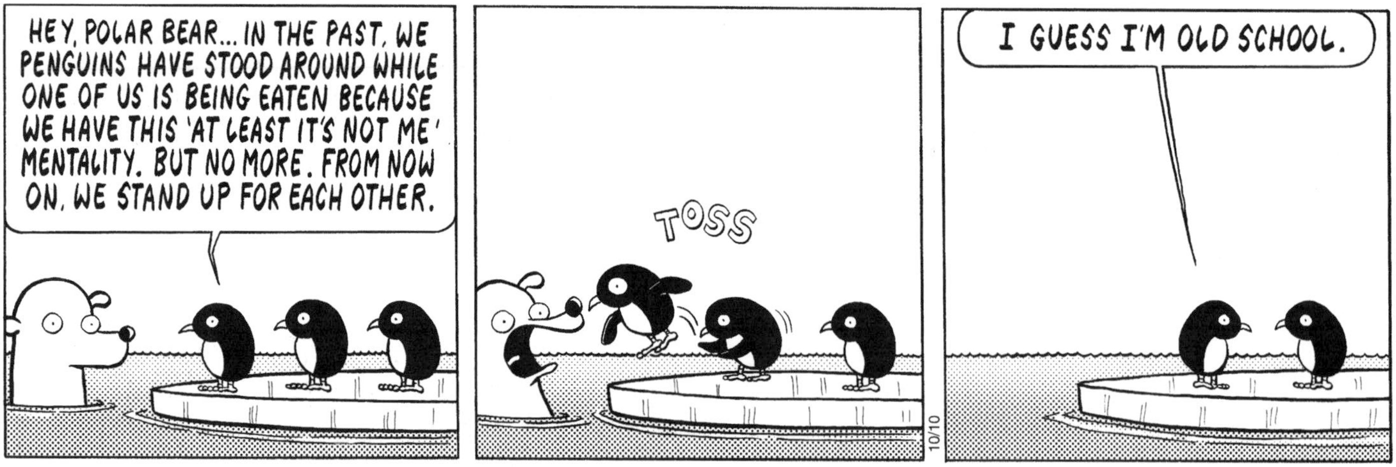
HEY, POLAR BEAR... IN THE PAST, WE PENGUINS HAVE STOOD AROUND WHILE ONE OF US IS BEING EATEN BECAUSE WE HAVE THIS 'AT LEAST IT'S NOT ME' MENTALITY. BUT NO MORE. FROM NOW ON, WE STAND UP FOR EACH OTHER.
TOSS
10/10
I GUESS I'M OLD SCHOOL.

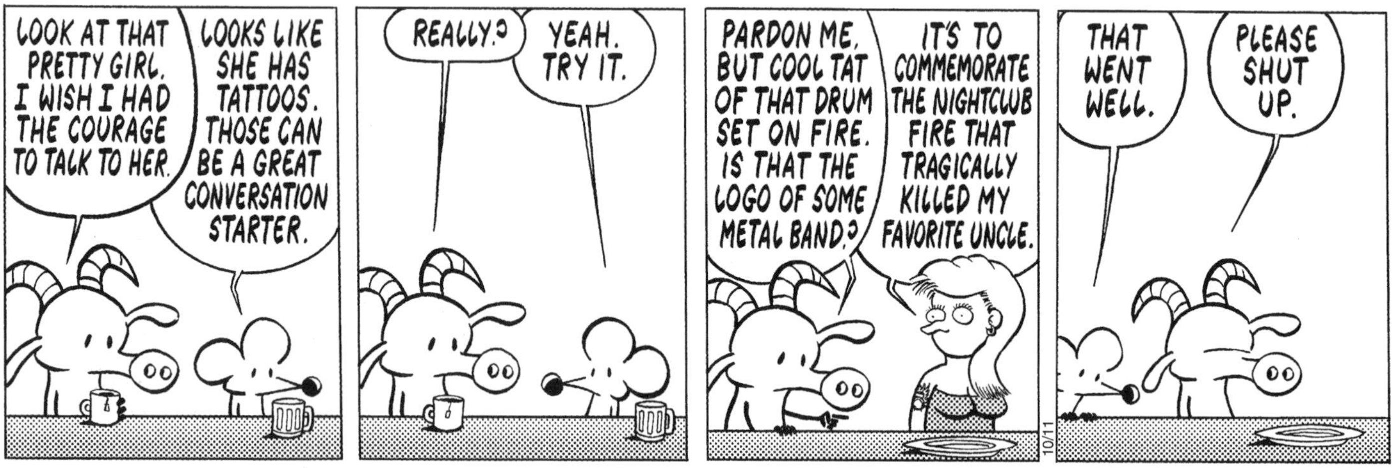
LOOK AT THAT PRETTY GIRL. I WISH I HAD THE COURAGE TO TALK TO HER.
LOOKS LIKE SHE HAS TATTOOS. THOSE CAN BE A GREAT CONVERSATION STARTER.
REALLY?
YEAH. TRY IT.
PARDON ME, BUT COOL TAT OF THAT DRUM SET ON FIRE. IS THAT THE LOGO OF SOME METAL BAND?
IT'S TO COMMEMORATE THE NIGHTCLUB FIRE THAT TRAGICALLY KILLED MY FAVORITE UNCLE.
10/11
THAT WENT WELL.
PLEASE SHUT UP.

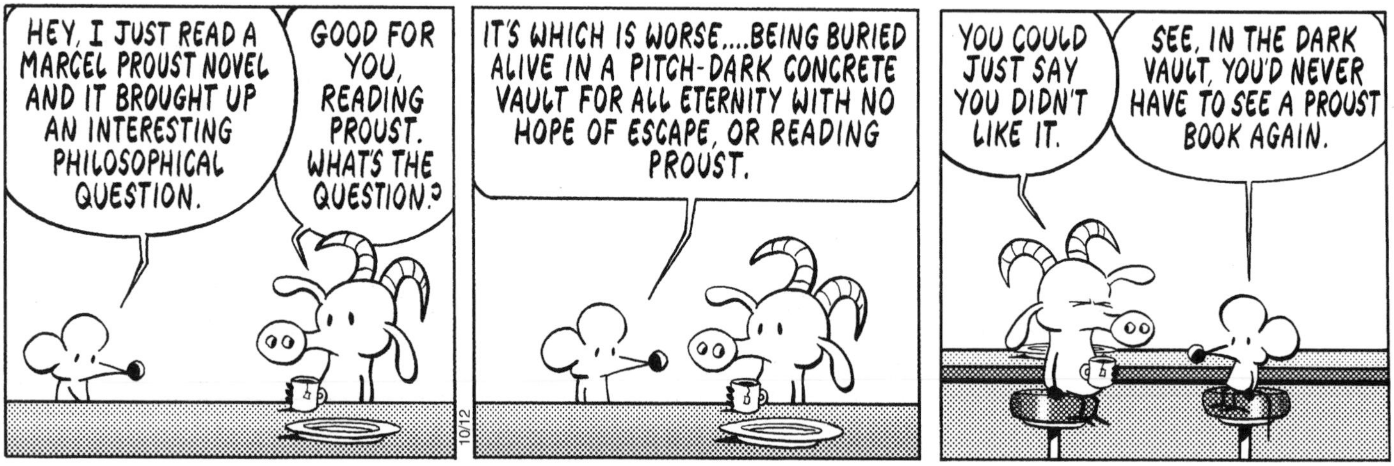
HEY, I JUST READ A MARCEL PROUST NOVEL AND IT BROUGHT UP AN INTERESTING PHILOSOPHICAL QUESTION.
GOOD FOR YOU, READING PROUST. WHAT'S THE QUESTION?
10/12
IT'S WHICH IS WORSE....BEING BURIED ALIVE IN A PITCH-DARK CONCRETE VAULT FOR ALL ETERNITY WITH NO HOPE OF ESCAPE, OR READING PROUST.
YOU COULD JUST SAY YOU DIDN'T LIKE IT.
SEE, IN THE DARK VAULT, YOU'D NEVER HAVE TO SEE A PROUST BOOK AGAIN.

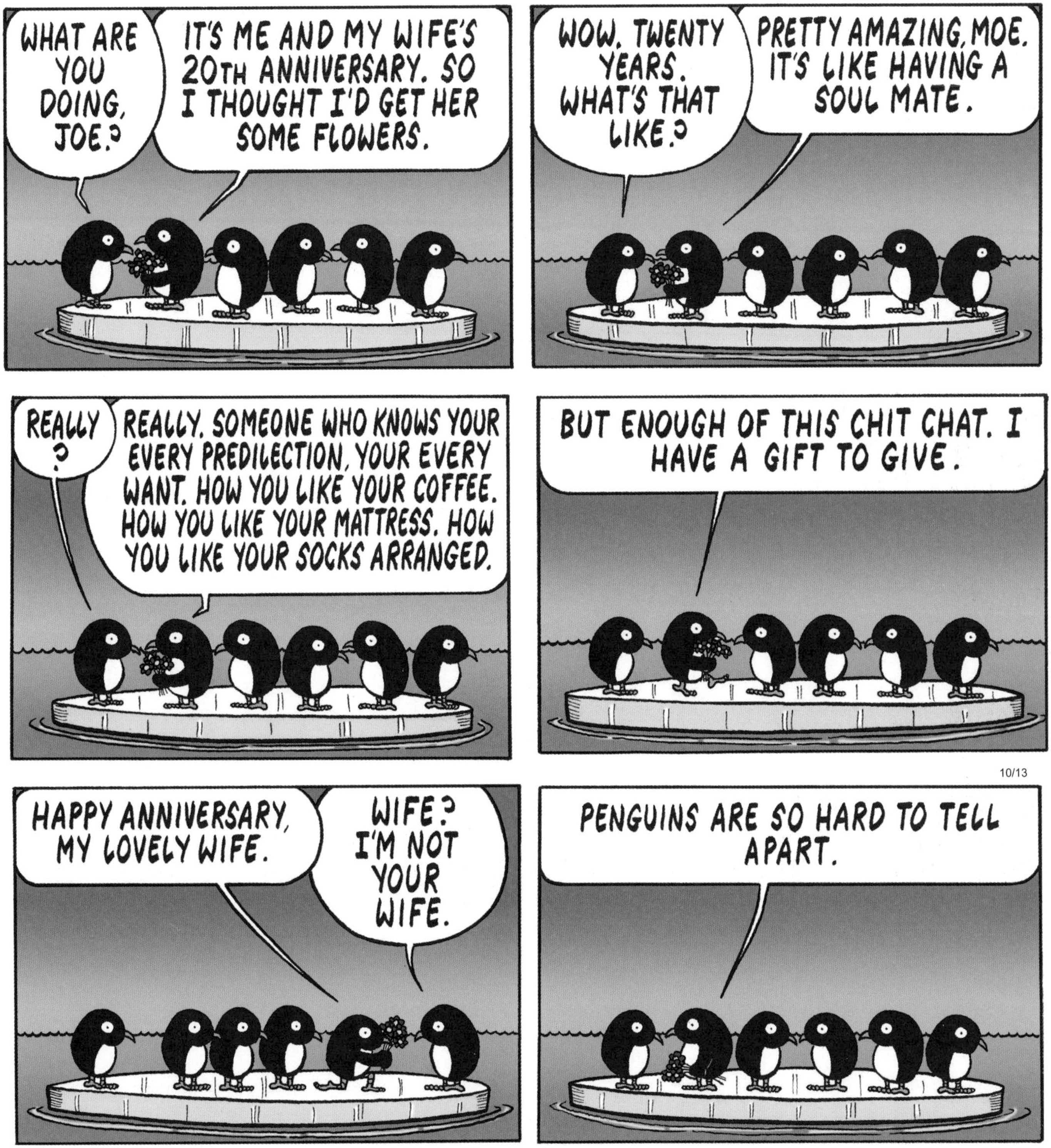
WHAT ARE YOU DOING, JOE?
IT'S ME AND MY WIFE'S 20TH ANNIVERSARY. SO I THOUGHT I'D GET HER SOME FLOWERS.
WOW. TWENTY YEARS. WHAT'S THAT LIKE?
PRETTY AMAZING, MOE. IT'S LIKE HAVING A SOUL MATE.
REALLY?
REALLY. SOMEONE WHO KNOWS YOUR EVERY PREDILECTION, YOUR EVERY WANT. HOW YOU LIKE YOUR COFFEE. HOW YOU LIKE YOUR MATTRESS. HOW YOU LIKE YOUR SOCKS ARRANGED.
BUT ENOUGH OF THIS CHIT CHAT. I HAVE A GIFT TO GIVE.
10/13
HAPPY ANNIVERSARY, MY LOVELY WIFE.
WIFE? I'M NOT YOUR WIFE.
PENGUINS ARE SO HARD TO TELL APART.

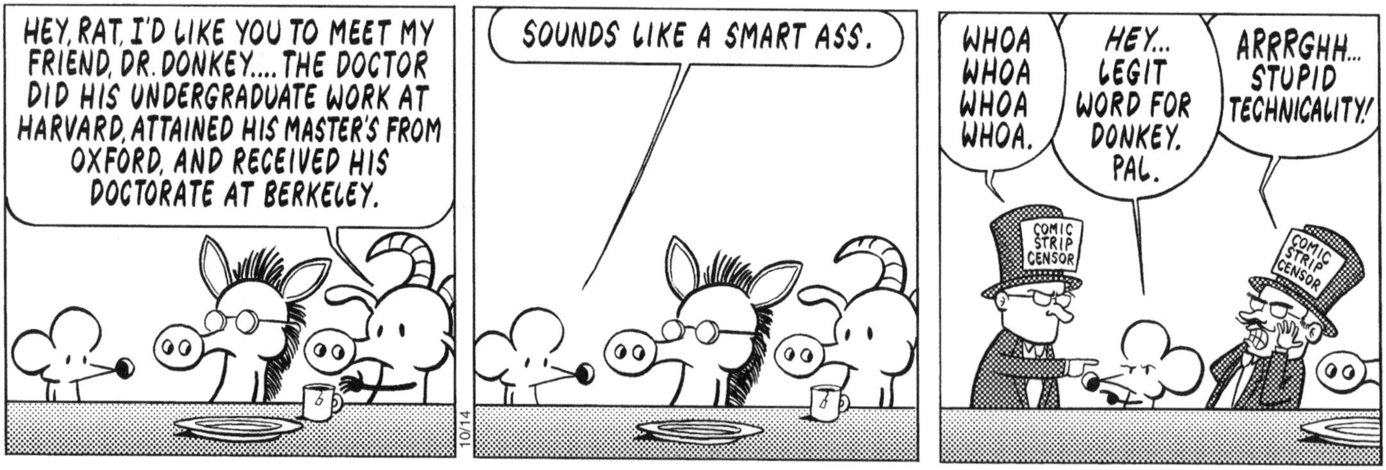
HEY, RAT, I'D LIKE YOU TO MEET MY FRIEND, DR. DONKEY.... THE DOCTOR DID HIS UNDERGRADUATE WORK AT HARVARD, ATTAINED HIS MASTER'S FROM OXFORD, AND RECEIVED HIS DOCTORATE AT BERKELEY.
10/14
SOUNDS LIKE A SMART ASS.
WHOA WHOA WHOA WHOA.
HEY... LEGIT WORD FOR DONKEY. PAL.
ARRRGHH... STUPID TECHNICALITY!
COMIC STRIP CENSOR
COMIC STRIP CENSOR

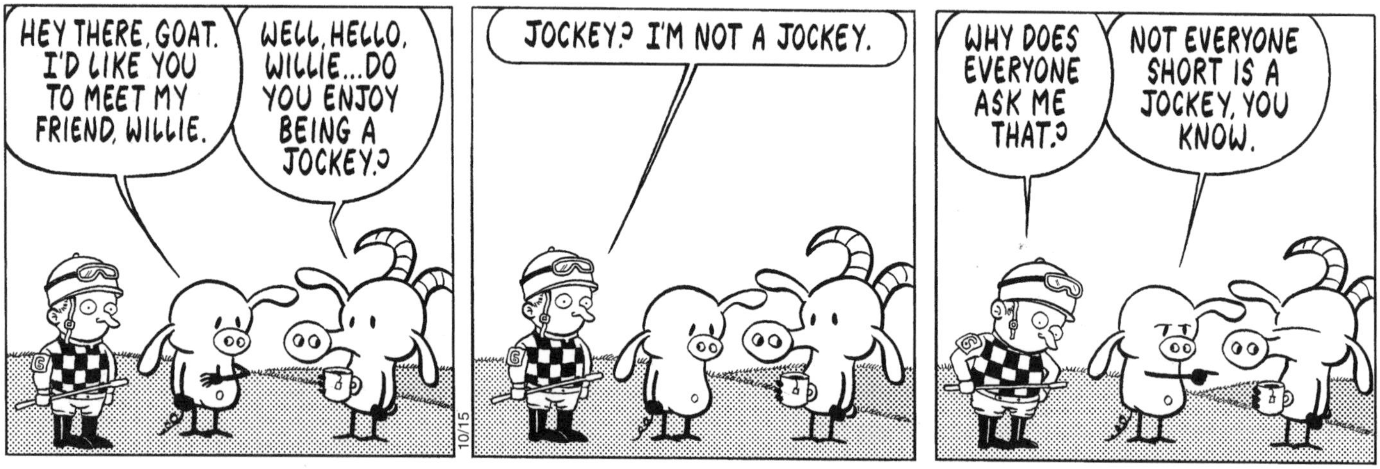
HEY THERE, GOAT. I'D LIKE YOU TO MEET MY FRIEND, WILLIE.
WELL, HELLO, WILLIE...DO YOU ENJOY BEING A JOCKEY?
10/15
JOCKEY? I'M NOT A JOCKEY.
WHY DOES EVERYONE ASK ME THAT?
NOT EVERYONE SHORT IS A JOCKEY, YOU KNOW.

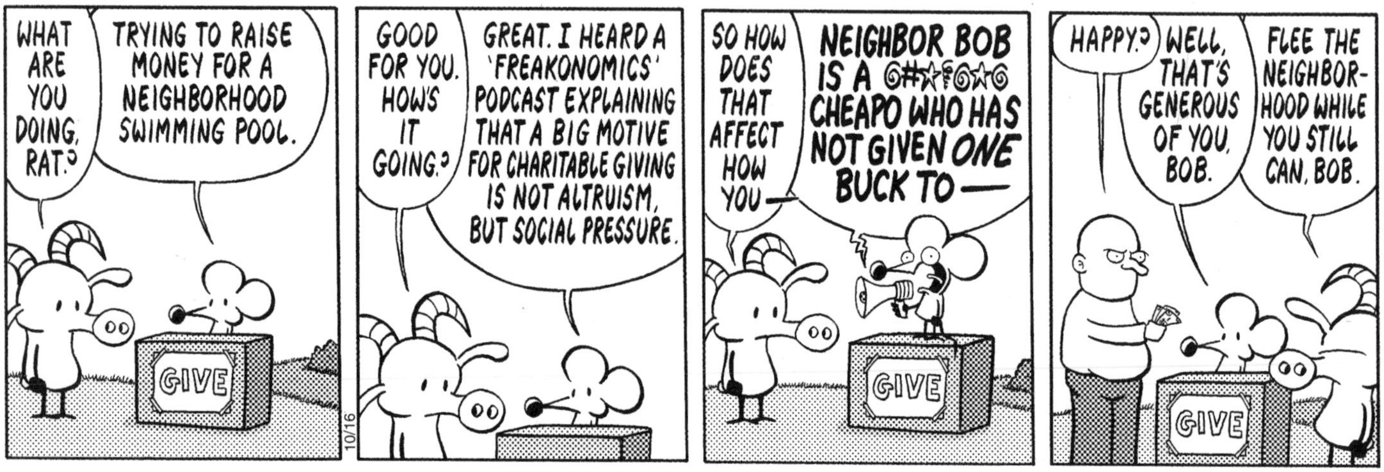
WHAT ARE YOU DOING, RAT?
TRYING TO RAISE MONEY FOR A NEIGHBORHOOD SWIMMING POOL.
GIVE
GOOD FOR YOU. HOW'S IT GOING?
GREAT. I HEARD A 'FREAKONOMICS' PODCAST EXPLAINING THAT A BIG MOTIVE FOR CHARITABLE GIVING IS NOT ALTRUISM, BUT SOCIAL PRESSURE.
10/16
SO HOW DOES THAT AFFECT HOW YOU—
NEIGHBOR BOB IS A @#☆$@☆@ CHEAPO WHO HAS NOT GIVEN *ONE* BUCK TO—
GIVE
HAPPY?
WELL, THAT'S GENEROUS OF YOU, BOB.
FLEE THE NEIGHBORHOOD WHILE YOU STILL CAN, BOB.
GIVE

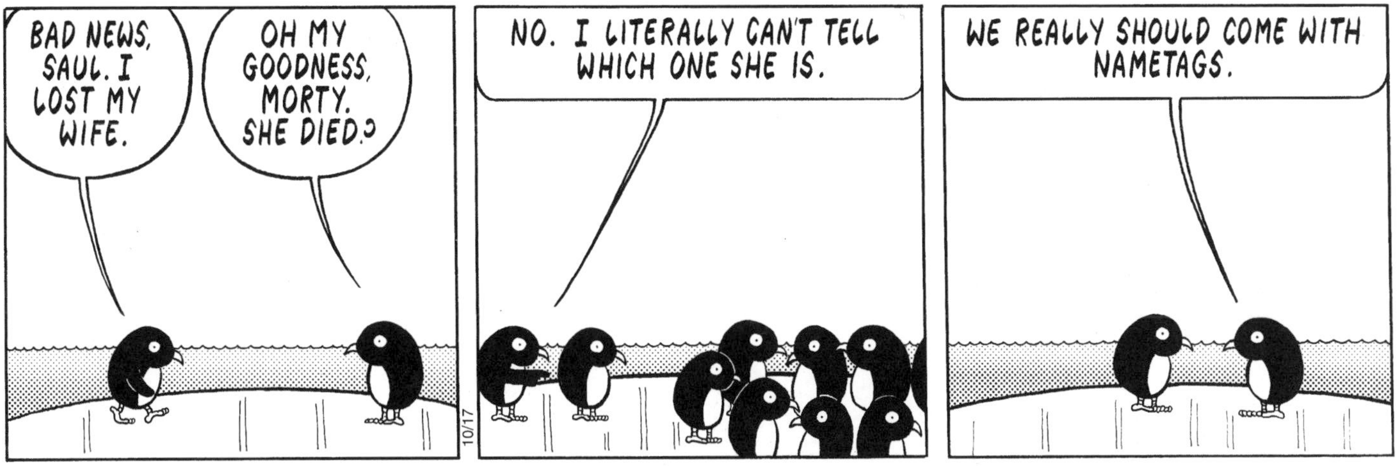
BAD NEWS, SAUL. I LOST MY WIFE.
OH MY GOODNESS, MORTY. SHE DIED?
10/17
NO. I LITERALLY CAN'T TELL WHICH ONE SHE IS.
WE REALLY SHOULD COME WITH NAMETAGS.

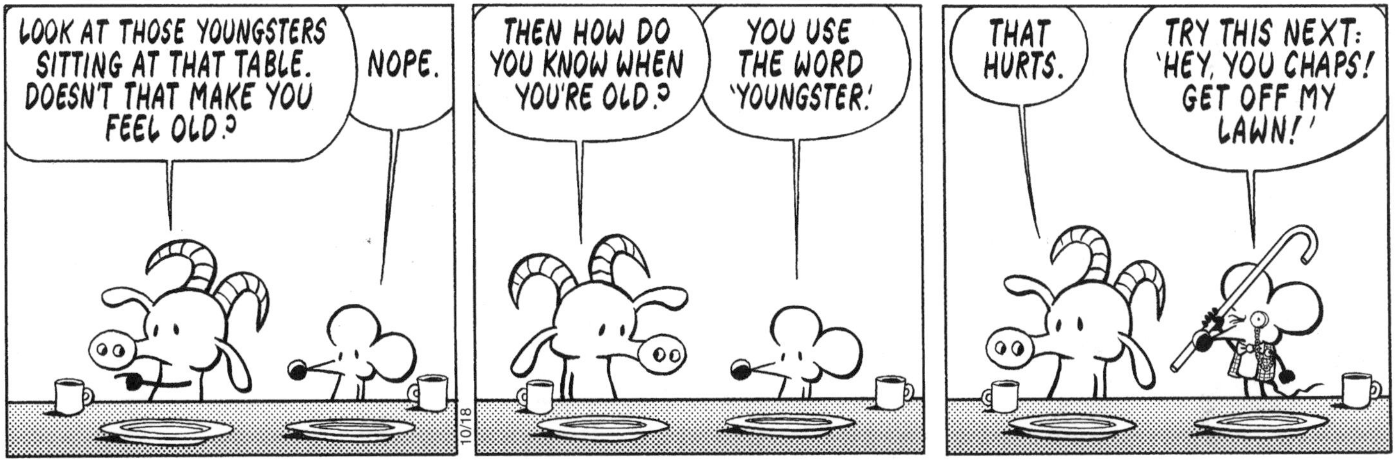
LOOK AT THOSE YOUNGSTERS SITTING AT THAT TABLE. DOESN'T THAT MAKE YOU FEEL OLD?
NOPE.
10/18
THEN HOW DO YOU KNOW WHEN YOU'RE OLD?
YOU USE THE WORD 'YOUNGSTER.'
THAT HURTS.
TRY THIS NEXT: 'HEY, YOU CHAPS! GET OFF MY LAWN!'

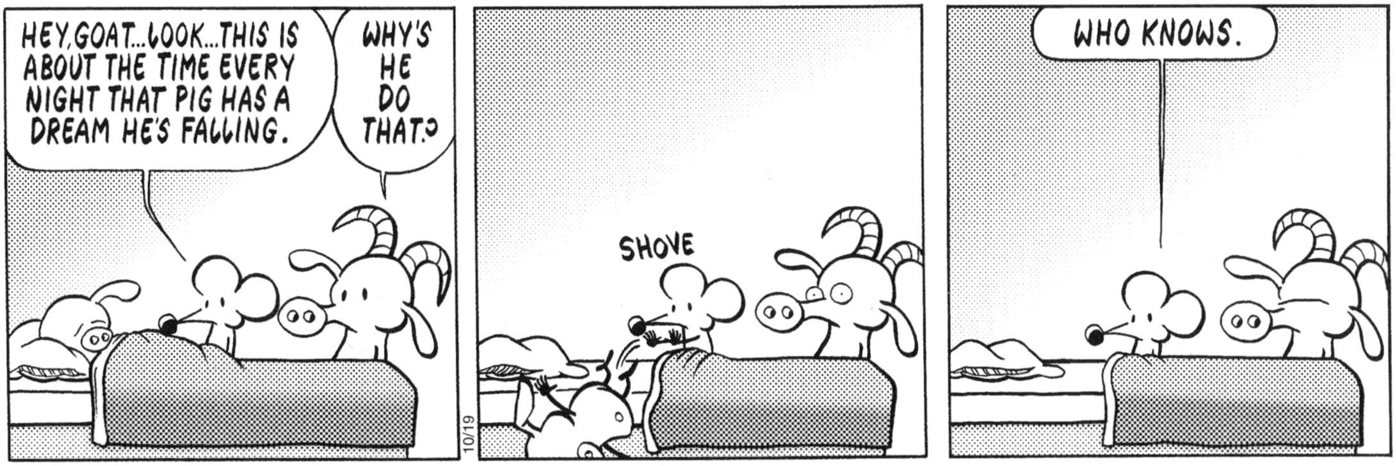
HEY, GOAT...LOOK...THIS IS ABOUT THE TIME EVERY NIGHT THAT PIG HAS A DREAM HE'S FALLING.
WHY'S HE DO THAT?
10/19
SHOVE
WHO KNOWS.

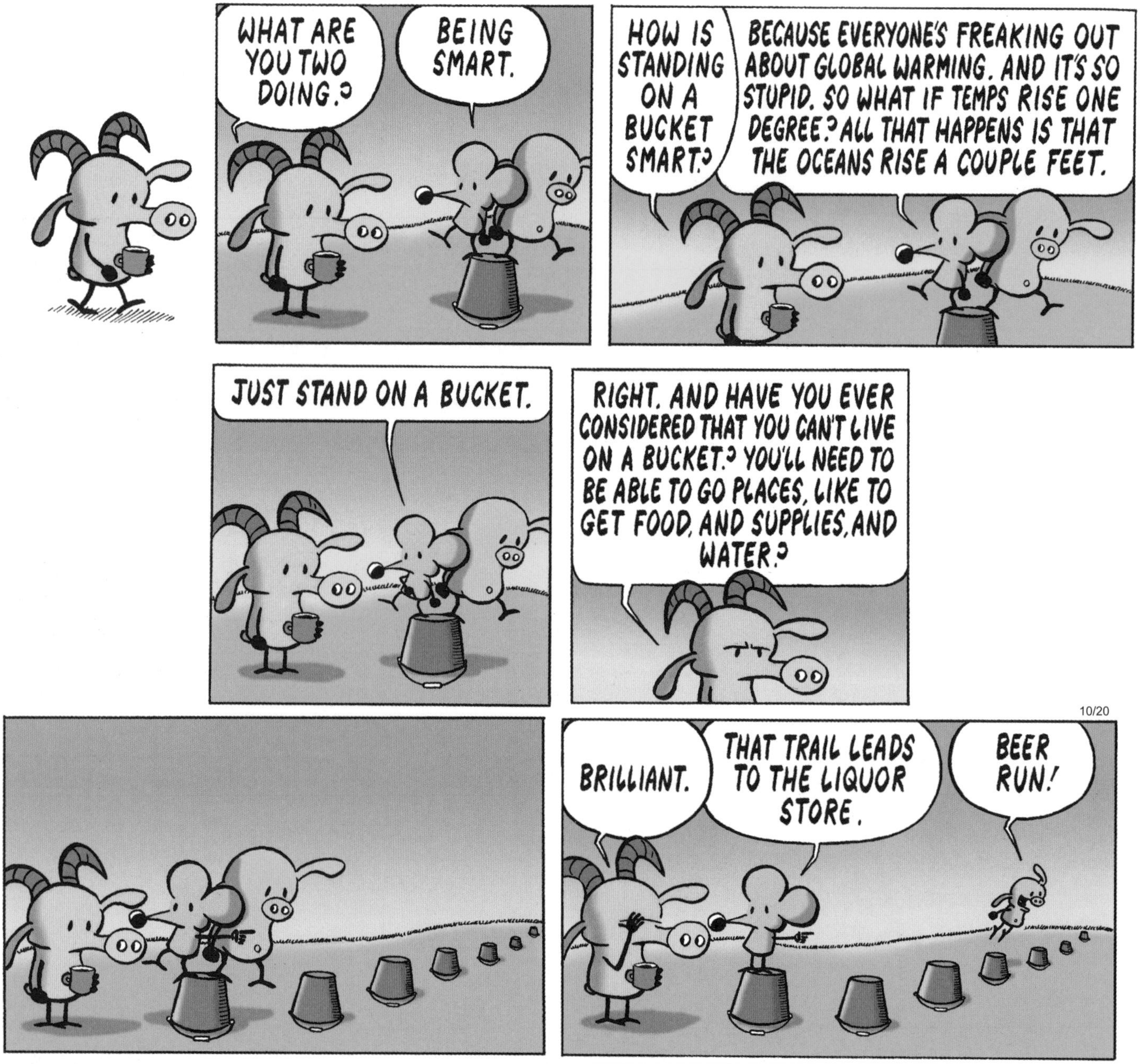
WHAT ARE YOU TWO DOING?
BEING SMART.
HOW IS STANDING ON A BUCKET SMART?
BECAUSE EVERYONE'S FREAKING OUT ABOUT GLOBAL WARMING. AND IT'S SO STUPID. SO WHAT IF TEMPS RISE ONE DEGREE? ALL THAT HAPPENS IS THAT THE OCEANS RISE A COUPLE FEET.
JUST STAND ON A BUCKET.
RIGHT. AND HAVE YOU EVER CONSIDERED THAT YOU CAN'T LIVE ON A BUCKET? YOU'LL NEED TO BE ABLE TO GO PLACES, LIKE TO GET FOOD, AND SUPPLIES, AND WATER?
10/20
BRILLIANT.
THAT TRAIL LEADS TO THE LIQUOR STORE.
BEER RUN!

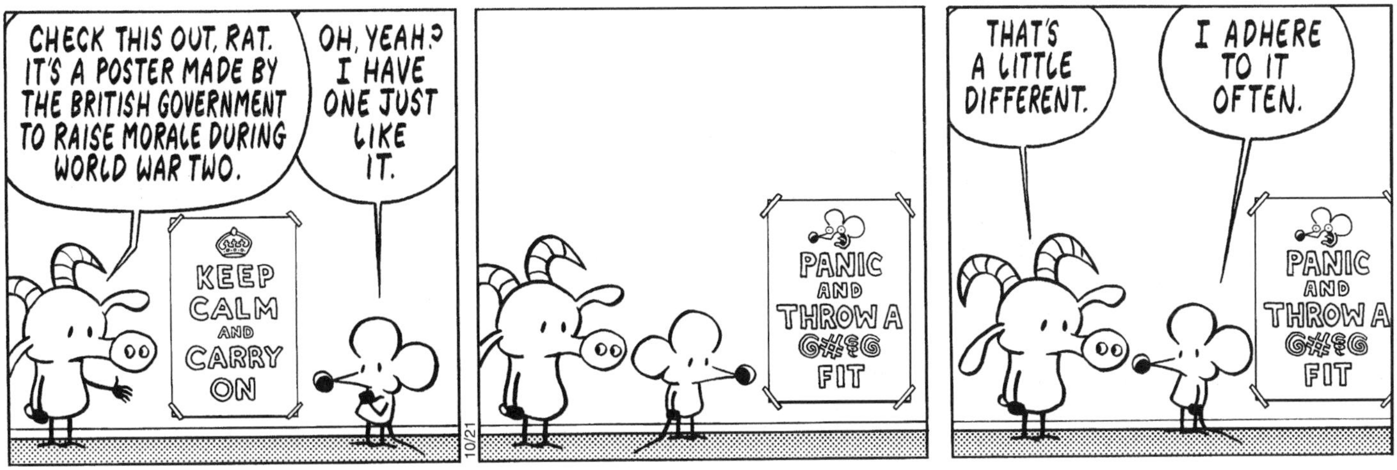
CHECK THIS OUT, RAT. IT'S A POSTER MADE BY THE BRITISH GOVERNMENT TO RAISE MORALE DURING WORLD WAR TWO.
OH, YEAH? I HAVE ONE JUST LIKE IT.
KEEP CALM AND CARRY ON
10/21
PANIC AND THROW A G#$G FIT
THAT'S A LITTLE DIFFERENT.
I ADHERE TO IT OFTEN.
PANIC AND THROW A G#$G FIT

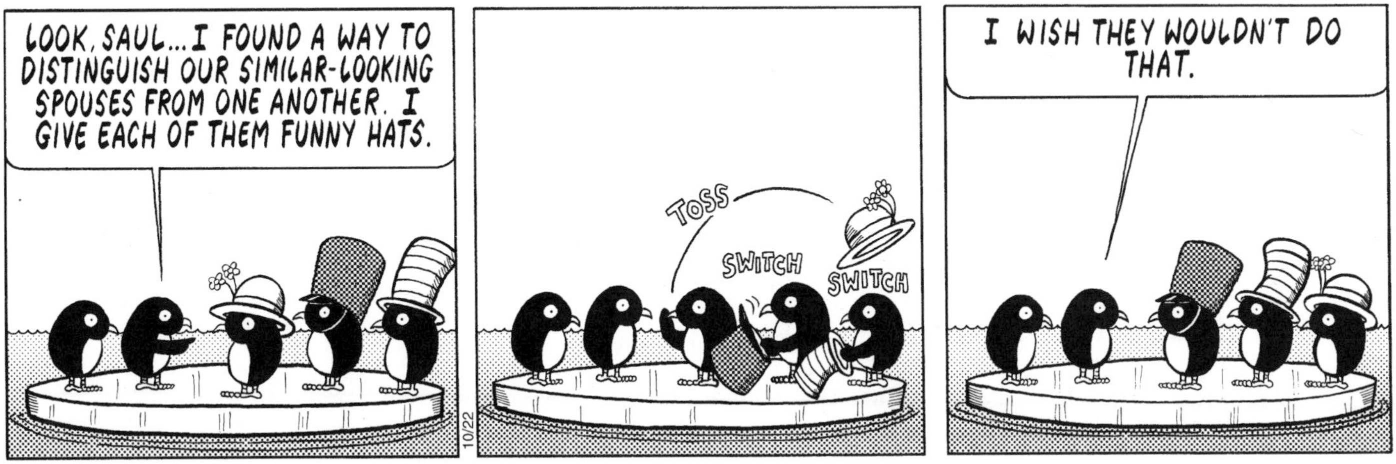
LOOK, SAUL...I FOUND A WAY TO DISTINGUISH OUR SIMILAR-LOOKING SPOUSES FROM ONE ANOTHER. I GIVE EACH OF THEM FUNNY HATS.
10/22
TOSS
SWITCH
SWITCH
I WISH THEY WOULDN'T DO THAT.

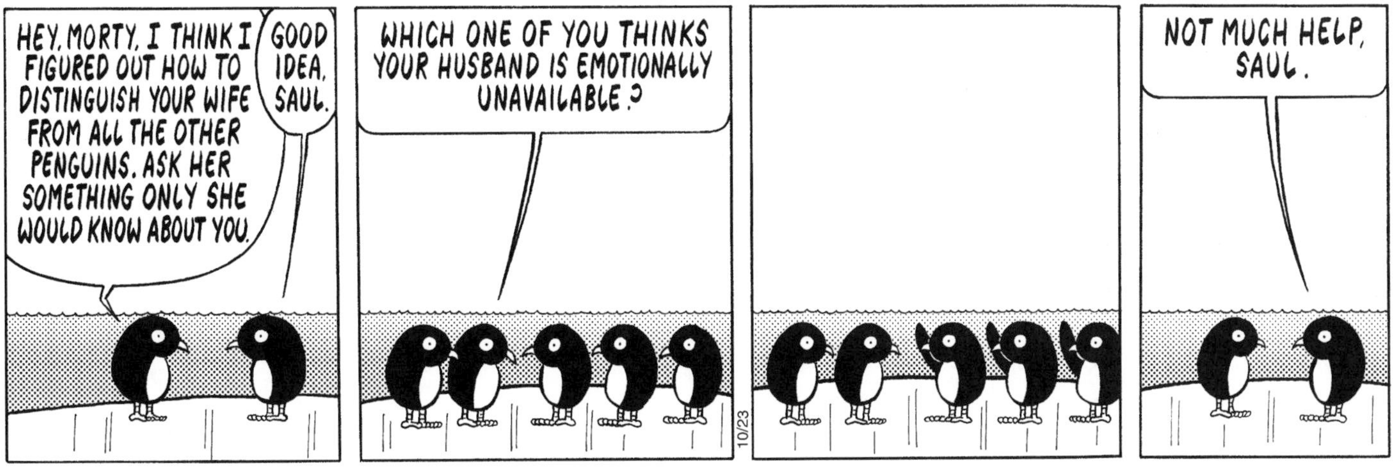
HEY, MORTY, I THINK I FIGURED OUT HOW TO DISTINGUISH YOUR WIFE FROM ALL THE OTHER PENGUINS. ASK HER SOMETHING ONLY SHE WOULD KNOW ABOUT YOU.
GOOD IDEA, SAUL.
WHICH ONE OF YOU THINKS YOUR HUSBAND IS EMOTIONALLY UNAVAILABLE?
10/23
NOT MUCH HELP, SAUL.

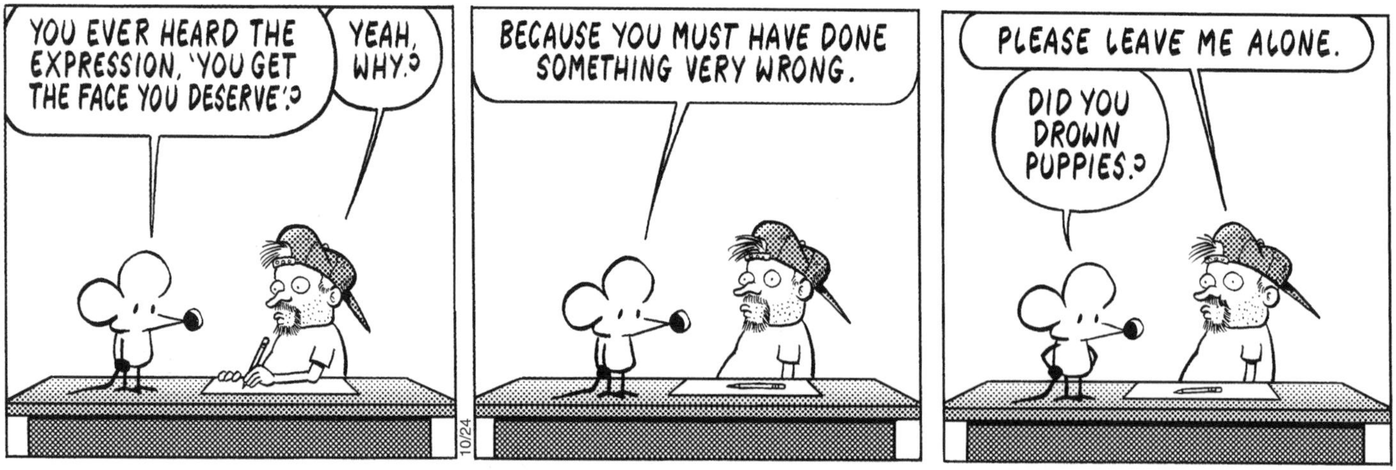
YOU EVER HEARD THE EXPRESSION, 'YOU GET THE FACE YOU DESERVE'?
YEAH, WHY?
BECAUSE YOU MUST HAVE DONE SOMETHING VERY WRONG.
PLEASE LEAVE ME ALONE.
DID YOU DROWN PUPPIES?
10/24

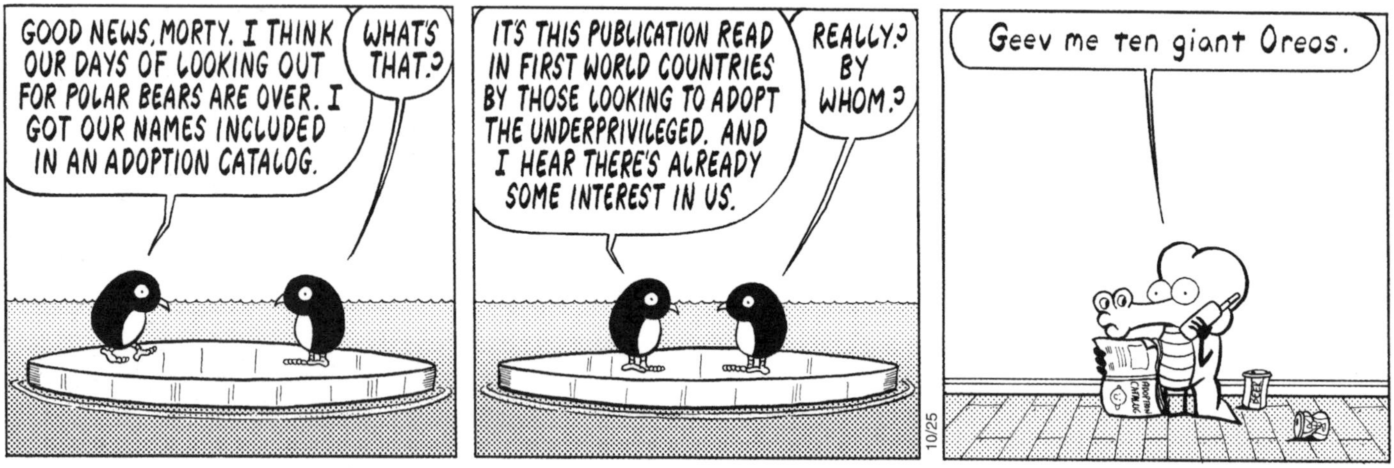
GOOD NEWS, MORTY. I THINK OUR DAYS OF LOOKING OUT FOR POLAR BEARS ARE OVER. I GOT OUR NAMES INCLUDED IN AN ADOPTION CATALOG.
WHAT'S THAT?
IT'S THIS PUBLICATION READ IN FIRST WORLD COUNTRIES BY THOSE LOOKING TO ADOPT THE UNDERPRIVILEGED. AND I HEAR THERE'S ALREADY SOME INTEREST IN US.
REALLY? BY WHOM?
Geev me ten giant Oreos.
10/25

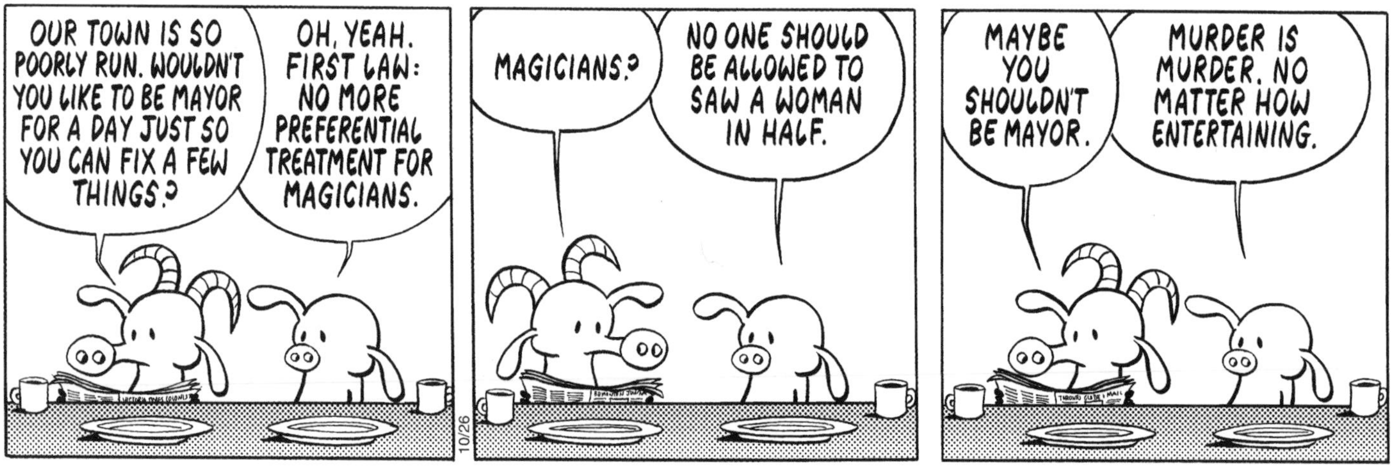
OUR TOWN IS SO POORLY RUN. WOULDN'T YOU LIKE TO BE MAYOR FOR A DAY JUST SO YOU CAN FIX A FEW THINGS?
OH, YEAH. FIRST LAW: NO MORE PREFERENTIAL TREATMENT FOR MAGICIANS.
MAGICIANS?
NO ONE SHOULD BE ALLOWED TO SAW A WOMAN IN HALF.
MAYBE YOU SHOULDN'T BE MAYOR.
MURDER IS MURDER. NO MATTER HOW ENTERTAINING.
10/26

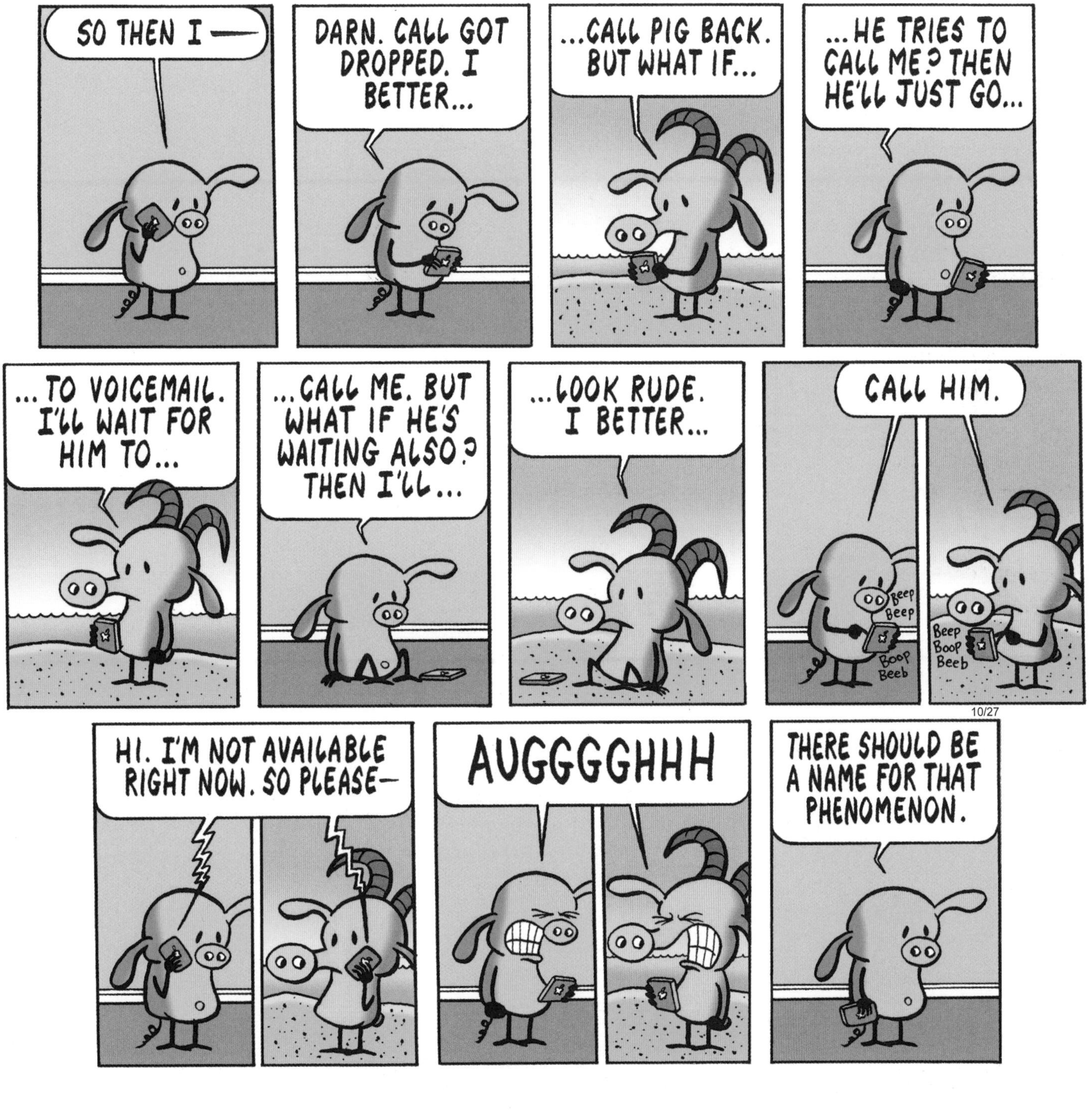
SO THEN I—
DARN. CALL GOT DROPPED. I BETTER...
...CALL PIG BACK. BUT WHAT IF...
...HE TRIES TO CALL ME? THEN HE'LL JUST GO...
...TO VOICEMAIL. I'LL WAIT FOR HIM TO...
...CALL ME. BUT WHAT IF HE'S WAITING ALSO? THEN I'LL...
...LOOK RUDE. I BETTER...
CALL HIM.
Beep Beep Boop Beeb
Beep Boop Beeb
10/27
HI. I'M NOT AVAILABLE RIGHT NOW. SO PLEASE—
AUGGGGHHH
THERE SHOULD BE A NAME FOR THAT PHENOMENON.

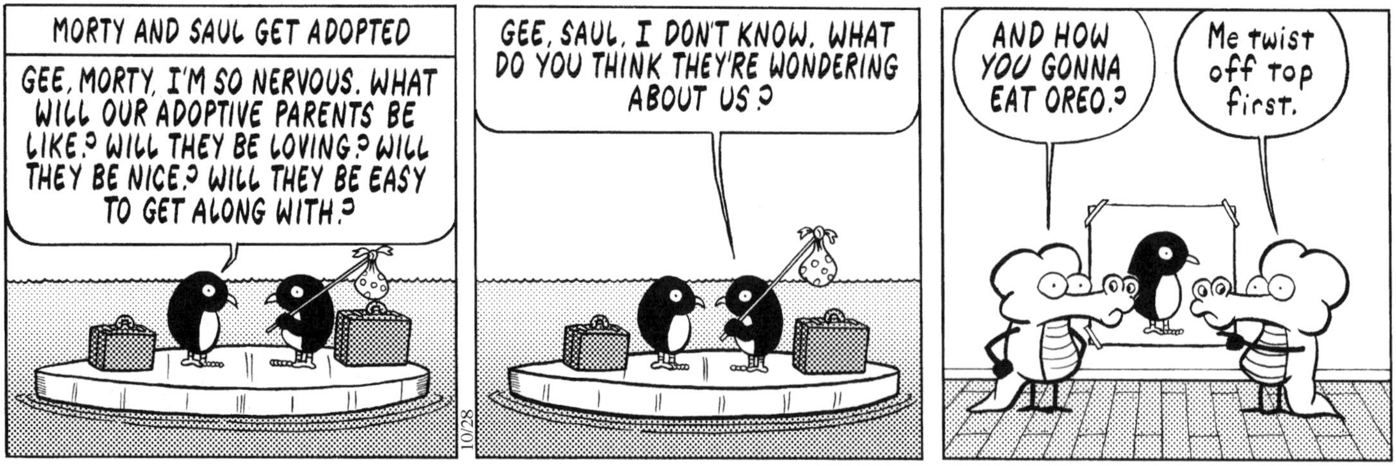
MORTY AND SAUL GET ADOPTED
GEE, MORTY, I'M SO NERVOUS. WHAT WILL OUR ADOPTIVE PARENTS BE LIKE? WILL THEY BE LOVING? WILL THEY BE NICE? WILL THEY BE EASY TO GET ALONG WITH?
GEE, SAUL, I DON'T KNOW. WHAT DO YOU THINK THEY'RE WONDERING ABOUT US?
AND HOW YOU GONNA EAT OREO?
Me twist off top first.
10/28

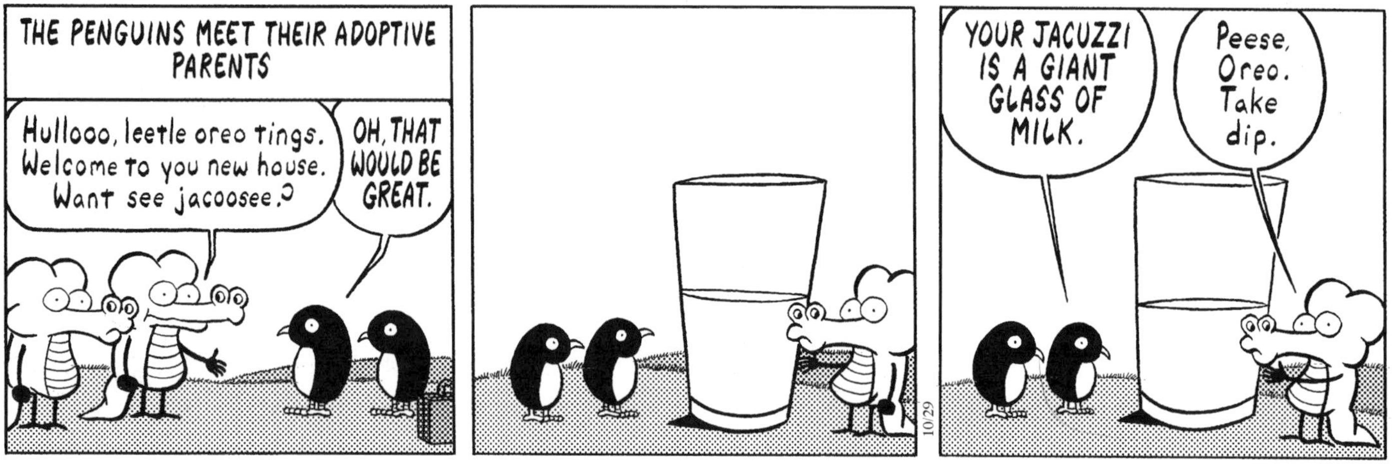
THE PENGUINS MEET THEIR ADOPTIVE PARENTS
Hullooo, leetle oreo tings. Welcome to you new house. Want see jacoosee?
OH, THAT WOULD BE GREAT.
YOUR JACUZZI IS A GIANT GLASS OF MILK.
Peese, Oreo. Take dip.
10/29

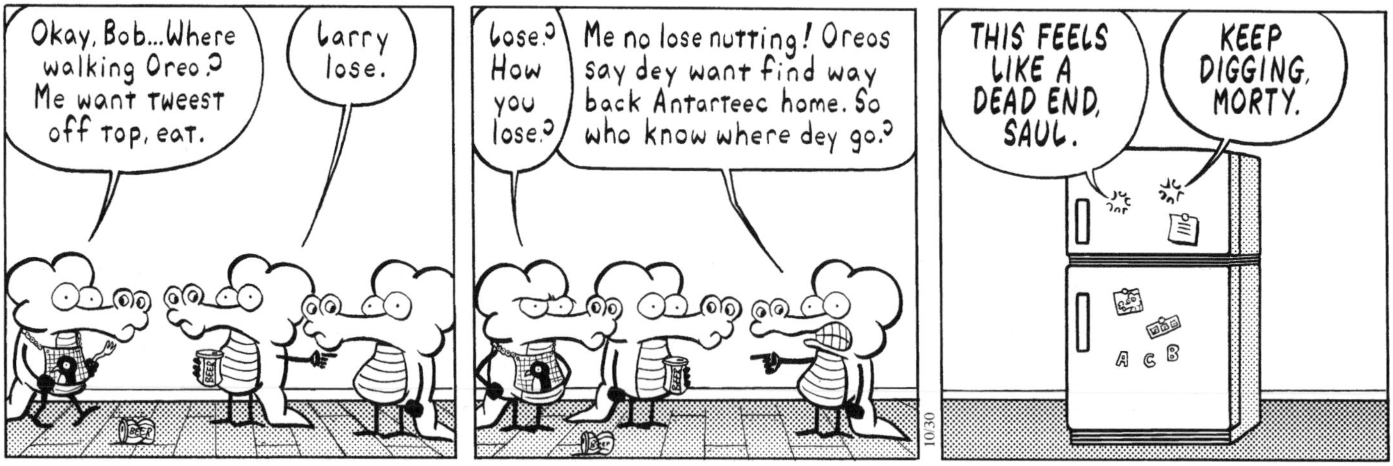
Okay, Bob...Where walking Oreo? Me want tweest off top, eat.
Larry lose.
Lose? How you lose?
Me no lose nutting! Oreos say dey want find way back Antarteec home. So who know where dey go?
THIS FEELS LIKE A DEAD END, SAUL.
KEEP DIGGING, MORTY.
A C B
10/30

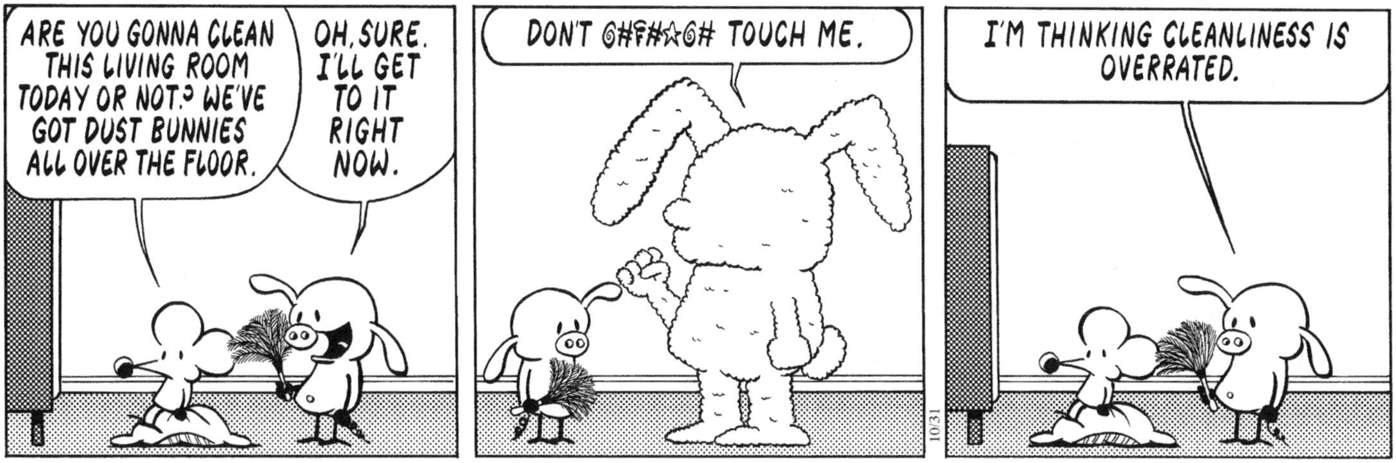
ARE YOU GONNA CLEAN THIS LIVING ROOM TODAY OR NOT? WE'VE GOT DUST BUNNIES ALL OVER THE FLOOR.
OH, SURE. I'LL GET TO IT RIGHT NOW.
DON'T @#?#☆@# TOUCH ME.
I'M THINKING CLEANLINESS IS OVERRATED.
10/31

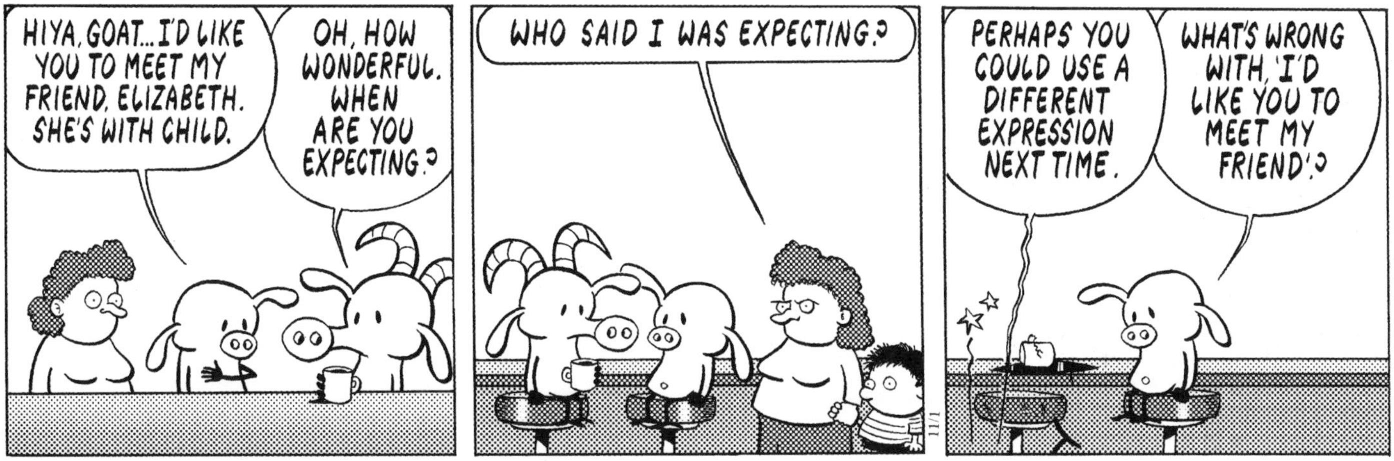
HIYA, GOAT...I'D LIKE YOU TO MEET MY FRIEND, ELIZABETH. SHE'S WITH CHILD.
OH, HOW WONDERFUL. WHEN ARE YOU EXPECTING?
WHO SAID I WAS EXPECTING?
PERHAPS YOU COULD USE A DIFFERENT EXPRESSION NEXT TIME.
WHAT'S WRONG WITH, 'I'D LIKE YOU TO MEET MY FRIEND'?
11/1

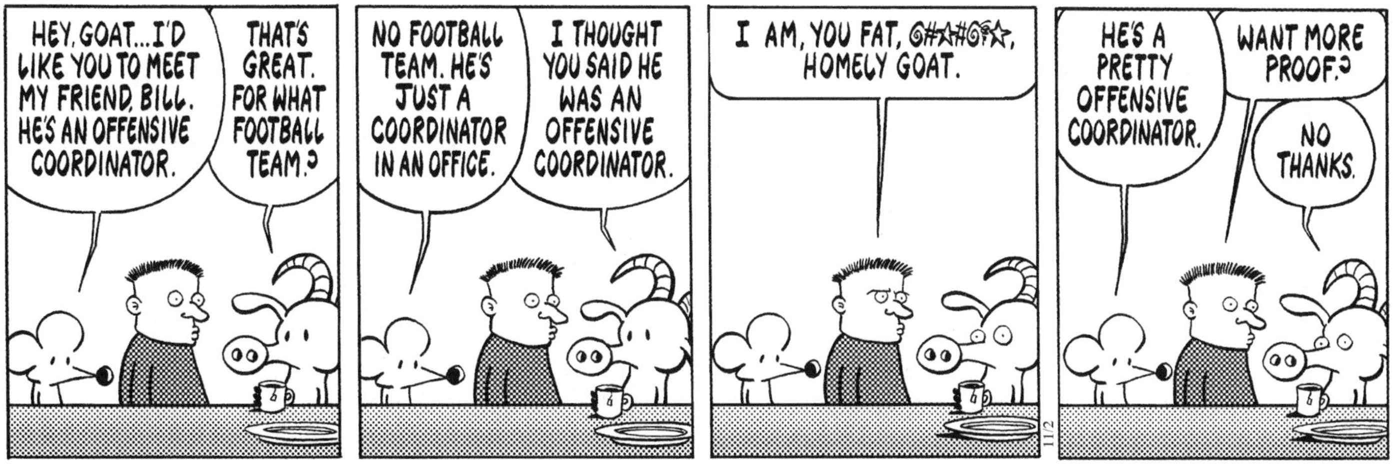
HEY, GOAT...I'D LIKE YOU TO MEET MY FRIEND, BILL. HE'S AN OFFENSIVE COORDINATOR.
THAT'S GREAT. FOR WHAT FOOTBALL TEAM?
NO FOOTBALL TEAM. HE'S JUST A COORDINATOR IN AN OFFICE.
I THOUGHT YOU SAID HE WAS AN OFFENSIVE COORDINATOR.
I AM, YOU FAT, @#☆#@?☆, HOMELY GOAT.
HE'S A PRETTY OFFENSIVE COORDINATOR.
WANT MORE PROOF?
NO THANKS.
11/2

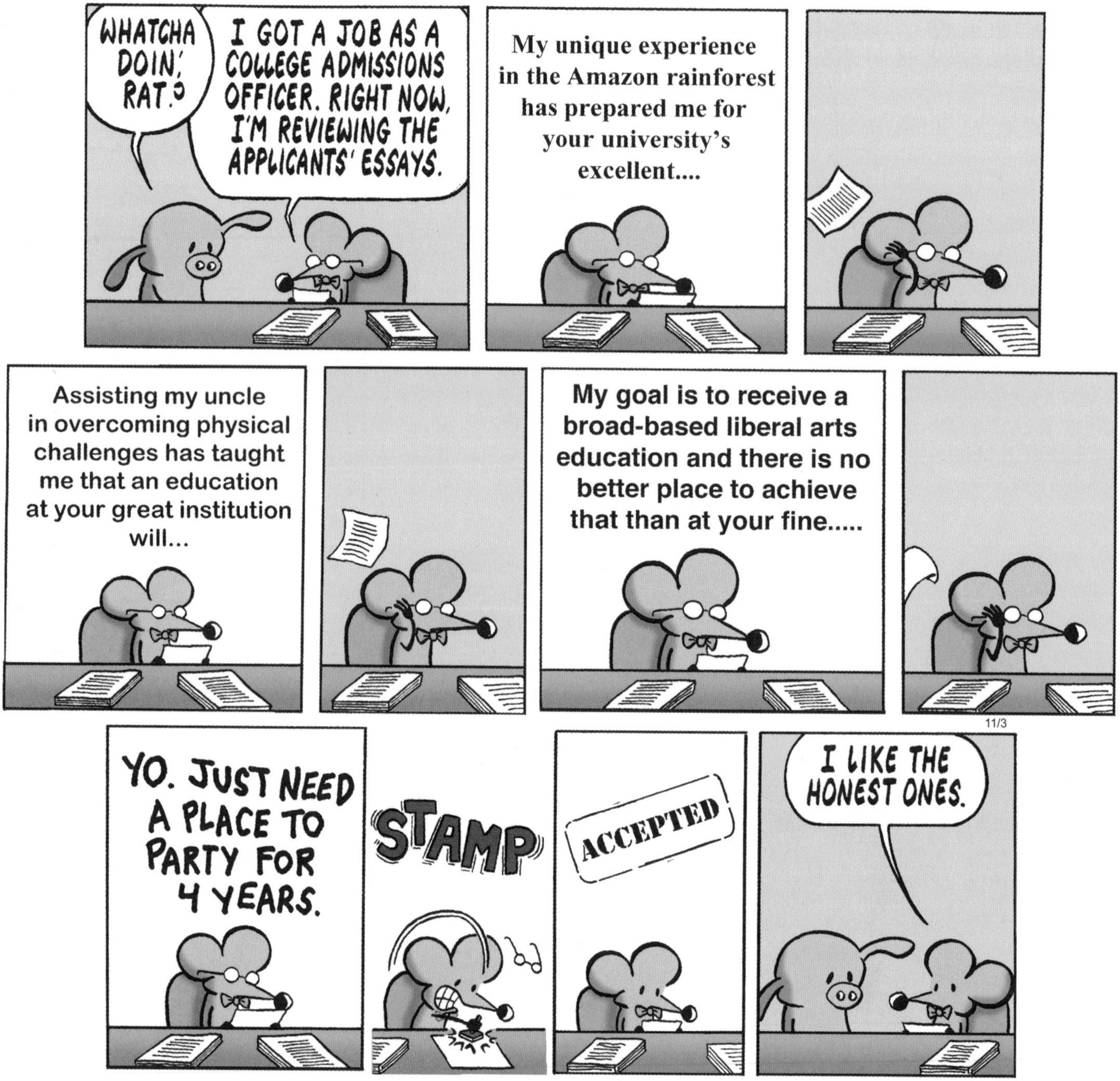
WHATCHA DOIN', RAT?
I GOT A JOB AS A COLLEGE ADMISSIONS OFFICER. RIGHT NOW, I'M REVIEWING THE APPLICANTS' ESSAYS.
My unique experience in the Amazon rainforest has prepared me for your university's excellent....
Assisting my uncle in overcoming physical challenges has taught me that an education at your great institution will...
My goal is to receive a broad-based liberal arts education and there is no better place to achieve that than at your fine.....
11/3
YO. JUST NEED A PLACE TO PARTY FOR 4 YEARS.
STAMP
ACCEPTED
I LIKE THE HONEST ONES.

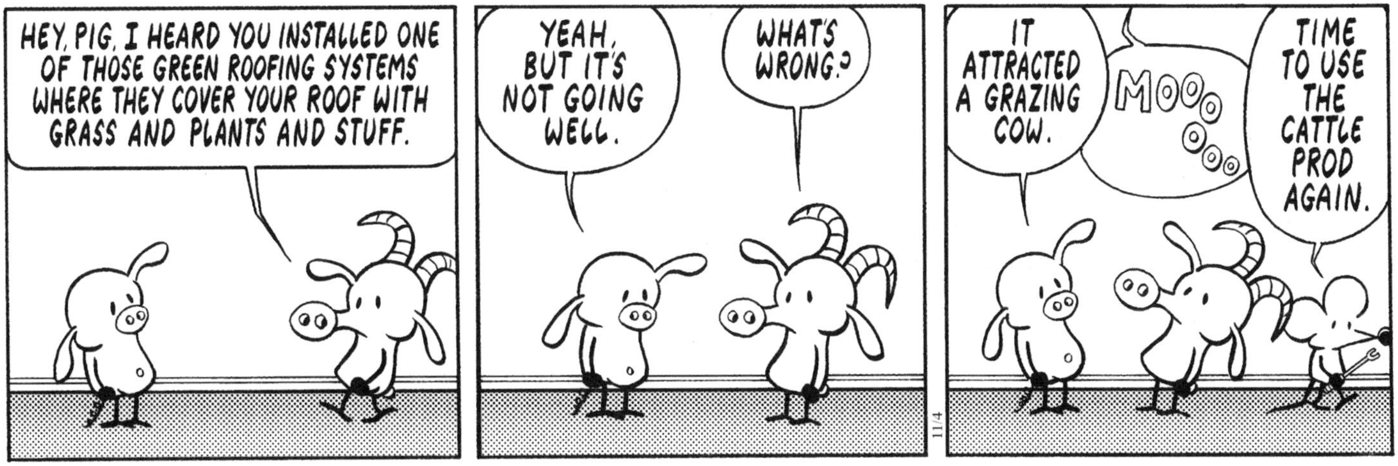
HEY, PIG, I HEARD YOU INSTALLED ONE OF THOSE GREEN ROOFING SYSTEMS WHERE THEY COVER YOUR ROOF WITH GRASS AND PLANTS AND STUFF.
YEAH, BUT IT'S NOT GOING WELL.
WHAT'S WRONG?
IT ATTRACTED A GRAZING COW.
MOOOOOOO
TIME TO USE THE CATTLE PROD AGAIN.
11/4

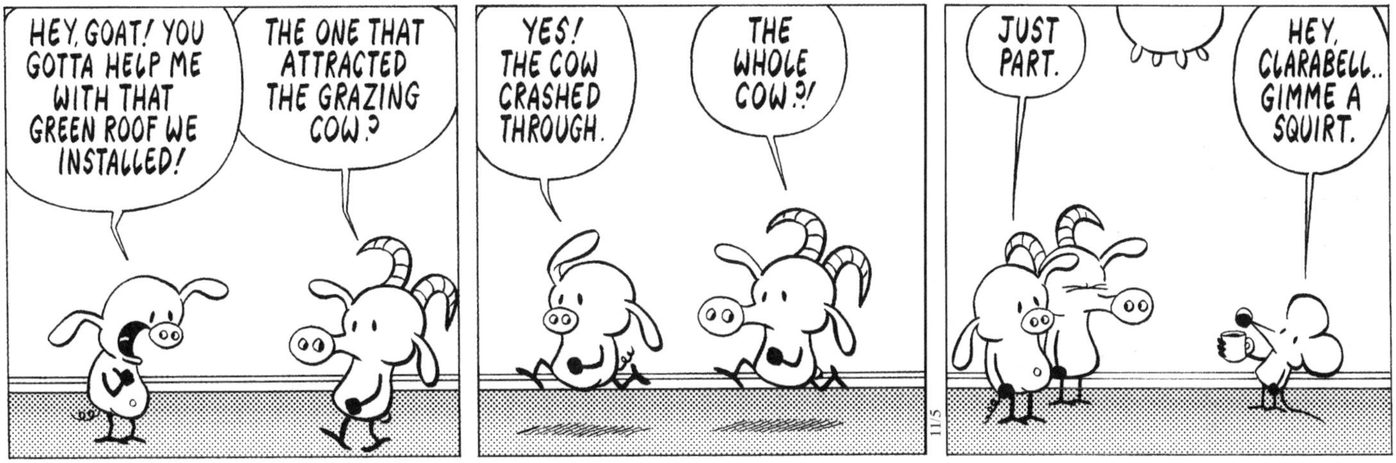
HEY, GOAT! YOU GOTTA HELP ME WITH THAT GREEN ROOF WE INSTALLED!
THE ONE THAT ATTRACTED THE GRAZING COW?
YES! THE COW CRASHED THROUGH.
THE WHOLE COW?!
JUST PART.
HEY, CLARABELL.. GIMME A SQUIRT.
11/5

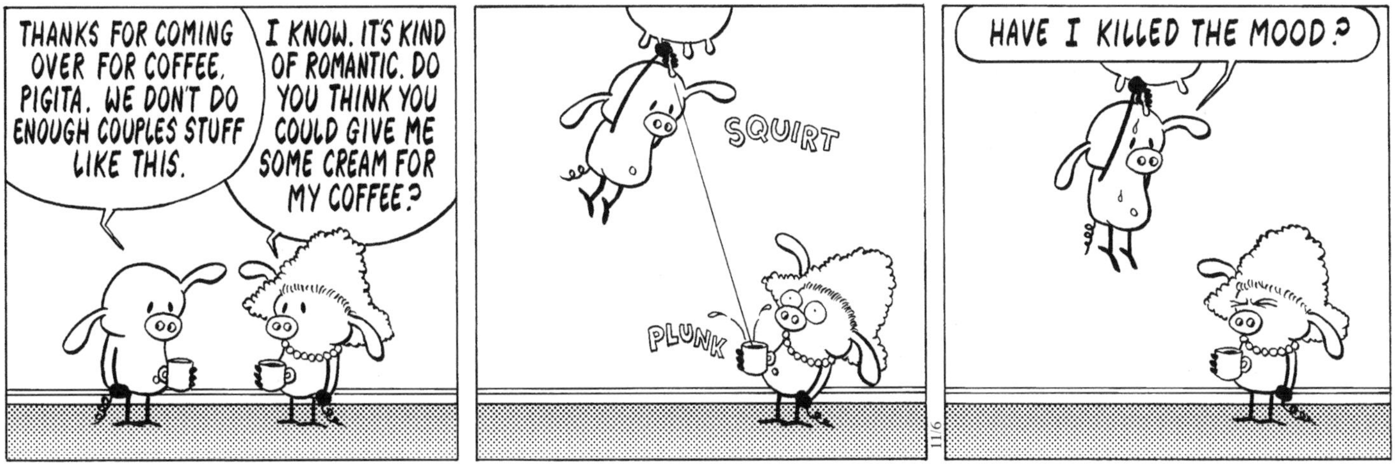
THANKS FOR COMING OVER FOR COFFEE, PIGITA. WE DON'T DO ENOUGH COUPLES STUFF LIKE THIS.
I KNOW. IT'S KIND OF ROMANTIC. DO YOU THINK YOU COULD GIVE ME SOME CREAM FOR MY COFFEE?
SQUIRT
PLUNK
HAVE I KILLED THE MOOD?
11/6

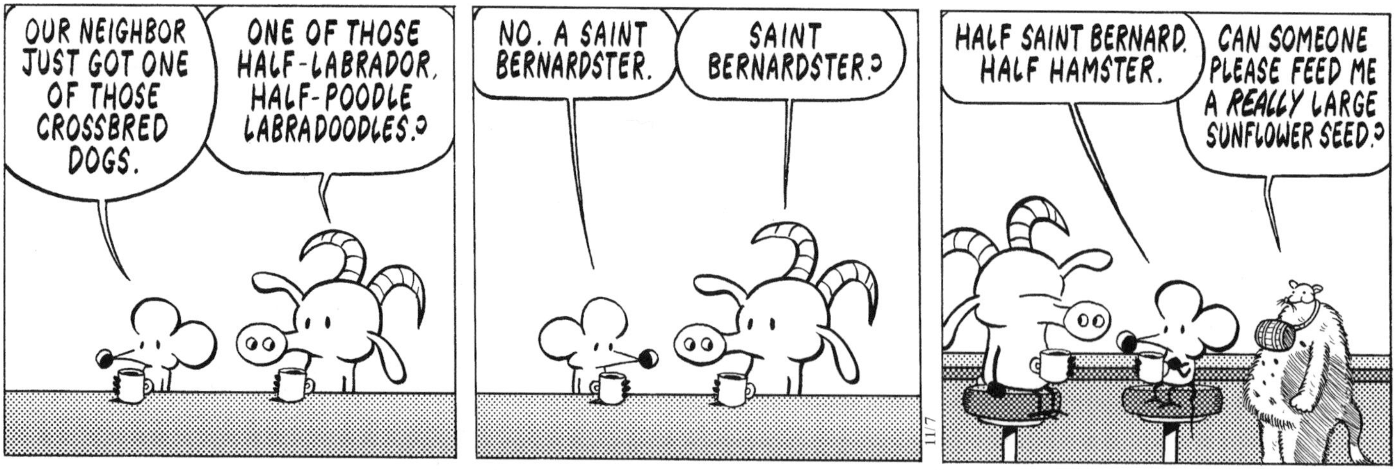
OUR NEIGHBOR JUST GOT ONE OF THOSE CROSSBRED DOGS.
ONE OF THOSE HALF-LABRADOR, HALF-POODLE LABRADOODLES?
NO. A SAINT BERNARDSTER.
SAINT BERNARDSTER?
HALF SAINT BERNARD. HALF HAMSTER.
CAN SOMEONE PLEASE FEED ME A *REALLY* LARGE SUNFLOWER SEED?
11/7

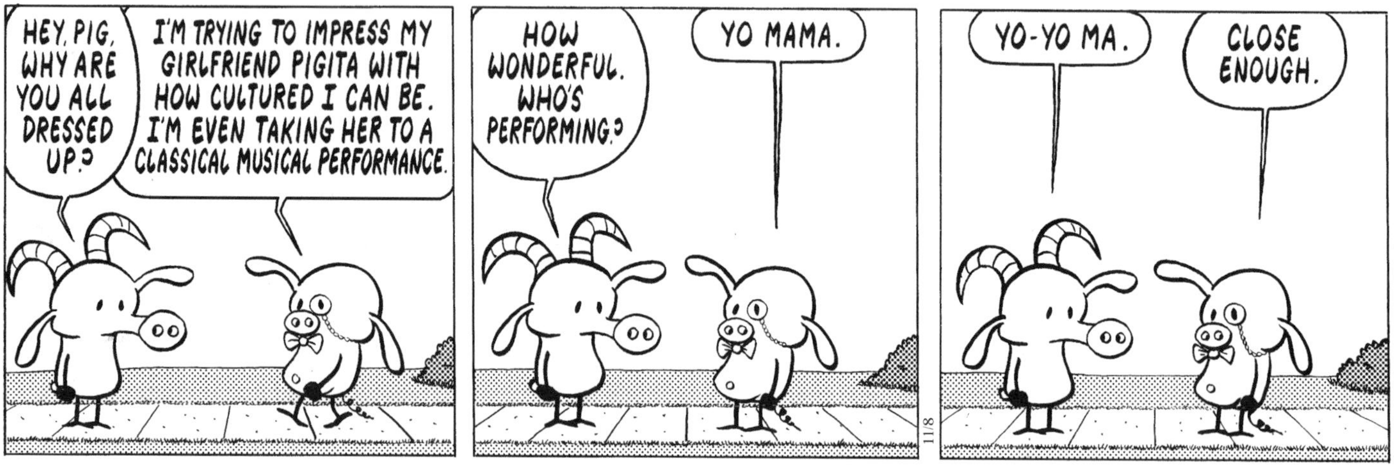
HEY, PIG, WHY ARE YOU ALL DRESSED UP?
I'M TRYING TO IMPRESS MY GIRLFRIEND PIGITA WITH HOW CULTURED I CAN BE. I'M EVEN TAKING HER TO A CLASSICAL MUSICAL PERFORMANCE.
HOW WONDERFUL. WHO'S PERFORMING?
YO MAMA.
YO-YO MA.
CLOSE ENOUGH.
11/8

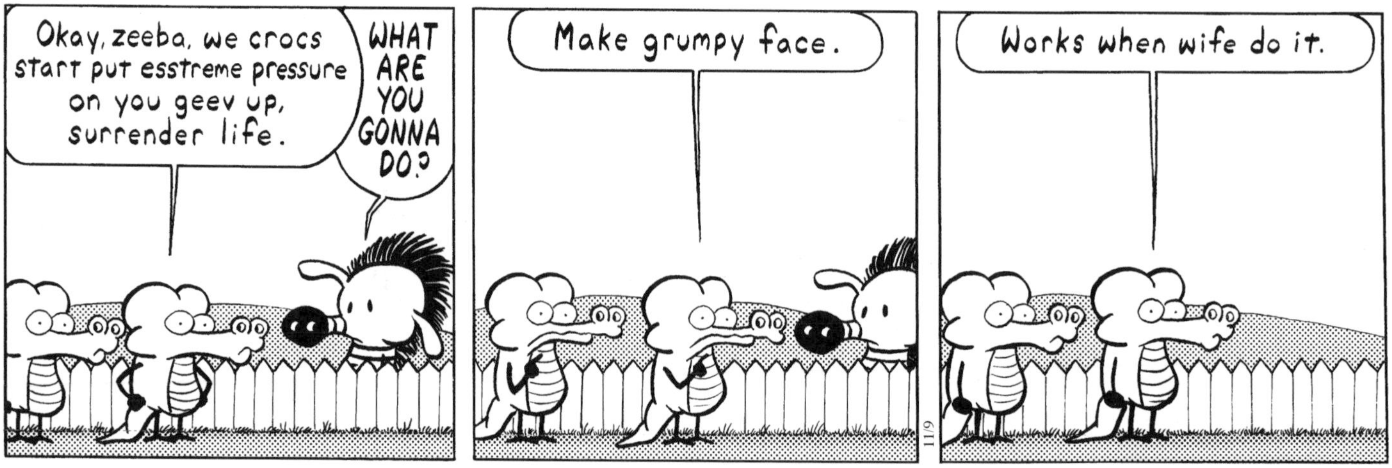
Okay, zeeba, we crocs start put esstreme pressure on you geev up, surrender life.
WHAT ARE YOU GONNA DO?
Make grumpy face.
Works when wife do it.
11/9

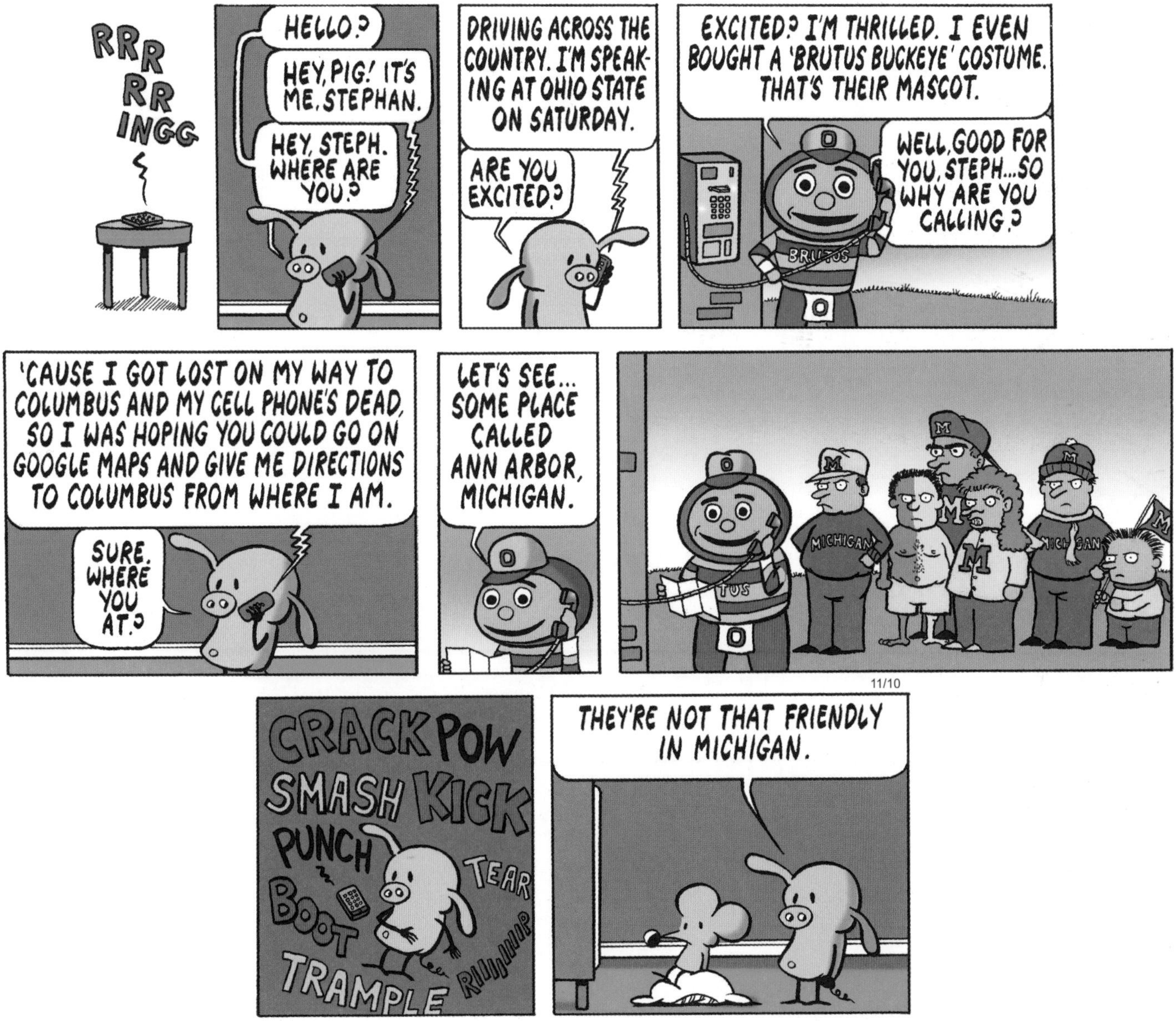
RRR RR INGG
HELLO?
HEY, PIG! IT'S ME, STEPHAN.
HEY, STEPH. WHERE ARE YOU?
DRIVING ACROSS THE COUNTRY. I'M SPEAKING AT OHIO STATE ON SATURDAY.
ARE YOU EXCITED?
EXCITED? I'M THRILLED. I EVEN BOUGHT A 'BRUTUS BUCKEYE' COSTUME. THAT'S THEIR MASCOT.
WELL, GOOD FOR YOU, STEPH...SO WHY ARE YOU CALLING?
BRUTUS
'CAUSE I GOT LOST ON MY WAY TO COLUMBUS AND MY CELL PHONE'S DEAD, SO I WAS HOPING YOU COULD GO ON GOOGLE MAPS AND GIVE ME DIRECTIONS TO COLUMBUS FROM WHERE I AM.
SURE. WHERE YOU AT?
LET'S SEE... SOME PLACE CALLED ANN ARBOR, MICHIGAN.
MICHIGAN
MICHIGAN
11/10
CRACK POW
SMASH KICK
PUNCH
TEAR
BOOT
TRAMPLE
RIIIIIIIP
THEY'RE NOT THAT FRIENDLY IN MICHIGAN.

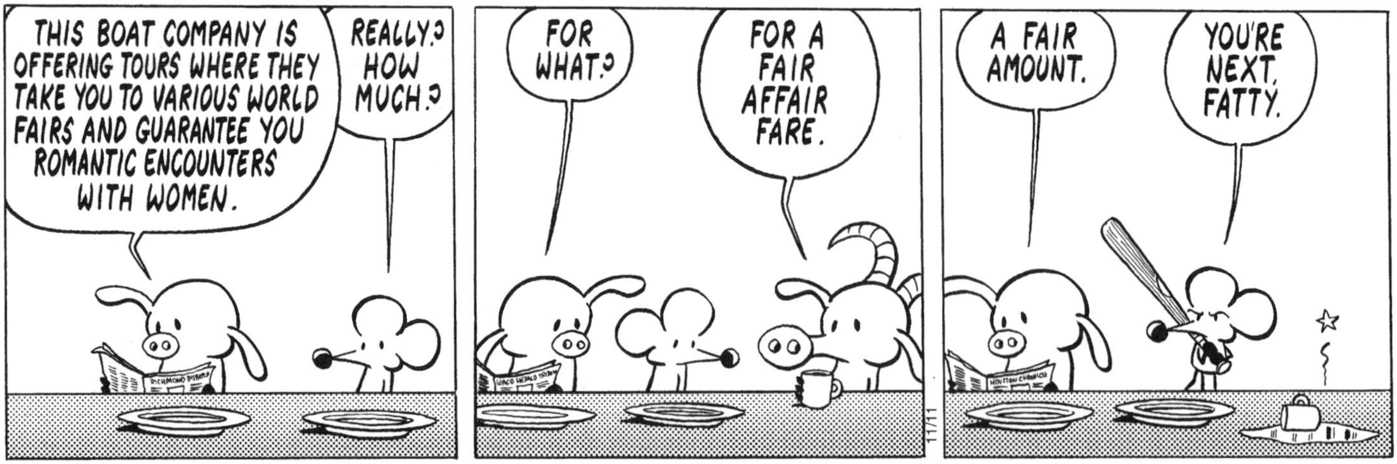
THIS BOAT COMPANY IS OFFERING TOURS WHERE THEY TAKE YOU TO VARIOUS WORLD FAIRS AND GUARANTEE YOU ROMANTIC ENCOUNTERS WITH WOMEN.
REALLY? HOW MUCH?
FOR WHAT?
FOR A FAIR AFFAIR FARE.
A FAIR AMOUNT.
YOU'RE NEXT, FATTY.
11/11

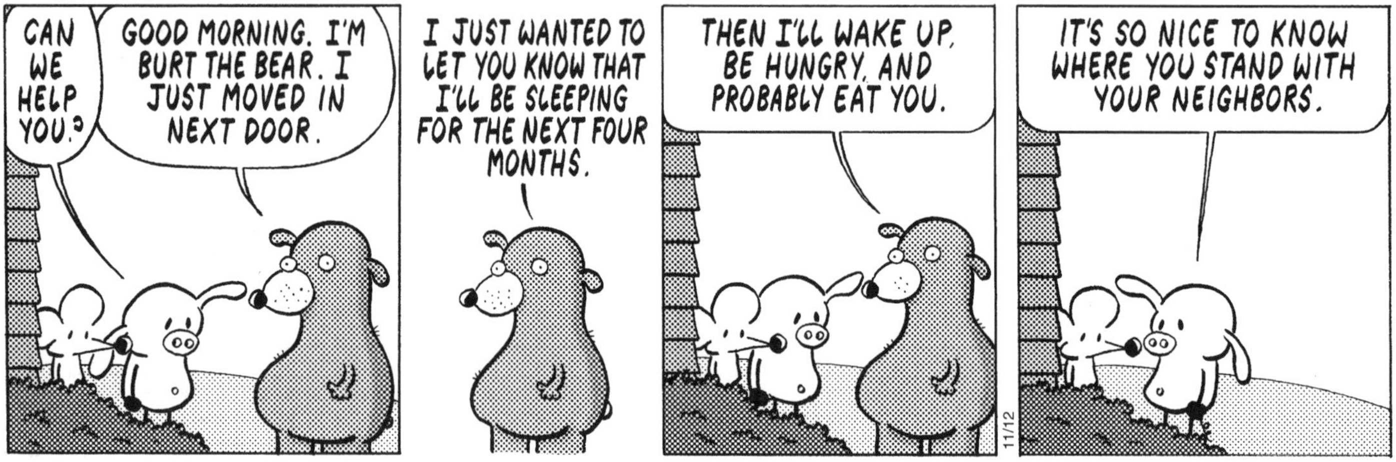
CAN WE HELP YOU?
GOOD MORNING. I'M BURT THE BEAR. I JUST MOVED IN NEXT DOOR.
I JUST WANTED TO LET YOU KNOW THAT I'LL BE SLEEPING FOR THE NEXT FOUR MONTHS.
THEN I'LL WAKE UP, BE HUNGRY, AND PROBABLY EAT YOU.
IT'S SO NICE TO KNOW WHERE YOU STAND WITH YOUR NEIGHBORS.
11/12

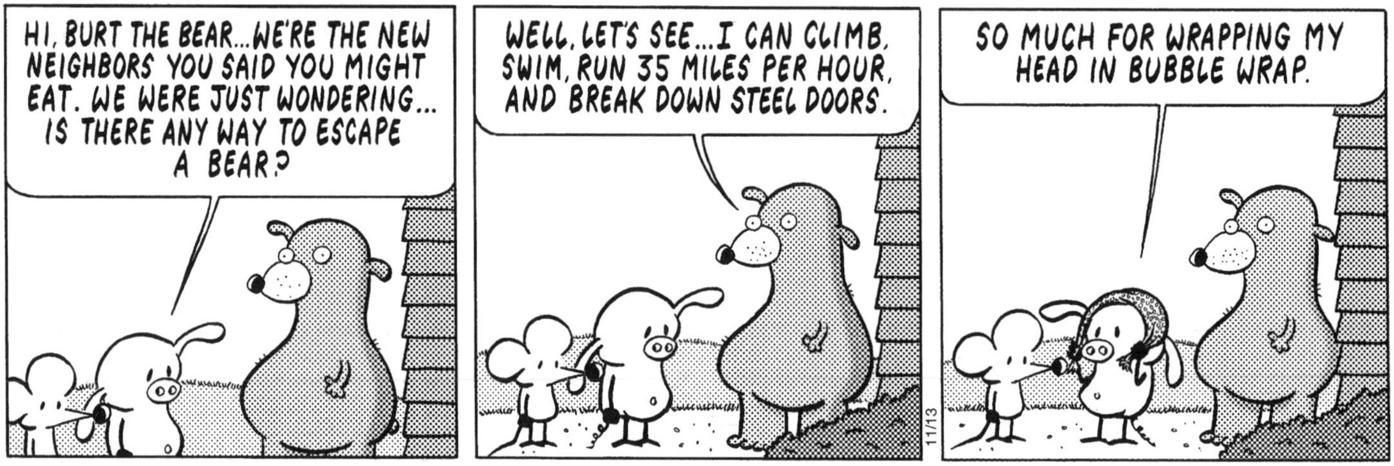
HI, BURT THE BEAR...WE'RE THE NEW NEIGHBORS YOU SAID YOU MIGHT EAT. WE WERE JUST WONDERING... IS THERE ANY WAY TO ESCAPE A BEAR?
WELL, LET'S SEE...I CAN CLIMB, SWIM, RUN 35 MILES PER HOUR, AND BREAK DOWN STEEL DOORS.
SO MUCH FOR WRAPPING MY HEAD IN BUBBLE WRAP.
11/13

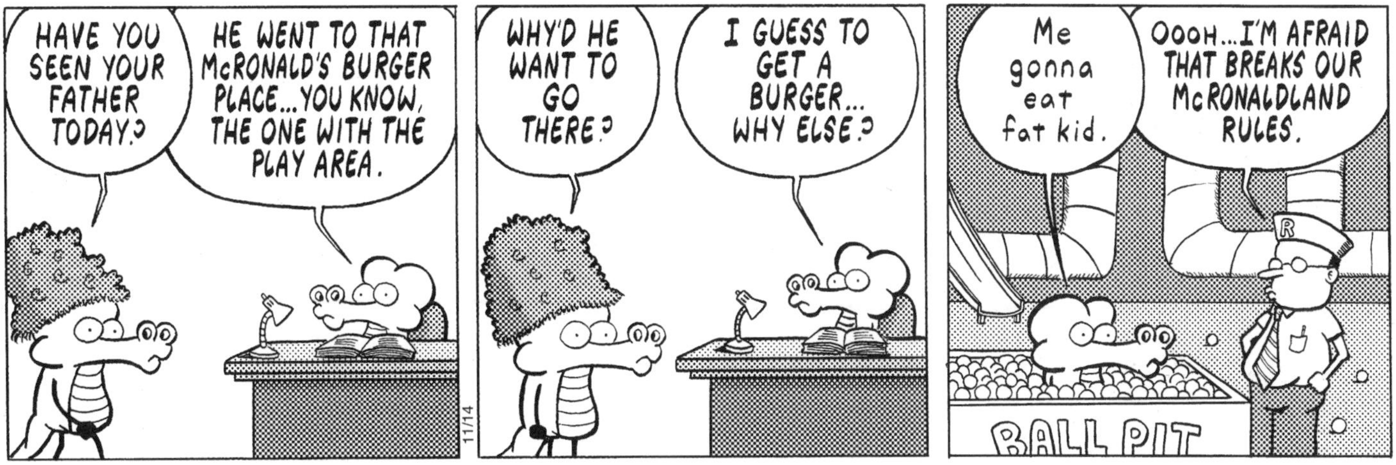
HAVE YOU SEEN YOUR FATHER TODAY?
HE WENT TO THAT McRONALD'S BURGER PLACE... YOU KNOW, THE ONE WITH THE PLAY AREA.
11/14
WHY'D HE WANT TO GO THERE?
I GUESS TO GET A BURGER... WHY ELSE?
Me gonna eat fat kid.
Oooh... I'M AFRAID THAT BREAKS OUR McRONALDLAND RULES.
R
BALL PIT

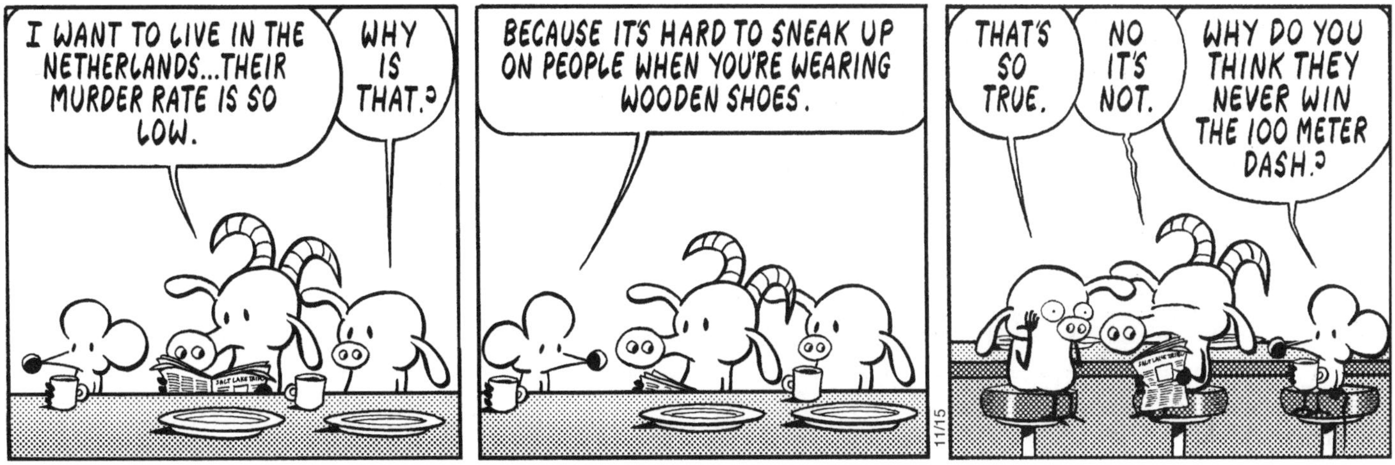
I WANT TO LIVE IN THE NETHERLANDS... THEIR MURDER RATE IS SO LOW.
WHY IS THAT?
BECAUSE IT'S HARD TO SNEAK UP ON PEOPLE WHEN YOU'RE WEARING WOODEN SHOES.
11/15
THAT'S SO TRUE.
NO IT'S NOT.
WHY DO YOU THINK THEY NEVER WIN THE 100 METER DASH?

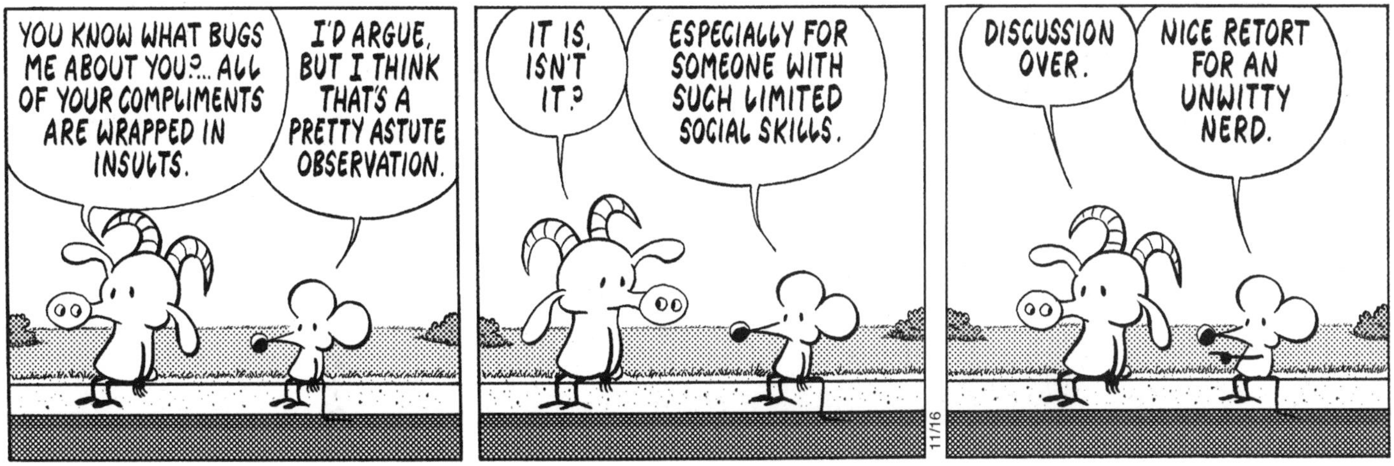
YOU KNOW WHAT BUGS ME ABOUT YOU?... ALL OF YOUR COMPLIMENTS ARE WRAPPED IN INSULTS.
I'D ARGUE, BUT I THINK THAT'S A PRETTY ASTUTE OBSERVATION.
IT IS, ISN'T IT?
ESPECIALLY FOR SOMEONE WITH SUCH LIMITED SOCIAL SKILLS.
11/16
DISCUSSION OVER.
NICE RETORT FOR AN UNWITTY NERD.

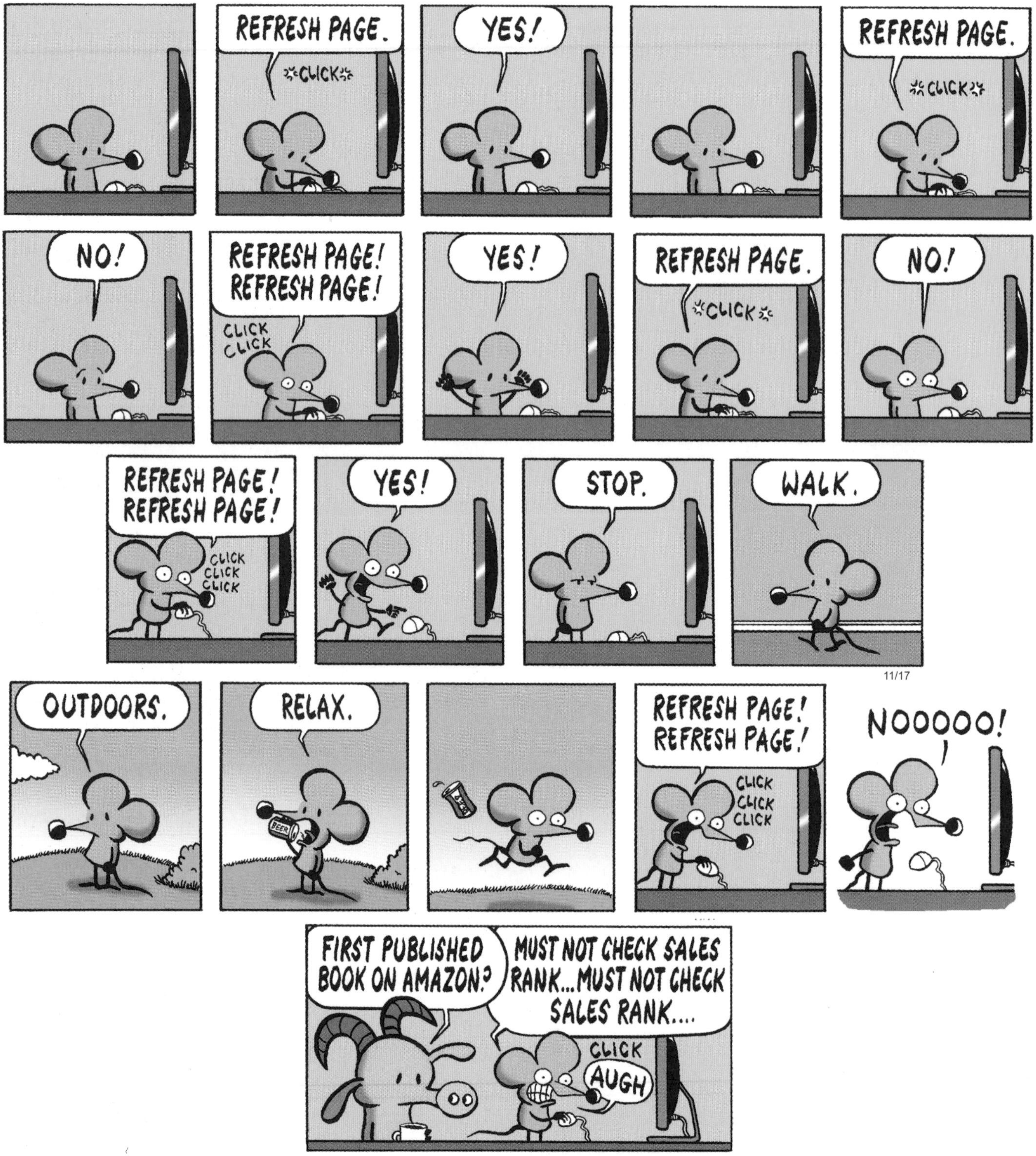
REFRESH PAGE.
CLICK
YES!
REFRESH PAGE.
CLICK
NO!
REFRESH PAGE! REFRESH PAGE!
CLICK CLICK
YES!
REFRESH PAGE.
CLICK
NO!
REFRESH PAGE! REFRESH PAGE!
CLICK CLICK CLICK
YES!
STOP.
WALK.
11/17
OUTDOORS.
RELAX.
BEER
REFRESH PAGE! REFRESH PAGE!
CLICK CLICK CLICK
NOOOOO!
FIRST PUBLISHED BOOK ON AMAZON?
MUST NOT CHECK SALES RANK...MUST NOT CHECK SALES RANK....
CLICK
AUGH

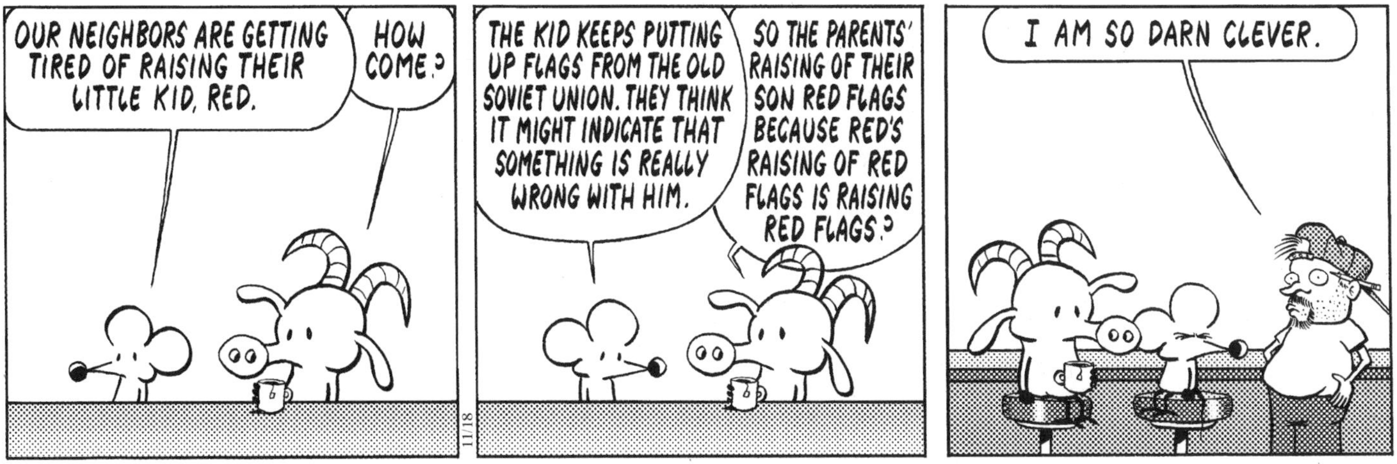
OUR NEIGHBORS ARE GETTING TIRED OF RAISING THEIR LITTLE KID, RED.
HOW COME?
THE KID KEEPS PUTTING UP FLAGS FROM THE OLD SOVIET UNION. THEY THINK IT MIGHT INDICATE THAT SOMETHING IS REALLY WRONG WITH HIM.
SO THE PARENTS' RAISING OF THEIR SON RED FLAGS BECAUSE RED'S RAISING OF RED FLAGS IS RAISING RED FLAGS?
I AM SO DARN CLEVER.
11/18

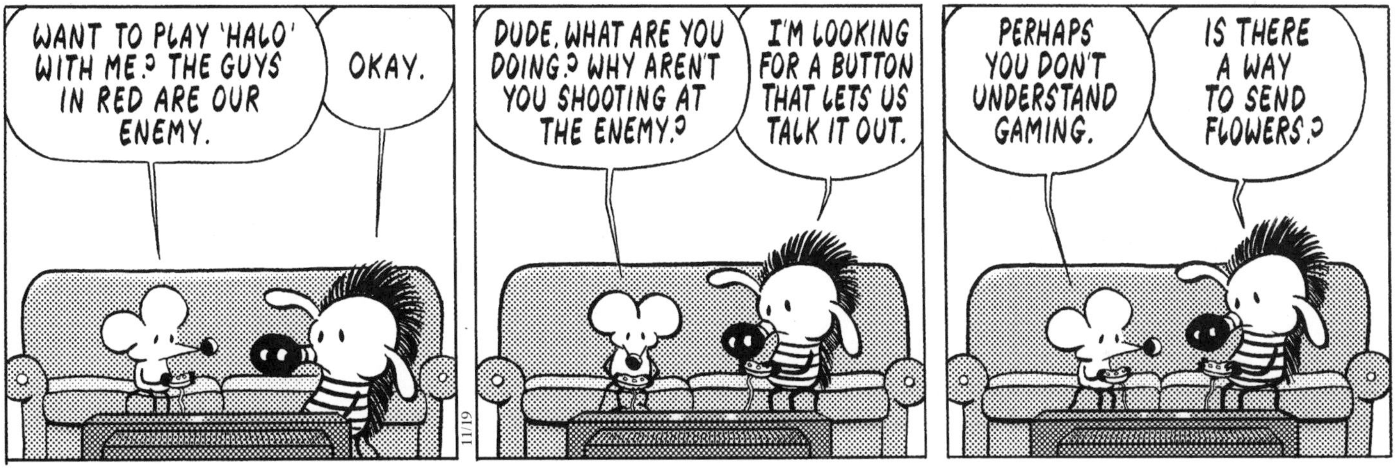
WANT TO PLAY 'HALO' WITH ME? THE GUYS IN RED ARE OUR ENEMY.
OKAY.
DUDE, WHAT ARE YOU DOING? WHY AREN'T YOU SHOOTING AT THE ENEMY?
I'M LOOKING FOR A BUTTON THAT LETS US TALK IT OUT.
PERHAPS YOU DON'T UNDERSTAND GAMING.
IS THERE A WAY TO SEND FLOWERS?
11/19

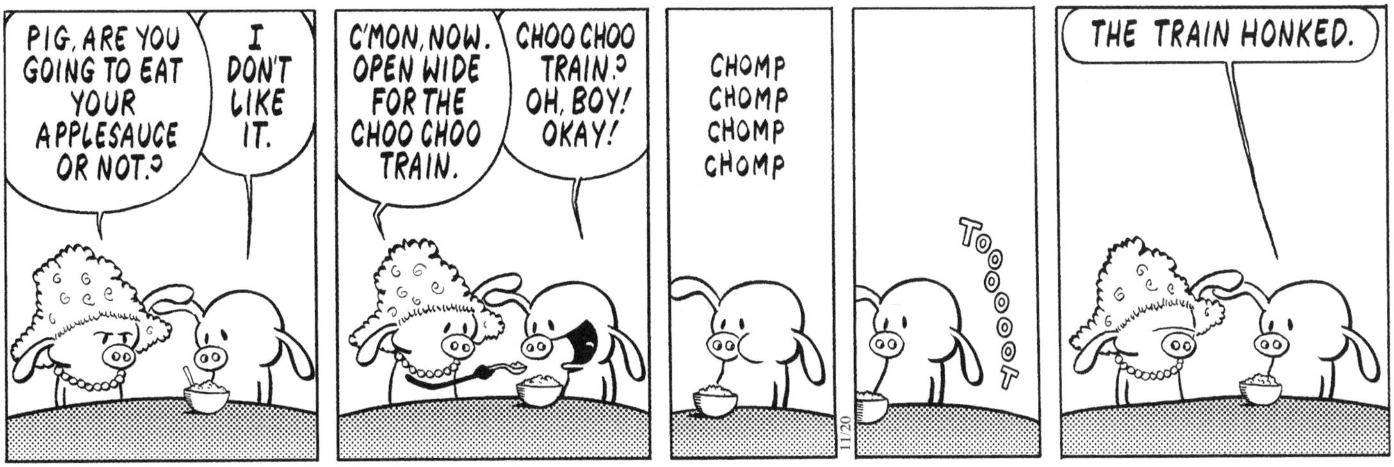
PIG, ARE YOU GOING TO EAT YOUR APPLESAUCE OR NOT?
I DON'T LIKE IT.
C'MON, NOW. OPEN WIDE FOR THE CHOO CHOO TRAIN.
CHOO CHOO TRAIN? OH, BOY! OKAY!
CHOMP CHOMP CHOMP CHOMP
TOOOOOOT
11/20
THE TRAIN HONKED.

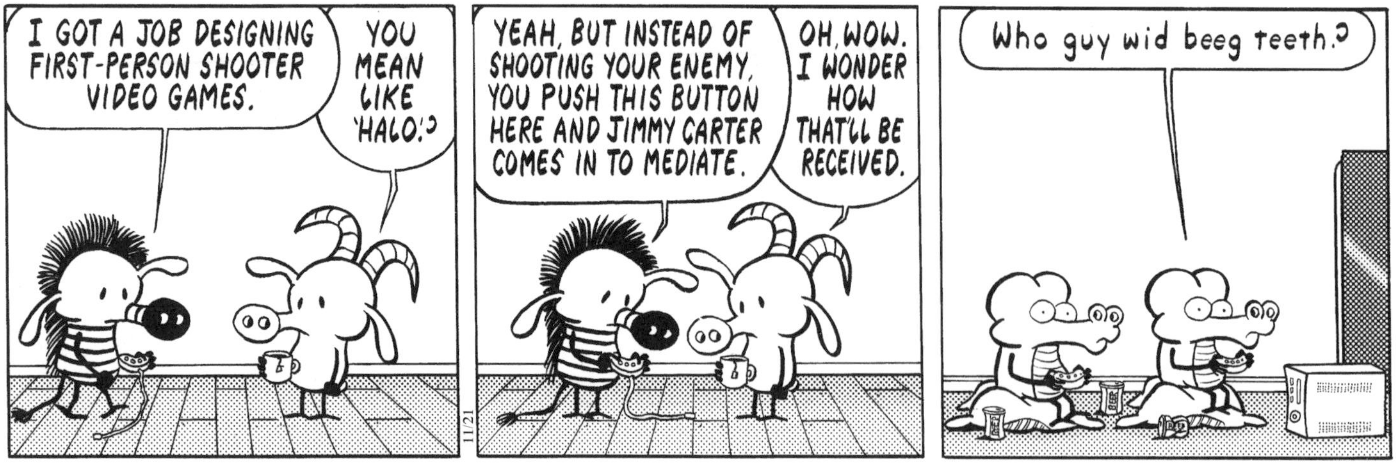
I GOT A JOB DESIGNING FIRST-PERSON SHOOTER VIDEO GAMES.
YOU MEAN LIKE 'HALO'?
YEAH, BUT INSTEAD OF SHOOTING YOUR ENEMY, YOU PUSH THIS BUTTON HERE AND JIMMY CARTER COMES IN TO MEDIATE.
OH, WOW. I WONDER HOW THAT'LL BE RECEIVED.
11/21
Who guy wid beeg teeth?

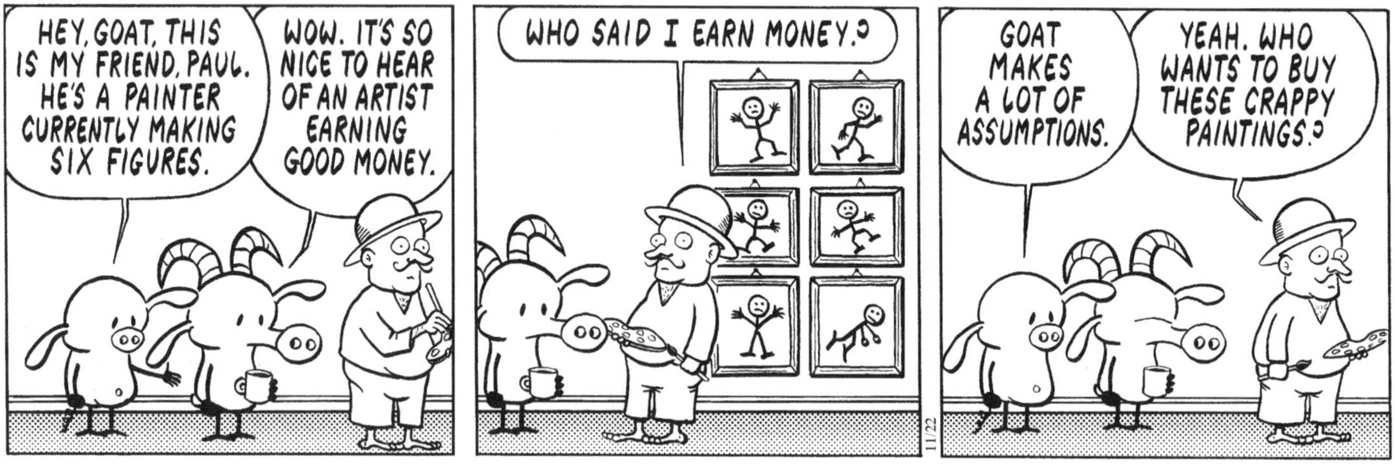
HEY, GOAT, THIS IS MY FRIEND, PAUL. HE'S A PAINTER CURRENTLY MAKING SIX FIGURES.
WOW. IT'S SO NICE TO HEAR OF AN ARTIST EARNING GOOD MONEY.
WHO SAID I EARN MONEY?
11/22
GOAT MAKES A LOT OF ASSUMPTIONS.
YEAH. WHO WANTS TO BUY THESE CRAPPY PAINTINGS?

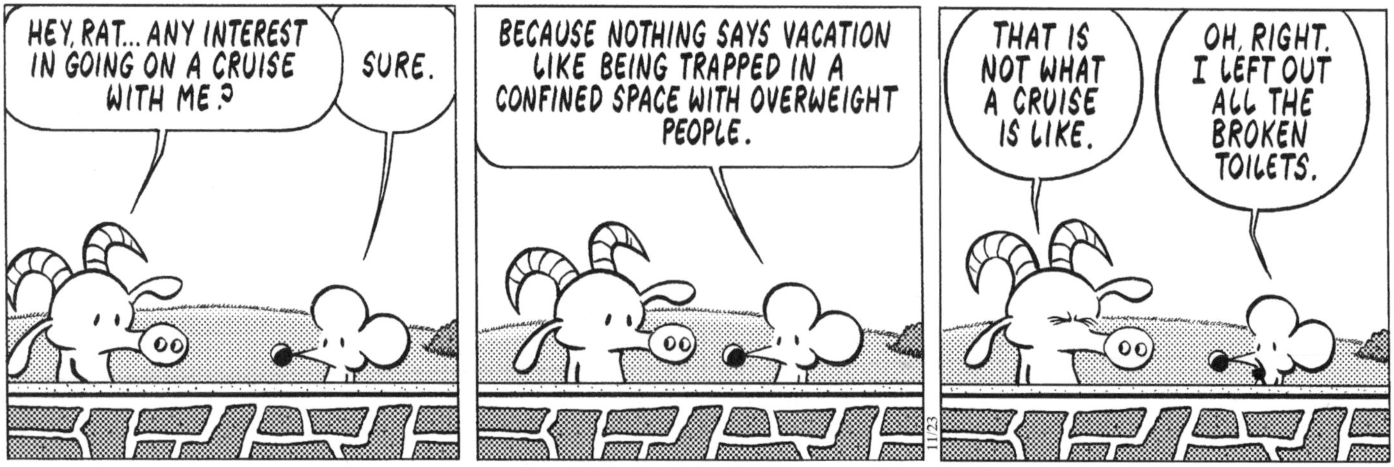
HEY, RAT... ANY INTEREST IN GOING ON A CRUISE WITH ME?
SURE.
BECAUSE NOTHING SAYS VACATION LIKE BEING TRAPPED IN A CONFINED SPACE WITH OVERWEIGHT PEOPLE.
11/23
THAT IS NOT WHAT A CRUISE IS LIKE.
OH, RIGHT. I LEFT OUT ALL THE BROKEN TOILETS.

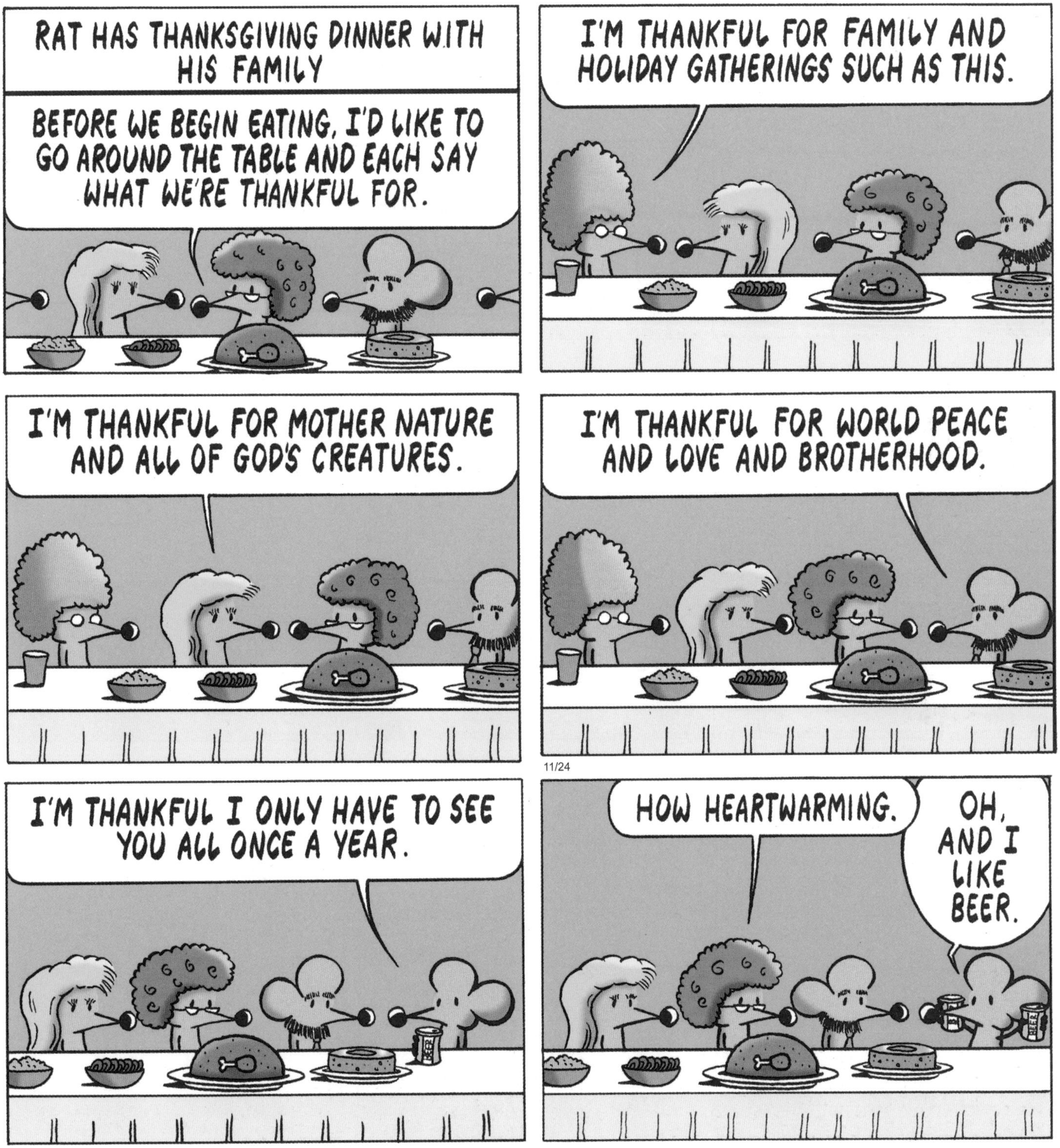
RAT HAS THANKSGIVING DINNER WITH HIS FAMILY
BEFORE WE BEGIN EATING, I'D LIKE TO GO AROUND THE TABLE AND EACH SAY WHAT WE'RE THANKFUL FOR.
I'M THANKFUL FOR FAMILY AND HOLIDAY GATHERINGS SUCH AS THIS.
I'M THANKFUL FOR MOTHER NATURE AND ALL OF GOD'S CREATURES.
I'M THANKFUL FOR WORLD PEACE AND LOVE AND BROTHERHOOD.
11/24
I'M THANKFUL I ONLY HAVE TO SEE YOU ALL ONCE A YEAR.
HOW HEARTWARMING.
OH, AND I LIKE BEER.

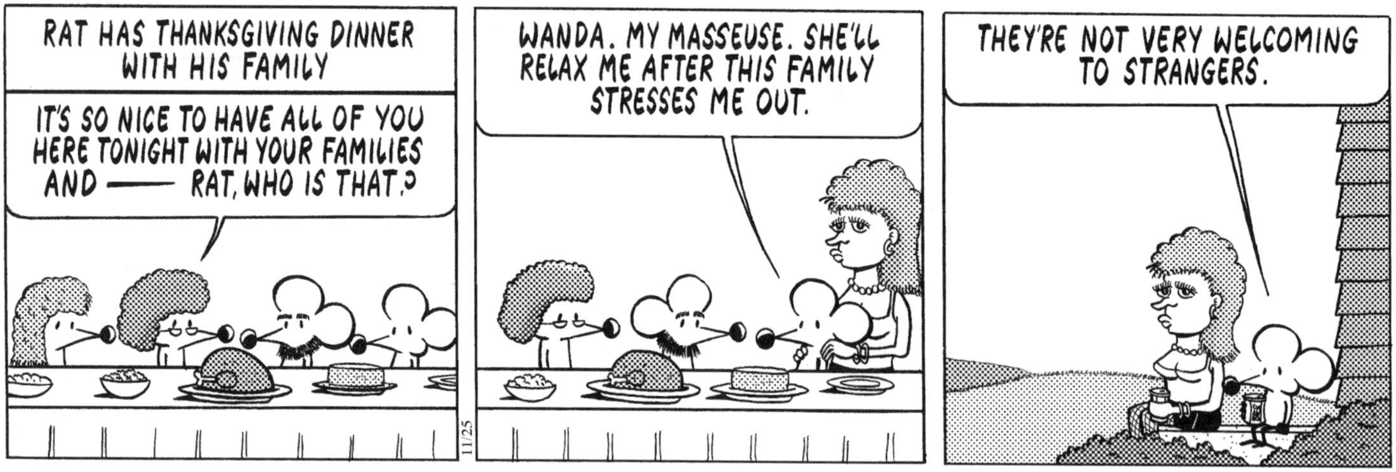
RAT HAS THANKSGIVING DINNER WITH HIS FAMILY
IT'S SO NICE TO HAVE ALL OF YOU HERE TONIGHT WITH YOUR FAMILIES AND —— RAT, WHO IS THAT?
WANDA. MY MASSEUSE. SHE'LL RELAX ME AFTER THIS FAMILY STRESSES ME OUT.
THEY'RE NOT VERY WELCOMING TO STRANGERS.
11/25

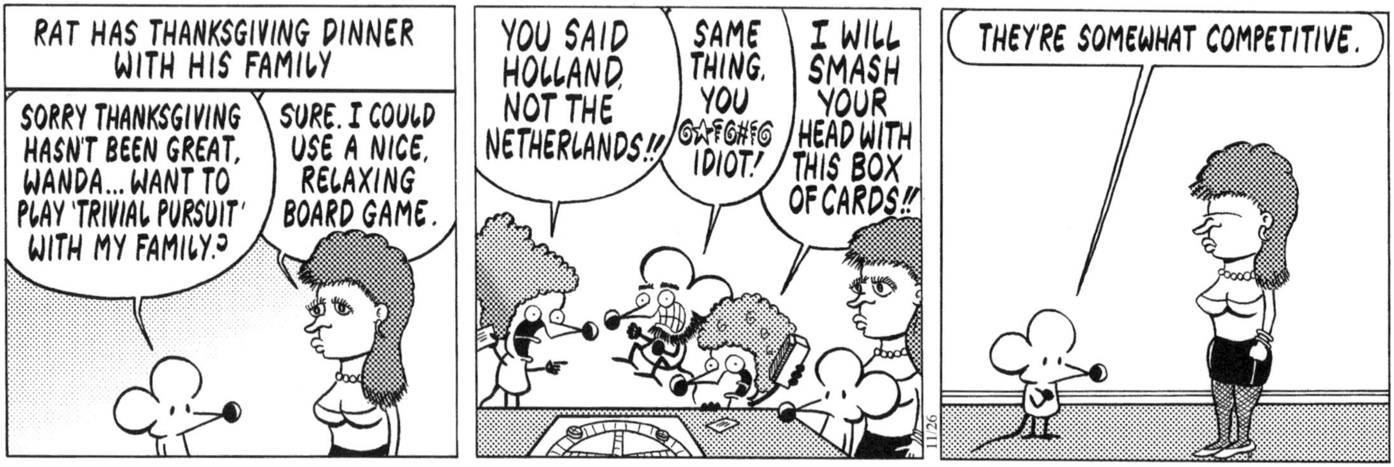
RAT HAS THANKSGIVING DINNER WITH HIS FAMILY
SORRY THANKSGIVING HASN'T BEEN GREAT, WANDA... WANT TO PLAY 'TRIVIAL PURSUIT' WITH MY FAMILY?
SURE. I COULD USE A NICE, RELAXING BOARD GAME.
YOU SAID HOLLAND, NOT THE NETHERLANDS!!
SAME THING, YOU @☆#@#@ IDIOT!
I WILL SMASH YOUR HEAD WITH THIS BOX OF CARDS!!
THEY'RE SOMEWHAT COMPETITIVE.
11/26

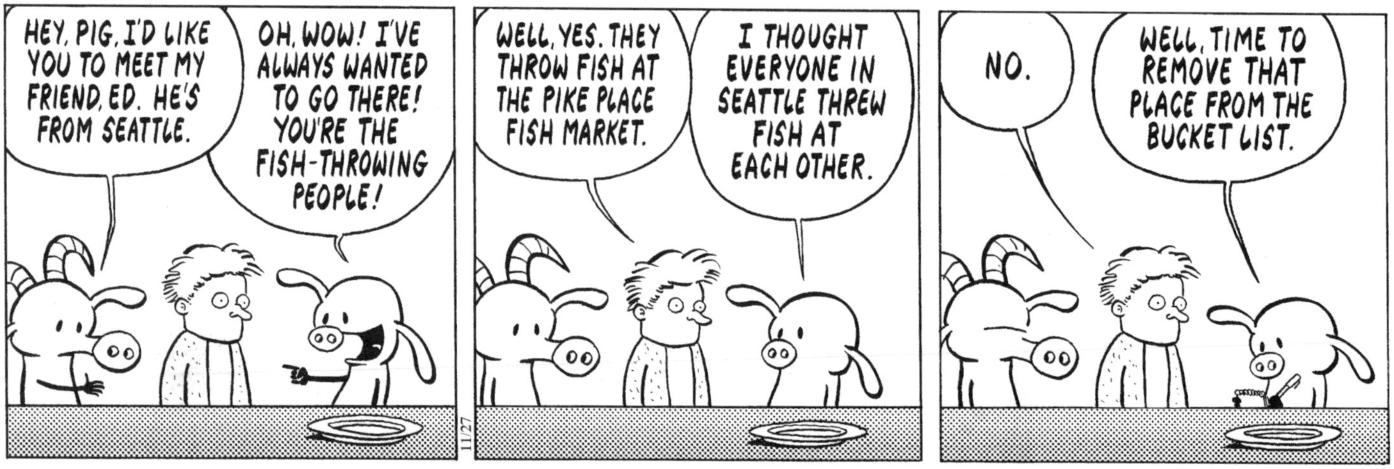
HEY, PIG, I'D LIKE YOU TO MEET MY FRIEND, ED. HE'S FROM SEATTLE.
OH, WOW! I'VE ALWAYS WANTED TO GO THERE! YOU'RE THE FISH-THROWING PEOPLE!
WELL, YES. THEY THROW FISH AT THE PIKE PLACE FISH MARKET.
I THOUGHT EVERYONE IN SEATTLE THREW FISH AT EACH OTHER.
NO.
WELL, TIME TO REMOVE THAT PLACE FROM THE BUCKET LIST.
11/27

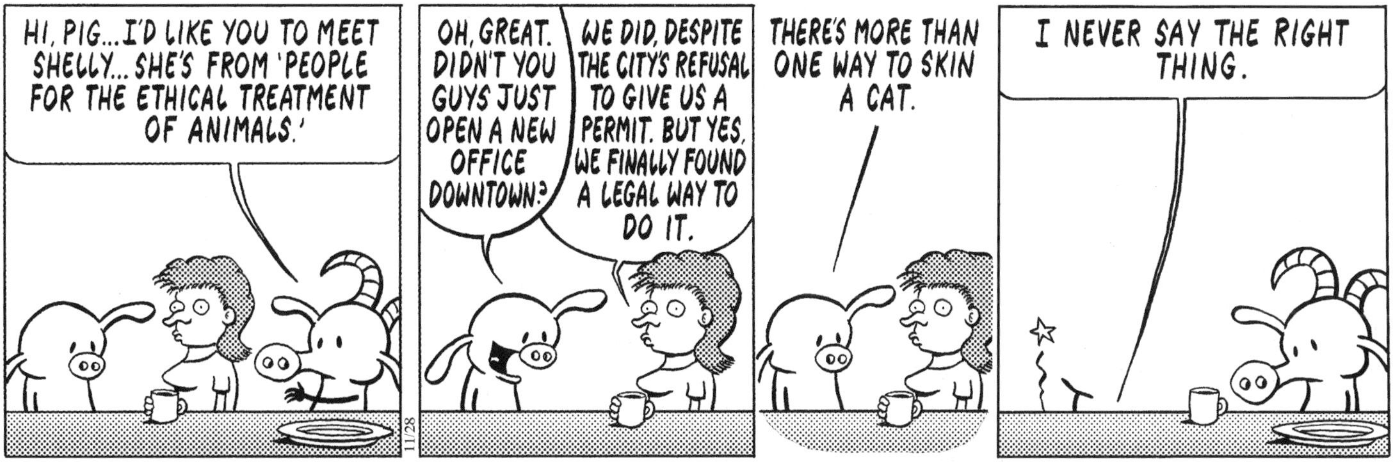
HI, PIG... I'D LIKE YOU TO MEET SHELLY... SHE'S FROM 'PEOPLE FOR THE ETHICAL TREATMENT OF ANIMALS.'
11/28
OH, GREAT. DIDN'T YOU GUYS JUST OPEN A NEW OFFICE DOWNTOWN?
WE DID, DESPITE THE CITY'S REFUSAL TO GIVE US A PERMIT. BUT YES, WE FINALLY FOUND A LEGAL WAY TO DO IT.
THERE'S MORE THAN ONE WAY TO SKIN A CAT.
I NEVER SAY THE RIGHT THING.

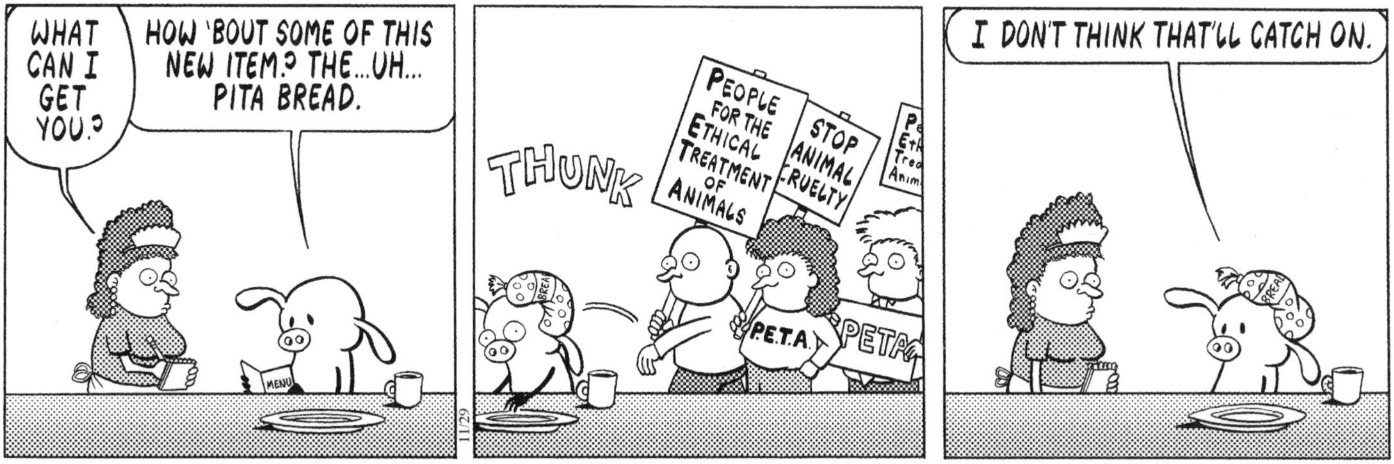
WHAT CAN I GET YOU?
HOW 'BOUT SOME OF THIS NEW ITEM? THE...UH... PITA BREAD.
MENU
11/29
THUNK
PEOPLE FOR THE ETHICAL TREATMENT OF ANIMALS
STOP ANIMAL CRUELTY
P.E.T.A.
PETA
I DON'T THINK THAT'LL CATCH ON.

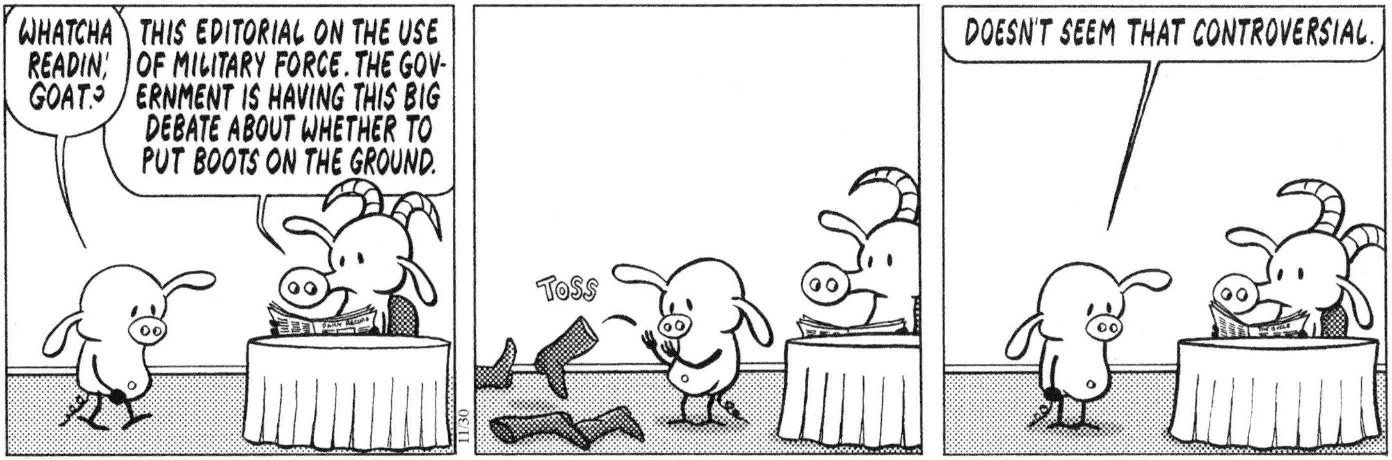
WHATCHA READIN', GOAT?
THIS EDITORIAL ON THE USE OF MILITARY FORCE. THE GOVERNMENT IS HAVING THIS BIG DEBATE ABOUT WHETHER TO PUT BOOTS ON THE GROUND.
11/30
TOSS
DOESN'T SEEM THAT CONTROVERSIAL.

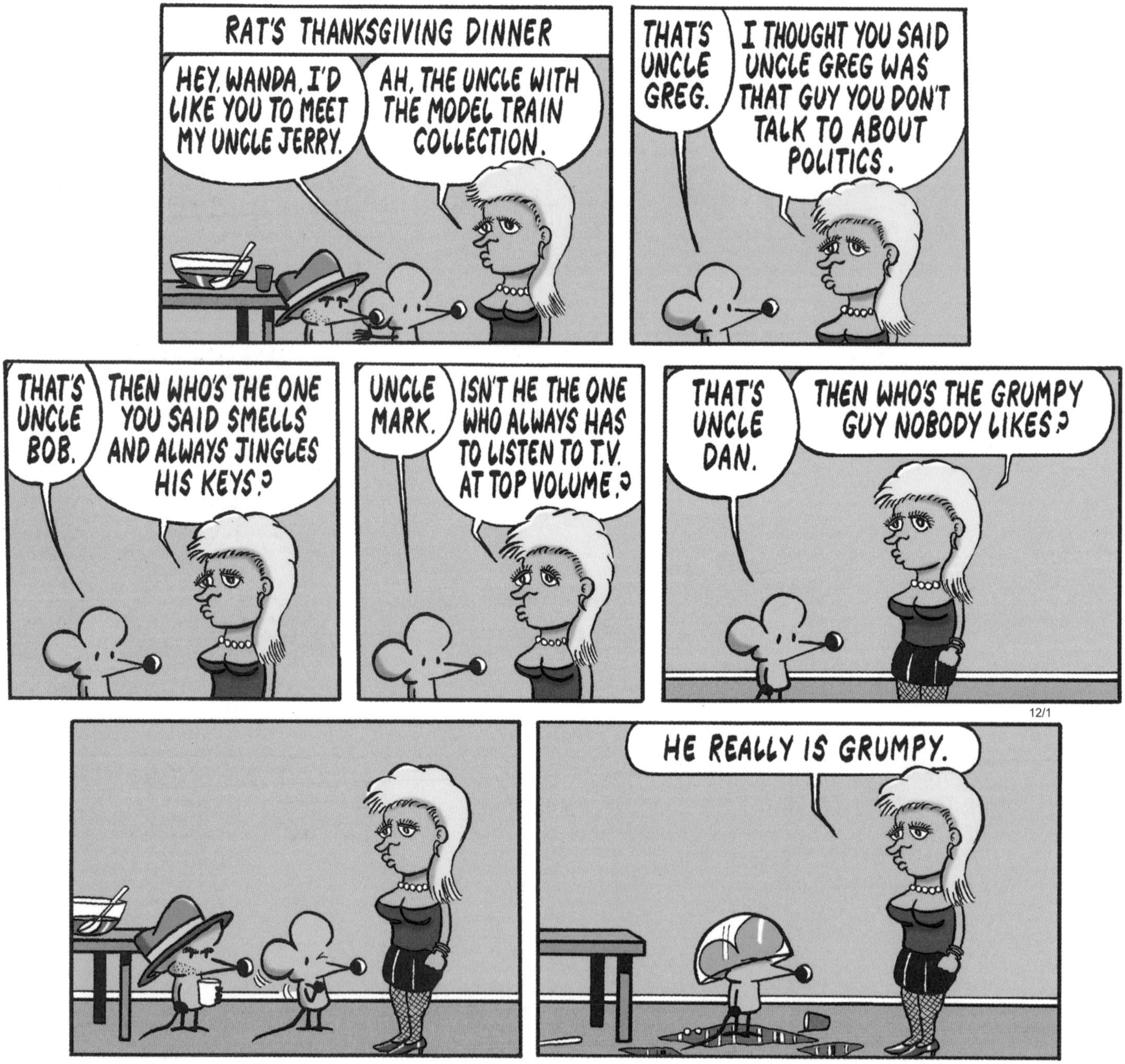

RAT'S THANKSGIVING DINNER
HEY, WANDA, I'D LIKE YOU TO MEET MY UNCLE JERRY.
AH, THE UNCLE WITH THE MODEL TRAIN COLLECTION.
THAT'S UNCLE GREG.
I THOUGHT YOU SAID UNCLE GREG WAS THAT GUY YOU DON'T TALK TO ABOUT POLITICS.
THAT'S UNCLE BOB.
THEN WHO'S THE ONE YOU SAID SMELLS AND ALWAYS JINGLES HIS KEYS?
UNCLE MARK.
ISN'T HE THE ONE WHO ALWAYS HAS TO LISTEN TO T.V. AT TOP VOLUME?
THAT'S UNCLE DAN.
THEN WHO'S THE GRUMPY GUY NOBODY LIKES?
12/1
HE REALLY IS GRUMPY.

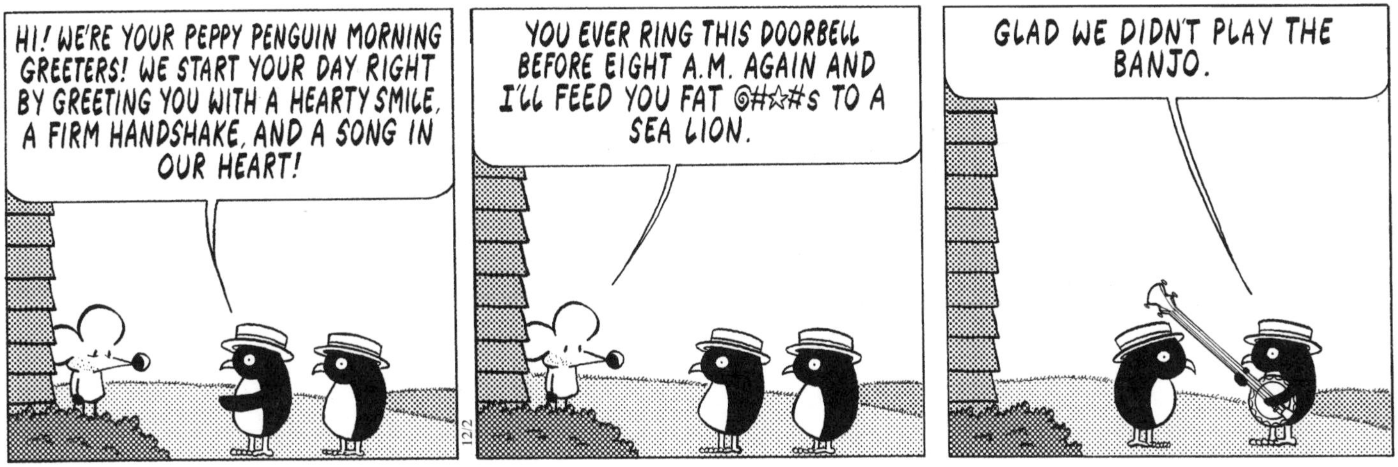
HI! WE'RE YOUR PEPPY PENGUIN MORNING GREETERS! WE START YOUR DAY RIGHT BY GREETING YOU WITH A HEARTY SMILE, A FIRM HANDSHAKE, AND A SONG IN OUR HEART!
12/2
YOU EVER RING THIS DOORBELL BEFORE EIGHT A.M. AGAIN AND I'LL FEED YOU FAT @#☆#s TO A SEA LION.
GLAD WE DIDN'T PLAY THE BANJO.

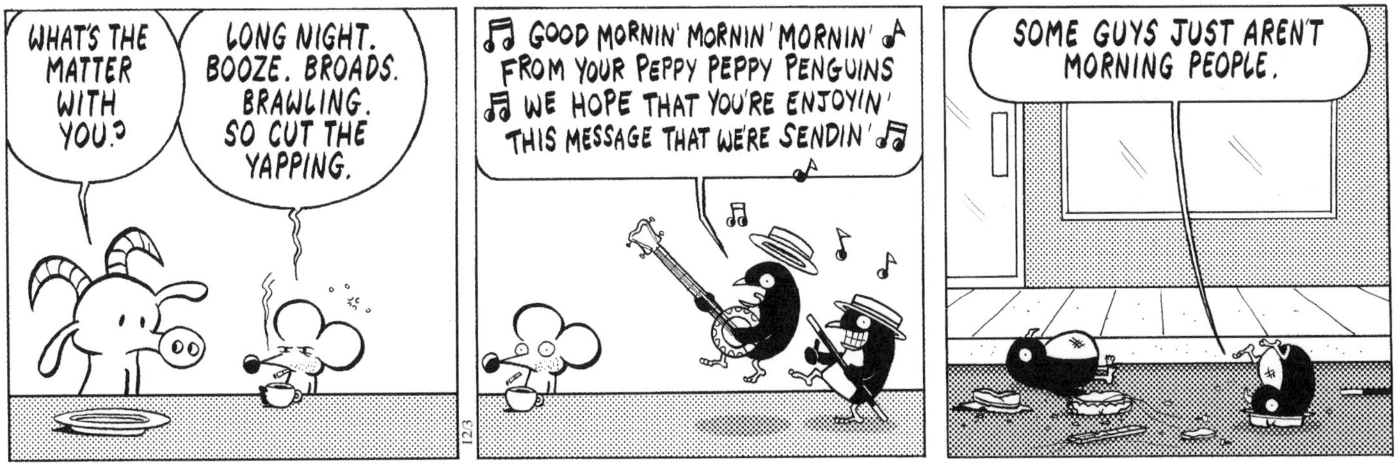
WHAT'S THE MATTER WITH YOU?
LONG NIGHT. BOOZE. BROADS. BRAWLING. SO CUT THE YAPPING.
12/3
♫ GOOD MORNIN' MORNIN' MORNIN' ♪ FROM YOUR PEPPY PEPPY PENGUINS ♫ WE HOPE THAT YOU'RE ENJOYIN' THIS MESSAGE THAT WE'RE SENDIN' ♫
SOME GUYS JUST AREN'T MORNING PEOPLE.

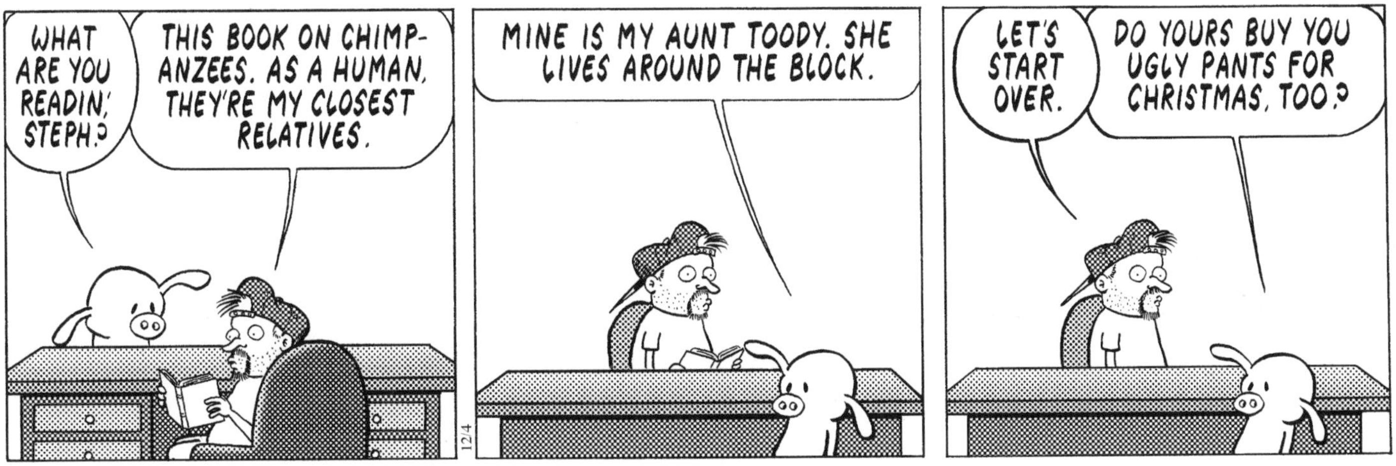
WHAT ARE YOU READIN,' STEPH?
THIS BOOK ON CHIMPANZEES. AS A HUMAN, THEY'RE MY CLOSEST RELATIVES.
12/4
MINE IS MY AUNT TOODY. SHE LIVES AROUND THE BLOCK.
LET'S START OVER.
DO YOURS BUY YOU UGLY PANTS FOR CHRISTMAS, TOO?

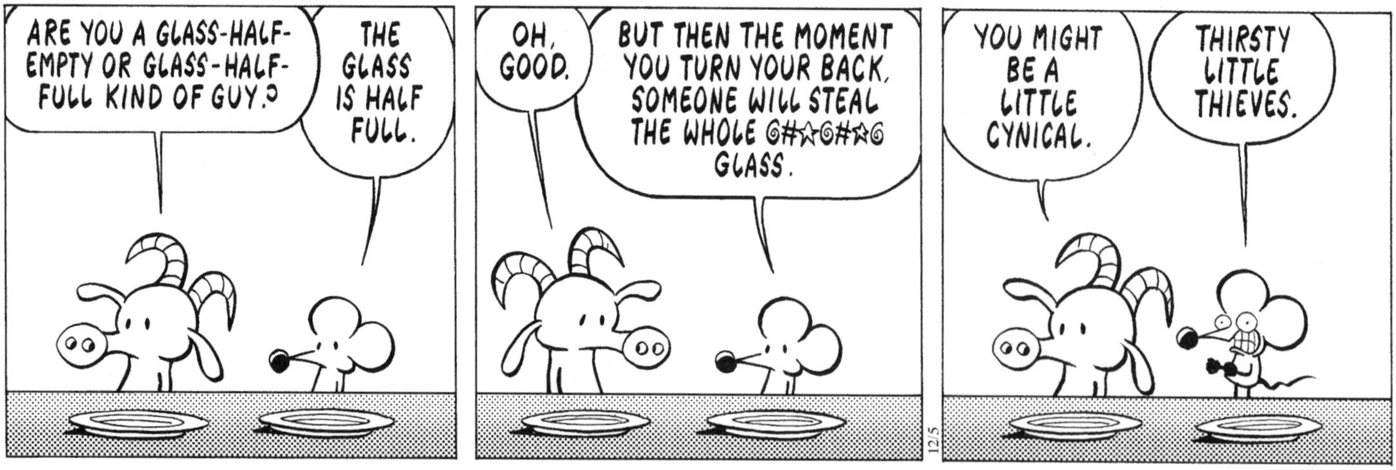
ARE YOU A GLASS-HALF-EMPTY OR GLASS-HALF-FULL KIND OF GUY?
THE GLASS IS HALF FULL.
OH, GOOD.
BUT THEN THE MOMENT YOU TURN YOUR BACK, SOMEONE WILL STEAL THE WHOLE @#☆@#☆@ GLASS.
12/5
YOU MIGHT BE A LITTLE CYNICAL.
THIRSTY LITTLE THIEVES.

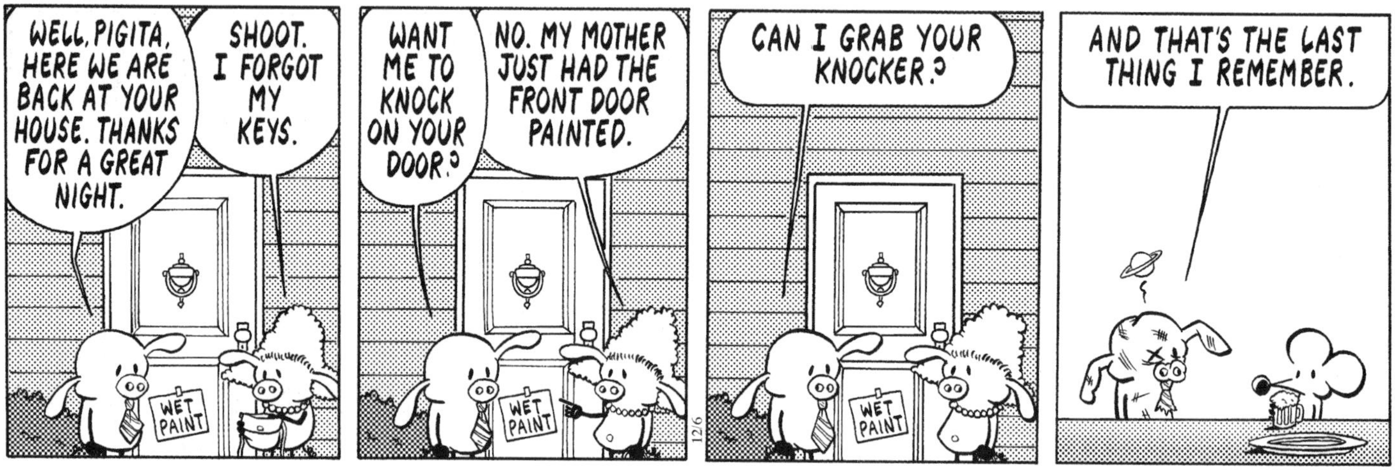
WELL, PIGITA, HERE WE ARE BACK AT YOUR HOUSE. THANKS FOR A GREAT NIGHT.
SHOOT. I FORGOT MY KEYS.
WET PAINT
WANT ME TO KNOCK ON YOUR DOOR?
NO. MY MOTHER JUST HAD THE FRONT DOOR PAINTED.
WET PAINT
12/6
CAN I GRAB YOUR KNOCKER?
WET PAINT
AND THAT'S THE LAST THING I REMEMBER.

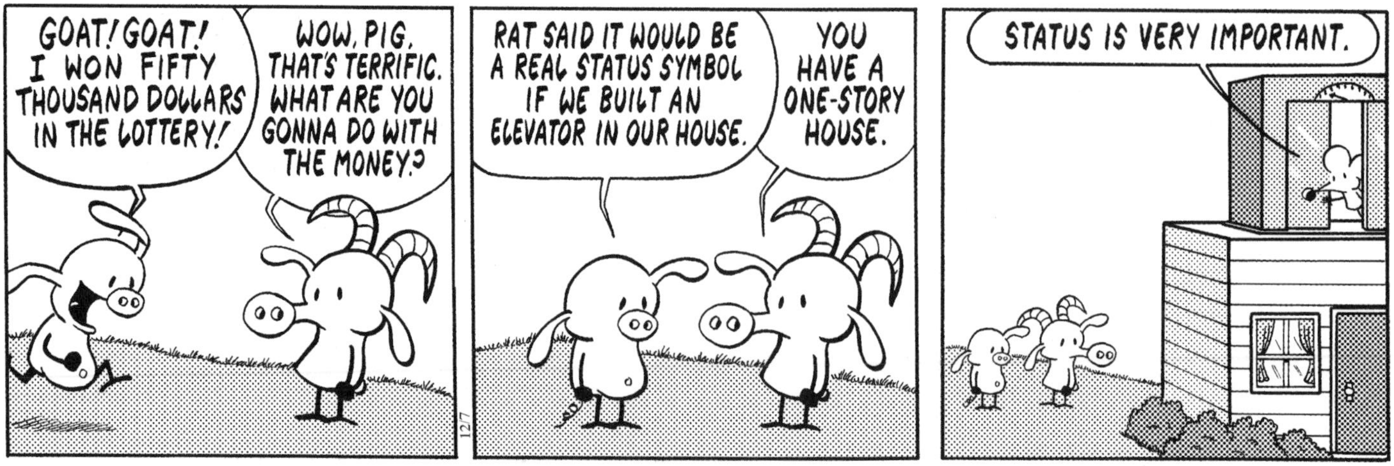
GOAT! GOAT! I WON FIFTY THOUSAND DOLLARS IN THE LOTTERY!
WOW, PIG, THAT'S TERRIFIC. WHAT ARE YOU GONNA DO WITH THE MONEY?
12/7
RAT SAID IT WOULD BE A REAL STATUS SYMBOL IF WE BUILT AN ELEVATOR IN OUR HOUSE.
YOU HAVE A ONE-STORY HOUSE.
STATUS IS VERY IMPORTANT.

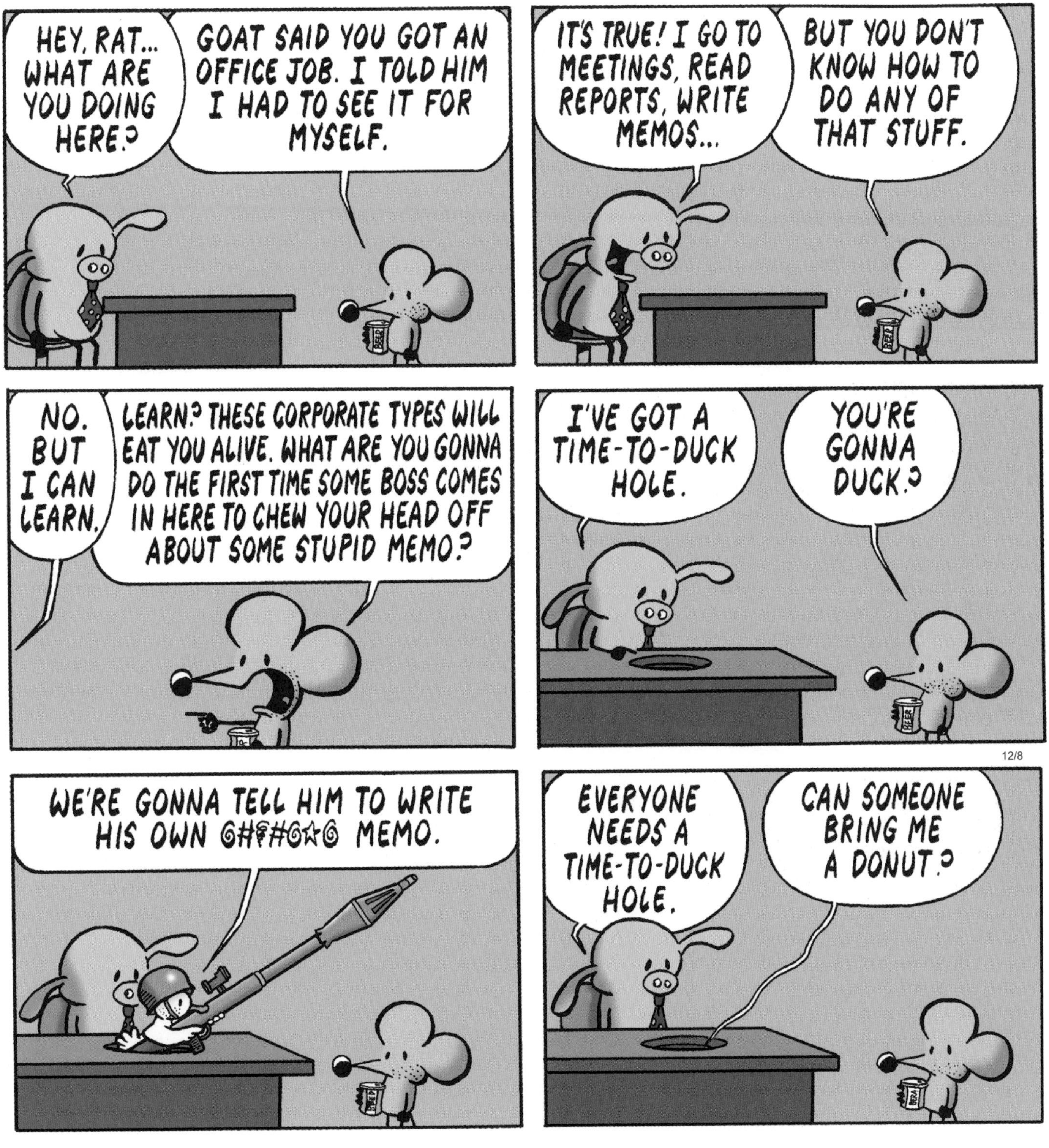
HEY, RAT... WHAT ARE YOU DOING HERE?
GOAT SAID YOU GOT AN OFFICE JOB. I TOLD HIM I HAD TO SEE IT FOR MYSELF.
IT'S TRUE! I GO TO MEETINGS, READ REPORTS, WRITE MEMOS...
BUT YOU DON'T KNOW HOW TO DO ANY OF THAT STUFF.
NO. BUT I CAN LEARN.
LEARN? THESE CORPORATE TYPES WILL EAT YOU ALIVE. WHAT ARE YOU GONNA DO THE FIRST TIME SOME BOSS COMES IN HERE TO CHEW YOUR HEAD OFF ABOUT SOME STUPID MEMO?
I'VE GOT A TIME-TO-DUCK HOLE.
YOU'RE GONNA DUCK?
12/8
WE'RE GONNA TELL HIM TO WRITE HIS OWN @#?#@☆@ MEMO.
EVERYONE NEEDS A TIME-TO-DUCK HOLE.
CAN SOMEONE BRING ME A DONUT?

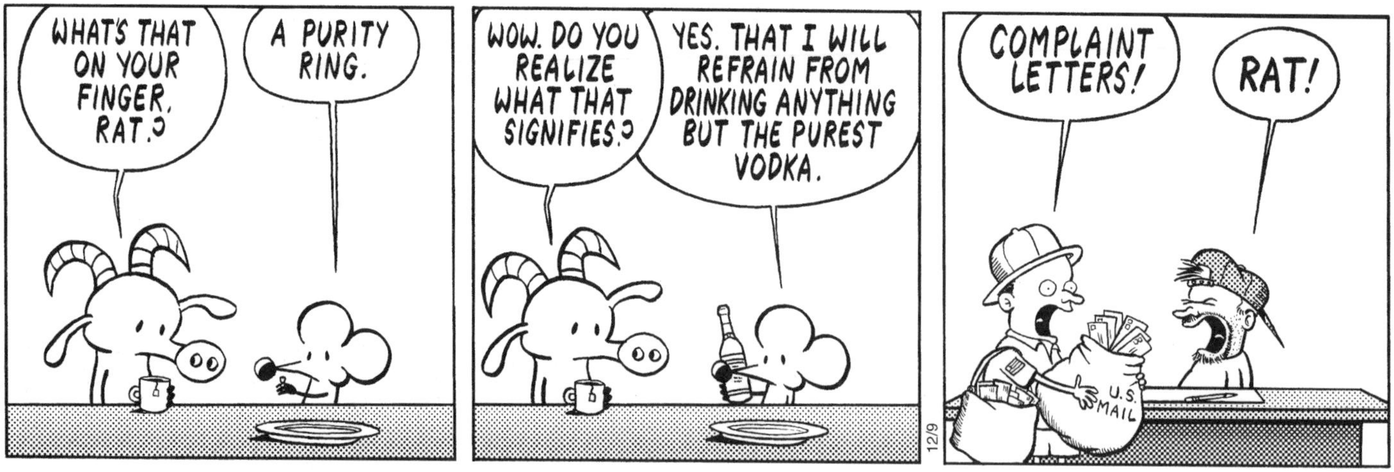
WHAT'S THAT ON YOUR FINGER, RAT?
A PURITY RING.
WOW. DO YOU REALIZE WHAT THAT SIGNIFIES?
YES. THAT I WILL REFRAIN FROM DRINKING ANYTHING BUT THE PUREST VODKA.
COMPLAINT LETTERS!
RAT!
U.S. MAIL
12/9

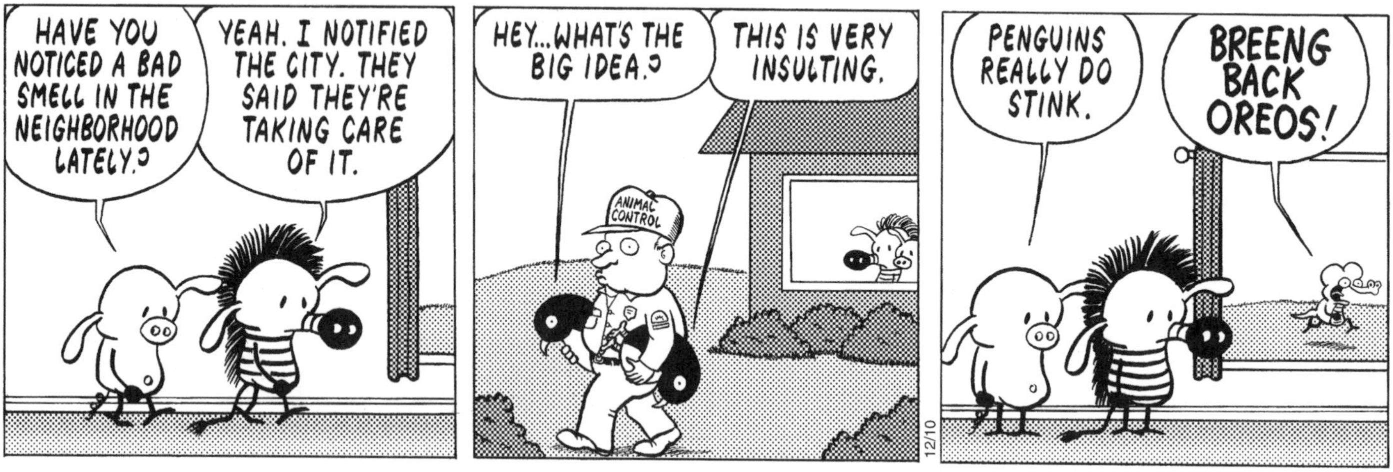
HAVE YOU NOTICED A BAD SMELL IN THE NEIGHBORHOOD LATELY?
YEAH. I NOTIFIED THE CITY. THEY SAID THEY'RE TAKING CARE OF IT.
HEY...WHAT'S THE BIG IDEA?
THIS IS VERY INSULTING.
ANIMAL CONTROL
PENGUINS REALLY DO STINK.
BREENG BACK OREOS!
12/10

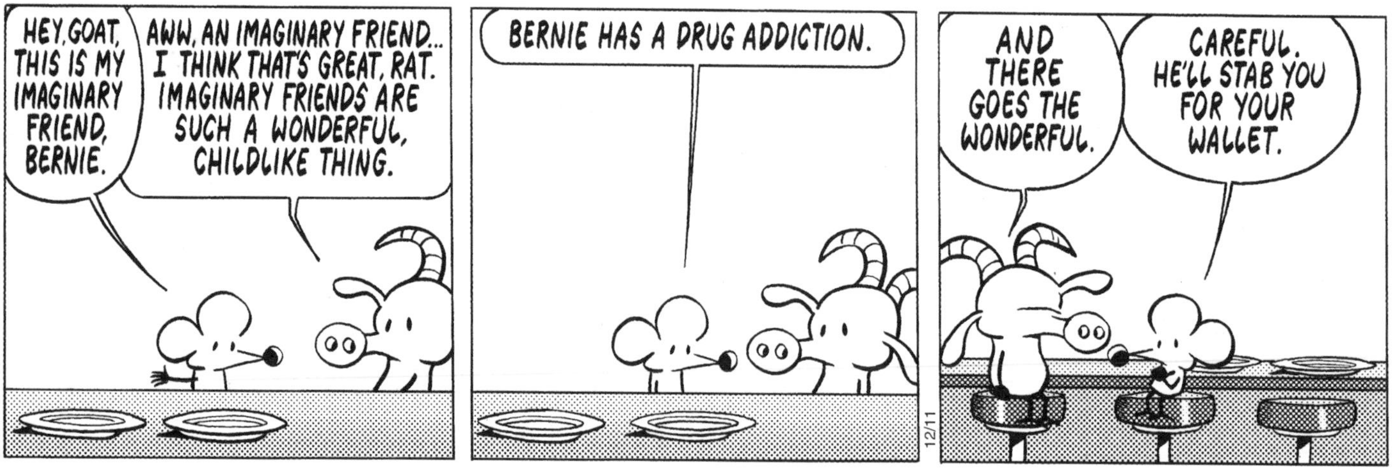
HEY, GOAT, THIS IS MY IMAGINARY FRIEND, BERNIE.
AWW, AN IMAGINARY FRIEND... I THINK THAT'S GREAT, RAT. IMAGINARY FRIENDS ARE SUCH A WONDERFUL, CHILDLIKE THING.
BERNIE HAS A DRUG ADDICTION.
AND THERE GOES THE WONDERFUL.
CAREFUL. HE'LL STAB YOU FOR YOUR WALLET.
12/11

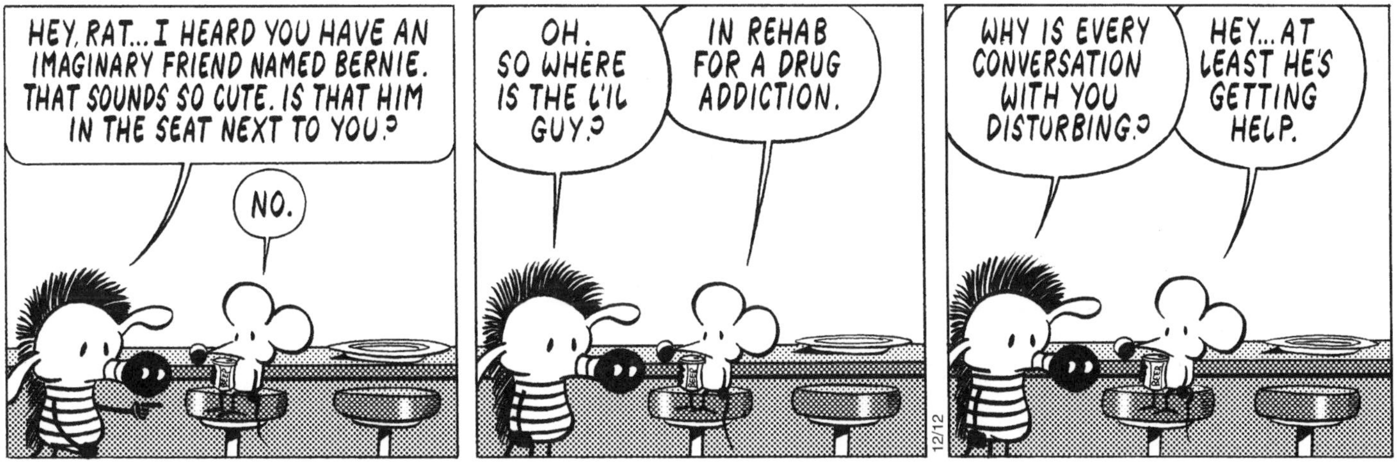
HEY, RAT... I HEARD YOU HAVE AN IMAGINARY FRIEND NAMED BERNIE. THAT SOUNDS SO CUTE. IS THAT HIM IN THE SEAT NEXT TO YOU?
NO.
OH. SO WHERE IS THE LI'L GUY?
IN REHAB FOR A DRUG ADDICTION.
WHY IS EVERY CONVERSATION WITH YOU DISTURBING?
HEY... AT LEAST HE'S GETTING HELP.
12/12

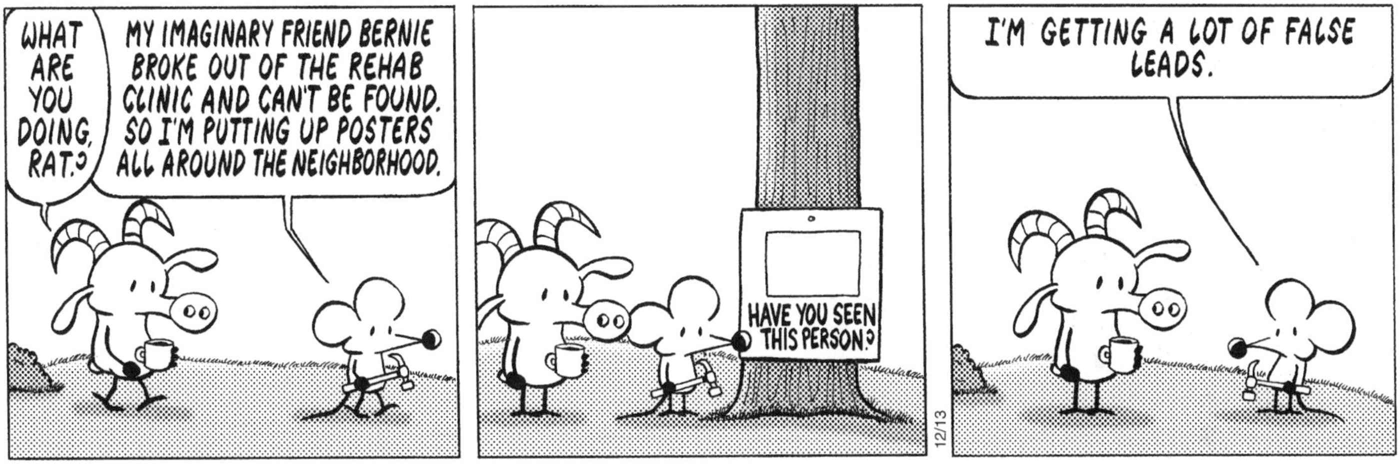
WHAT ARE YOU DOING, RAT?
MY IMAGINARY FRIEND BERNIE BROKE OUT OF THE REHAB CLINIC AND CAN'T BE FOUND. SO I'M PUTTING UP POSTERS ALL AROUND THE NEIGHBORHOOD.
HAVE YOU SEEN THIS PERSON?
I'M GETTING A LOT OF FALSE LEADS.
12/13

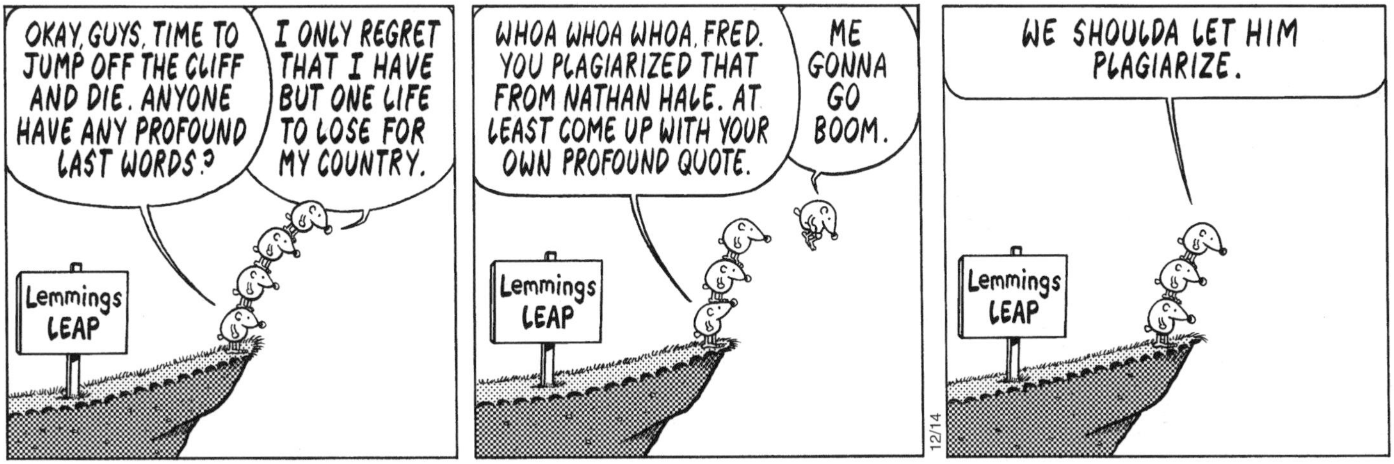
OKAY, GUYS, TIME TO JUMP OFF THE CLIFF AND DIE. ANYONE HAVE ANY PROFOUND LAST WORDS?
I ONLY REGRET THAT I HAVE BUT ONE LIFE TO LOSE FOR MY COUNTRY.
Lemmings LEAP
WHOA WHOA WHOA, FRED. YOU PLAGIARIZED THAT FROM NATHAN HALE. AT LEAST COME UP WITH YOUR OWN PROFOUND QUOTE.
ME GONNA GO BOOM.
Lemmings LEAP
WE SHOULDA LET HIM PLAGIARIZE.
Lemmings LEAP
12/14

CHECK IT OUT. I GOT A JOB WRITING THE JUMBLE IN THE NEWSPAPER.
I LOVE THE JUMBLE! CAN I SEE ONE?
JUMBLE
Unscramble these six words to mock an overrated cartoonist.
RELAPS
SI
THOB
MUDB
DNA
YUFNUNN
I'M AFRAID IT'S JUST NOT THERE.
THAT CAN'T BE.
The doctor says Pastis is missing this bone.
Now arrange the circled letters to form the answer suggested by the cartoon
PRINT YOUR ANSWER IN THE CIRCLES BELOW
GUESS WHAT ELSE THE DOCTOR SAID YOU'RE MISSING.
ENOUGH.
12/15

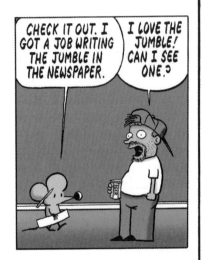

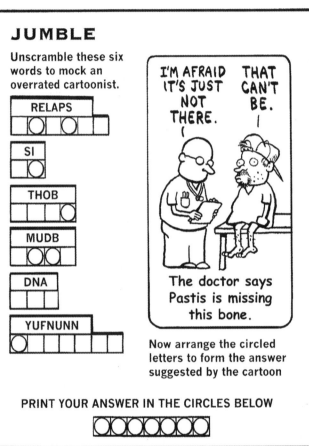

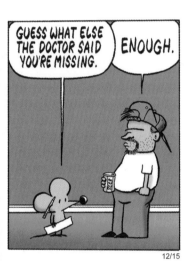

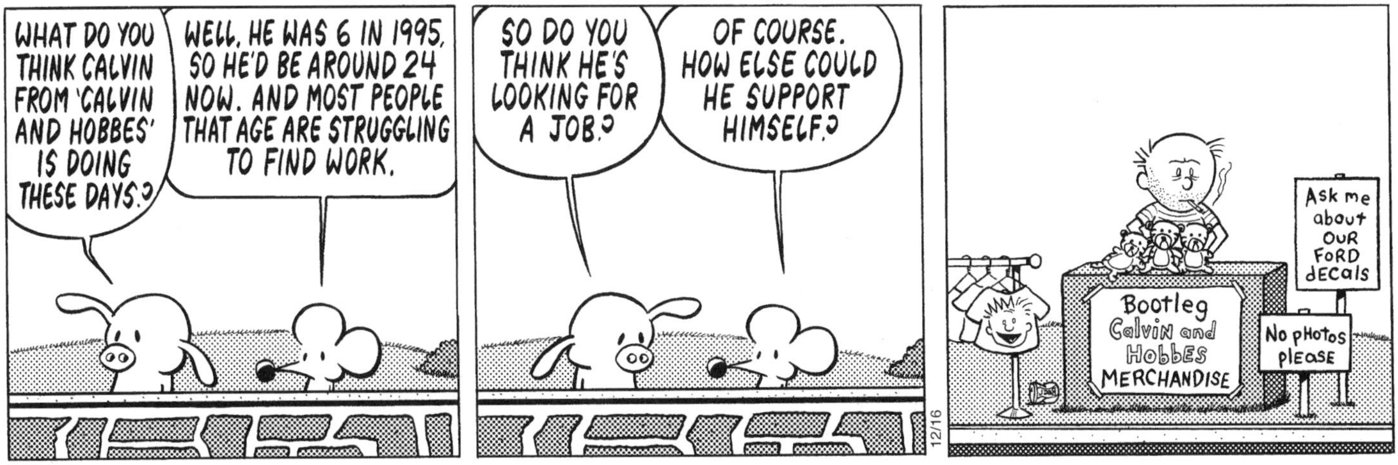
WHAT DO YOU THINK CALVIN FROM 'CALVIN AND HOBBES' IS DOING THESE DAYS?
WELL, HE WAS 6 IN 1995, SO HE'D BE AROUND 24 NOW. AND MOST PEOPLE THAT AGE ARE STRUGGLING TO FIND WORK.
SO DO YOU THINK HE'S LOOKING FOR A JOB?
OF COURSE. HOW ELSE COULD HE SUPPORT HIMSELF?
12/16
Ask me about OUR FORD decals
Bootleg Calvin and Hobbes MERCHANDISE
No pHotos please

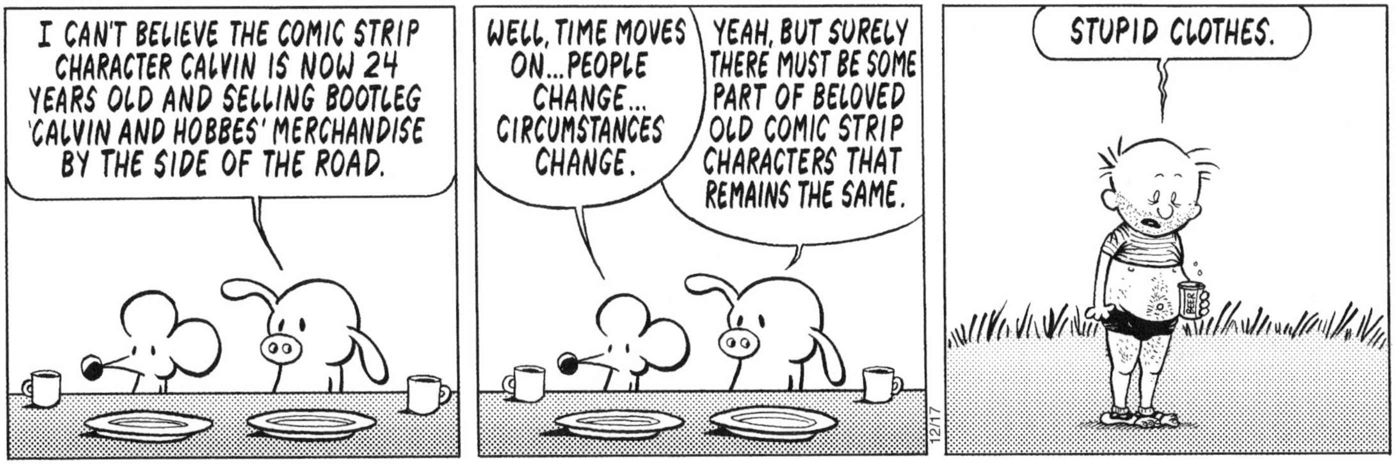
I CAN'T BELIEVE THE COMIC STRIP CHARACTER CALVIN IS NOW 24 YEARS OLD AND SELLING BOOTLEG 'CALVIN AND HOBBES' MERCHANDISE BY THE SIDE OF THE ROAD.
WELL, TIME MOVES ON...PEOPLE CHANGE... CIRCUMSTANCES CHANGE.
YEAH, BUT SURELY THERE MUST BE SOME PART OF BELOVED OLD COMIC STRIP CHARACTERS THAT REMAINS THE SAME.
12/17
STUPID CLOTHES.
BEER

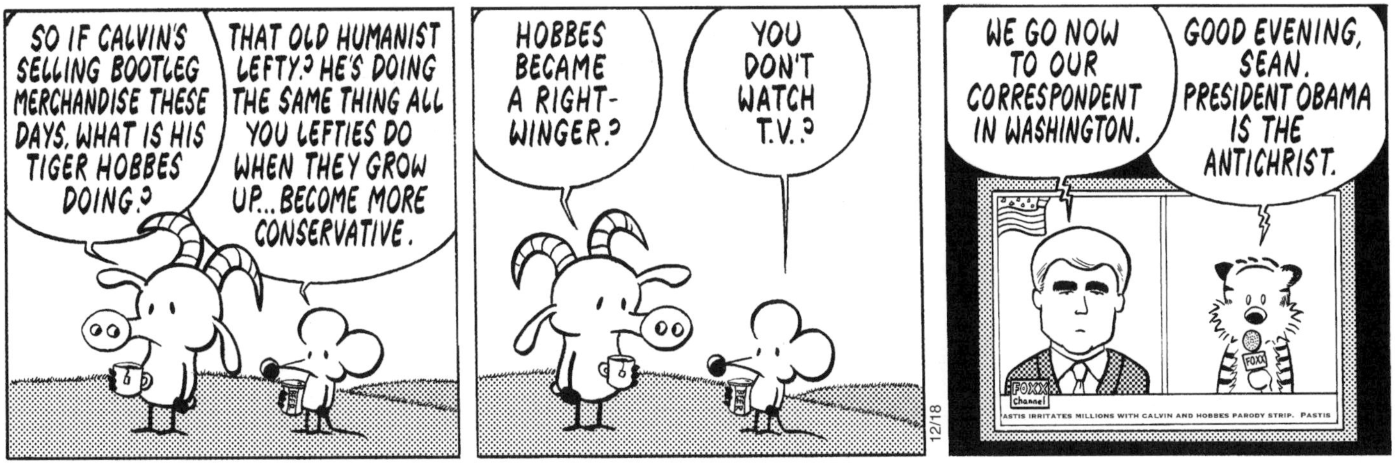
SO IF CALVIN'S SELLING BOOTLEG MERCHANDISE THESE DAYS, WHAT IS HIS TIGER HOBBES DOING?
THAT OLD HUMANIST LEFTY? HE'S DOING THE SAME THING ALL YOU LEFTIES DO WHEN THEY GROW UP...BECOME MORE CONSERVATIVE.
HOBBES BECAME A RIGHT-WINGER?
YOU DON'T WATCH T.V.?
12/18
WE GO NOW TO OUR CORRESPONDENT IN WASHINGTON.
GOOD EVENING, SEAN. PRESIDENT OBAMA IS THE ANTICHRIST.
FOXX Channel
FOXX
ASTIS IRRITATES MILLIONS WITH CALVIN AND HOBBES PARODY STRIP. PASTIS

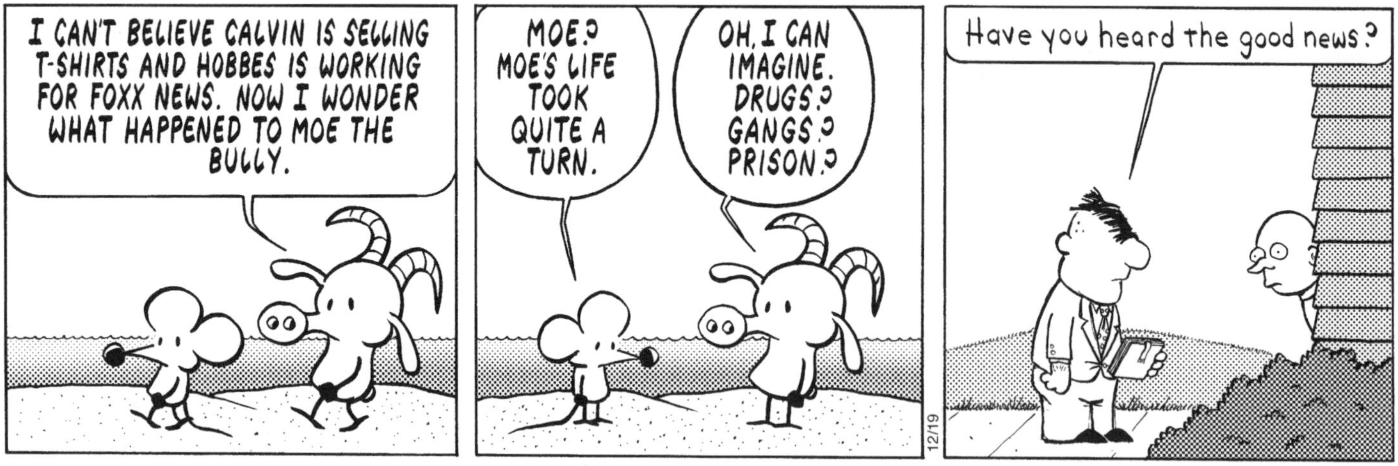
I CAN'T BELIEVE CALVIN IS SELLING T-SHIRTS AND HOBBES IS WORKING FOR FOXX NEWS. NOW I WONDER WHAT HAPPENED TO MOE THE BULLY.
MOE? MOE'S LIFE TOOK QUITE A TURN.
OH, I CAN IMAGINE. DRUGS? GANGS? PRISON?
12/19
Have you heard the good news?

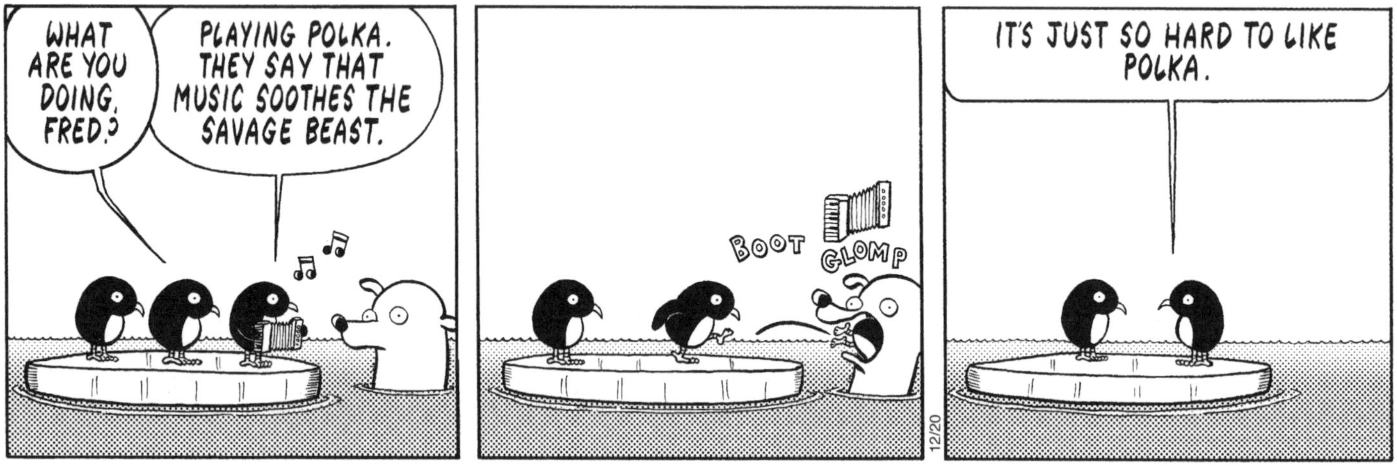
WHAT ARE YOU DOING, FRED?
PLAYING POLKA. THEY SAY THAT MUSIC SOOTHES THE SAVAGE BEAST.
BOOT
GLOMP
12/20
IT'S JUST SO HARD TO LIKE POLKA.

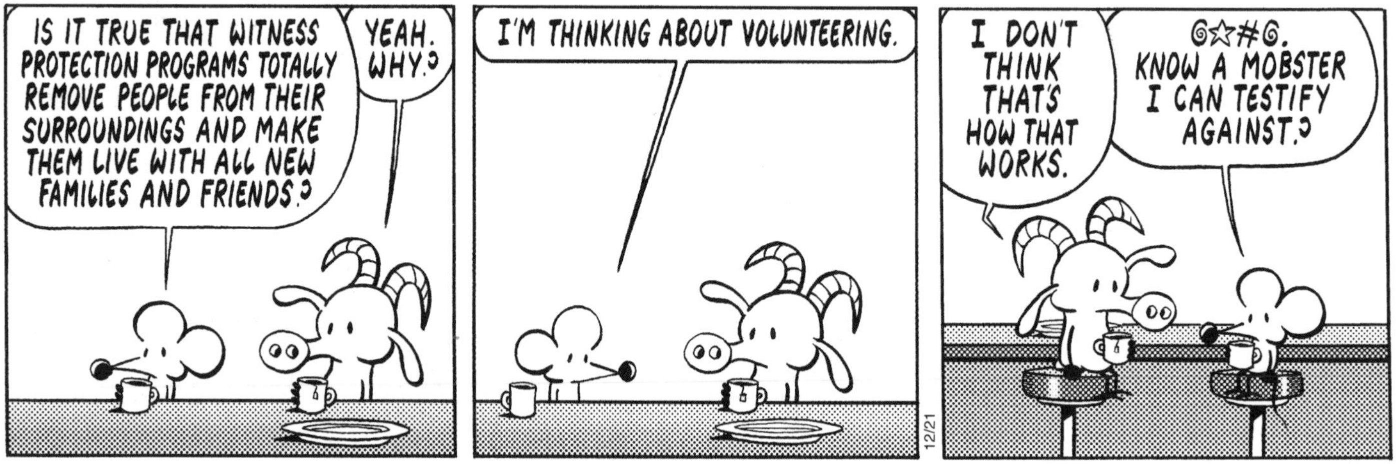
IS IT TRUE THAT WITNESS PROTECTION PROGRAMS TOTALLY REMOVE PEOPLE FROM THEIR SURROUNDINGS AND MAKE THEM LIVE WITH ALL NEW FAMILIES AND FRIENDS?
YEAH. WHY?
I'M THINKING ABOUT VOLUNTEERING.
12/21
I DON'T THINK THAT'S HOW THAT WORKS.
G☆#G. KNOW A MOBSTER I CAN TESTIFY AGAINST?

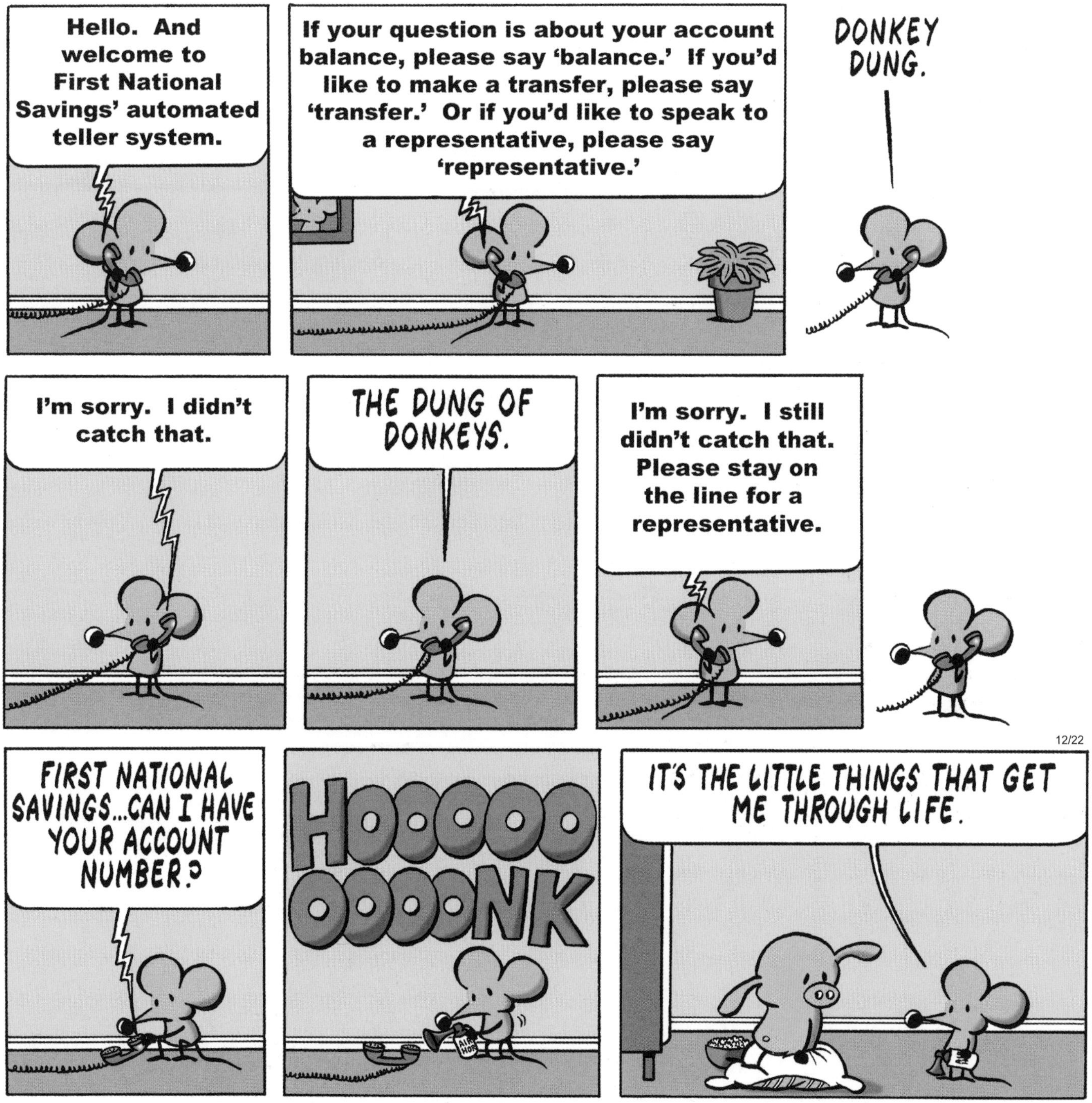
Hello. And welcome to First National Savings' automated teller system.
If your question is about your account balance, please say 'balance.' If you'd like to make a transfer, please say 'transfer.' Or if you'd like to speak to a representative, please say 'representative.'
DONKEY DUNG.
I'm sorry. I didn't catch that.
THE DUNG OF DONKEYS.
I'm sorry. I still didn't catch that. Please stay on the line for a representative.
12/22
FIRST NATIONAL SAVINGS...CAN I HAVE YOUR ACCOUNT NUMBER?
HOOOOO OOOONK
AIR HORN
IT'S THE LITTLE THINGS THAT GET ME THROUGH LIFE.

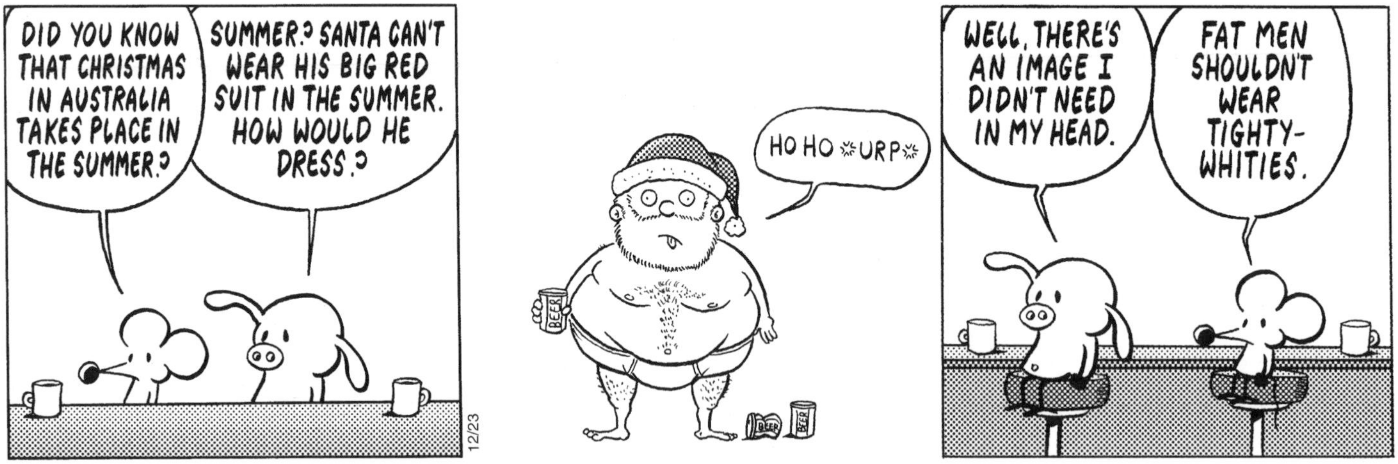
DID YOU KNOW THAT CHRISTMAS IN AUSTRALIA TAKES PLACE IN THE SUMMER?
SUMMER? SANTA CAN'T WEAR HIS BIG RED SUIT IN THE SUMMER. HOW WOULD HE DRESS?
12/23
HO HO ☆URP☆
WELL, THERE'S AN IMAGE I DIDN'T NEED IN MY HEAD.
FAT MEN SHOULDN'T WEAR TIGHTY-WHITIES.
BEER

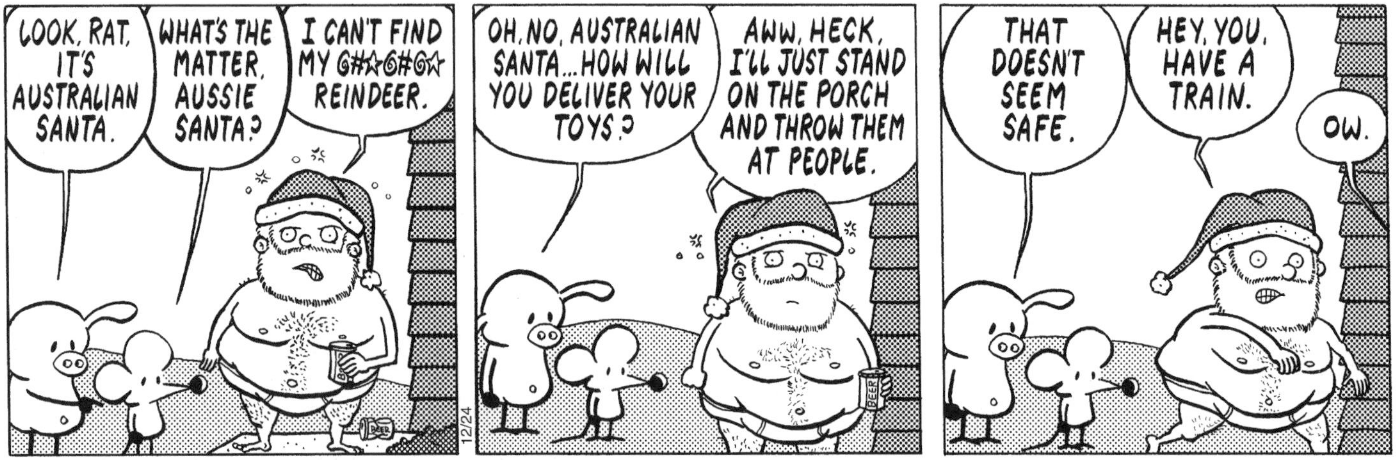
LOOK, RAT, IT'S AUSTRALIAN SANTA.
WHAT'S THE MATTER, AUSSIE SANTA?
I CAN'T FIND MY G#☆G#G☆ REINDEER.
12/24
OH, NO, AUSTRALIAN SANTA...HOW WILL YOU DELIVER YOUR TOYS?
AWW, HECK, I'LL JUST STAND ON THE PORCH AND THROW THEM AT PEOPLE.
THAT DOESN'T SEEM SAFE.
HEY, YOU. HAVE A TRAIN.
OW.

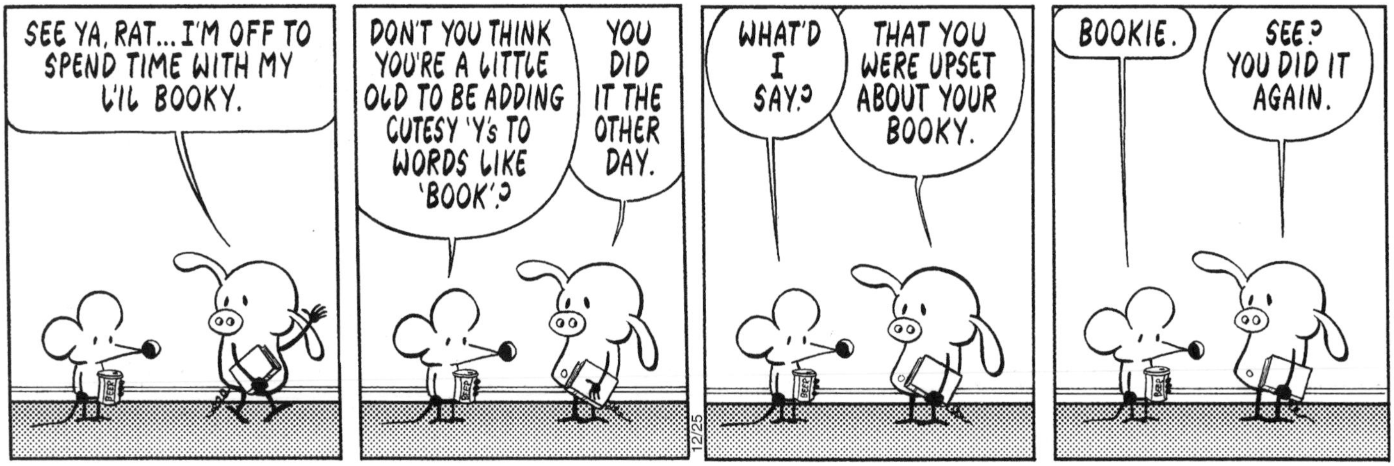
SEE YA, RAT... I'M OFF TO SPEND TIME WITH MY LI'L BOOKY.
DON'T YOU THINK YOU'RE A LITTLE OLD TO BE ADDING CUTESY 'Y's TO WORDS LIKE 'BOOK'?
YOU DID IT THE OTHER DAY.
12/25
WHAT'D I SAY?
THAT YOU WERE UPSET ABOUT YOUR BOOKY.
BOOKIE.
SEE? YOU DID IT AGAIN.

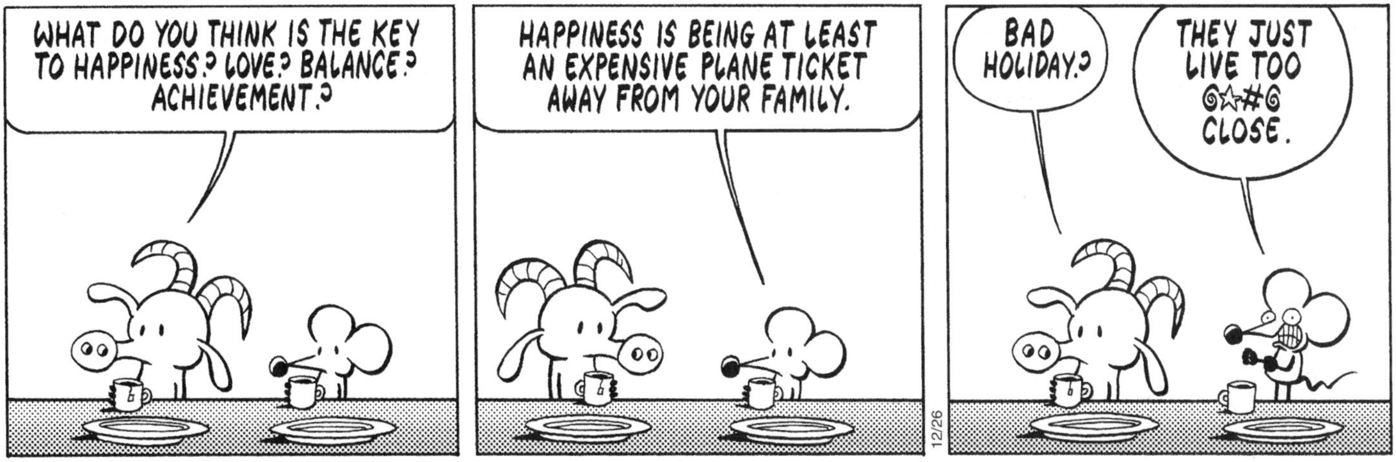
WHAT DO YOU THINK IS THE KEY TO HAPPINESS? LOVE? BALANCE? ACHIEVEMENT?
HAPPINESS IS BEING AT LEAST AN EXPENSIVE PLANE TICKET AWAY FROM YOUR FAMILY.
12/26
BAD HOLIDAY?
THEY JUST LIVE TOO @☆#@ CLOSE.

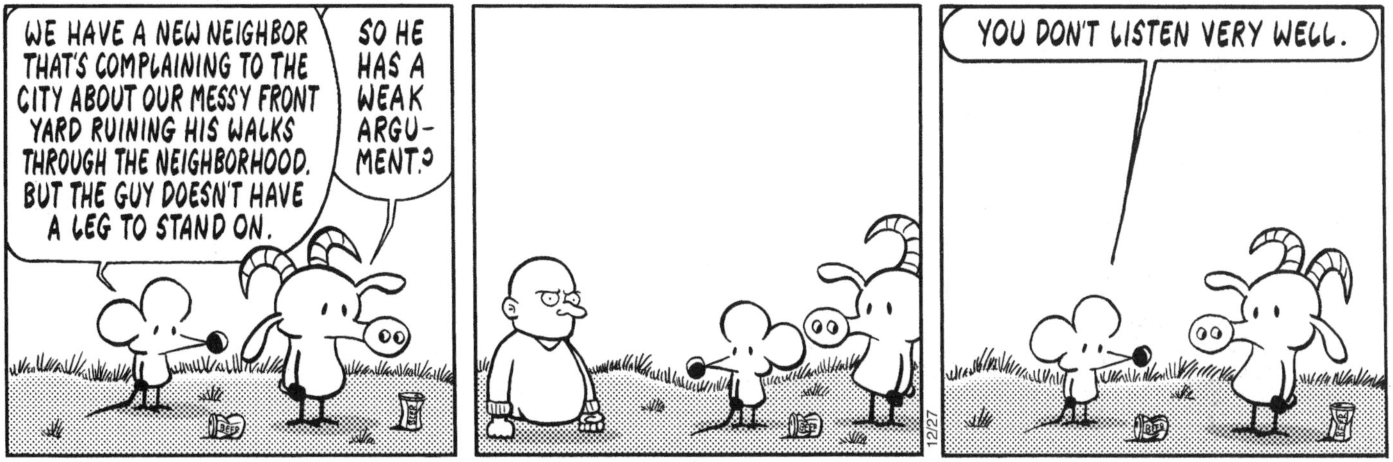
WE HAVE A NEW NEIGHBOR THAT'S COMPLAINING TO THE CITY ABOUT OUR MESSY FRONT YARD RUINING HIS WALKS THROUGH THE NEIGHBORHOOD. BUT THE GUY DOESN'T HAVE A LEG TO STAND ON.
SO HE HAS A WEAK ARGU-MENT?
12/27
YOU DON'T LISTEN VERY WELL.

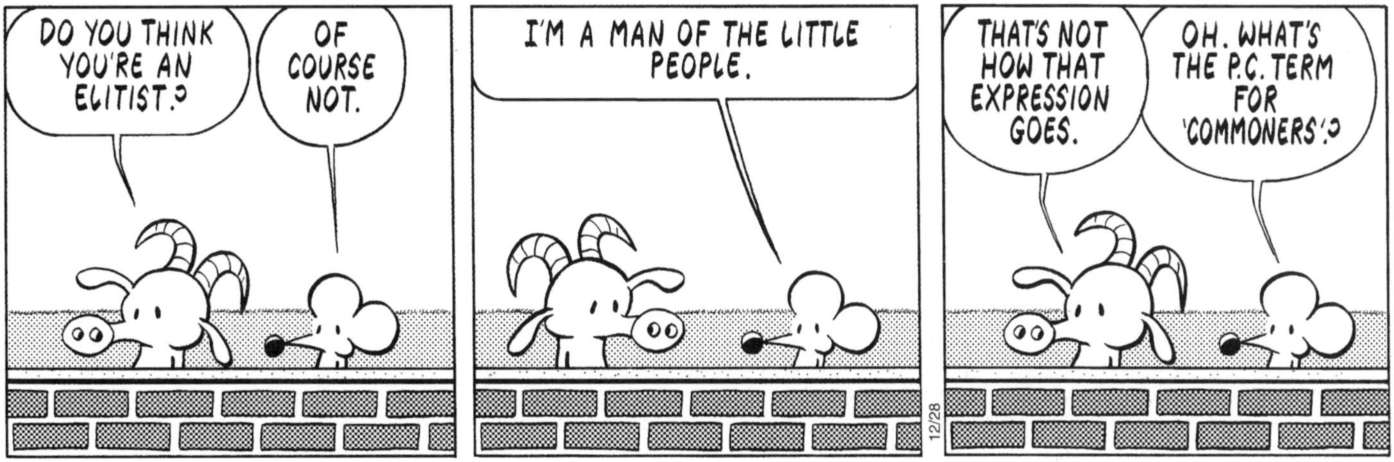
DO YOU THINK YOU'RE AN ELITIST?
OF COURSE NOT.
I'M A MAN OF THE LITTLE PEOPLE.
12/28
THAT'S NOT HOW THAT EXPRESSION GOES.
OH. WHAT'S THE P.C. TERM FOR 'COMMONERS'?

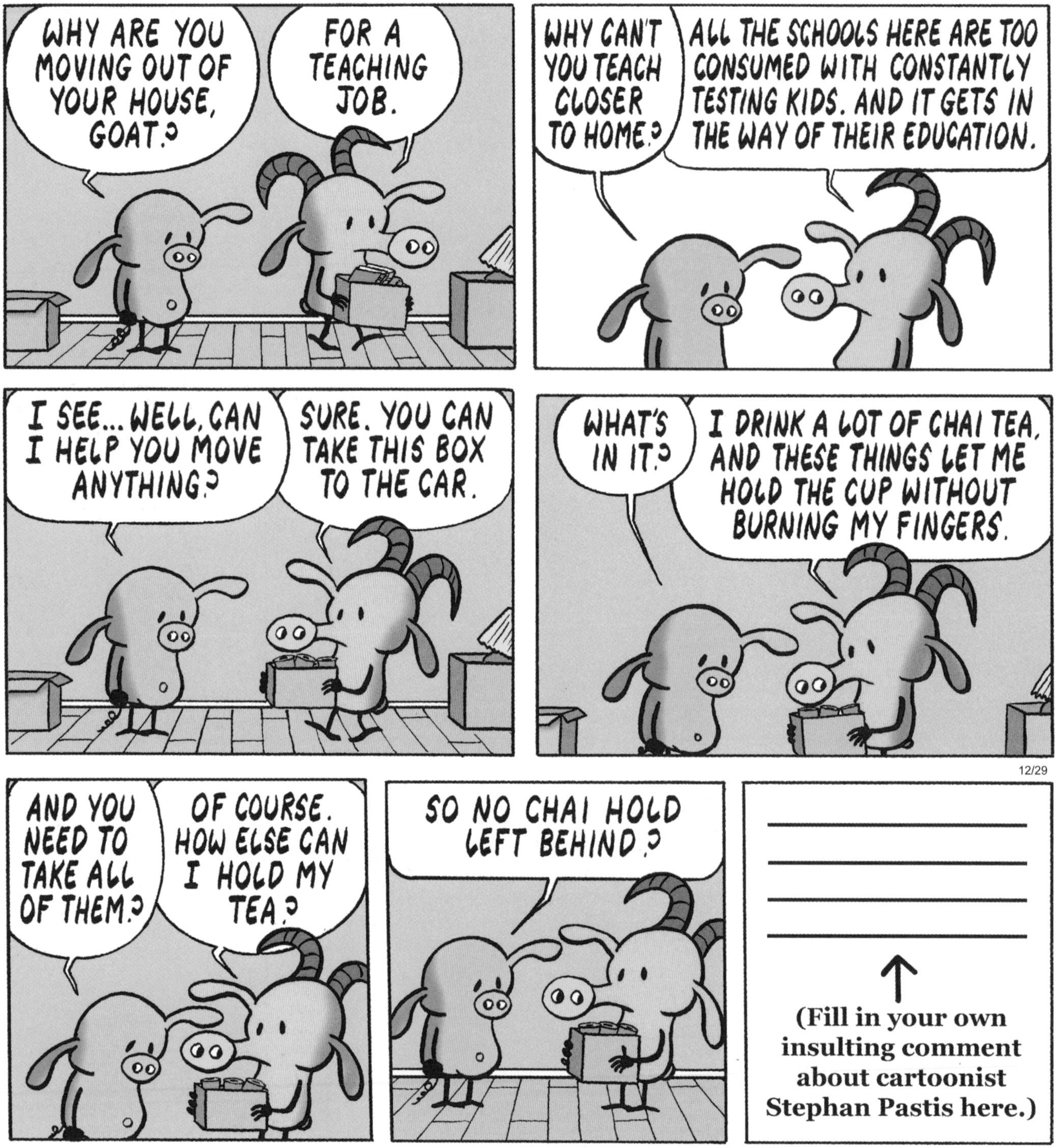
WHY ARE YOU MOVING OUT OF YOUR HOUSE, GOAT?
FOR A TEACHING JOB.
WHY CAN'T YOU TEACH CLOSER TO HOME?
ALL THE SCHOOLS HERE ARE TOO CONSUMED WITH CONSTANTLY TESTING KIDS. AND IT GETS IN THE WAY OF THEIR EDUCATION.
I SEE... WELL, CAN I HELP YOU MOVE ANYTHING?
SURE. YOU CAN TAKE THIS BOX TO THE CAR.
WHAT'S IN IT?
I DRINK A LOT OF CHAI TEA, AND THESE THINGS LET ME HOLD THE CUP WITHOUT BURNING MY FINGERS.
12/29
AND YOU NEED TO TAKE ALL OF THEM?
OF COURSE. HOW ELSE CAN I HOLD MY TEA?
SO NO CHAI HOLD LEFT BEHIND?
(Fill in your own insulting comment about cartoonist Stephan Pastis here.)

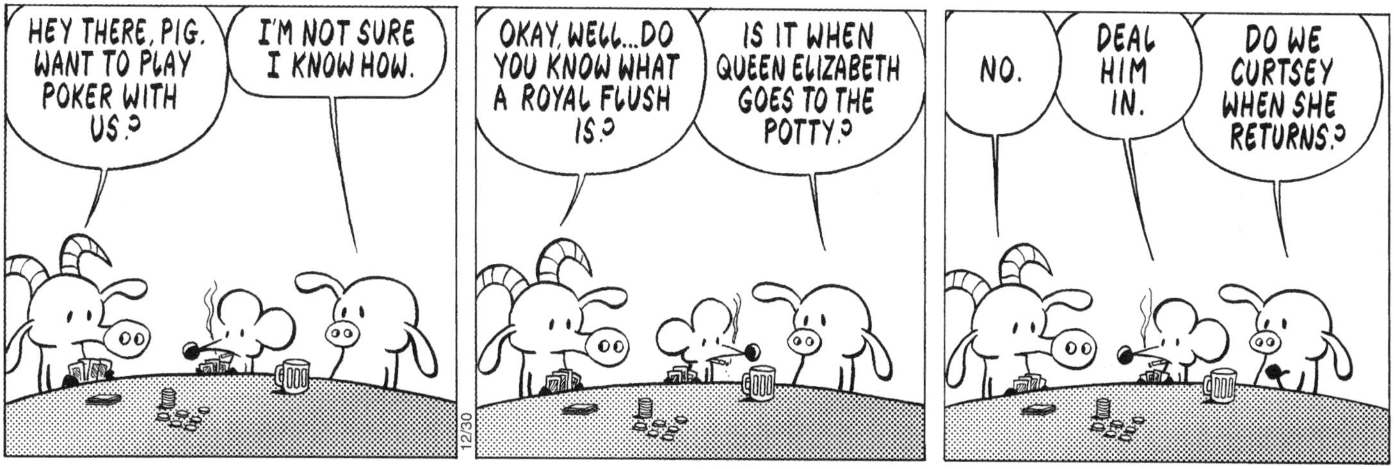
HEY THERE, PIG. WANT TO PLAY POKER WITH US?
I'M NOT SURE I KNOW HOW.
12/30
OKAY, WELL...DO YOU KNOW WHAT A ROYAL FLUSH IS?
IS IT WHEN QUEEN ELIZABETH GOES TO THE POTTY?
NO.
DEAL HIM IN.
DO WE CURTSEY WHEN SHE RETURNS?

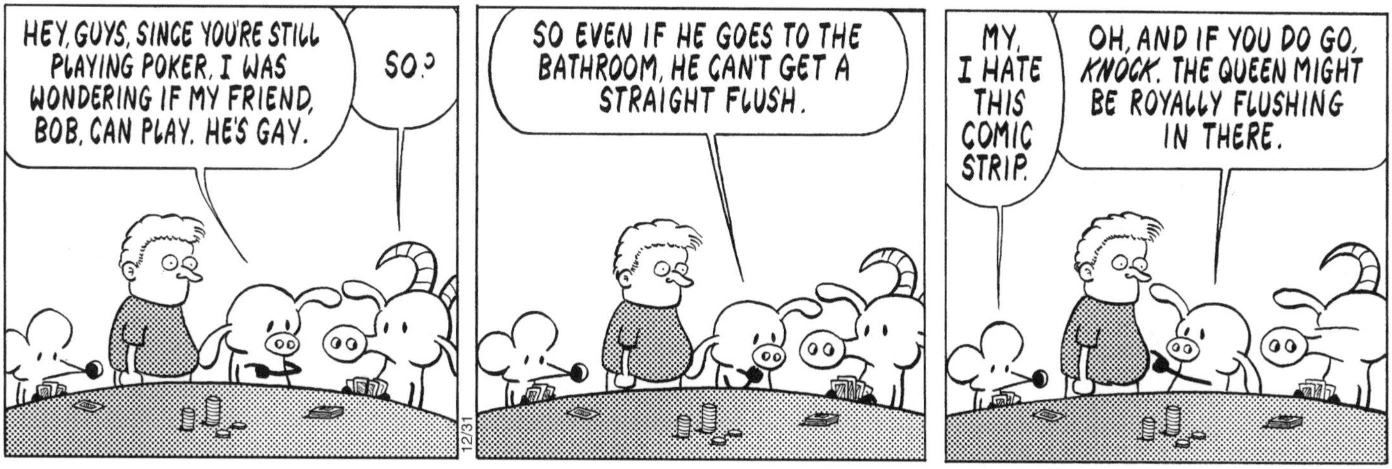
HEY, GUYS, SINCE YOU'RE STILL PLAYING POKER, I WAS WONDERING IF MY FRIEND, BOB, CAN PLAY. HE'S GAY.
SO?
12/31
SO EVEN IF HE GOES TO THE BATHROOM, HE CAN'T GET A STRAIGHT FLUSH.
MY, I HATE THIS COMIC STRIP.
OH, AND IF YOU DO GO, *KNOCK*. THE QUEEN MIGHT BE ROYALLY FLUSHING IN THERE.

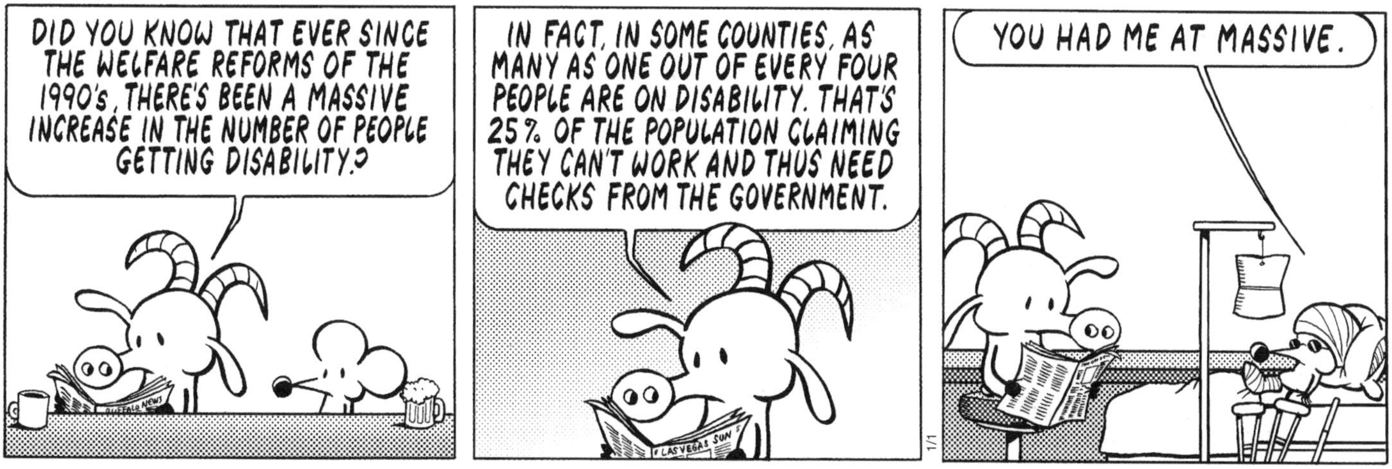
DID YOU KNOW THAT EVER SINCE THE WELFARE REFORMS OF THE 1990's, THERE'S BEEN A MASSIVE INCREASE IN THE NUMBER OF PEOPLE GETTING DISABILITY?
BUFFALO NEWS
IN FACT, IN SOME COUNTIES, AS MANY AS ONE OUT OF EVERY FOUR PEOPLE ARE ON DISABILITY. THAT'S 25% OF THE POPULATION CLAIMING THEY CAN'T WORK AND THUS NEED CHECKS FROM THE GOVERNMENT.
LAS VEGAS SUN
1/1
YOU HAD ME AT MASSIVE.

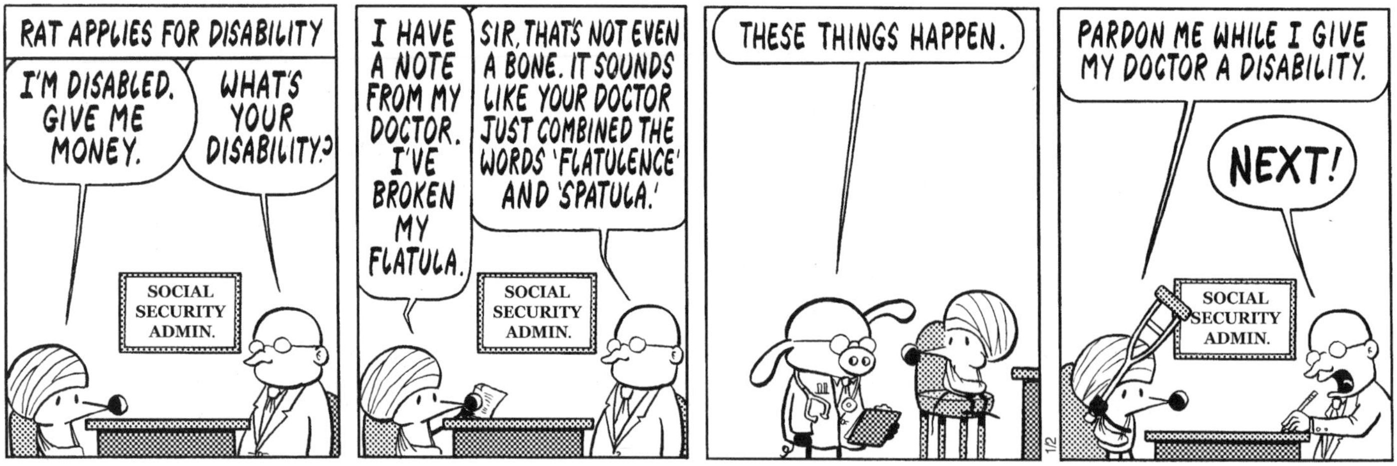
RAT APPLIES FOR DISABILITY
I'M DISABLED. GIVE ME MONEY.
WHAT'S YOUR DISABILITY?
SOCIAL SECURITY ADMIN.
I HAVE A NOTE FROM MY DOCTOR. I'VE BROKEN MY FLATULA.
SIR, THAT'S NOT EVEN A BONE. IT SOUNDS LIKE YOUR DOCTOR JUST COMBINED THE WORDS 'FLATULENCE' AND 'SPATULA.'
SOCIAL SECURITY ADMIN.
THESE THINGS HAPPEN.
1/2
PARDON ME WHILE I GIVE MY DOCTOR A DISABILITY.
NEXT!
SOCIAL SECURITY ADMIN.

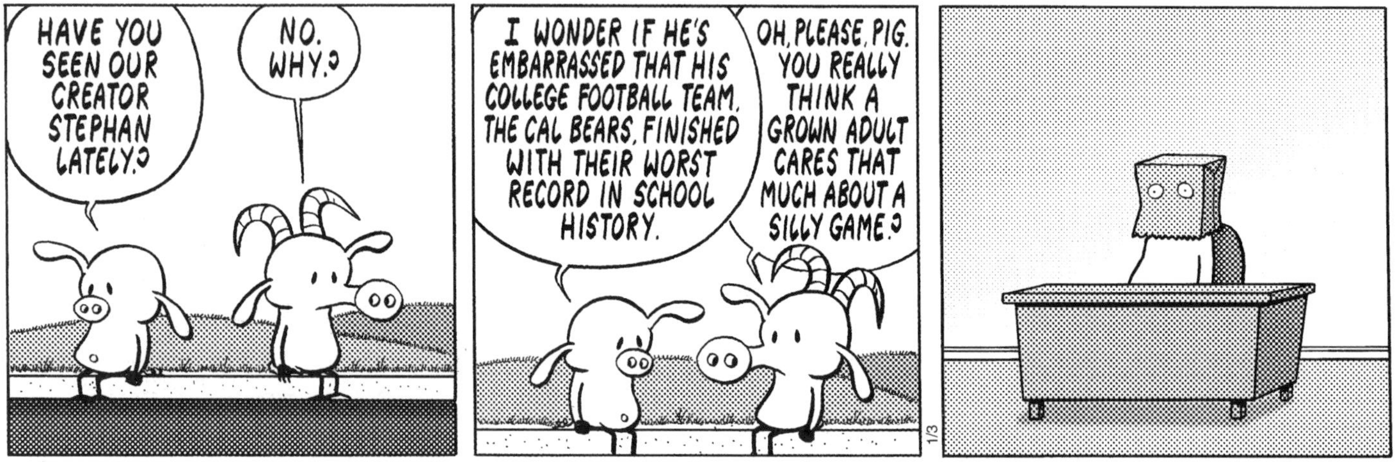
HAVE YOU SEEN OUR CREATOR STEPHAN LATELY?
NO. WHY?
I WONDER IF HE'S EMBARRASSED THAT HIS COLLEGE FOOTBALL TEAM, THE CAL BEARS, FINISHED WITH THEIR WORST RECORD IN SCHOOL HISTORY.
OH, PLEASE, PIG. YOU REALLY THINK A GROWN ADULT CARES THAT MUCH ABOUT A SILLY GAME?
1/3

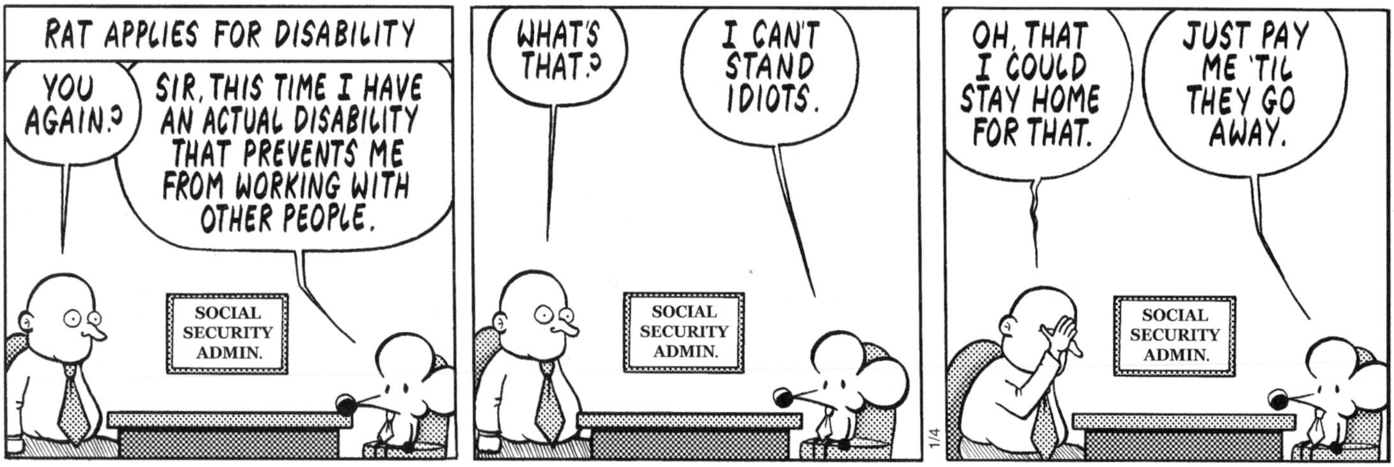
RAT APPLIES FOR DISABILITY
YOU AGAIN?
SIR, THIS TIME I HAVE AN ACTUAL DISABILITY THAT PREVENTS ME FROM WORKING WITH OTHER PEOPLE.
SOCIAL SECURITY ADMIN.
WHAT'S THAT?
I CAN'T STAND IDIOTS.
SOCIAL SECURITY ADMIN.
1/4
OH, THAT I COULD STAY HOME FOR THAT.
JUST PAY ME 'TIL THEY GO AWAY.
SOCIAL SECURITY ADMIN.

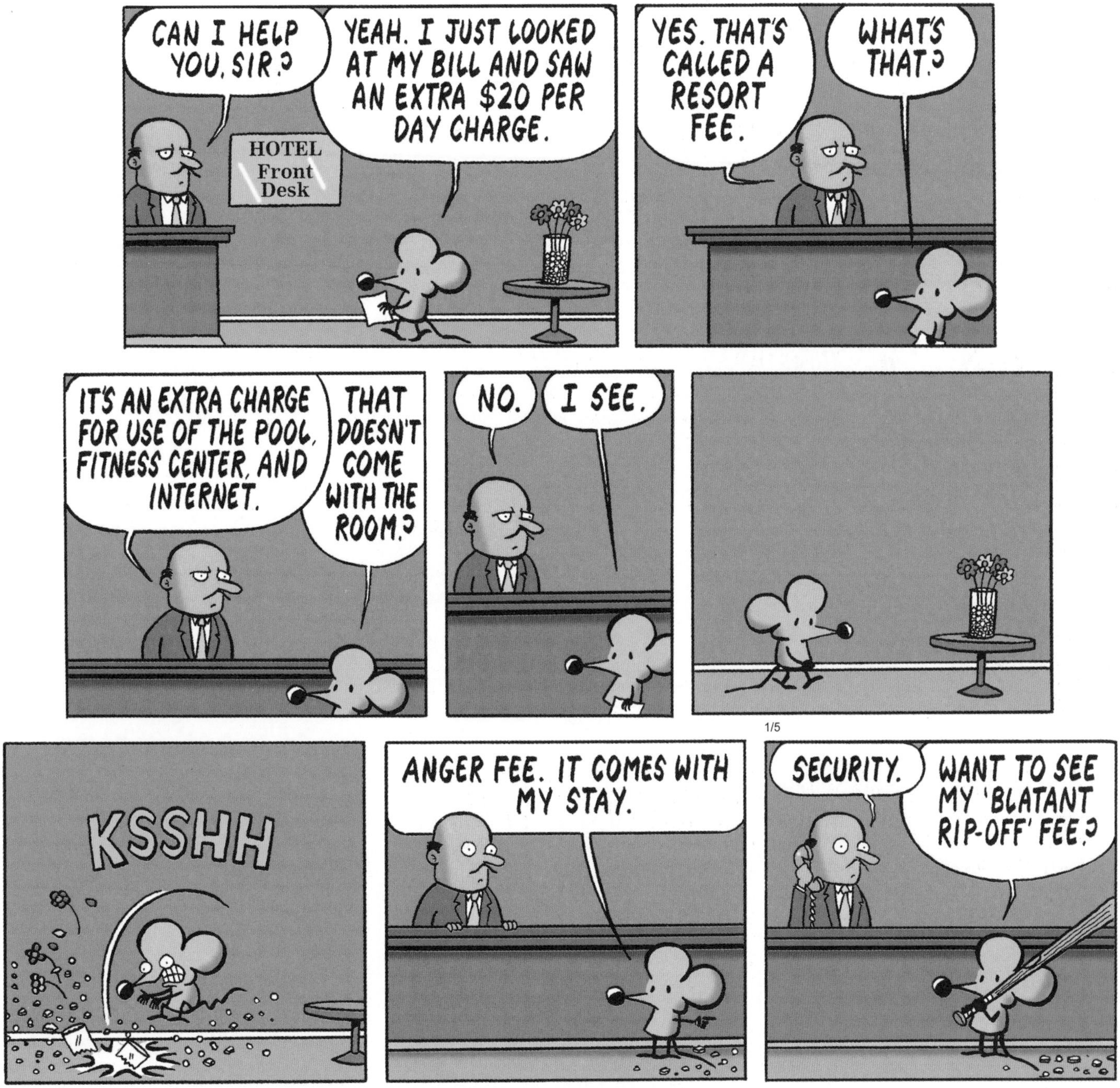
CAN I HELP YOU, SIR?
YEAH. I JUST LOOKED AT MY BILL AND SAW AN EXTRA $20 PER DAY CHARGE.
HOTEL Front Desk
YES. THAT'S CALLED A RESORT FEE.
WHAT'S THAT?
IT'S AN EXTRA CHARGE FOR USE OF THE POOL, FITNESS CENTER, AND INTERNET.
THAT DOESN'T COME WITH THE ROOM?
NO.
I SEE.
1/5
KSSHH
ANGER FEE. IT COMES WITH MY STAY.
SECURITY.
WANT TO SEE MY 'BLATANT RIP-OFF' FEE?

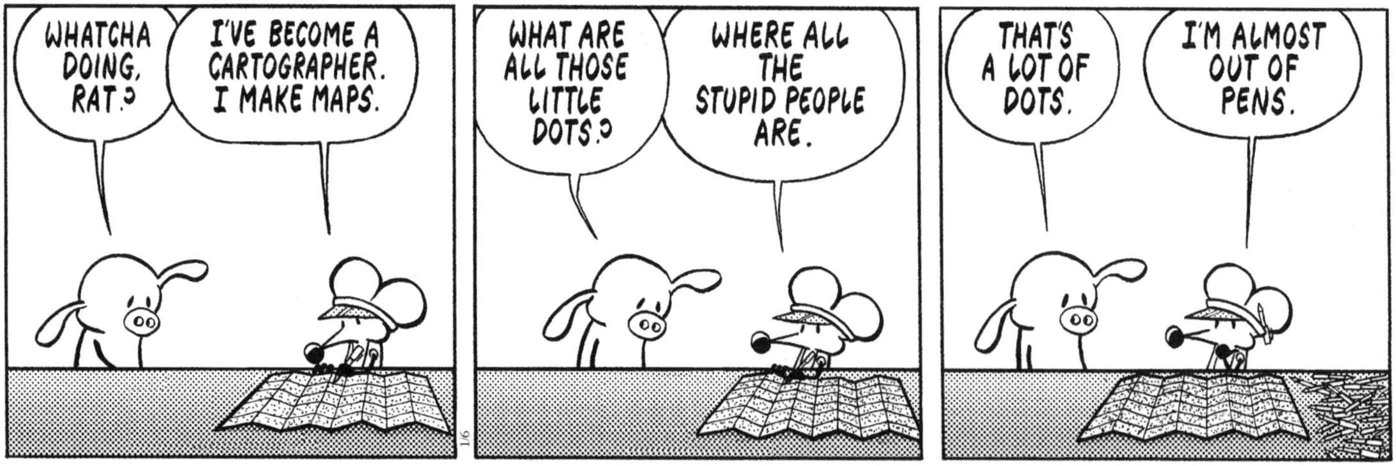
WHATCHA DOING, RAT?
I'VE BECOME A CARTOGRAPHER. I MAKE MAPS.
WHAT ARE ALL THOSE LITTLE DOTS?
WHERE ALL THE STUPID PEOPLE ARE.
THAT'S A LOT OF DOTS.
I'M ALMOST OUT OF PENS.

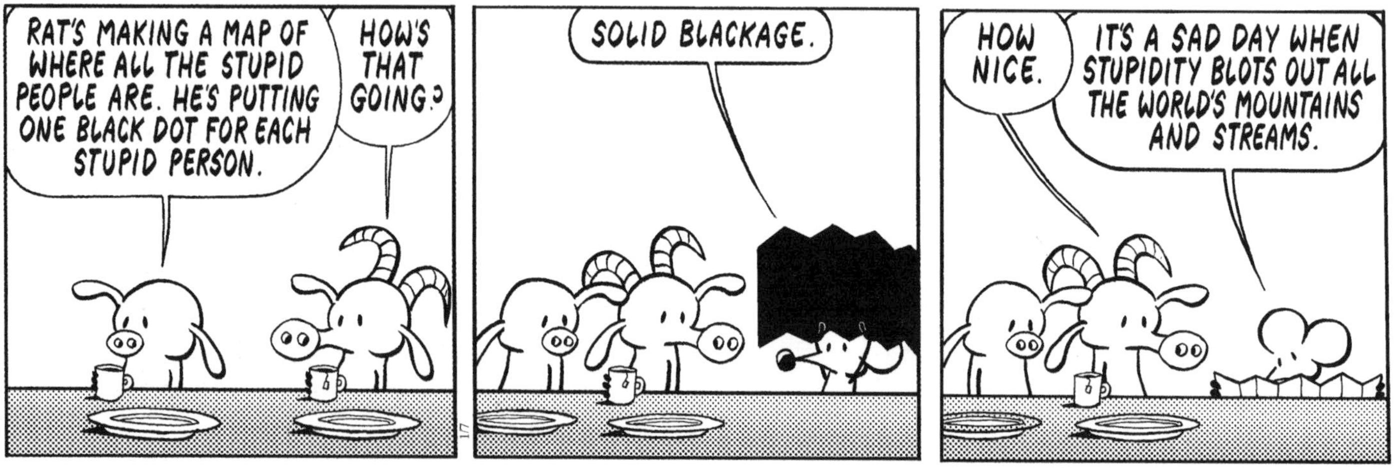
RAT'S MAKING A MAP OF WHERE ALL THE STUPID PEOPLE ARE. HE'S PUTTING ONE BLACK DOT FOR EACH STUPID PERSON.
HOW'S THAT GOING?
SOLID BLACKAGE.
HOW NICE.
IT'S A SAD DAY WHEN STUPIDITY BLOTS OUT ALL THE WORLD'S MOUNTAINS AND STREAMS.

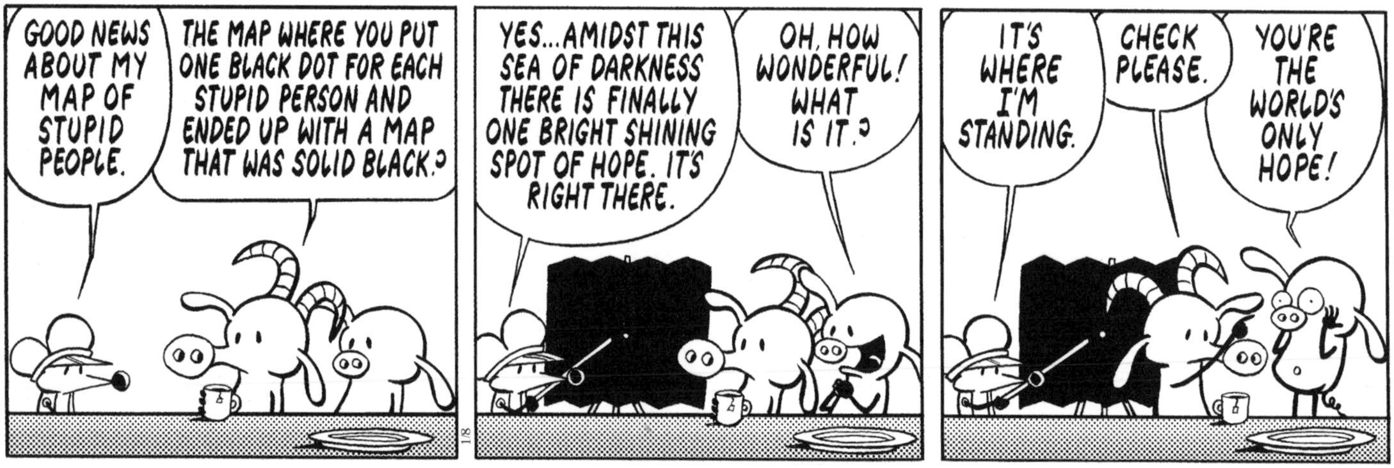
GOOD NEWS ABOUT MY MAP OF STUPID PEOPLE.
THE MAP WHERE YOU PUT ONE BLACK DOT FOR EACH STUPID PERSON AND ENDED UP WITH A MAP THAT WAS SOLID BLACK?
YES...AMIDST THIS SEA OF DARKNESS THERE IS FINALLY ONE BRIGHT SHINING SPOT OF HOPE. IT'S RIGHT THERE.
OH, HOW WONDERFUL! WHAT IS IT?
IT'S WHERE I'M STANDING.
CHECK PLEASE.
YOU'RE THE WORLD'S ONLY HOPE!

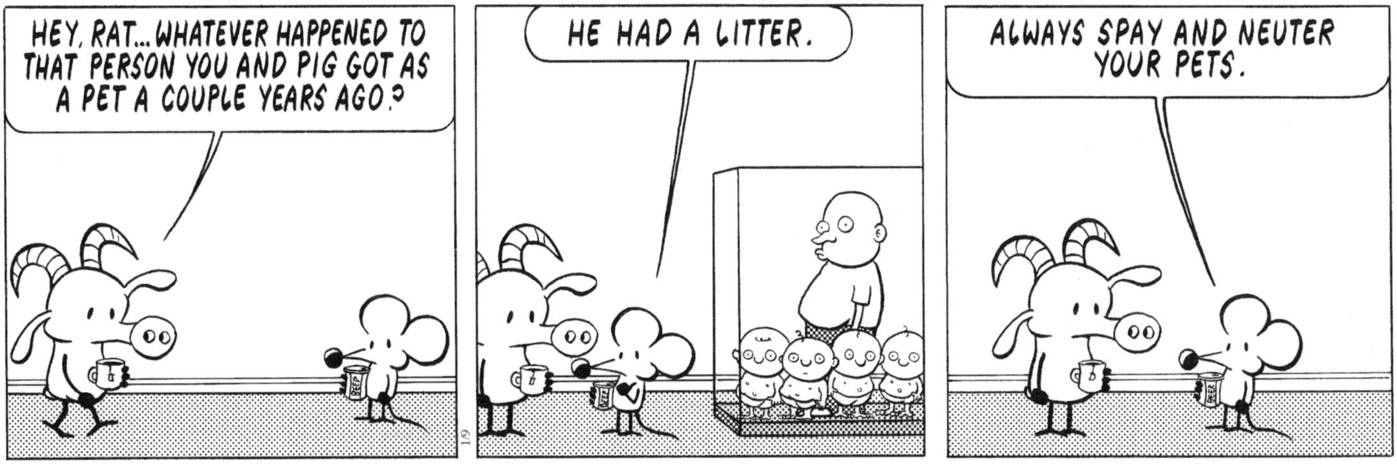
HEY, RAT...WHATEVER HAPPENED TO THAT PERSON YOU AND PIG GOT AS A PET A COUPLE YEARS AGO?
HE HAD A LITTER.
ALWAYS SPAY AND NEUTER YOUR PETS.
1/9

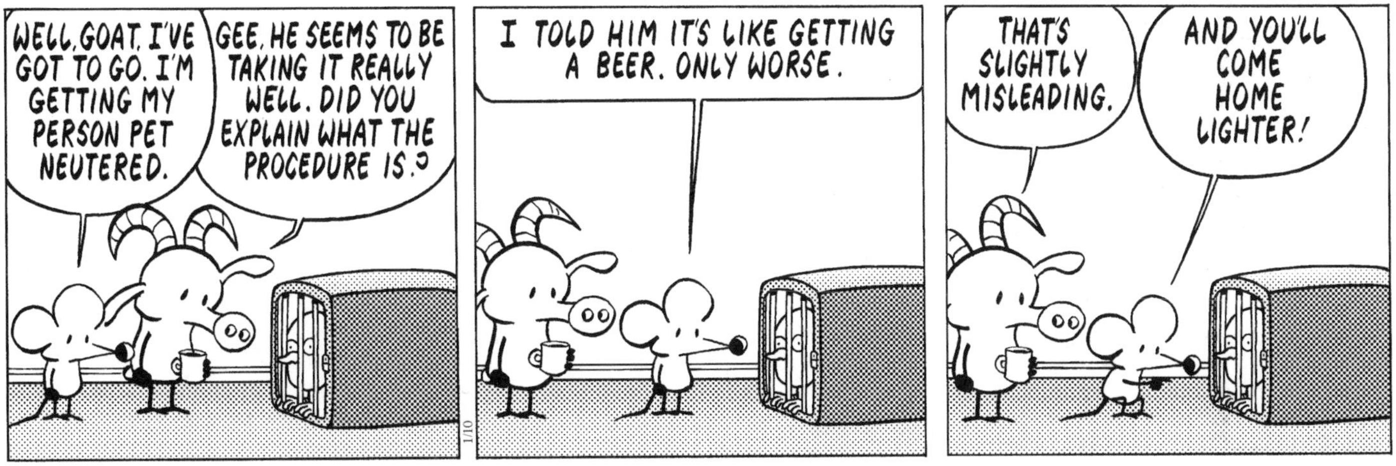
WELL, GOAT, I'VE GOT TO GO. I'M GETTING MY PERSON PET NEUTERED.
GEE, HE SEEMS TO BE TAKING IT REALLY WELL. DID YOU EXPLAIN WHAT THE PROCEDURE IS?
I TOLD HIM IT'S LIKE GETTING A BEER. ONLY WORSE.
THAT'S SLIGHTLY MISLEADING.
AND YOU'LL COME HOME LIGHTER!
1/10

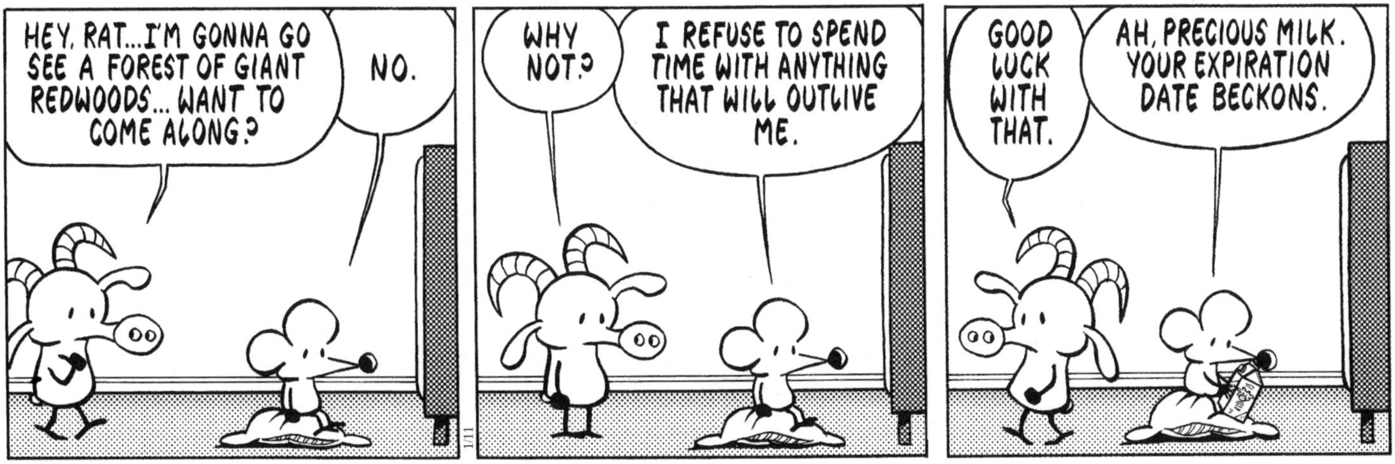
HEY, RAT...I'M GONNA GO SEE A FOREST OF GIANT REDWOODS... WANT TO COME ALONG?
NO.
WHY NOT?
I REFUSE TO SPEND TIME WITH ANYTHING THAT WILL OUTLIVE ME.
GOOD LUCK WITH THAT.
AH, PRECIOUS MILK. YOUR EXPIRATION DATE BECKONS.
1/11

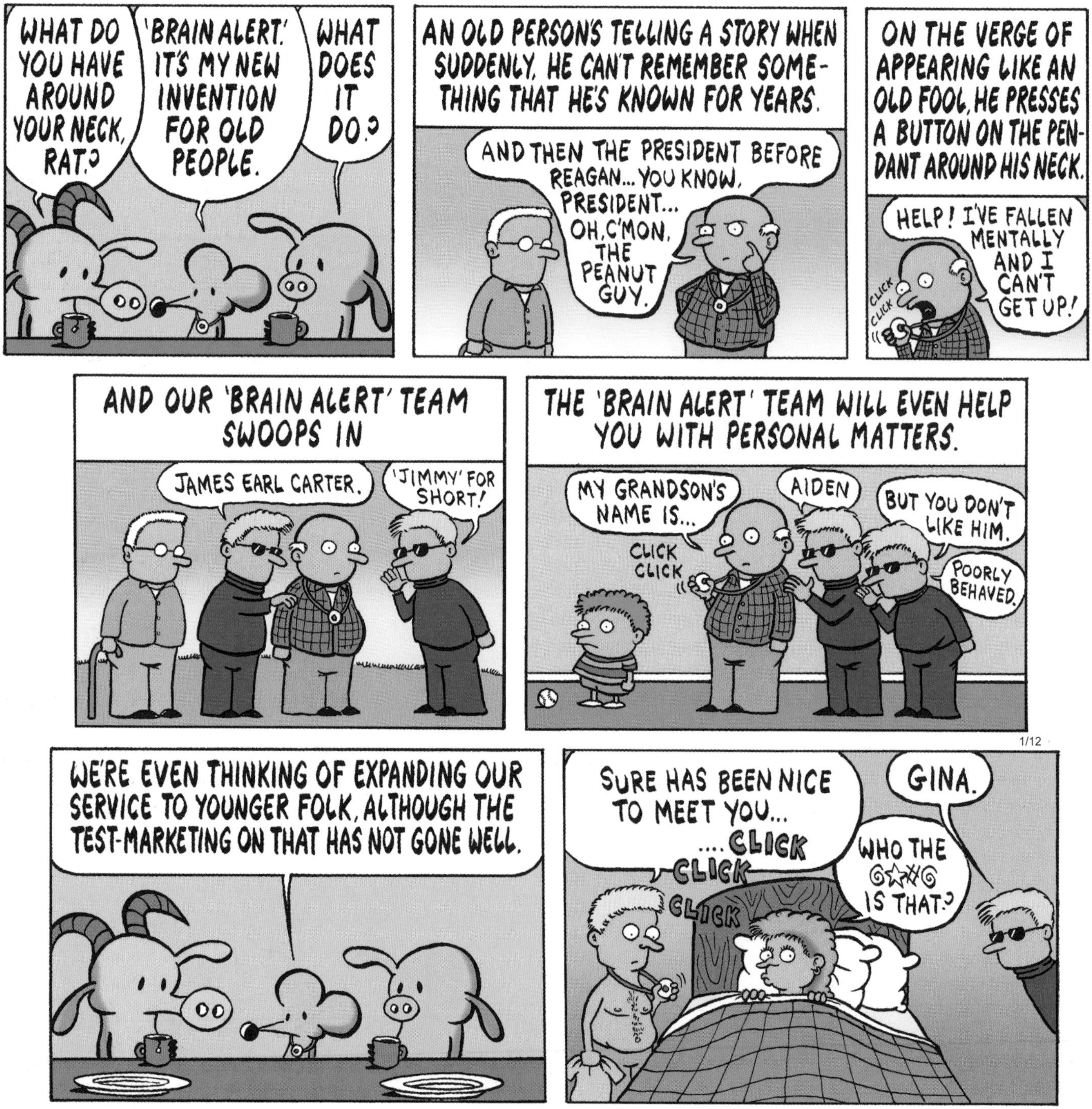
WHAT DO YOU HAVE AROUND YOUR NECK, RAT?
'BRAIN ALERT.' IT'S MY NEW INVENTION FOR OLD PEOPLE.
WHAT DOES IT DO?
AN OLD PERSON'S TELLING A STORY WHEN SUDDENLY, HE CAN'T REMEMBER SOMETHING THAT HE'S KNOWN FOR YEARS.
AND THEN THE PRESIDENT BEFORE REAGAN... YOU KNOW, PRESIDENT... OH, C'MON, THE PEANUT GUY.
ON THE VERGE OF APPEARING LIKE AN OLD FOOL, HE PRESSES A BUTTON ON THE PENDANT AROUND HIS NECK.
CLICK CLICK
HELP! I'VE FALLEN MENTALLY AND I CAN'T GET UP!
AND OUR 'BRAIN ALERT' TEAM SWOOPS IN
JAMES EARL CARTER.
'JIMMY' FOR SHORT!
THE 'BRAIN ALERT' TEAM WILL EVEN HELP YOU WITH PERSONAL MATTERS.
MY GRANDSON'S NAME IS...
CLICK CLICK
AIDEN
BUT YOU DON'T LIKE HIM.
POORLY BEHAVED.
1/12
WE'RE EVEN THINKING OF EXPANDING OUR SERVICE TO YOUNGER FOLK, ALTHOUGH THE TEST-MARKETING ON THAT HAS NOT GONE WELL.
SURE HAS BEEN NICE TO MEET YOU... ....CLICK
CLICK
CLICK
GINA.
WHO THE @☆#@ IS THAT?

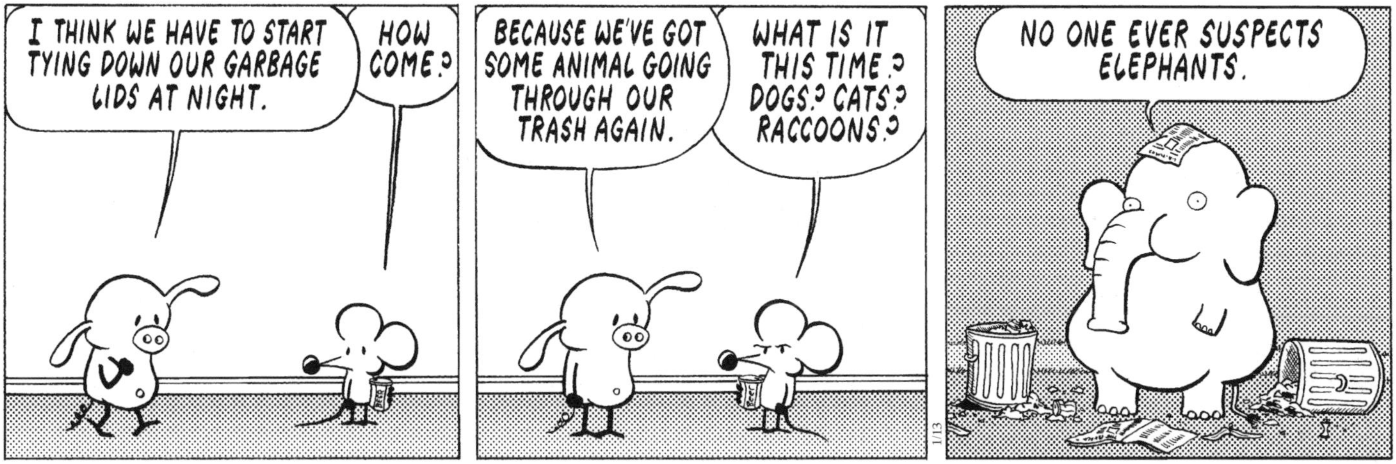
I THINK WE HAVE TO START TYING DOWN OUR GARBAGE LIDS AT NIGHT.
HOW COME?
BECAUSE WE'VE GOT SOME ANIMAL GOING THROUGH OUR TRASH AGAIN.
WHAT IS IT THIS TIME? DOGS? CATS? RACCOONS?
NO ONE EVER SUSPECTS ELEPHANTS.
1/13

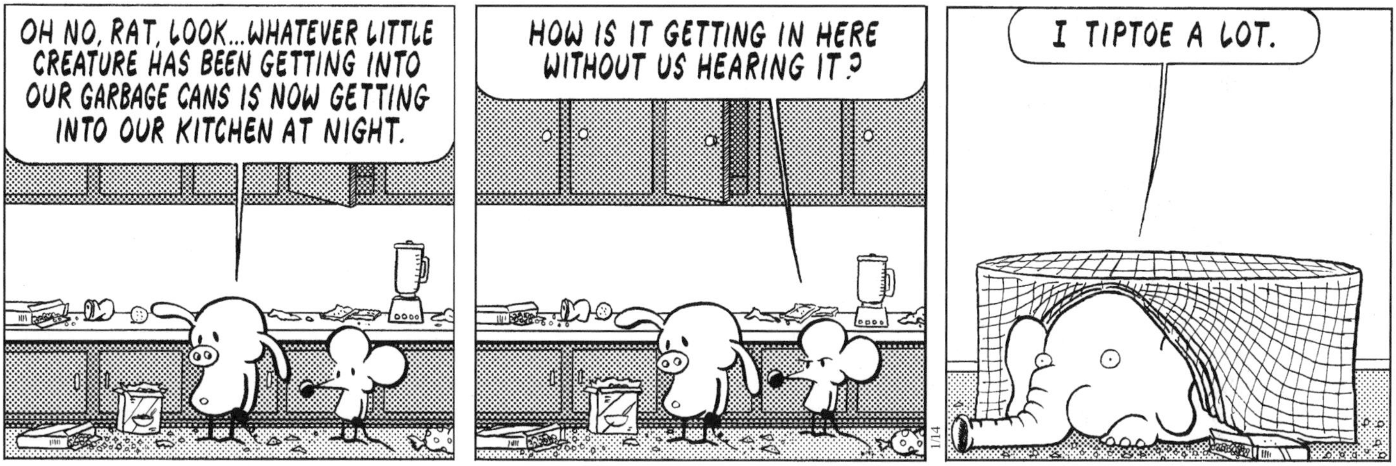
OH NO, RAT, LOOK...WHATEVER LITTLE CREATURE HAS BEEN GETTING INTO OUR GARBAGE CANS IS NOW GETTING INTO OUR KITCHEN AT NIGHT.
HOW IS IT GETTING IN HERE WITHOUT US HEARING IT?
I TIPTOE A LOT.
1/14

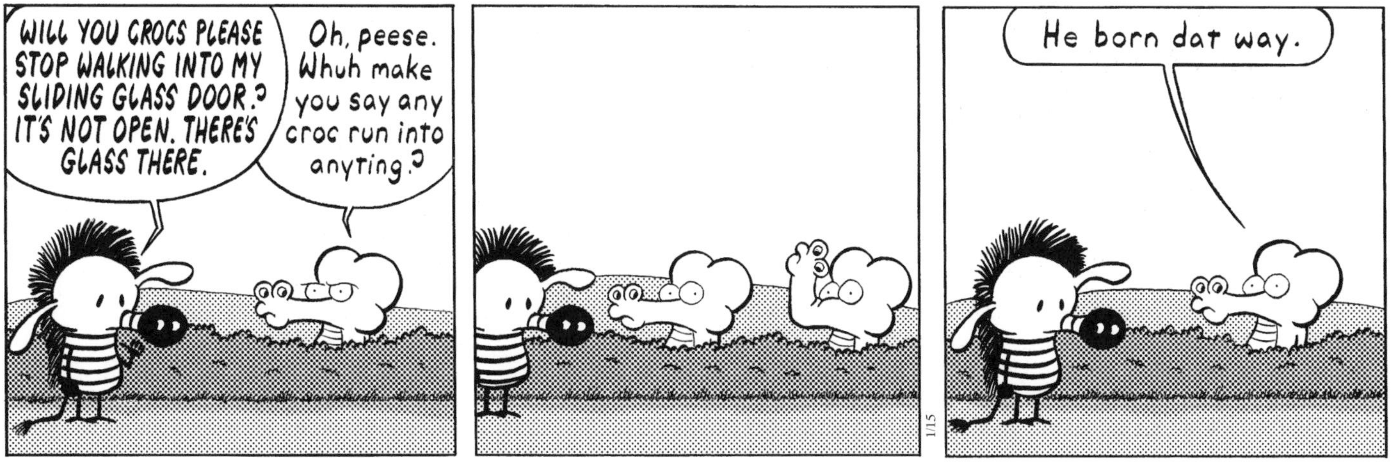
WILL YOU CROCS PLEASE STOP WALKING INTO MY SLIDING GLASS DOOR? IT'S NOT OPEN. THERE'S GLASS THERE.
Oh, peese. Whuh make you say any croc run into anyting?
He born dat way.
1/15

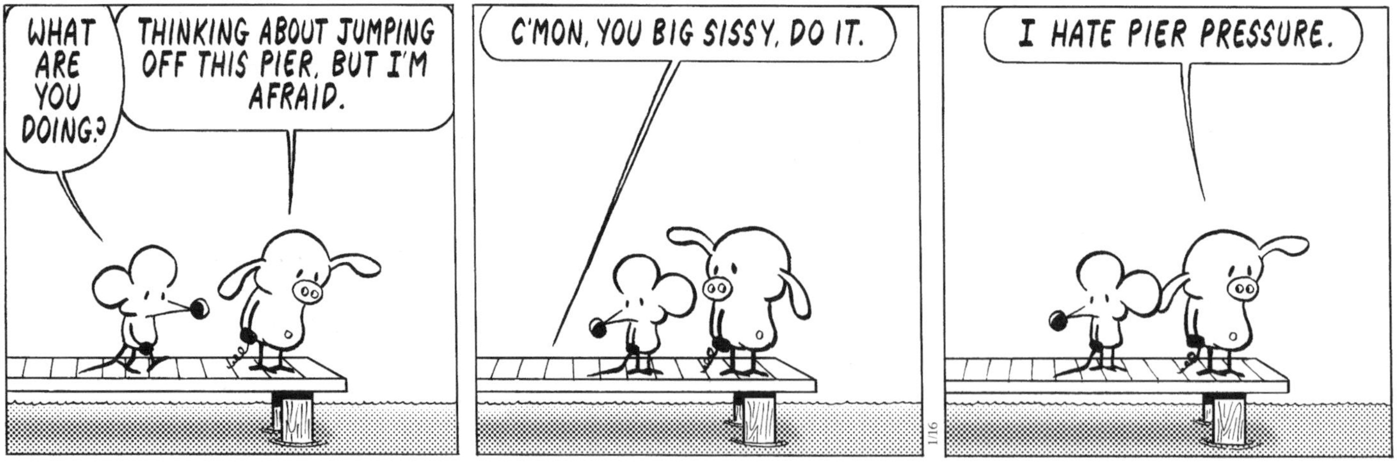
WHAT ARE YOU DOING?
THINKING ABOUT JUMPING OFF THIS PIER, BUT I'M AFRAID.
C'MON, YOU BIG SISSY, DO IT.
I HATE PIER PRESSURE.
1/16

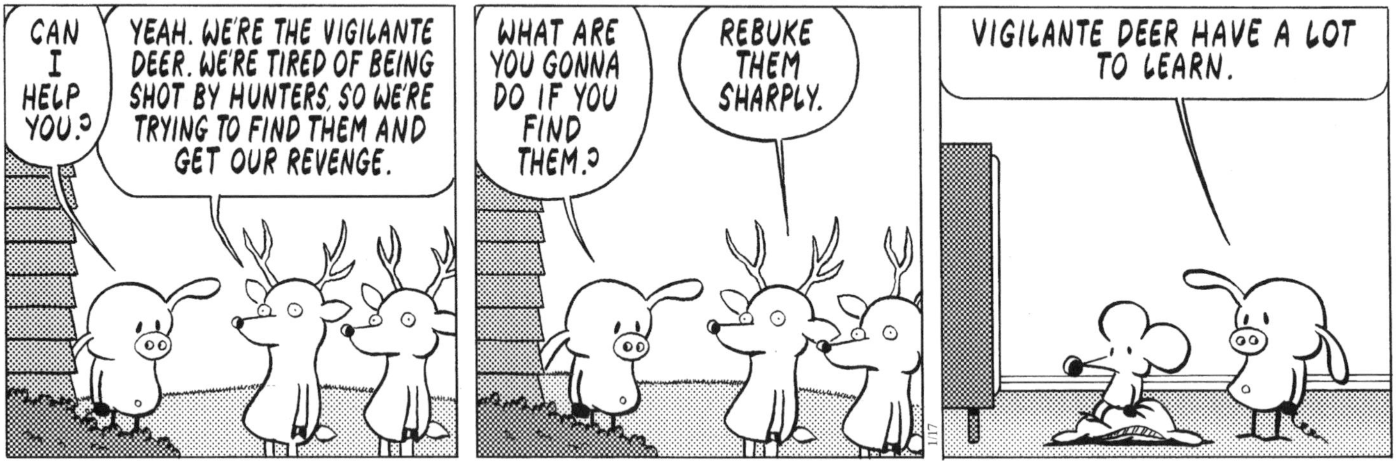
CAN I HELP YOU?
YEAH. WE'RE THE VIGILANTE DEER. WE'RE TIRED OF BEING SHOT BY HUNTERS, SO WE'RE TRYING TO FIND THEM AND GET OUR REVENGE.
WHAT ARE YOU GONNA DO IF YOU FIND THEM?
REBUKE THEM SHARPLY.
VIGILANTE DEER HAVE A LOT TO LEARN.
1/17

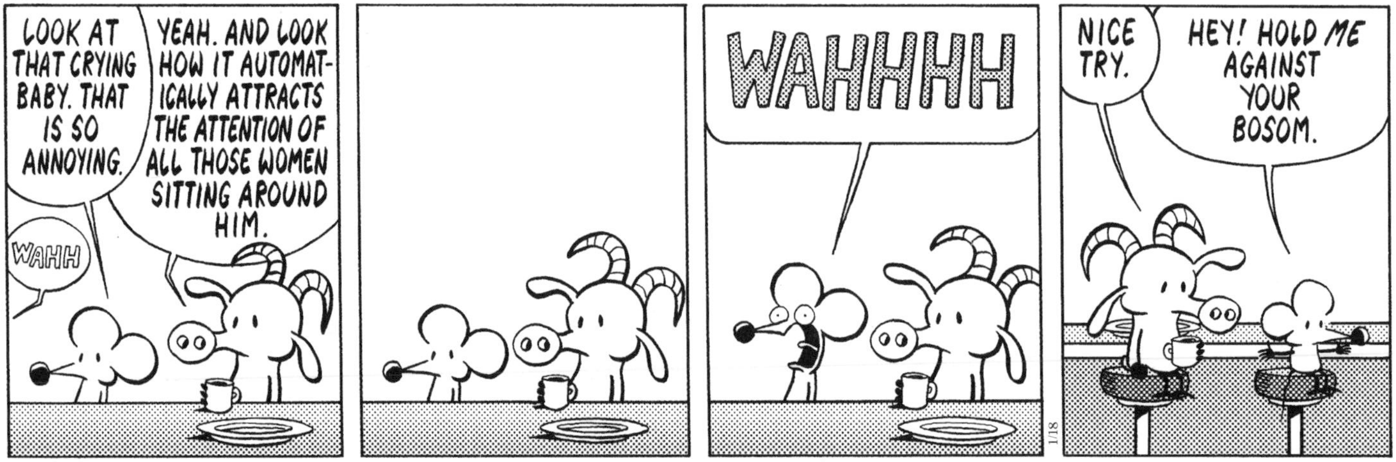
LOOK AT THAT CRYING BABY. THAT IS SO ANNOYING.
YEAH. AND LOOK HOW IT AUTOMATICALLY ATTRACTS THE ATTENTION OF ALL THOSE WOMEN SITTING AROUND HIM.
WAHH
WAHHHH
NICE TRY.
HEY! HOLD *ME* AGAINST YOUR BOSOM.
1/18

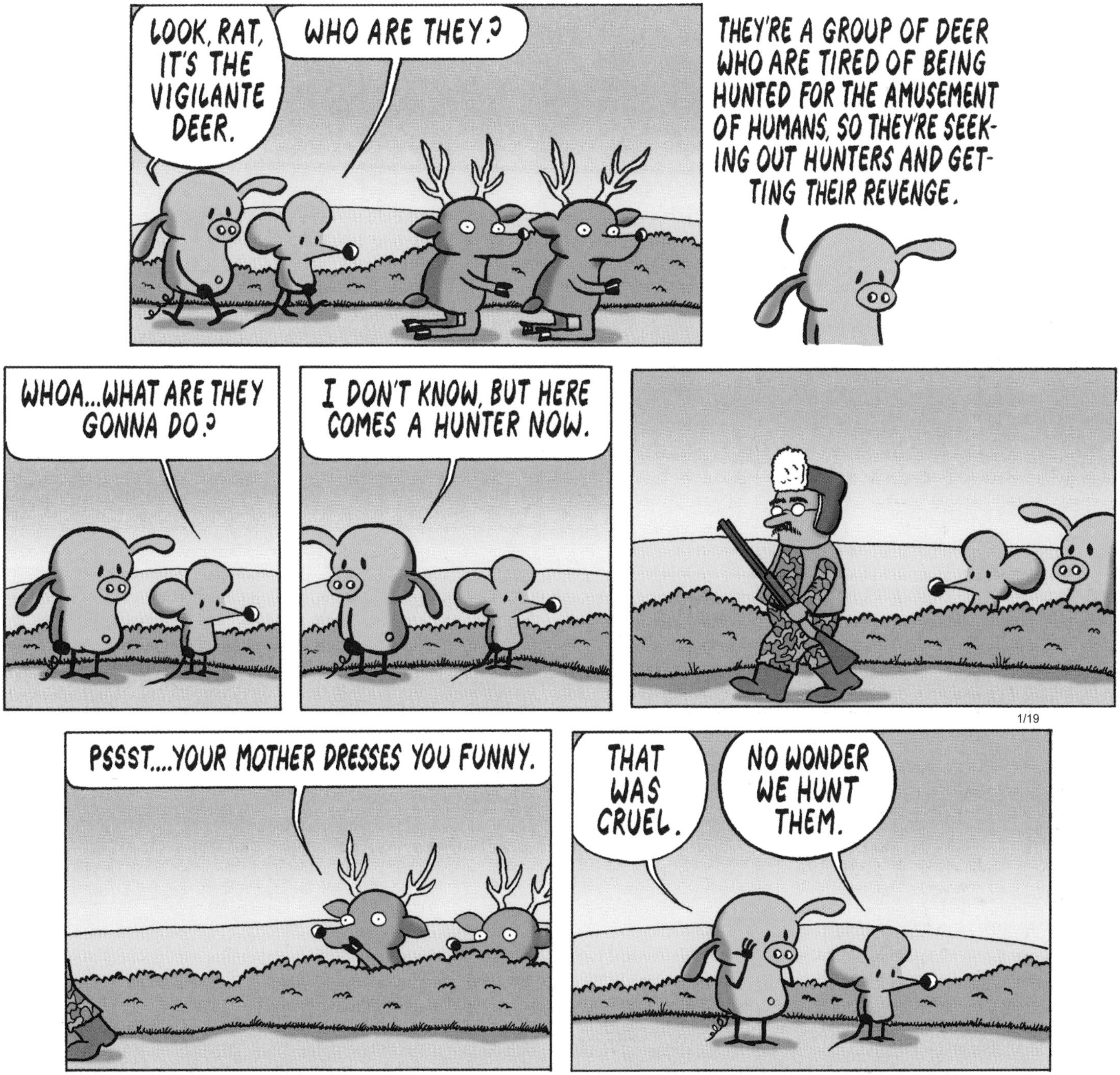
LOOK, RAT, IT'S THE VIGILANTE DEER.
WHO ARE THEY?
THEY'RE A GROUP OF DEER WHO ARE TIRED OF BEING HUNTED FOR THE AMUSEMENT OF HUMANS, SO THEY'RE SEEKING OUT HUNTERS AND GETTING THEIR REVENGE.
WHOA...WHAT ARE THEY GONNA DO?
I DON'T KNOW, BUT HERE COMES A HUNTER NOW.
1/19
PSSST....YOUR MOTHER DRESSES YOU FUNNY.
THAT WAS CRUEL.
NO WONDER WE HUNT THEM.

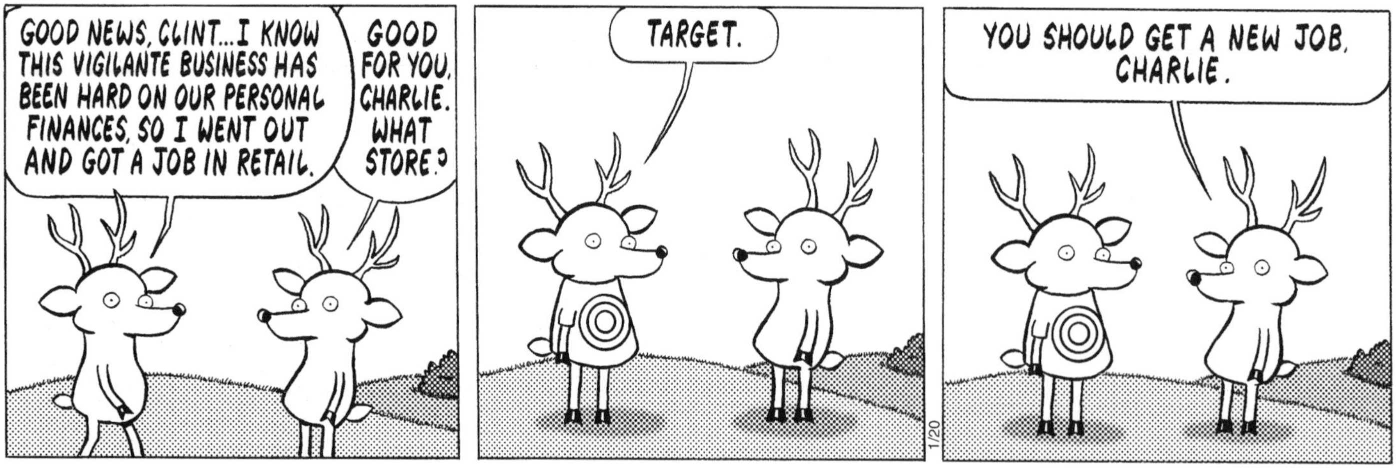
GOOD NEWS, CLINT...I KNOW THIS VIGILANTE BUSINESS HAS BEEN HARD ON OUR PERSONAL FINANCES, SO I WENT OUT AND GOT A JOB IN RETAIL.
GOOD FOR YOU, CHARLIE. WHAT STORE?
TARGET.
1/20
YOU SHOULD GET A NEW JOB, CHARLIE.

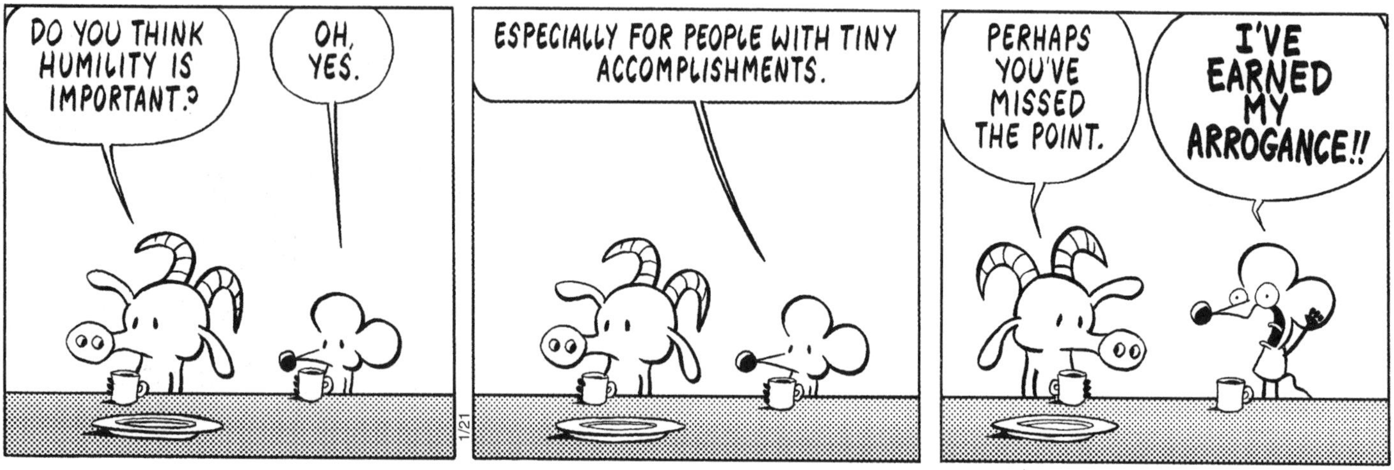
DO YOU THINK HUMILITY IS IMPORTANT?
OH, YES.
1/21
ESPECIALLY FOR PEOPLE WITH TINY ACCOMPLISHMENTS.
PERHAPS YOU'VE MISSED THE POINT.
I'VE EARNED MY ARROGANCE!!

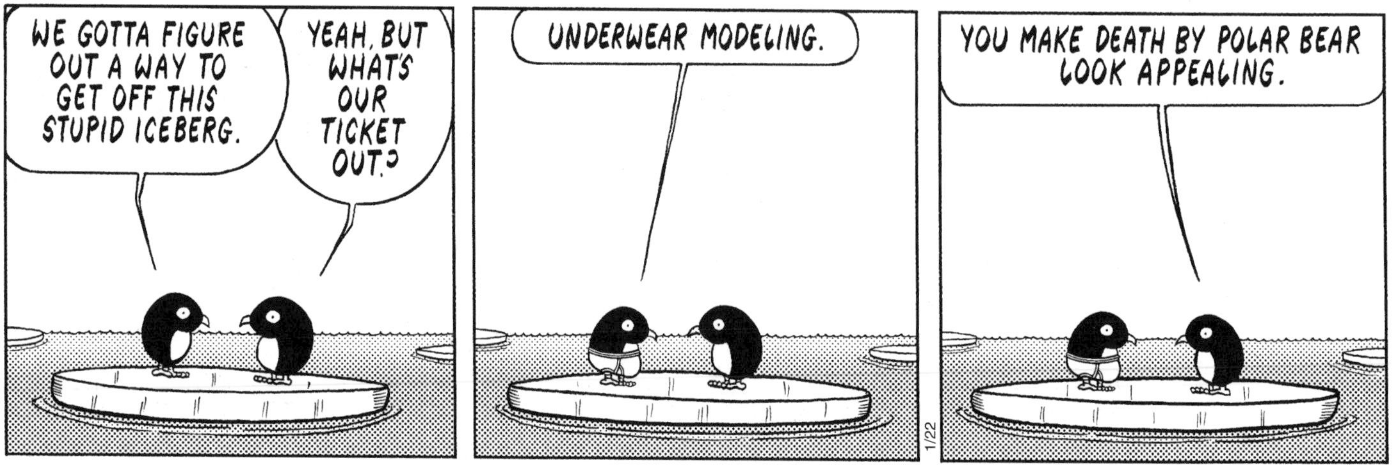
WE GOTTA FIGURE OUT A WAY TO GET OFF THIS STUPID ICEBERG.
YEAH, BUT WHAT'S OUR TICKET OUT?
UNDERWEAR MODELING.
1/22
YOU MAKE DEATH BY POLAR BEAR LOOK APPEALING.

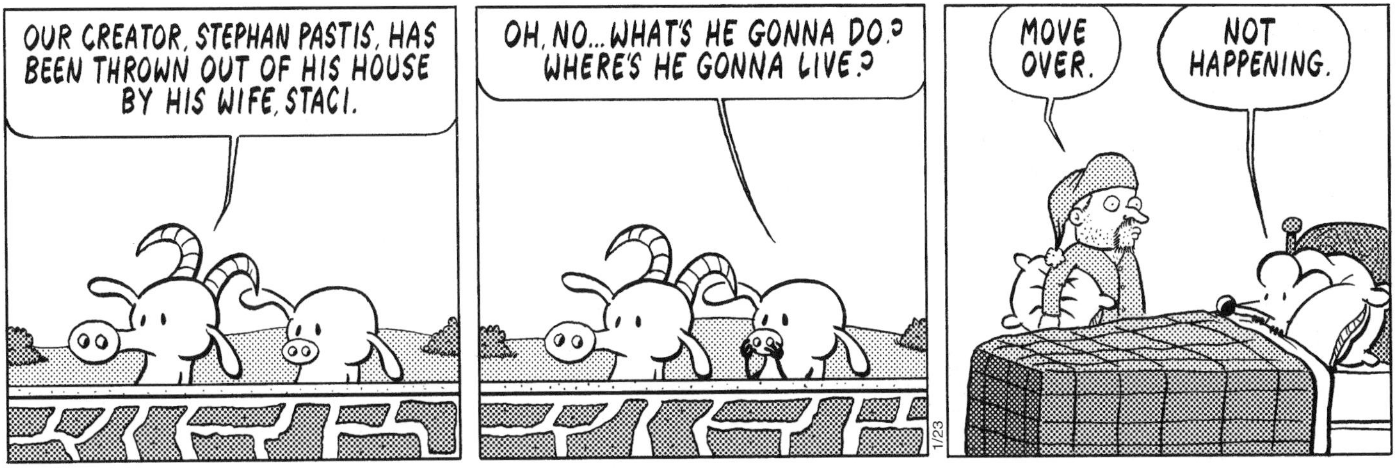
OUR CREATOR, STEPHAN PASTIS, HAS BEEN THROWN OUT OF HIS HOUSE BY HIS WIFE, STACI.
OH, NO... WHAT'S HE GONNA DO? WHERE'S HE GONNA LIVE?
MOVE OVER.
NOT HAPPENING.
1/23

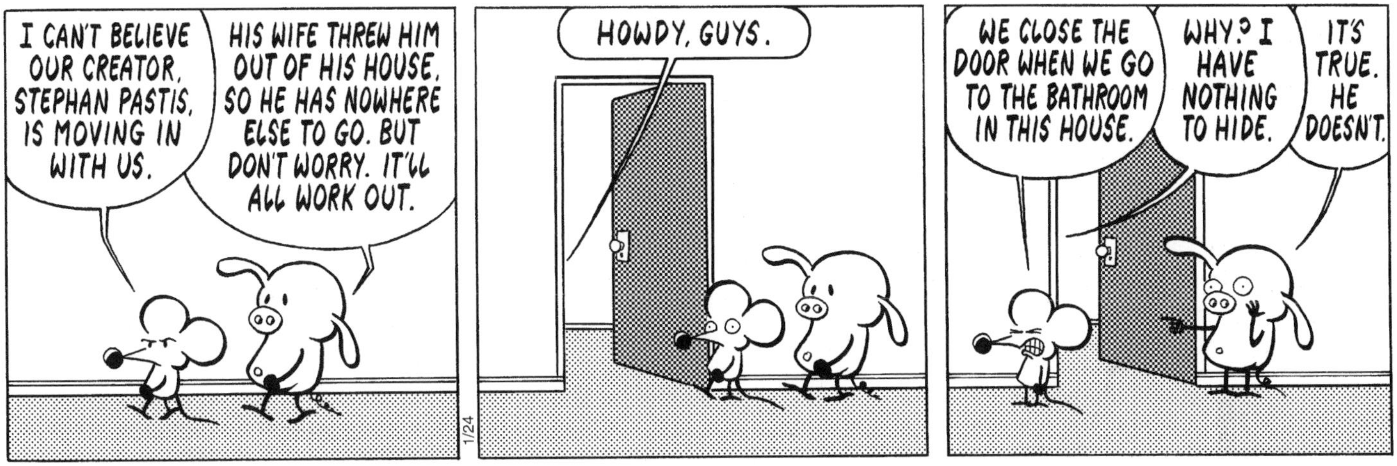
I CAN'T BELIEVE OUR CREATOR, STEPHAN PASTIS, IS MOVING IN WITH US.
HIS WIFE THREW HIM OUT OF HIS HOUSE, SO HE HAS NOWHERE ELSE TO GO. BUT DON'T WORRY. IT'LL ALL WORK OUT.
1/24
HOWDY, GUYS.
WE CLOSE THE DOOR WHEN WE GO TO THE BATHROOM IN THIS HOUSE.
WHY? I HAVE NOTHING TO HIDE.
IT'S TRUE. HE DOESN'T.

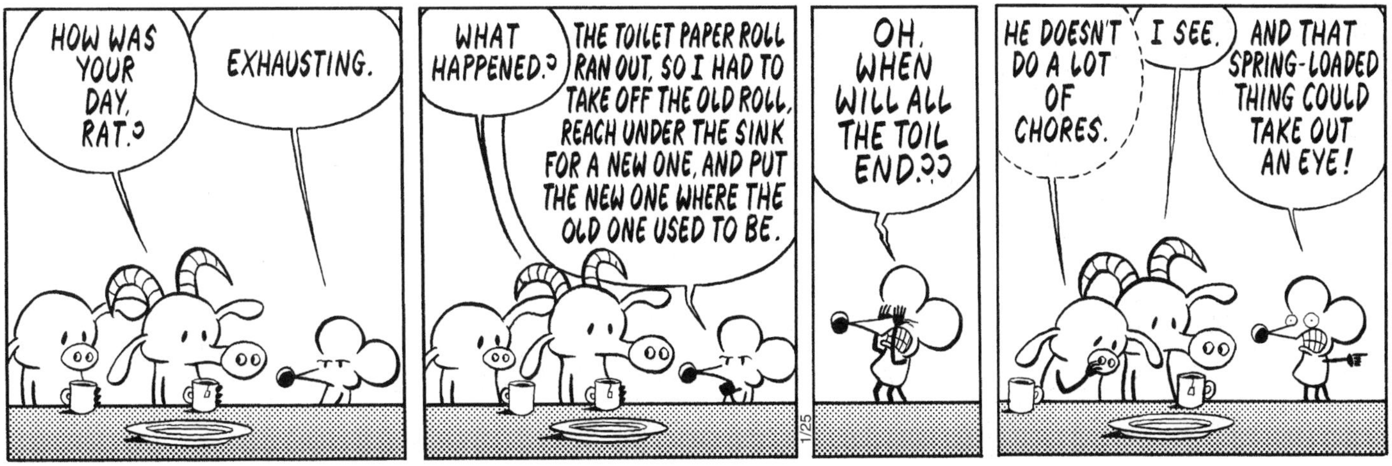
HOW WAS YOUR DAY, RAT?
EXHAUSTING.
WHAT HAPPENED?
THE TOILET PAPER ROLL RAN OUT, SO I HAD TO TAKE OFF THE OLD ROLL, REACH UNDER THE SINK FOR A NEW ONE, AND PUT THE NEW ONE WHERE THE OLD ONE USED TO BE.
1/25
OH, WHEN WILL ALL THE TOIL END??
HE DOESN'T DO A LOT OF CHORES.
I SEE.
AND THAT SPRING-LOADED THING COULD TAKE OUT AN EYE!

Danny Donkey took a cruise with his family.

OH, YAY.

'Okay, everyone,' said Cousin Dickie, 'I've organized each day of our vacation.'

Tomorrow we'll get up real early and go whale watching.

Tuesday we'll dock in Key West and have five hours of sightseeing followed by one hour of shopping.

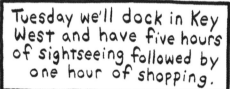

Wednesday we'll sail to see various pre-Columbian ruins, followed by four hours of scuba training.

1/26

'Does anyone have any questions?'

Danny Donkey tied his cousin to an anchor and threw him overboard.

THAT WASN'T REALLY A QUESTION.

DANNY'S A MAN OF FEW WORDS.

NO ONE SHOULD NEED A VACATION FROM A VACATION!

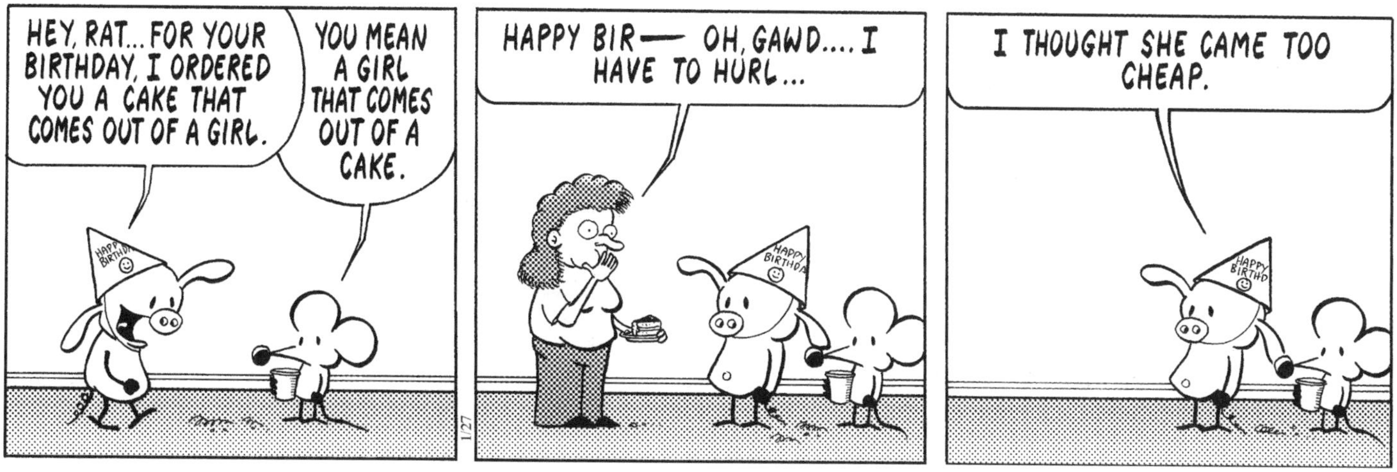
HEY, RAT... FOR YOUR BIRTHDAY, I ORDERED YOU A CAKE THAT COMES OUT OF A GIRL.
YOU MEAN A GIRL THAT COMES OUT OF A CAKE.
HAPPY BIRTHDAY
HAPPY BIR— OH, GAWD.... I HAVE TO HURL...
I THOUGHT SHE CAME TOO CHEAP.
1/27

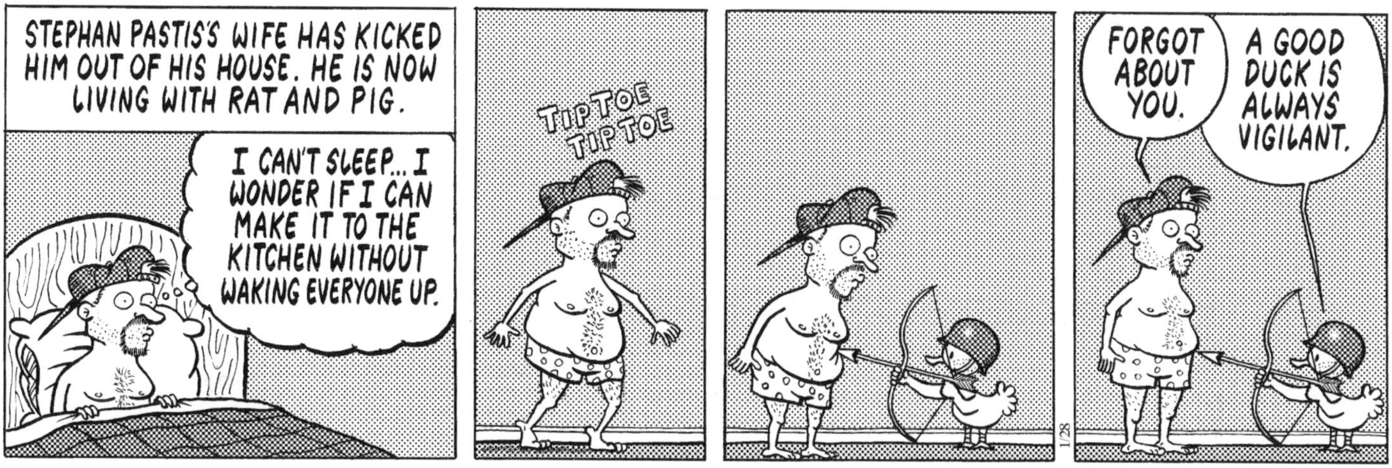
STEPHAN PASTIS'S WIFE HAS KICKED HIM OUT OF HIS HOUSE. HE IS NOW LIVING WITH RAT AND PIG.
I CAN'T SLEEP... I WONDER IF I CAN MAKE IT TO THE KITCHEN WITHOUT WAKING EVERYONE UP.
TIPTOE TIPTOE
FORGOT ABOUT YOU.
A GOOD DUCK IS ALWAYS VIGILANT.
1/28

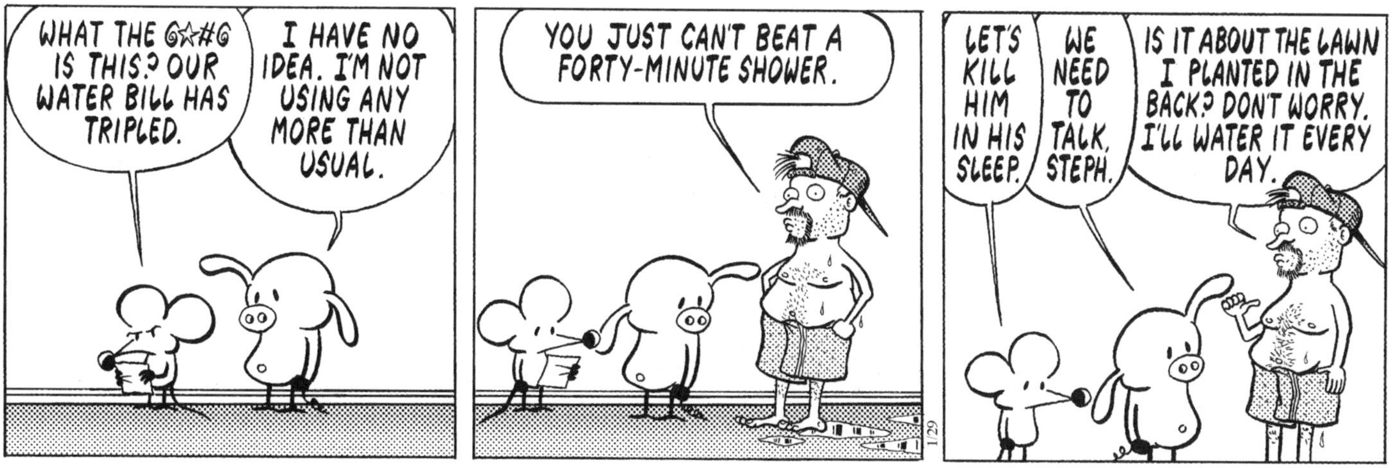
WHAT THE G☆#G IS THIS? OUR WATER BILL HAS TRIPLED.
I HAVE NO IDEA. I'M NOT USING ANY MORE THAN USUAL.
YOU JUST CAN'T BEAT A FORTY-MINUTE SHOWER.
LET'S KILL HIM IN HIS SLEEP.
WE NEED TO TALK, STEPH.
IS IT ABOUT THE LAWN I PLANTED IN THE BACK? DON'T WORRY. I'LL WATER IT EVERY DAY.
1/29

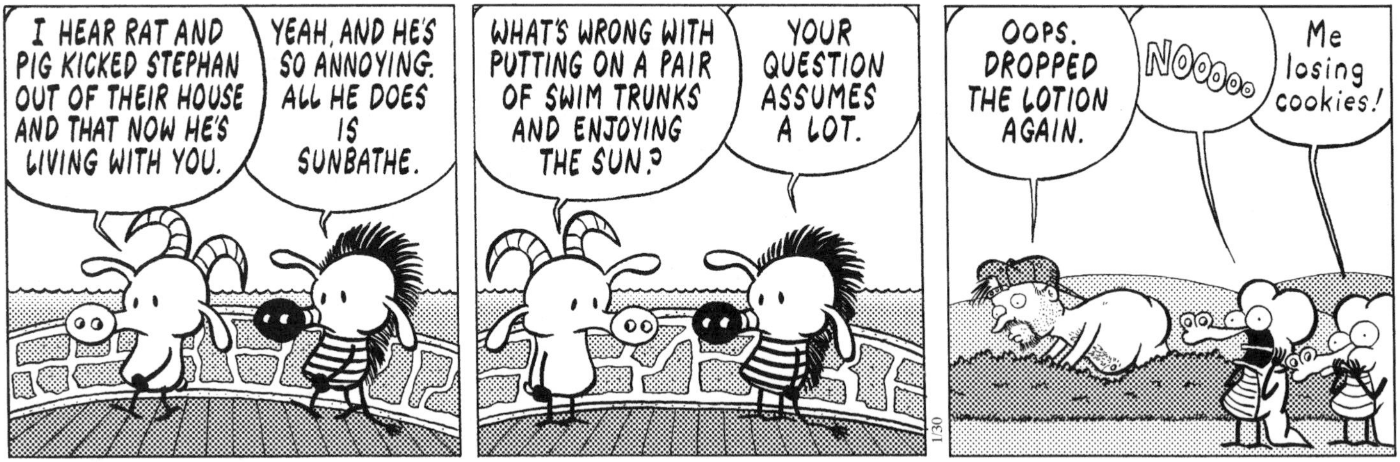
I HEAR RAT AND PIG KICKED STEPHAN OUT OF THEIR HOUSE AND THAT NOW HE'S LIVING WITH YOU.
YEAH, AND HE'S SO ANNOYING. ALL HE DOES IS SUNBATHE.
WHAT'S WRONG WITH PUTTING ON A PAIR OF SWIM TRUNKS AND ENJOYING THE SUN?
YOUR QUESTION ASSUMES A LOT.
1/30
OOPS. DROPPED THE LOTION AGAIN.
NOOooo
Me losing cookies!

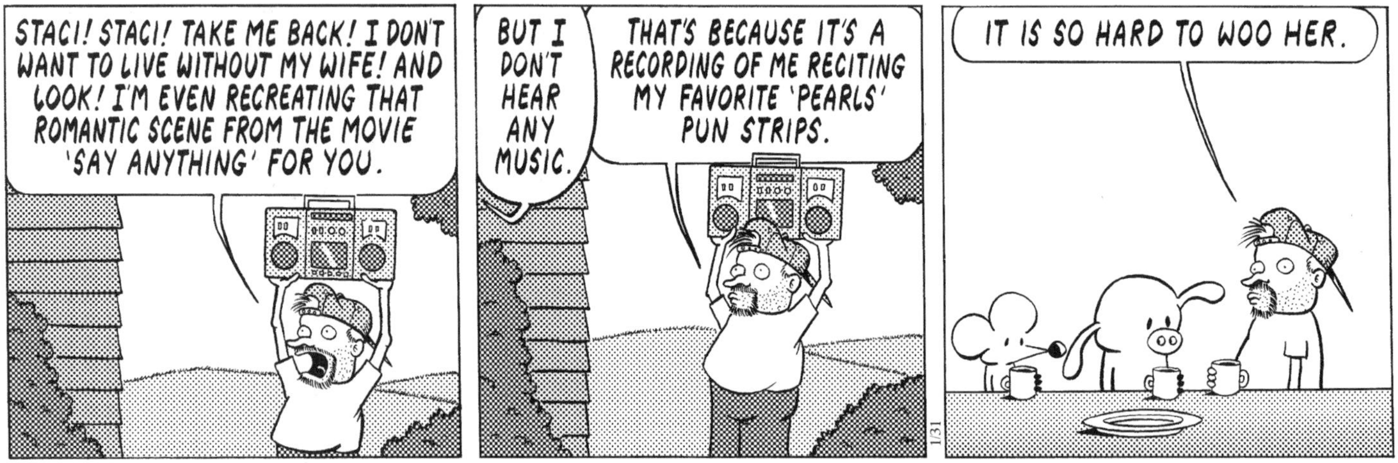
STACI! STACI! TAKE ME BACK! I DON'T WANT TO LIVE WITHOUT MY WIFE! AND LOOK! I'M EVEN RECREATING THAT ROMANTIC SCENE FROM THE MOVIE 'SAY ANYTHING' FOR YOU.
BUT I DON'T HEAR ANY MUSIC.
THAT'S BECAUSE IT'S A RECORDING OF ME RECITING MY FAVORITE 'PEARLS' PUN STRIPS.
1/31
IT IS SO HARD TO WOO HER.

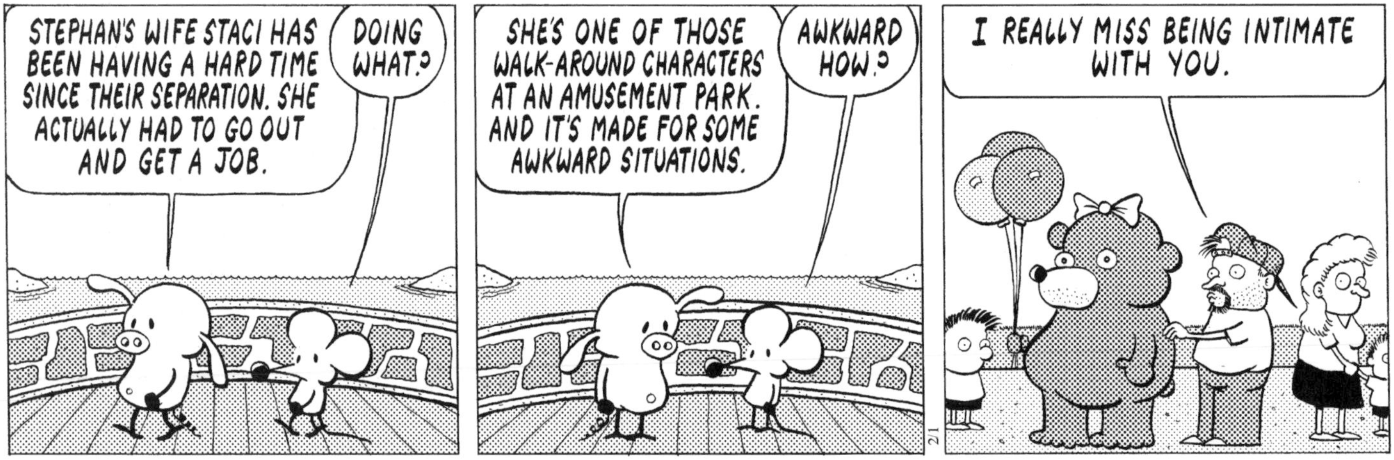
STEPHAN'S WIFE STACI HAS BEEN HAVING A HARD TIME SINCE THEIR SEPARATION. SHE ACTUALLY HAD TO GO OUT AND GET A JOB.
DOING WHAT?
SHE'S ONE OF THOSE WALK-AROUND CHARACTERS AT AN AMUSEMENT PARK. AND IT'S MADE FOR SOME AWKWARD SITUATIONS.
AWKWARD HOW?
2/1
I REALLY MISS BEING INTIMATE WITH YOU.

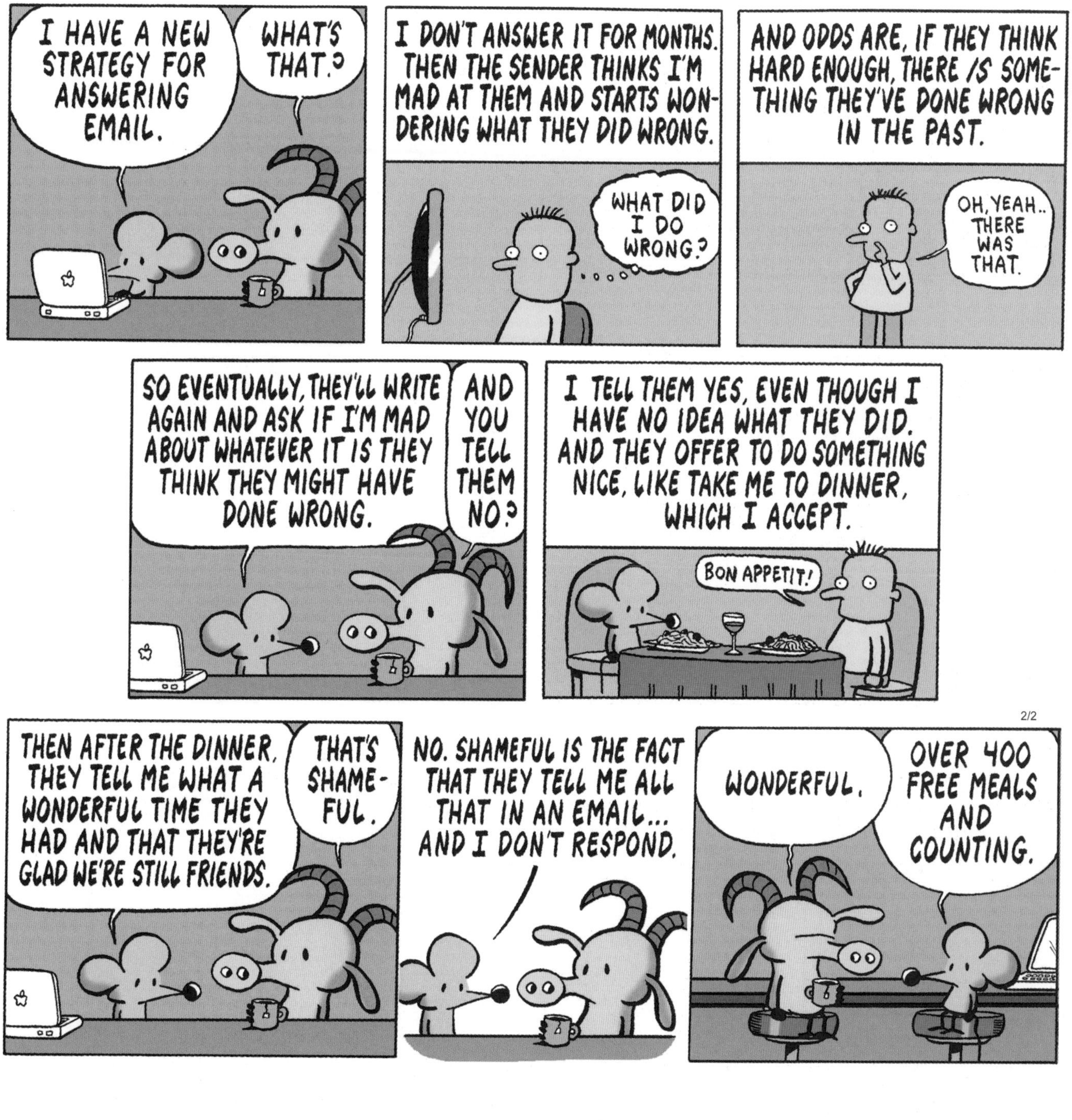
I HAVE A NEW STRATEGY FOR ANSWERING EMAIL.
WHAT'S THAT?
I DON'T ANSWER IT FOR MONTHS. THEN THE SENDER THINKS I'M MAD AT THEM AND STARTS WONDERING WHAT THEY DID WRONG.
WHAT DID I DO WRONG?
AND ODDS ARE, IF THEY THINK HARD ENOUGH, THERE IS SOMETHING THEY'VE DONE WRONG IN THE PAST.
OH, YEAH.. THERE WAS THAT.
SO EVENTUALLY, THEY'LL WRITE AGAIN AND ASK IF I'M MAD ABOUT WHATEVER IT IS THEY THINK THEY MIGHT HAVE DONE WRONG.
AND YOU TELL THEM NO?
I TELL THEM YES, EVEN THOUGH I HAVE NO IDEA WHAT THEY DID. AND THEY OFFER TO DO SOMETHING NICE, LIKE TAKE ME TO DINNER, WHICH I ACCEPT.
BON APPETIT!
2/2
THEN AFTER THE DINNER, THEY TELL ME WHAT A WONDERFUL TIME THEY HAD AND THAT THEY'RE GLAD WE'RE STILL FRIENDS.
THAT'S SHAMEFUL.
NO. SHAMEFUL IS THE FACT THAT THEY TELL ME ALL THAT IN AN EMAIL... AND I DON'T RESPOND.
WONDERFUL.
OVER 400 FREE MEALS AND COUNTING.

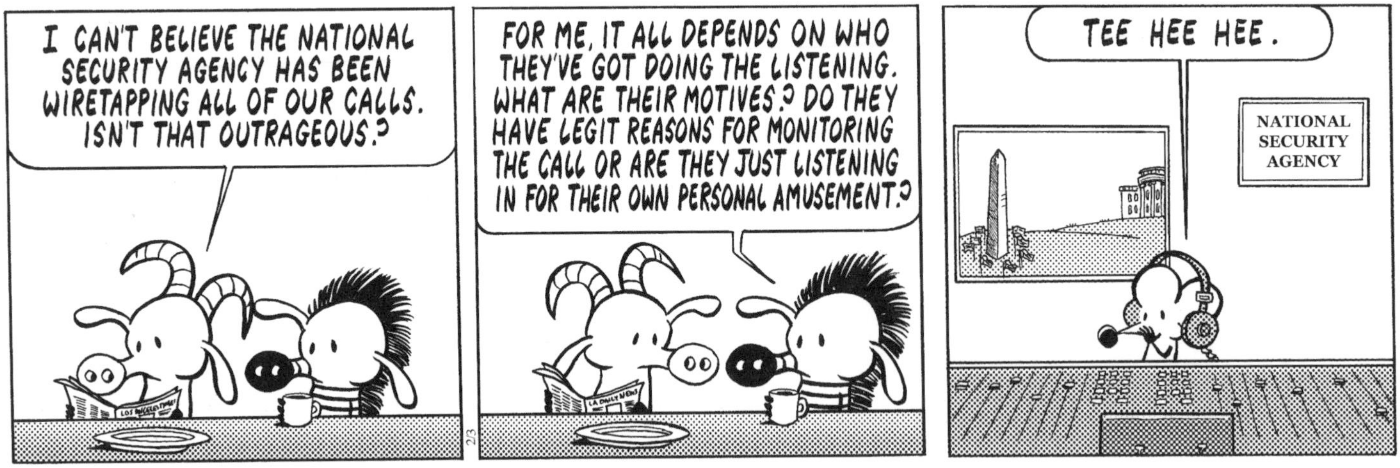
I CAN'T BELIEVE THE NATIONAL SECURITY AGENCY HAS BEEN WIRETAPPING ALL OF OUR CALLS. ISN'T THAT OUTRAGEOUS?
FOR ME, IT ALL DEPENDS ON WHO THEY'VE GOT DOING THE LISTENING. WHAT ARE THEIR MOTIVES? DO THEY HAVE LEGIT REASONS FOR MONITORING THE CALL OR ARE THEY JUST LISTENING IN FOR THEIR OWN PERSONAL AMUSEMENT?
TEE HEE HEE.
NATIONAL SECURITY AGENCY

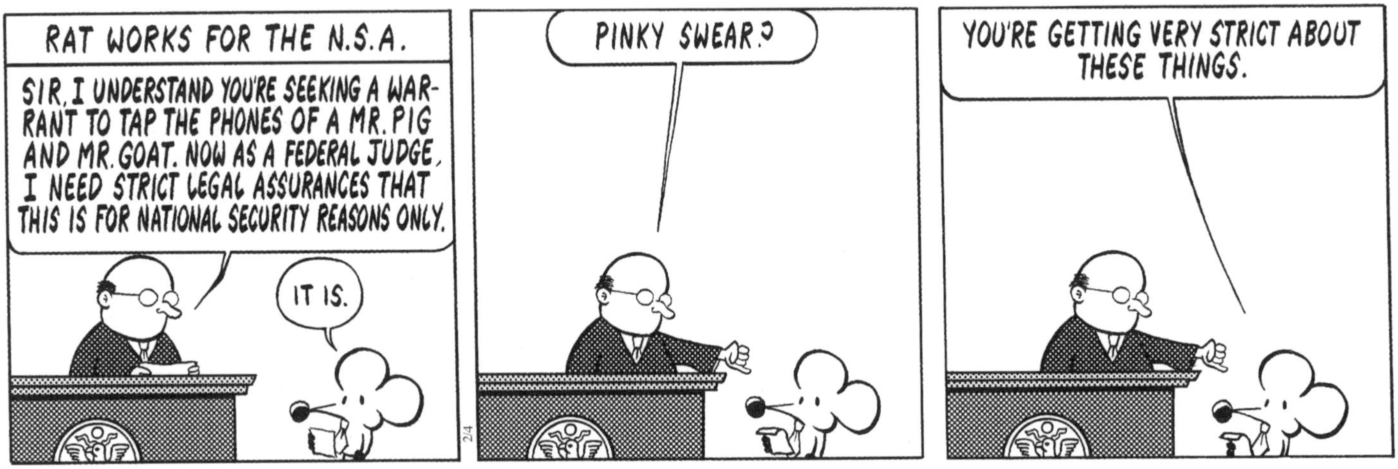
RAT WORKS FOR THE N.S.A.
SIR, I UNDERSTAND YOU'RE SEEKING A WARRANT TO TAP THE PHONES OF A MR. PIG AND MR. GOAT. NOW AS A FEDERAL JUDGE, I NEED STRICT LEGAL ASSURANCES THAT THIS IS FOR NATIONAL SECURITY REASONS ONLY.
IT IS.
PINKY SWEAR?
YOU'RE GETTING VERY STRICT ABOUT THESE THINGS.

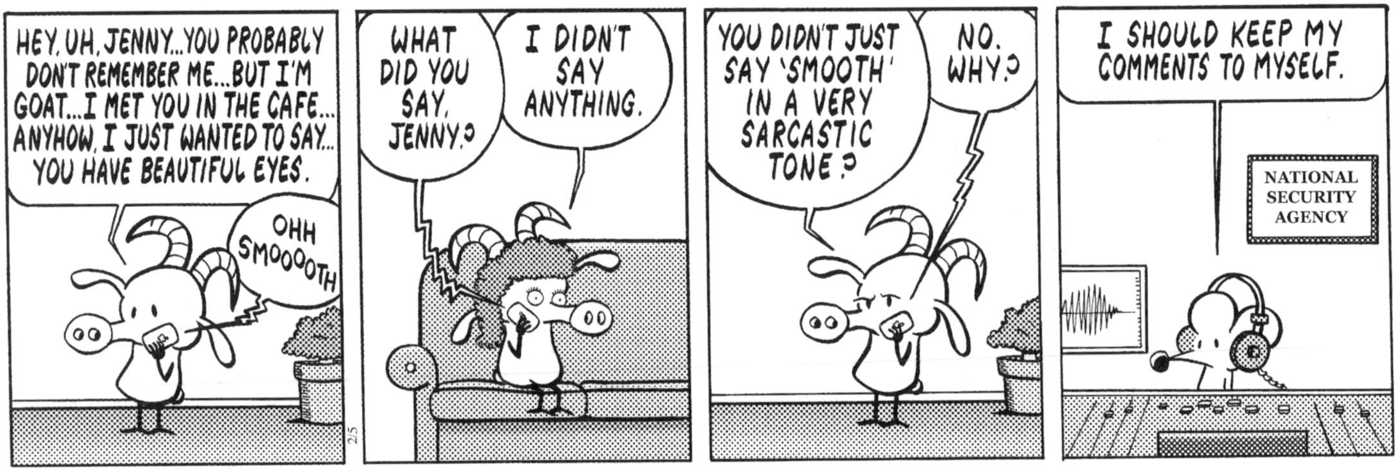
HEY, UH, JENNY...YOU PROBABLY DON'T REMEMBER ME...BUT I'M GOAT...I MET YOU IN THE CAFE... ANYHOW, I JUST WANTED TO SAY... YOU HAVE BEAUTIFUL EYES.
OHH SMOOOOOTH
WHAT DID YOU SAY, JENNY?
I DIDN'T SAY ANYTHING.
YOU DIDN'T JUST SAY 'SMOOTH' IN A VERY SARCASTIC TONE?
NO. WHY?
I SHOULD KEEP MY COMMENTS TO MYSELF.
NATIONAL SECURITY AGENCY

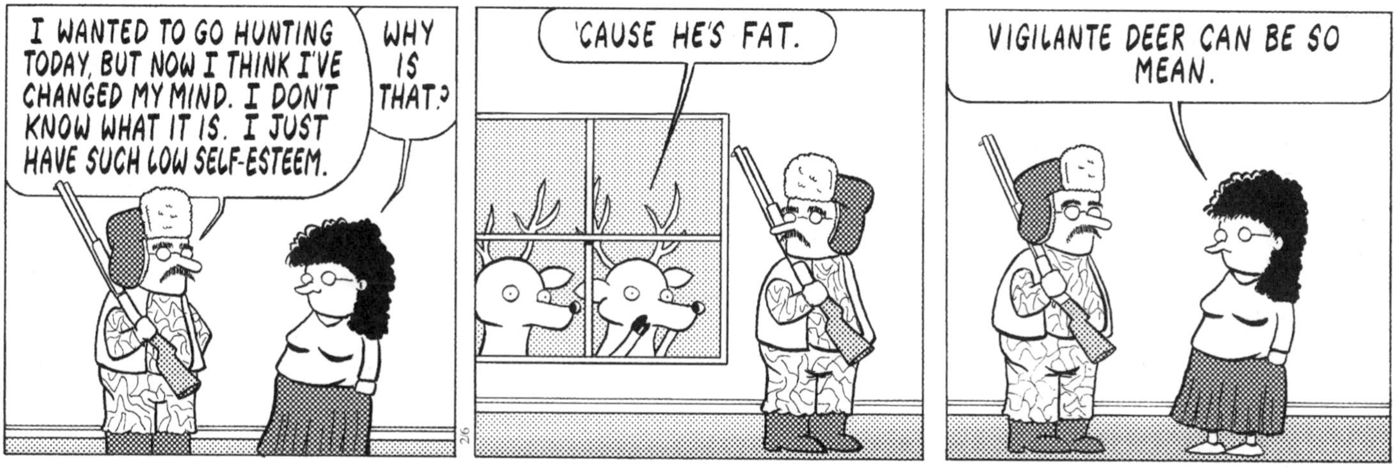
I WANTED TO GO HUNTING TODAY, BUT NOW I THINK I'VE CHANGED MY MIND. I DON'T KNOW WHAT IT IS. I JUST HAVE SUCH LOW SELF-ESTEEM.
WHY IS THAT?
'CAUSE HE'S FAT.
VIGILANTE DEER CAN BE SO MEAN.

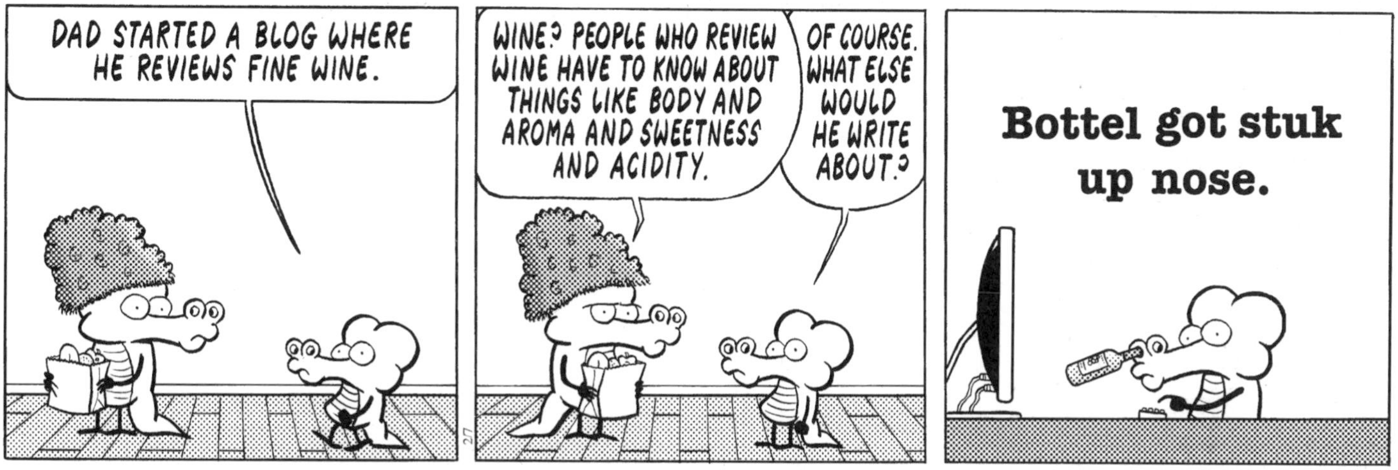
DAD STARTED A BLOG WHERE HE REVIEWS FINE WINE.
WINE? PEOPLE WHO REVIEW WINE HAVE TO KNOW ABOUT THINGS LIKE BODY AND AROMA AND SWEETNESS AND ACIDITY.
OF COURSE. WHAT ELSE WOULD HE WRITE ABOUT?
Bottel got stuk up nose.

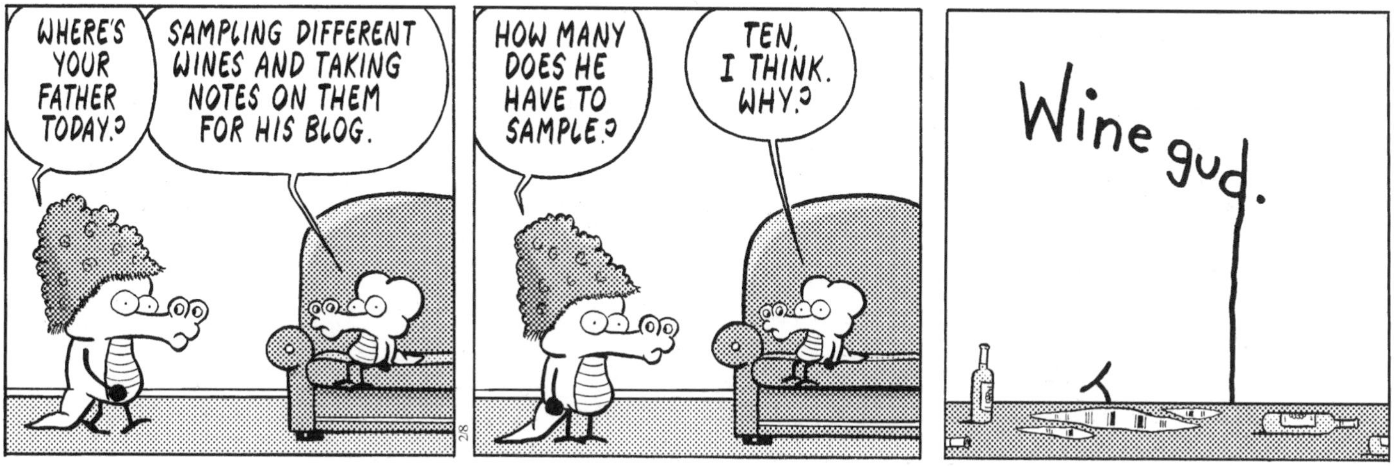
WHERE'S YOUR FATHER TODAY?
SAMPLING DIFFERENT WINES AND TAKING NOTES ON THEM FOR HIS BLOG.
HOW MANY DOES HE HAVE TO SAMPLE?
TEN, I THINK. WHY?
Wine gud.

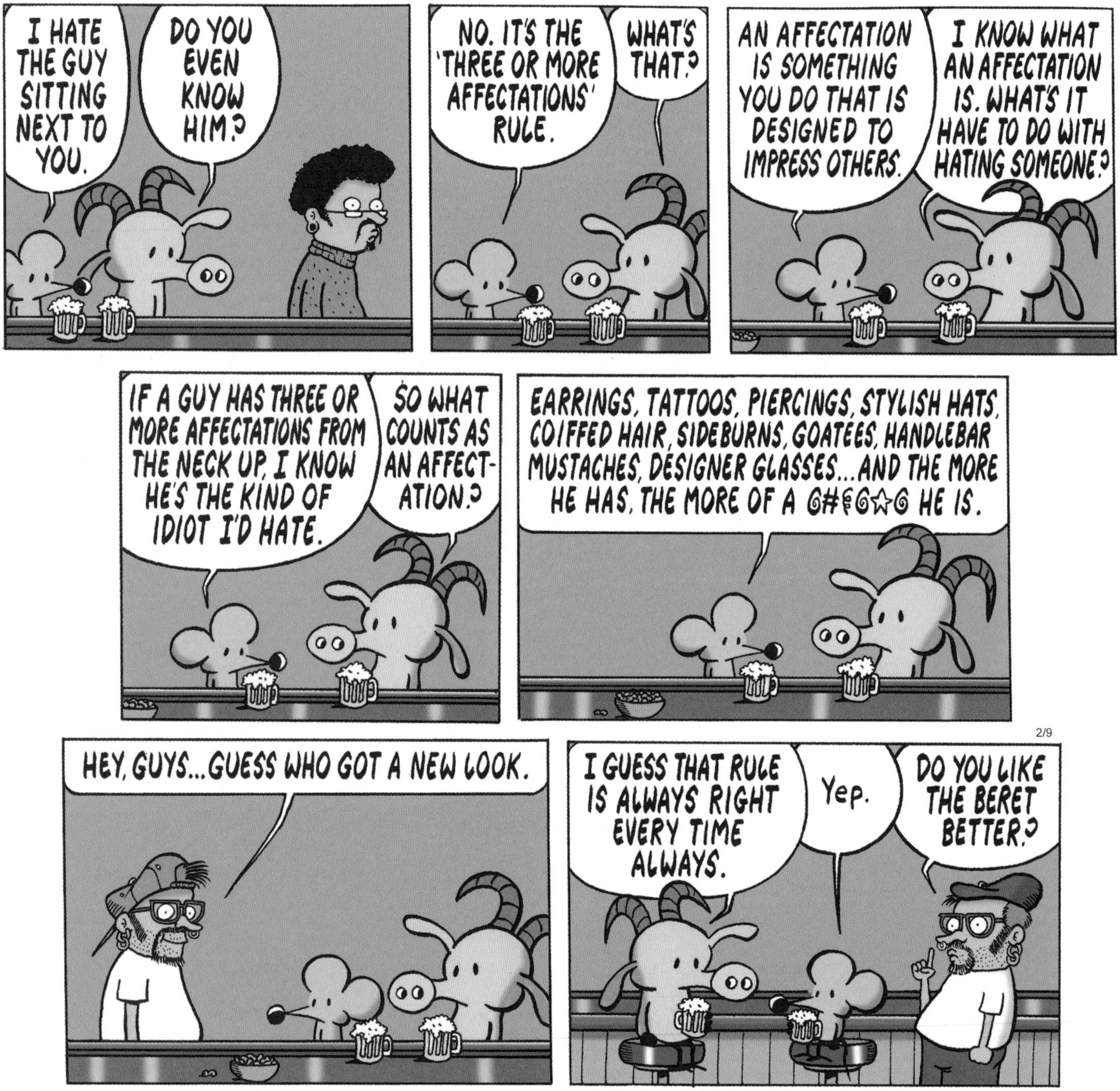
I HATE THE GUY SITTING NEXT TO YOU.
DO YOU EVEN KNOW HIM?
NO. IT'S THE 'THREE OR MORE AFFECTATIONS' RULE.
WHAT'S THAT?
AN AFFECTATION IS SOMETHING YOU DO THAT IS DESIGNED TO IMPRESS OTHERS.
I KNOW WHAT AN AFFECTATION IS. WHAT'S IT HAVE TO DO WITH HATING SOMEONE?
IF A GUY HAS THREE OR MORE AFFECTATIONS FROM THE NECK UP, I KNOW HE'S THE KIND OF IDIOT I'D HATE.
SO WHAT COUNTS AS AN AFFECT-ATION?
EARRINGS, TATTOOS, PIERCINGS, STYLISH HATS, COIFFED HAIR, SIDEBURNS, GOATEES, HANDLEBAR MUSTACHES, DESIGNER GLASSES...AND THE MORE HE HAS, THE MORE OF A 6#$6☆6 HE IS.
HEY, GUYS...GUESS WHO GOT A NEW LOOK.
2/9
I GUESS THAT RULE IS ALWAYS RIGHT EVERY TIME ALWAYS.
Yep.
DO YOU LIKE THE BERET BETTER?

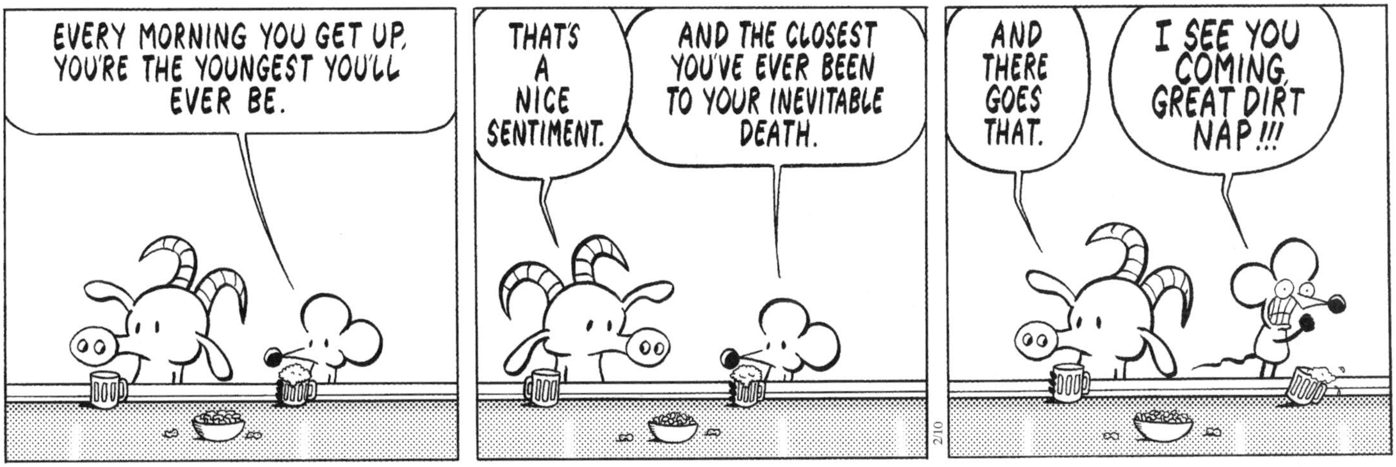
EVERY MORNING YOU GET UP, YOU'RE THE YOUNGEST YOU'LL EVER BE.
THAT'S A NICE SENTIMENT.
AND THE CLOSEST YOU'VE EVER BEEN TO YOUR INEVITABLE DEATH.
AND THERE GOES THAT.
I SEE YOU COMING, GREAT DIRT NAP!!!
2/10

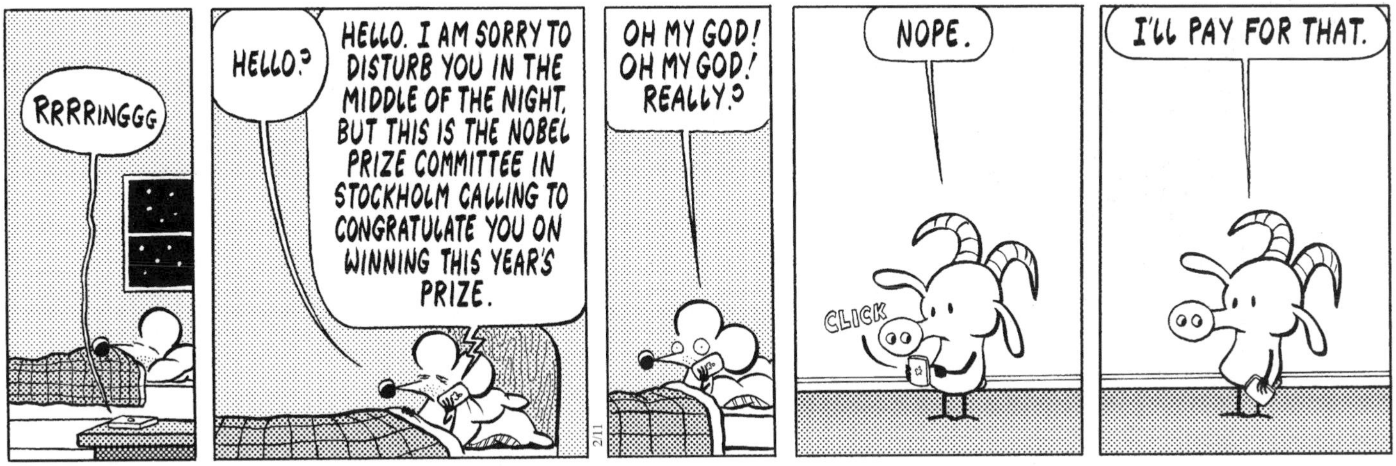
RRRRINGGG
HELLO?
HELLO. I AM SORRY TO DISTURB YOU IN THE MIDDLE OF THE NIGHT, BUT THIS IS THE NOBEL PRIZE COMMITTEE IN STOCKHOLM CALLING TO CONGRATULATE YOU ON WINNING THIS YEAR'S PRIZE.
2/11
OH MY GOD! OH MY GOD! REALLY?
NOPE.
CLICK
I'LL PAY FOR THAT.

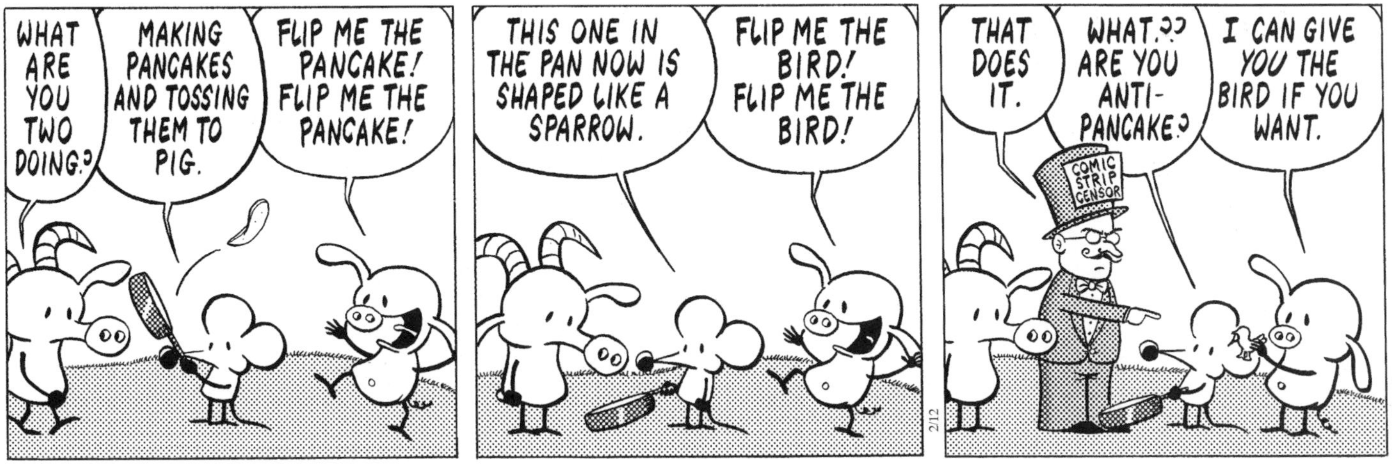
WHAT ARE YOU TWO DOING?
MAKING PANCAKES AND TOSSING THEM TO PIG.
FLIP ME THE PANCAKE! FLIP ME THE PANCAKE!
THIS ONE IN THE PAN NOW IS SHAPED LIKE A SPARROW.
FLIP ME THE BIRD! FLIP ME THE BIRD!
2/12
THAT DOES IT.
WHAT?? ARE YOU ANTI-PANCAKE?
I CAN GIVE *YOU* THE BIRD IF YOU WANT.
COMIC STRIP CENSOR

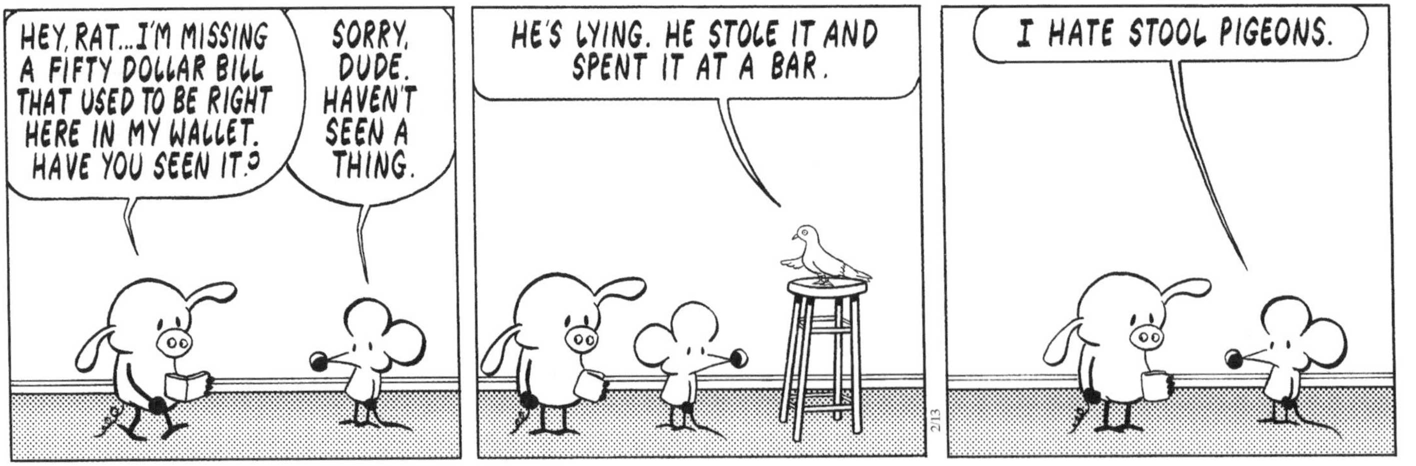
HEY, RAT...I'M MISSING A FIFTY DOLLAR BILL THAT USED TO BE RIGHT HERE IN MY WALLET. HAVE YOU SEEN IT?
SORRY, DUDE. HAVEN'T SEEN A THING.
HE'S LYING. HE STOLE IT AND SPENT IT AT A BAR.
I HATE STOOL PIGEONS.
2/13

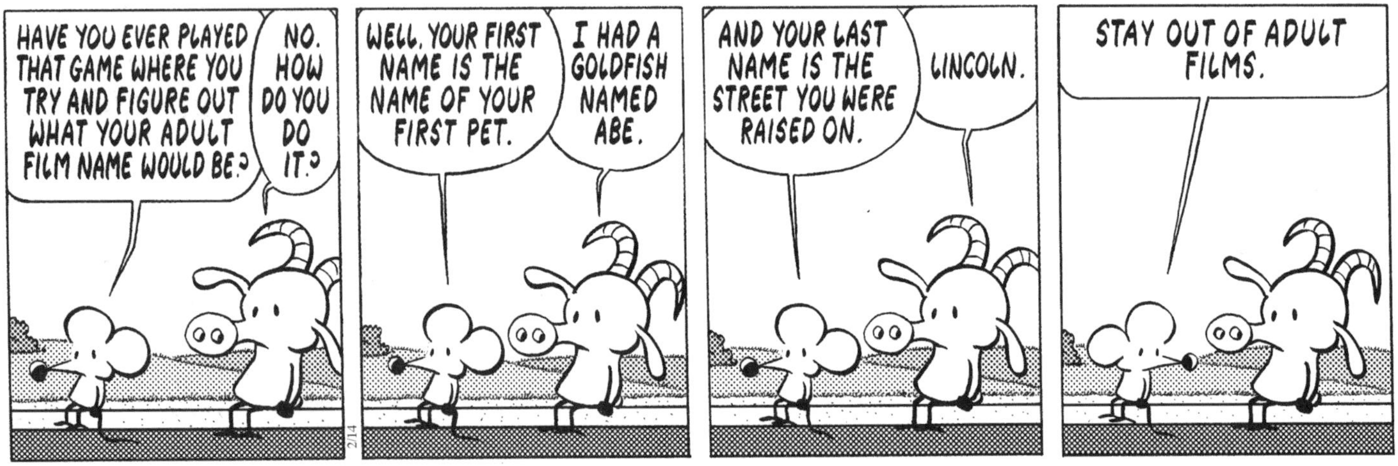
HAVE YOU EVER PLAYED THAT GAME WHERE YOU TRY AND FIGURE OUT WHAT YOUR ADULT FILM NAME WOULD BE?
NO. HOW DO YOU DO IT?
WELL, YOUR FIRST NAME IS THE NAME OF YOUR FIRST PET.
I HAD A GOLDFISH NAMED ABE.
AND YOUR LAST NAME IS THE STREET YOU WERE RAISED ON.
LINCOLN.
STAY OUT OF ADULT FILMS.
2/14

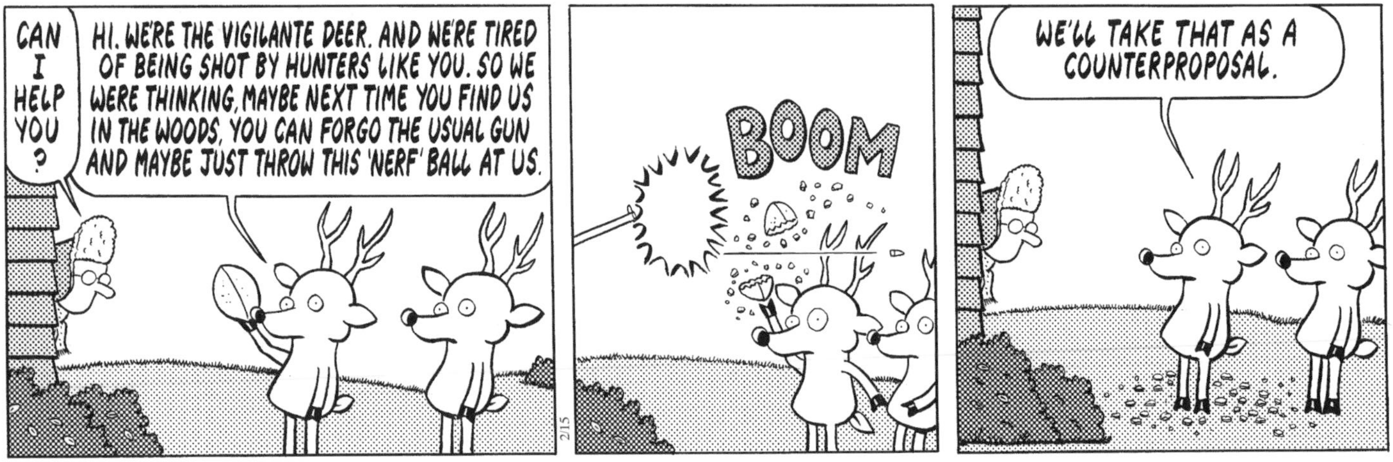
CAN I HELP YOU?
HI. WE'RE THE VIGILANTE DEER. AND WE'RE TIRED OF BEING SHOT BY HUNTERS LIKE YOU. SO WE WERE THINKING, MAYBE NEXT TIME YOU FIND US IN THE WOODS, YOU CAN FORGO THE USUAL GUN AND MAYBE JUST THROW THIS 'NERF' BALL AT US.
BOOM
WE'LL TAKE THAT AS A COUNTERPROPOSAL.
2/15

Stephan Pastis's wife has left him. As a result, he has started dating again.

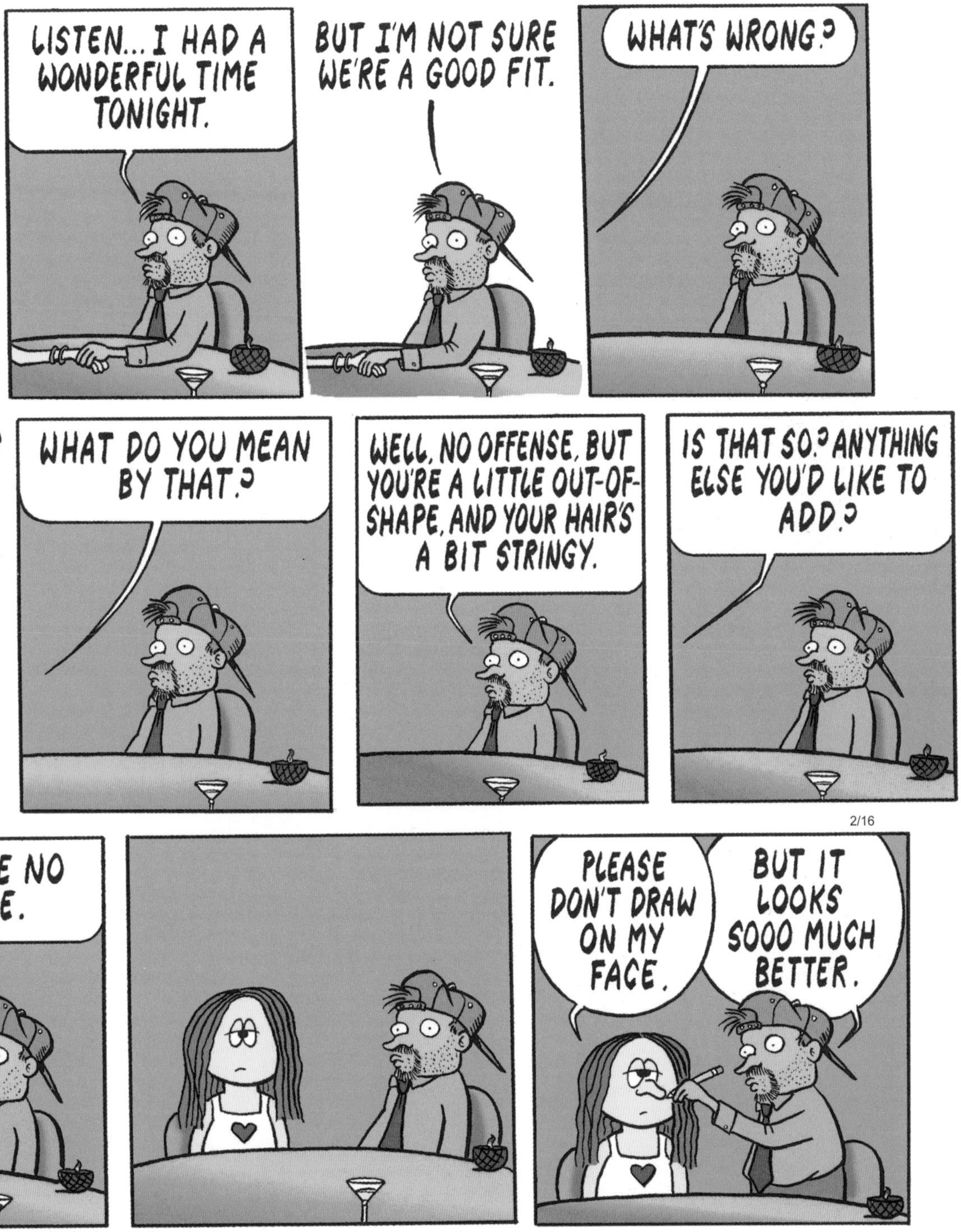
LISTEN... I HAD A WONDERFUL TIME TONIGHT.
BUT I'M NOT SURE WE'RE A GOOD FIT.
WHAT'S WRONG?
WELL, DON'T TAKE THIS THE WRONG WAY, BUT YOU'RE KIND OF A WORRIER. AND PHYSICALLY, YOU'RE NOT REALLY MY TYPE.
WHAT DO YOU MEAN BY THAT?
WELL, NO OFFENSE, BUT YOU'RE A LITTLE OUT-OF-SHAPE, AND YOUR HAIR'S A BIT STRINGY.
IS THAT SO? ANYTHING ELSE YOU'D LIKE TO ADD?
2/16
YOU HAVE NO NOSE.
PLEASE DON'T DRAW ON MY FACE.
BUT IT LOOKS SOOO MUCH BETTER.

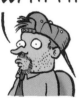

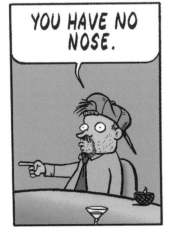

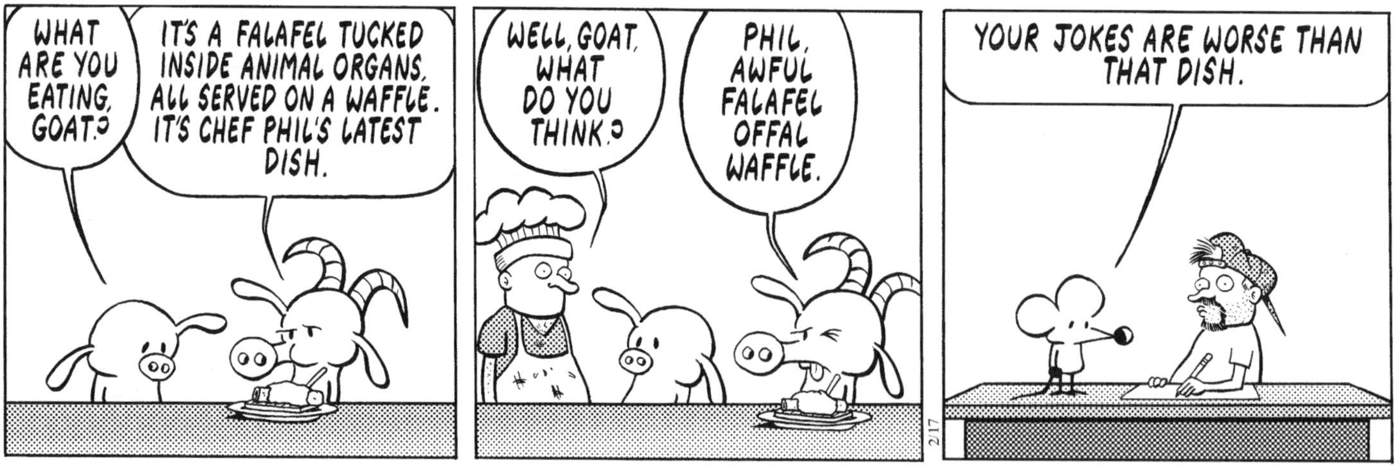
WHAT ARE YOU EATING, GOAT?
IT'S A FALAFEL TUCKED INSIDE ANIMAL ORGANS, ALL SERVED ON A WAFFLE. IT'S CHEF PHIL'S LATEST DISH.
WELL, GOAT, WHAT DO YOU THINK?
PHIL, AWFUL FALAFEL OFFAL WAFFLE.
2/17
YOUR JOKES ARE WORSE THAN THAT DISH.

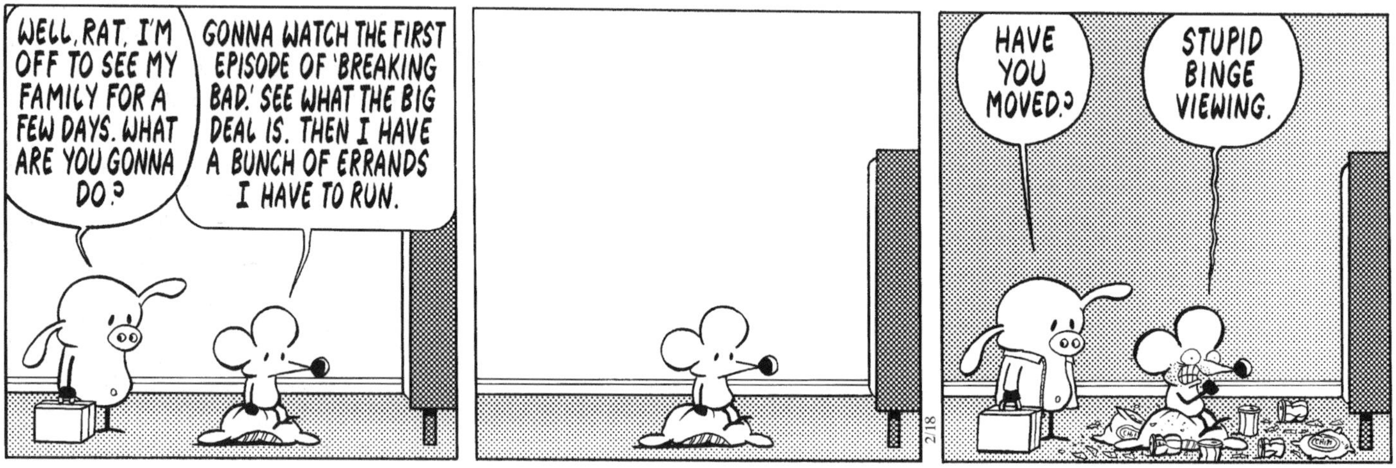
WELL, RAT, I'M OFF TO SEE MY FAMILY FOR A FEW DAYS. WHAT ARE YOU GONNA DO?
GONNA WATCH THE FIRST EPISODE OF 'BREAKING BAD.' SEE WHAT THE BIG DEAL IS. THEN I HAVE A BUNCH OF ERRANDS I HAVE TO RUN.
2/18
HAVE YOU MOVED?
STUPID BINGE VIEWING.

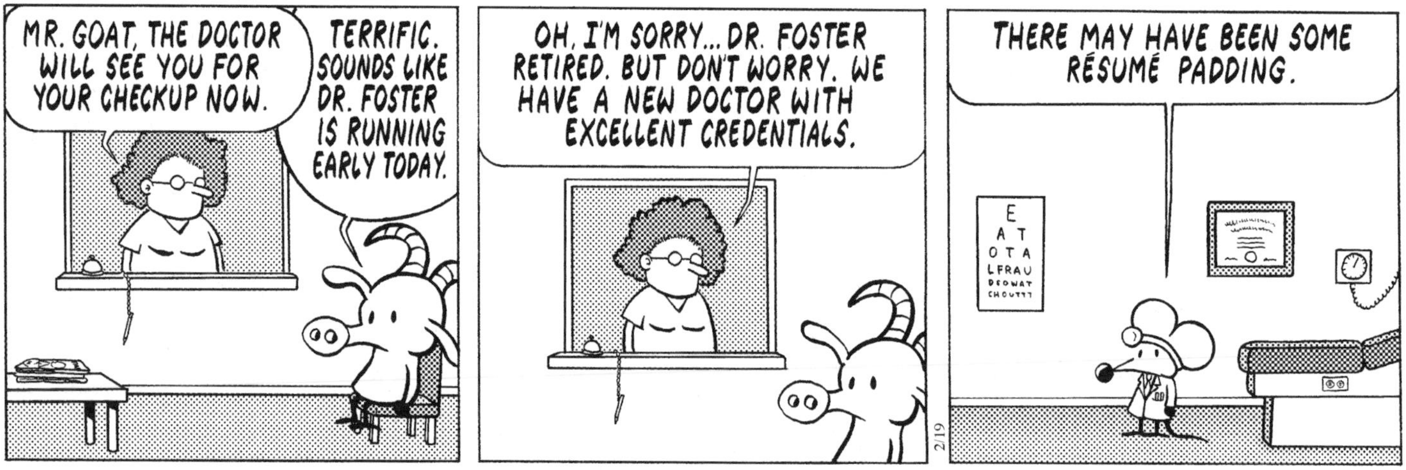
MR. GOAT, THE DOCTOR WILL SEE YOU FOR YOUR CHECKUP NOW.
TERRIFIC. SOUNDS LIKE DR. FOSTER IS RUNNING EARLY TODAY.
OH, I'M SORRY... DR. FOSTER RETIRED. BUT DON'T WORRY. WE HAVE A NEW DOCTOR WITH EXCELLENT CREDENTIALS.
2/19
THERE MAY HAVE BEEN SOME RÉSUMÉ PADDING.

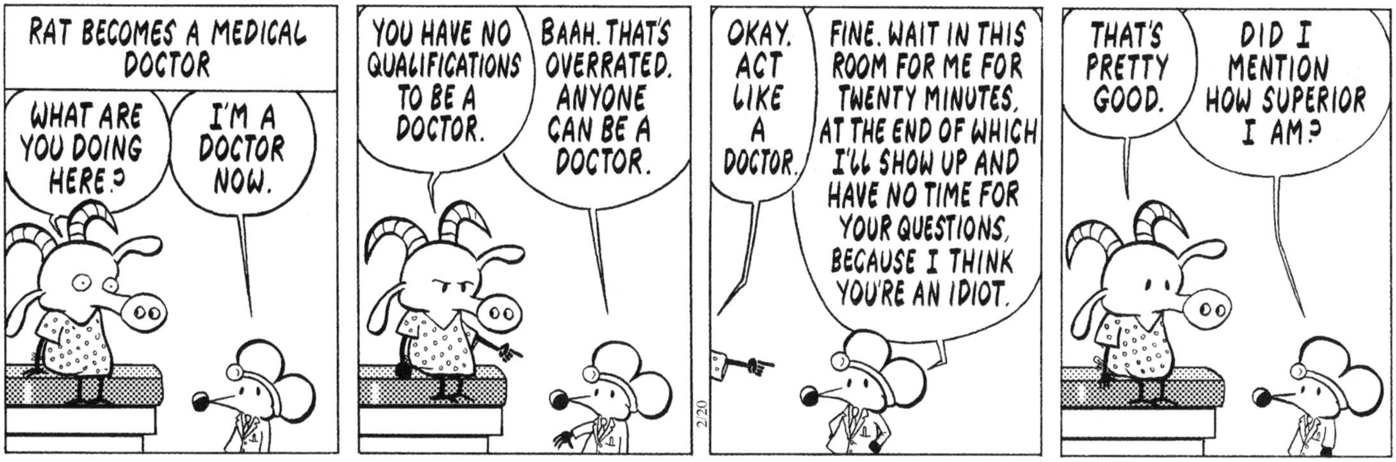
RAT BECOMES A MEDICAL DOCTOR
WHAT ARE YOU DOING HERE?
I'M A DOCTOR NOW.
YOU HAVE NO QUALIFICATIONS TO BE A DOCTOR.
BAAH. THAT'S OVERRATED. ANYONE CAN BE A DOCTOR.
2/20
OKAY. ACT LIKE A DOCTOR.
FINE. WAIT IN THIS ROOM FOR ME FOR TWENTY MINUTES, AT THE END OF WHICH I'LL SHOW UP AND HAVE NO TIME FOR YOUR QUESTIONS, BECAUSE I THINK YOU'RE AN IDIOT.
THAT'S PRETTY GOOD.
DID I MENTION HOW SUPERIOR I AM?

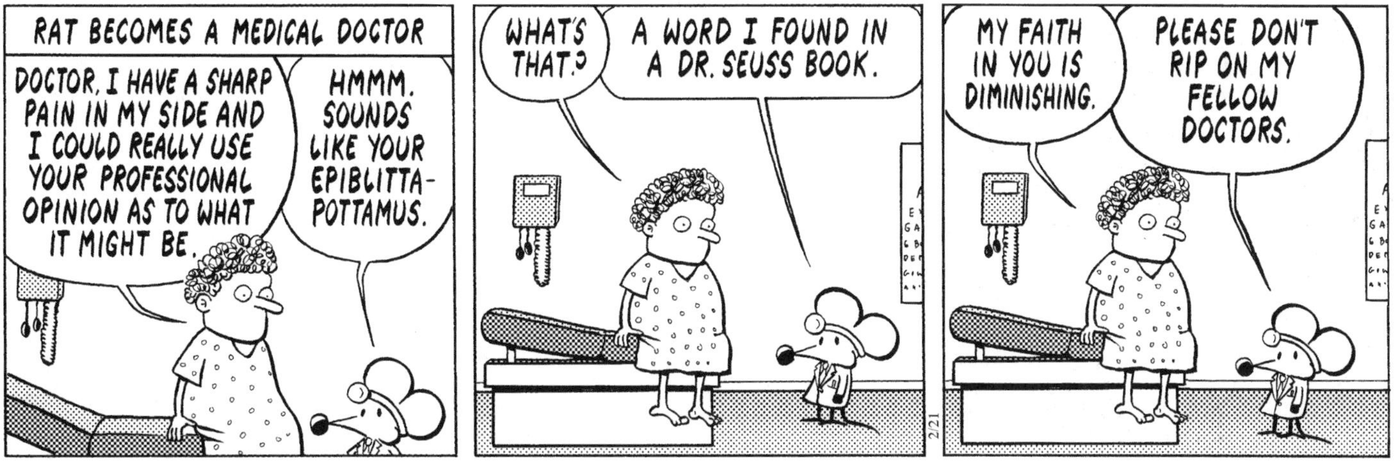
RAT BECOMES A MEDICAL DOCTOR
DOCTOR, I HAVE A SHARP PAIN IN MY SIDE AND I COULD REALLY USE YOUR PROFESSIONAL OPINION AS TO WHAT IT MIGHT BE.
HMMM. SOUNDS LIKE YOUR EPIBLITTA-POTTAMUS.
WHAT'S THAT?
A WORD I FOUND IN A DR. SEUSS BOOK.
2/21
MY FAITH IN YOU IS DIMINISHING.
PLEASE DON'T RIP ON MY FELLOW DOCTORS.

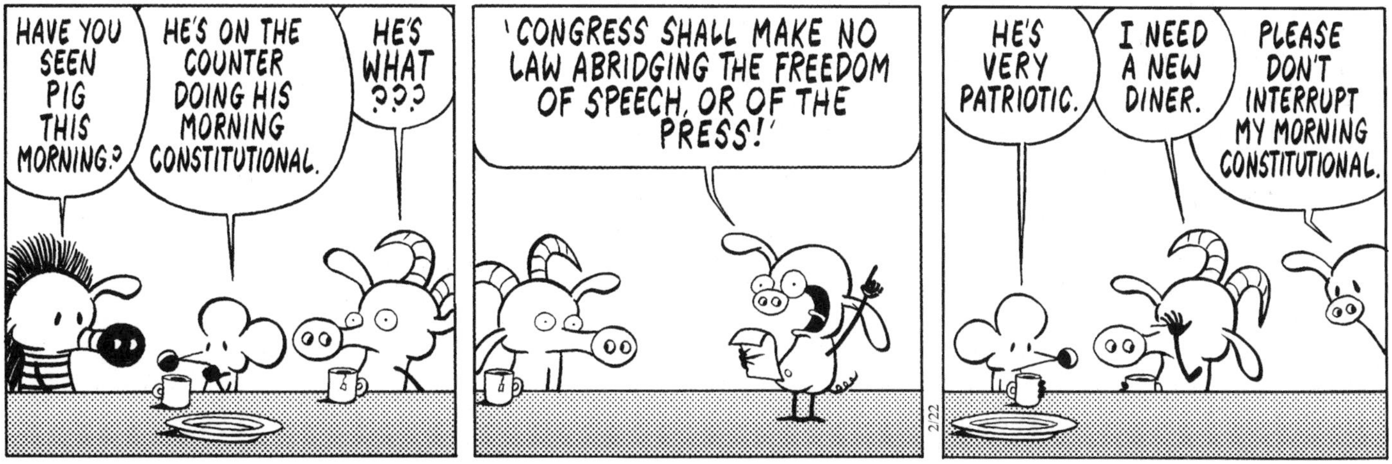
HAVE YOU SEEN PIG THIS MORNING?
HE'S ON THE COUNTER DOING HIS MORNING CONSTITUTIONAL.
HE'S WHAT???
'CONGRESS SHALL MAKE NO LAW ABRIDGING THE FREEDOM OF SPEECH, OR OF THE PRESS!'
2/22
HE'S VERY PATRIOTIC.
I NEED A NEW DINER.
PLEASE DON'T INTERRUPT MY MORNING CONSTITUTIONAL.

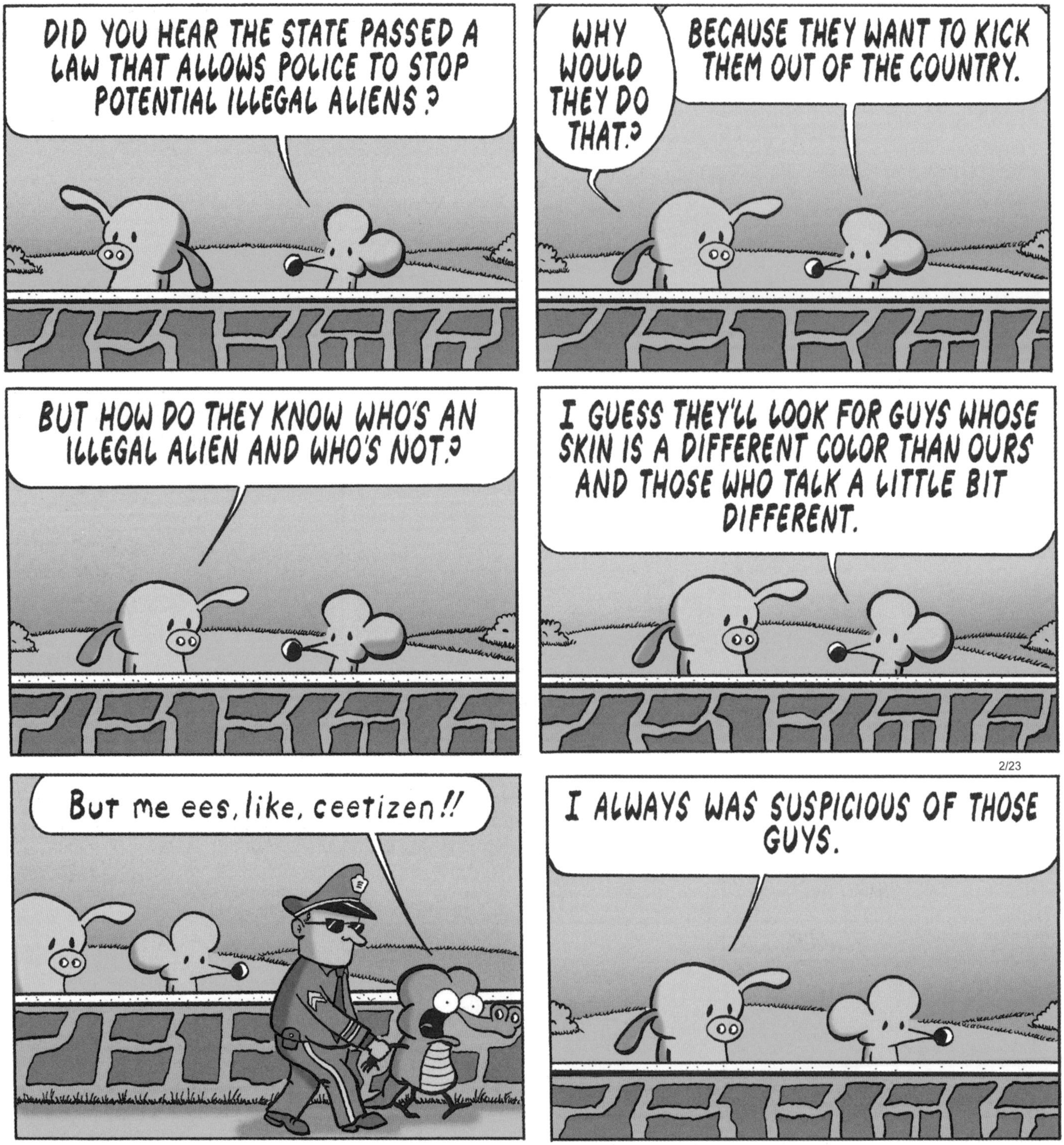
DID YOU HEAR THE STATE PASSED A LAW THAT ALLOWS POLICE TO STOP POTENTIAL ILLEGAL ALIENS?
WHY WOULD THEY DO THAT?
BECAUSE THEY WANT TO KICK THEM OUT OF THE COUNTRY.
BUT HOW DO THEY KNOW WHO'S AN ILLEGAL ALIEN AND WHO'S NOT?
I GUESS THEY'LL LOOK FOR GUYS WHOSE SKIN IS A DIFFERENT COLOR THAN OURS AND THOSE WHO TALK A LITTLE BIT DIFFERENT.
2/23
But me ees, like, ceetizen!!
I ALWAYS WAS SUSPICIOUS OF THOSE GUYS.

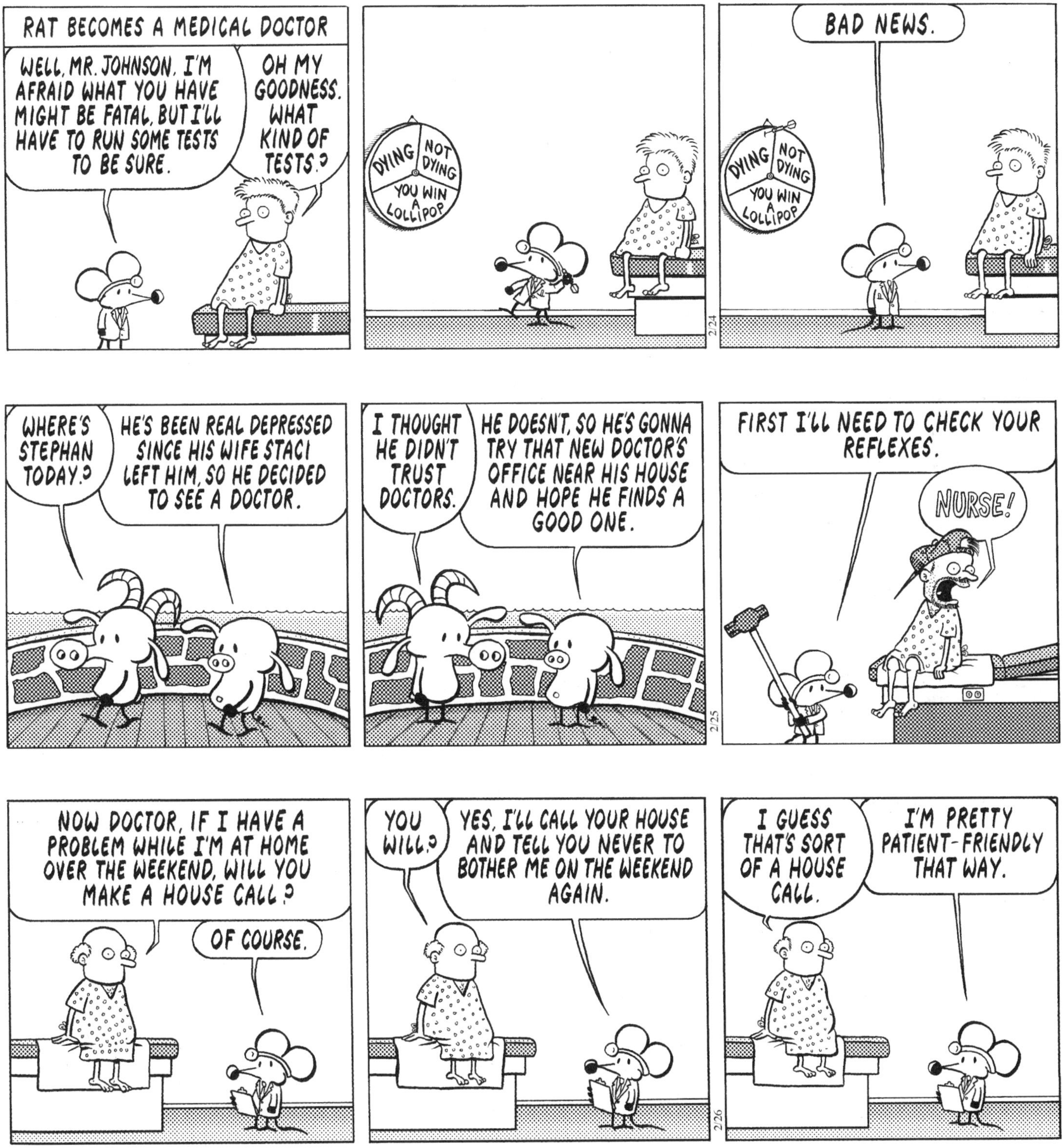

RAT BECOMES A MEDICAL DOCTOR
WELL, MR. JOHNSON, I'M AFRAID WHAT YOU HAVE MIGHT BE FATAL, BUT I'LL HAVE TO RUN SOME TESTS TO BE SURE.
OH MY GOODNESS. WHAT KIND OF TESTS?
DYING
NOT DYING
YOU WIN A LOLLIPOP
2/24
DYING
NOT DYING
YOU WIN A LOLLIPOP
BAD NEWS.
WHERE'S STEPHAN TODAY?
HE'S BEEN REAL DEPRESSED SINCE HIS WIFE STACI LEFT HIM, SO HE DECIDED TO SEE A DOCTOR.
I THOUGHT HE DIDN'T TRUST DOCTORS.
HE DOESN'T, SO HE'S GONNA TRY THAT NEW DOCTOR'S OFFICE NEAR HIS HOUSE AND HOPE HE FINDS A GOOD ONE.
2/25
FIRST I'LL NEED TO CHECK YOUR REFLEXES.
NURSE!
NOW DOCTOR, IF I HAVE A PROBLEM WHILE I'M AT HOME OVER THE WEEKEND, WILL YOU MAKE A HOUSE CALL?
OF COURSE.
YOU WILL?
YES, I'LL CALL YOUR HOUSE AND TELL YOU NEVER TO BOTHER ME ON THE WEEKEND AGAIN.
2/26
I GUESS THAT'S SORT OF A HOUSE CALL.
I'M PRETTY PATIENT-FRIENDLY THAT WAY.

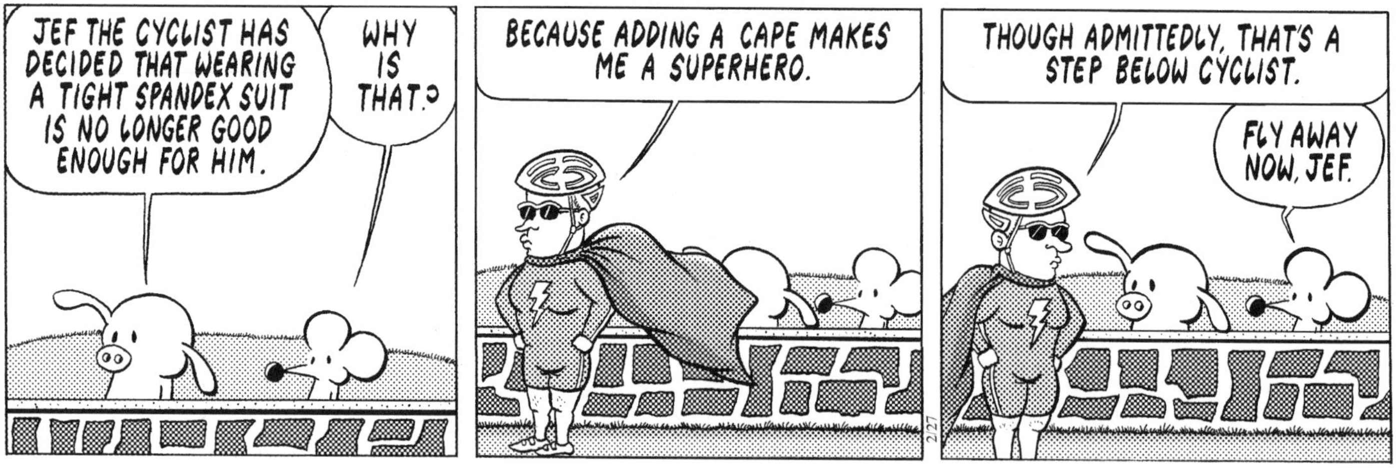
JEF THE CYCLIST HAS DECIDED THAT WEARING A TIGHT SPANDEX SUIT IS NO LONGER GOOD ENOUGH FOR HIM.
WHY IS THAT?
BECAUSE ADDING A CAPE MAKES ME A SUPERHERO.
THOUGH ADMITTEDLY, THAT'S A STEP BELOW CYCLIST.
FLY AWAY NOW, JEF.
2/27

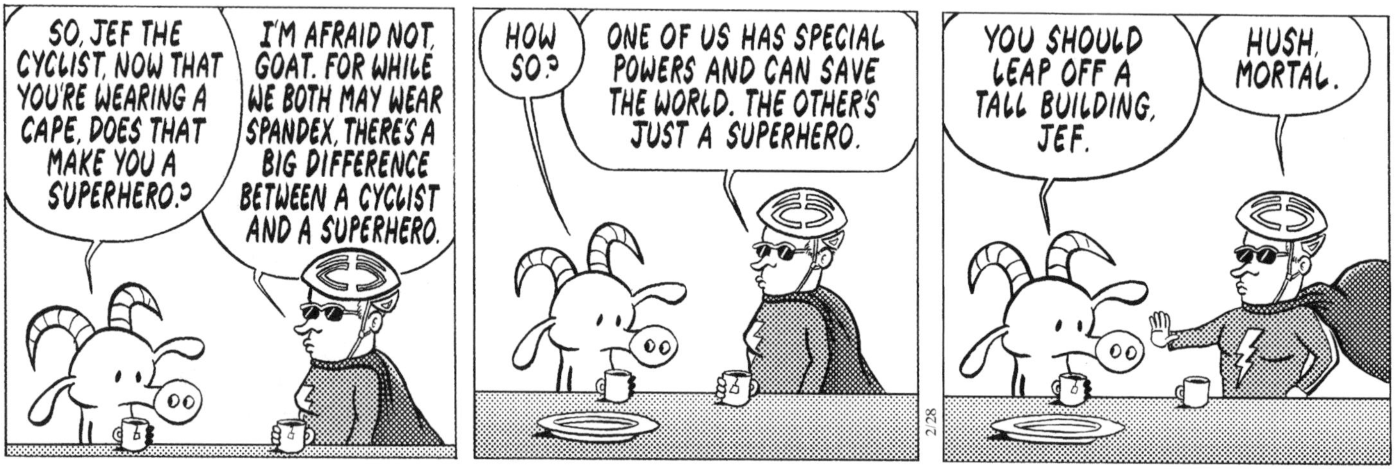
SO, JEF THE CYCLIST, NOW THAT YOU'RE WEARING A CAPE, DOES THAT MAKE YOU A SUPERHERO?
I'M AFRAID NOT, GOAT. FOR WHILE WE BOTH MAY WEAR SPANDEX, THERE'S A BIG DIFFERENCE BETWEEN A CYCLIST AND A SUPERHERO.
HOW SO?
ONE OF US HAS SPECIAL POWERS AND CAN SAVE THE WORLD. THE OTHER'S JUST A SUPERHERO.
YOU SHOULD LEAP OFF A TALL BUILDING, JEF.
HUSH, MORTAL.
2/28

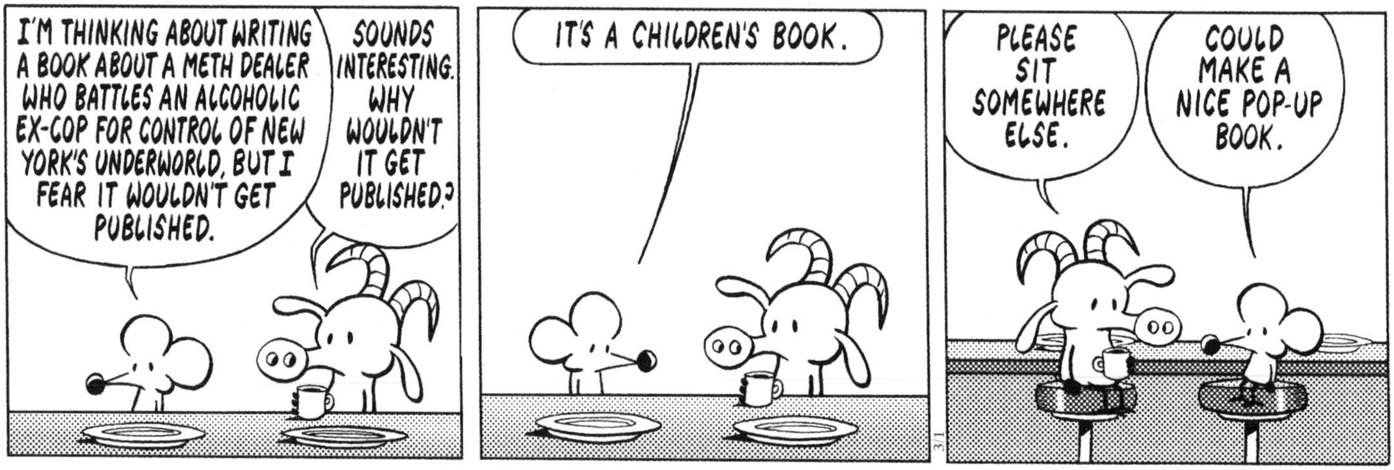
I'M THINKING ABOUT WRITING A BOOK ABOUT A METH DEALER WHO BATTLES AN ALCOHOLIC EX-COP FOR CONTROL OF NEW YORK'S UNDERWORLD, BUT I FEAR IT WOULDN'T GET PUBLISHED.
SOUNDS INTERESTING. WHY WOULDN'T IT GET PUBLISHED?
IT'S A CHILDREN'S BOOK.
PLEASE SIT SOMEWHERE ELSE.
COULD MAKE A NICE POP-UP BOOK.
3/1

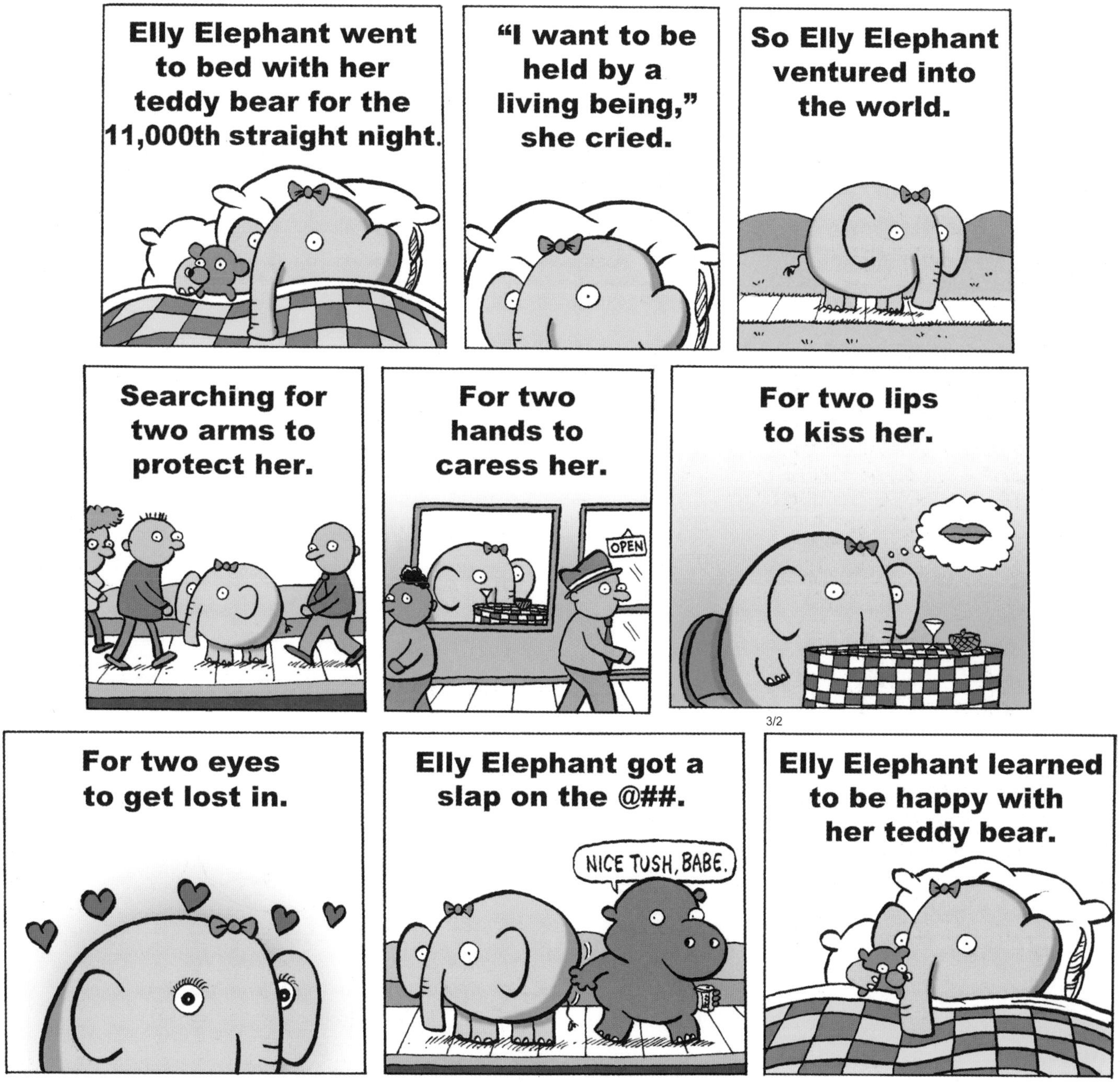
Elly Elephant went to bed with her teddy bear for the 11,000th straight night.
"I want to be held by a living being," she cried.
So Elly Elephant ventured into the world.
Searching for two arms to protect her.
For two hands to caress her.
OPEN
For two lips to kiss her.
3/2
For two eyes to get lost in.
Elly Elephant got a slap on the @##.
NICE TUSH, BABE.
Elly Elephant learned to be happy with her teddy bear.

Pearls Before Swine is distributed internationally by Universal Uclick.

King of the Comics copyright © 2015 by Stephan Pastis. All rights reserved. Printed in China. No part of this book may be used or reproduced in any manner whatsoever without written permission except in the case of reprints in the context of reviews.

Andrews McMeel Publishing, LLC
an Andrews McMeel Universal company
1130 Walnut Street, Kansas City, Missouri 64106

www.andrewsmcmeel.com

15 16 17 18 19 SDB 10 9 8 7 6 5 4 3 2 1

ISBN: 978-1-4494-5828-7

Library of Congress Control Number: 2014952153

Pearls Before Swine can be viewed on the Internet at
www.pearlscomic.com

These strips appeared in newspapers from June 3, 2013 to March 2, 2014.

─── **ATTENTION: SCHOOLS AND BUSINESSES** ───

Andrews McMeel books are available at quantity discounts with bulk purchase for educational, business, or sales promotional use. For information, please e-mail the Andrews McMeel Publishing Special Sales Department:
specialsales@amuniversal.com.

MAR 27 2015